Corporate Social and Human Rights Responsibilities

Corporate Social and Human Rights Responsibilities

Global Legal and Management Perspectives

Edited by

Karin Buhmann
Associate Professor, University of Copenhagen

Lynn Roseberry
Associate Professor, Copenhagen Business School

Mette Morsing
Professor of Corporate Social Responsibility, Copenhagen Business School

The Academy of Business in Society

Selection and editorial content © Karin Buhmann, Lynn Roseberry and Mette Morsing 2011
Individual chapters © the contributors 2011
Preface © Victor Kjaer 2011

All rights reserved. No reproduction, copy or transmission of this publication may be made without written permission.

No portion of this publication may be reproduced, copied or transmitted save with written permission or in accordance with the provisions of the Copyright, Designs and Patents Act 1988, or under the terms of any licence permitting limited copying issued by the Copyright Licensing Agency, Saffron House, 6-10 Kirby Street, London EC1N 8TS.

Any person who does any unauthorized act in relation to this publication may be liable to criminal prosecution and civil claims for damages.

The authors have asserted their rights to be identified as the authors of this work in accordance with the Copyright, Designs and Patents Act 1988.

First published 2011 by
PALGRAVE MACMILLAN

Palgrave Macmillan in the UK is an imprint of Macmillan Publishers Limited, registered in England, company number 785998, of Houndmills, Basingstoke, Hampshire RG21 6XS.

Palgrave Macmillan in the US is a division of St Martin's Press LLC, 175 Fifth Avenue, New York, NY 10010.

Palgrave Macmillan is the global academic imprint of the above companies and has companies and representatives throughout the world.

Palgrave® and Macmillan® are registered trademarks in the United States, the United Kingdom, Europe and other countries.

ISBN 978–0–230–23089–7 hardback

This book is printed on paper suitable for recycling and made from fully managed and sustained forest sources. Logging, pulping and manufacturing processes are expected to conform to the environmental regulations of the country of origin.

A catalogue record for this book is available from the British Library.

Library of Congress Cataloging-in-Publication Data
Corporate social and human rights responsibilities : global legal and
  management perspectives / edited by Karin Buhmann, Lynn Roseberry, Mette Morsing.
     p. cm.
  Includes bibliographical references.
  ISBN 978–0–230–23089–7
  1. Social responsibility of business.   2. Corporate governance—Social aspects.   3. Human rights.   I. Buhmann, Karin.   II. Roseberry, Lynn M.   III. Morsing, Mette.
  HD60.C674 2011
  658.4′08—dc22   2010033956

10 9 8 7 6 5 4 3 2 1
20 19 18 17 16 15 14 13 12 11

Printed and bound in Great Britain by
CPI Antony Rowe, Chippenham and Eastbourne

Contents

List of Tables and Figures	vii
Preface	viii
Acknowledgements	xi
Contributors	xii
Introduction Karin Buhmann, Lynn Roseberry, and Mette Morsing	1

Part I Setting the Stage

1. Conceptualizing the Home State Duty to Protect Human Rights — Sara L. Seck — 25
2. 'A *Necessary* Supplement' – What the United Nations Global Compact Is (and Is Not) — Andreas Rasche — 52
3. Balancing Power Interests in Reflexive Law Public-Private CSR Schemes: The Global Compact and the EU's Multi-Stakeholder Forum on CSR — Karin Buhmann — 77
4. 'Protect, Respect and Remedy': A Critique of the SRSG's Framework for Business and Human Rights — Surya Deva — 108

Part II Regional Perspectives

5. Corporate Social Responsibility in Africa: A Fig Leaf or a New Development Path Worth Pursuing? — Wambui Kimathi — 129
6. It's Our Business: Ensuring Inclusiveness in the Process of Regulating and Enforcing Corporate Social Responsibility — Chris Sidoti — 144

7 Public Procurement, International Labour Law and Free
   Movement in EU Law: Protect, Respect and Remedy   165
   Ruth Nielsen

8 Business Responsibilities and Human Rights in Latin America:
   Lessons and Inspiration for the Future   185
   Cecilia Anicama

Part III Combining Law and Management

9   Business Commitments in CSR Codes of Conduct and
    International Framework Agreements: The Case of
    Human Rights   205
    Dominique Bé

10 Regulating the Levers of Globalization: Integrating Corporate
    Social Responsibility into the Capital-Raising Process   222
    Lauren Caplan

11 Institutionalization of Corporate Ethics and Corporate Social
    Responsibility Programmes in Firms   244
    Jacob D. Rendtorff

12 The Organization of CSR as a Means of Corporate
    Control: From Do-Gooding Sideshow to Mainstream?   266
    Jette S. Knudsen

Index   288

List of Tables and Figures

Tables

5.1	Development approaches compared	138
Annex I	Acronyms	218
Annex II	References to human rights and implementing provisions in IFAs and CSR codes	219
Annex III	List of IFAs and CSR codes	220
12.1	CSR impact on corporate functions: business-driven and image-making CSR	278
12.2	CSR impact on corporate functions in HP: business-driven and image-making CSR	284
12.3	CSR impact on corporate functions in Ben & Jerry's: business-driven and image-making CSR	285
12.4	Recommendations to managers	286

Figures

2.1	The ten universal principles	55
2.2	The three engagement mechanisms and their role at the global and national/regional level	60

Preface

Since the mid-1990s, the world has experienced increasing public attention to corporate social responsibility (CSR) and the impact of corporations on global welfare. The challenge of how best to ensure the strategic business potential for individual businesses in assuming social responsibility, improving environmental protection, supporting human rights and so forth has been heavily debated and as a consequence the business management literature on CSR has exploded.

This anthology, however, is not just another among many, since it features two special qualities. First, it offers a special focus on human rights and second, it combines legal and management perspectives.

The contributions given by the distinguished panel of authors were originally presented at the international conference 'Corporate Social Responsibility, Business Responsibilities for Human Rights, and International Law', which was organised by the University of Copenhagen and the Copenhagen Business School and held in Copenhagen in November 2008. The conference was financially supported by the Danish government.

This is a selection of the perspectives presented at the conference, focusing especially on the influence of law on management decisions on CSR and including corporate responsibilities relating to violations of human rights.

From a Danish perspective this development is especially interesting as Denmark and the Danish government have decided to look for new ways of strengthening legal influence on CSR management decisions without violating the fundamental principle of CSR as a voluntary management policy. One particular legal instrument, which was issued as a part of the Danish National Action Plan on CSR, has apparently attracted considerable international attention.

I am referring to the so-called 'Act amending the Danish Financial Statements Act'. This single amendment (§99a) to the financial statements Act requires (in short) that Danish companies and investors over a certain size report on their CSR policies.

The Act has a special bearing on this anthology as it refers explicitly to international principles for corporate responsibility, in particular the UN Global Compact, the UN-backed Principles for Responsible Investment (PRI) and (in the accompanying guidelines to the Act) the Global Reporting Initiative (GRI). In this way the Act adds a global legal perspective to national legislation on financial statements and reporting in general, and, in particular, on corporate responsibility and business management.

The purpose of the Act itself is to exert what you might call reflective influence on business management decisions. More specifically, the purpose is to urge companies to develop a business strategy on corporate responsibility including corporate social and human rights responsibilities when operating on global markets. The Act strikes a delicate balance between voluntary business action on CSR and action mandated by law and it does this in a very simple way.

First of all, the Act does not require Danish companies to do anything in particular. It is strictly a law on reporting, that is, on transparency. In short, companies are only required to report on their CSR policies in so far as they have such policies in place. However, the 'trick' and the 'reflective inducement' embedded in the Act is that companies can only avoid reporting on their CSR policies by explicitly stating that they do *not* have such policies. The point is, of course, that companies given such a choice will be motivated to reflect on the benefits of adopting a CSR strategy and communicating it to stakeholders.

The potential outcome is twofold. One is that companies which do not yet have a policy or a strategy on CSR will get one. The process of formulating a CSR policy would then ideally also motivate the companies to reflect more actively on their role in society and on their individual business potential of integrating CSR as a part of their business strategy. The other potential outcome is that, by virtue of the specific reporting requirements of the law, the reports will contain a minimum standard of critical information.

In order to meet the statutory requirements, the reporting of the companies will, as a minimum, have to include the following information:

First, the report must describe the CSR policy in terms of in-house guidelines, objectives and strategies. This also includes information about any standards, guidelines or principles for CSR applied.

Second, the report must contain information about how the policies are implemented and translated into concrete action. Apart from the concrete activities this may involve, reporting on implementation includes describing any relevant management systems, control systems, evaluations or other measures of corporate governance securing and reviewing implementation of the policies.

Third, the companies must disclose their own evaluation of the results of their CSR efforts during the financial year including an evaluation of the expected future results. This evaluation may be of a qualitative nature and does not need to be measured in terms of financial results or performance.

These requirements set a minimum standard for the amount and quality of information disclosed. However, since the law explicitly refers to the reporting standards of the UN Global Compact and PRI as an optional reporting format this also reflects the hope on the part of the Danish government that these reporting standards will eventually become the standard format.

While this anthology is not about the Danish legislative initiative on CSR reporting as such, the thematic approach to the subject seems particularly relevant as seen from the perspective of the Danish government and the concept of CSR behind the Danish 'Action Plan for Corporate Social Responsibility'.

As such, both the theoretical approach to CSR of this anthology and the amendment of the Danish Financial Statements Act serve to break down the conceptual premise that since CSR is by definition is voluntary it is therefore also outside the realm of legislation. This premise contains a paradox, as the scope of regulation automatically decreases the scope for CSR. In other words, regulation automatically reduces CSR and what may count as CSR in one country may be a legal requirement in another country.

This is, for obvious reasons, a dubious approach. It narrows the perspective of CSR and the potential of public-private partnerships in solving the social and environmental challenges of globalisation including the challenge of strengthening human rights on a global scale. It also blinds one to the many different ways, other than 'command-and-control' regulation, in which the state (and governments) may involve private businesses in solving social problems.

The new Danish law on CSR reporting demonstrates that it is indeed possible to reconcile regulation with business-driven CSR, and that voluntary CSR can go hand-in-hand with a principles based legislation. The new Danish law also demonstrates that national legislation can be used to encourage companies to align their CSR strategies with international principles, not least human rights.

With special reference to human rights: this includes the potential of globally accepted standards, guidelines and principles of corporate responsibility such as the UN Global Compact. To use a concept developed under international relations theory back in the 1980s, you might call them 'international regimes'.[1]

I therefore urge anyone interested in the interface between regulation and CSR and, in particular, in the potential of globally accepted principles of CSR in strengthening human rights to continue reading beyond this preface.

Victor Kjaer
Deputy General, Director of Danish
Commerce and Companies Agency,
Copenhagen, Denmark

---

[1] Stephen D. Krasner (ed.) (1983) *International Regimes*, Ithaca: Cornell University Press.

Acknowledgements

We extend our warmest thanks to the contributors to this volume, conference participants whose lively debate helped shape the editorial process and our institutions. We are particularly grateful to the Danish Agency for Commerce and Companies and the Danish Research Council for the Social Sciences, whose financial support made the 2008 conference possible; to Jonas Eder-Hansen and student assistants at the Centre for Corporate Social Responsibility at Copenhagen Business School for professional support in organising the conference; to Director Henrik Zobbe at the Institute of Food and Resource Economics at the University of Copenhagen for practical and moral support for the conference; to Paul Milner and Virginia Thorp at Palgrave for being our editors and very helpful assistance throughout; and to The Academy of Business in Society (EABIS) for branding support. We also warmly thank our families, friends and colleagues for bearing with us at times when we have worked at this project, especially for putting up with seemingly never-ending working days around deadlines and during the 2008 conference.

Frederiksberg,
May 2010

Contributors

Cecilia Anicama is an international lawyer. She is currently the programme coordinator at Save the Children Sweden in Peru; former Human Rights Specialist at Inter-American Commission on Human Rights, Head of Human Rights Office at Andean Commission of Jurists; Coordinator of Human Rights Summer Session at International Institute of Human Rights. She is the author of *State Responsibilities to Regulate and Adjudicate Corporate Activities under the Inter-American Human Rights System. Report on the American Convention on Human Rights* prepared to inform the mandate of the Special Representative of the UN Secretary-General (SRSG) on Business and Human Rights, Professor John Ruggie; and *A human rights approach to the concept of social license*, among other papers published in English, Portuguese, Spanish and French. The views expressed in the chapter in this book are those of the author in her personal capacity as an international lawyer.

Dominique Bé, an economist by training, is deputy head of the European Social Fund coordination unit, in the directorate general for employment, social affairs and equal opportunities of the European Commission. Previously he was involved in the development of EU policies related to corporate social responsibility and social dialogue.

Karin Buhmann obtained her Ph.D. at the Institute of Law, Aarhus University, and a Master's in International Law at the Raoul Wallenberg Institute, Lund University. She is an Associate Professor at the Institute of Food and Resource Economics, the University of Copenhagen. She specializes in human rights law, business responsibilities for human rights (BRHR) and CSR, approaching CSR from the perspective of public law. Her current research is on emerging international, transnational and national regulation of CSR and BRHR. She is particularly interested in the interrelationship between international law and emerging forms of law and regulatory modalities related to corporate social and human rights responsibilities. She also works on CSR in a Chinese context and on development law. She has been invited to present her research at several Nordic, European and international conferences.

Lauren Caplan is Counsel to an investment management company primarily serving nonprofit institutional investors and was previously an Associate at Chadbourne & Parke LLP in New York and London, focusing on corporate transactions and project finance.

Surya Deva is an Associate Professor at the School of Law, City University of Hong Kong, Hong Kong; Visiting Research Fellow, University of New South Wales, Sydney. BA (Hons.), LLB, LLM (Delhi); PhD (Sydney). Formerly, Assistant Professor, National Law Institute University, Bhopal; Lecturer, Faculty of Law, University of Delhi, Delhi.

Wambui Kimathi is a Commissioner at the Kenya National Commission for Human Rights (KNCHR), where she has worked since its establishment in July, 2003. While at the Commission she has mostly been involved in economic and social rights programs and increasingly in the Project on Business and Human Rights. She has several years of experience in human rights and democracy, having worked in senior positions in the NGO sector first with the Institute for Education in Democracy and later with the Kenya Human Rights Commission (KHRC).

Victor Kjaer is Deputy General Director of the Danish Commerce and Companies Agency (the DCCA), which belongs to the Danish Ministry of Economic and Business Affairs. The DCCA is responsible for implementing the Danish Governments Action Plan for Corporate Social Responsibility (CSR), including the Danish Act from 2008 on CSR reporting, and acts as a secretariat for the Danish Council for Corporate Responsibility. He is responsible for the CSR activities of the DCCA, as well as for company law regulation and control of financial reports from listed companies.

Jette S. Knudsen is an Associate Professor at the Department for International Economics and Management at Copenhagen Business School. She holds a PhD from MIT and has been employed as a consultant with PwC and with the think tank Centre for European Policy Studies (CEPS) in Brussels. For four years she served as the director of the Copenhagen Centre for Corporate Responsibility, a think tank financed by the Danish government. In the Copenhagen Centre she worked closely with several leading Danish and international companies on evaluation, strategy development and implementation of CSR initiatives. She has been project leader with the Danish shipping conglomerate A.P. Moller Maersk (CEO office), where she headed a task force evaluating CSR risks and opportunities.

Mette Morsing is a Professor, PhD, Director of CBS Centre for Corporate Social Responsibility (cbsCSR). Professor Morsing researches, teaches and consults on CSR. In particular, her research interests focus on internal-external communication, identity, corporate branding, stakeholder relations and responsible leadership. She has published extensively on these issues in international journals and books. She is a member of several international and national committees and boards with relation to CSR. For many years she served on the Management Board of EABIS, and recently joined the Board of the LEGO Foundation, the Advisory Board of Academy of Responsible Management based in Malaysia and Abu Dhabi and the National Council for Corporate Responsibility under the Minister for Economy and Trade.

Ruth Nielsen, dr jur., jur is a dr honoris causa 2000 from the Law Faculty, University of Lund, Professor at the CBS Department of Law. Her primary fields of research and teaching are EU law, labour law, procurement law, contract law, e-commerce law and legal theory. Professor Nielsen is a member of the European Commission's Legal Expert Group on the Application of European Law on Equal Treatment between Men and Women, a member of the Danish Equality Complaints Board set up under the Equality Act 2000, and a member of the board of the Danish Association for Labour Law.

Andreas Rasche is Assistant Professor of Business in Society at the Governance and Public Management Group at Warwick Business School. He previously taught at Helmut-Schmidt-University, University of the Federal Armed Forces in Hamburg. He holds a PhD (Dr. rer. pol.) from European Business School, Germany and a Habilitation (Dr. habil.) from Helmut-Schmidt-University Hamburg. He regularly publishes in international journals on corporate responsibility and is also the author of *The Paradoxical Foundation of Strategic Management* (Springer) and is currently editing, together with Georg Kell, the book *The United Nations Global Compact: Achievements, Trends and Challenges* (Cambridge University Press). More information is available at: http:///www.arasche.com.

Jacob D. Rendtorff, Dr. scient. adm., PhD, mag. art., Diplom Pol is Professor of Responsibility, Ethics and Legitimacy of Corporations, at the Department of Communication, Business and Information Technologies, Roskilde University, Denmark. Rendtorff is Director of Studies and Director of Research of the research group on management, change and business. Rendtorff has, in Danish, English, French and German, written more than 50 articles, authored 7 books and been editor or co-editor on more than ten other books; in particular, *Basic Ethical Principles in European Bioethics and Biolaw, Copenhagen and Barcelona* (2000) (written together with Peter Kemp). His latest book is *Responsibility, Ethics and Legitimacy of Corporations*, Copenhagen Business School Press, 2009.

Lynn Roseberry is an Associate professor, JD, LLM, PhD, and Head of the CBS Department of Law. Lynn Roseberry holds law degrees from Arizona State University and Harvard Law School and a PhD in law from CBS. She teaches and researches in Danish, EU and international labour and human rights law. She is particularly interested in anti-discrimination law and has contributed to several books on the subject. She has been invited to present her research at numerous regional and European conferences on various aspects of anti-discrimination law.

Sara L. Seck joined the Faculty of Law at the University of Western Ontario in July 2007. She completed a PhD in law at Osgoode Hall Law School, York University, Canada in 2008. Her PhD research concerned home State obligations to regulate transnational mining companies under international environmental and human rights law. She has participated in several expert consultations with the SRSG, and in November 2009 co-convened a multi-stakeholder consultation in support of Corporate Law Tools project. In 2009 she was the recipient of a Social Sciences and Humanities Research Council of Canada (SSHRC) research grant for a project entitled 'A Critical Analysis of the Home State Duty to Protect Human Rights'.

Chris Sidoti is a human rights lawyer, activist and teacher. He has been Australian Human Rights Commissioner (1995–2000), Australian Law Reform Commissioner (1992–1995) and Foundation Director of the Australian Human Rights Commission (1987–1992). He has also worked in non-government organisations, including the International Service for Human Rights, in Geneva, the Human Rights Council of Australia and the Australian Catholic Commission for Justice and Peace. He is an Adjunct Professor at the University of Western Sydney, Griffith University (Queensland) and the Australian Catholic University, a Fellow of the Castan Centre for Human Rights Law at Monash University and an Affiliate at the Sydney Centre for International Law at the University of Sydney.

Introduction

Karin Buhmann, Lynn Roseberry, and Mette Morsing

1 Overview

What has the law to do with corporate social responsibility? Corporate social responsibility (CSR) is generally defined as voluntary business action, i.e. action not mandated by law. In 2001 the EU Commission defined the concept of CSR as 'essentially a concept whereby companies decide voluntarily to contribute to a better society and a cleaner environment'.[1] Other definitions, however, take a more inclusive approach to CSR and law, suggesting that CSR need not only be action beyond the requirements of law.[2] Indeed, Archie B. Carroll's oft-cited 1979 definition of CSR considers compliance with law as being part of CSR.[3] Carroll and Mark Schwartz have expanded this idea to cover not only action in accordance with the letter of the law but also at least some types of action in accordance with the law's (current or future) spirit.[4]

Increasingly CSR takes on a legal character that necessarily reflects on management decisions: more and more European and other governments, most recently those of the United Kingdom and Denmark, have taken to imposing legal requirements on businesses to prepare non-financial reports

---

[1] Commission of the European Commission (2001) *Promoting a European Framework for Corporate Social Responsibility*, EU Doc. COM(2001) 366, paragraph 8 compare para. 20.
[2] For example, Blowfield, Michael and Jedrzej George Frynas (2005) Setting new agendas: critical perspectives on corporate social responsibility in the developing world. *International Affairs*, Vol. 81, No. 3: 499–513, at 503; Ward, Halina (2004) *Public Sector Roles in Strengthening Corporate Social Responsibility: Taking Stock*. Washington DC: The World Bank Group: 3; compare also Zerk, Jennifer A. (2006) *Multinationals and Corporate Social Responsibility: Limitations and Opportunities in International Law*. Cambridge: Cambridge University Press.
[3] Carroll, Archie B. (1979) A three-dimensional conceptual model of corporate performance. *The Academy of Management Review*, Vol. 4: 497–505, at 500.
[4] Schwartz, Mark S. and Archie B. Carroll (2003) Corporate social responsibility: a three-domain approach. *Business Ethics Quarterly*, Vol. 13, No. 4: 503–530.

of their impact on society and environment. In Europe, the US and elsewhere civil society and individuals increasingly resort to litigation to hold corporations accountable for alleged violations of their human, labour or environmental rights.

This book seeks to take up the challenges that emergent juridification of CSR poses to conventional conceptions of CSR developed in a management context. In particular, the book sheds light on areas of convergence and divergence, complementarities and differences between management and legal perspectives on CSR. The book also explores the emerging institutionalization of business responsibilities for human rights as a distinct part of the general CSR paradigm. In this chapter, we address this challenge from the point of view that the boundaries between conventional law and CSR and between management practices and institutionalizing processes that drive management action to meet societal expectations seem to be softening.

The purpose of this book is to take a step towards bringing management and legal perspectives of CSR together and to test some approaches towards integrating law in the ongoing promotion of CSR. We have noticed that managers and students are trying to understand connections between law and CSR, and to understand what relationships there may be between law, CSR and business responsibilities for human rights. We believe that the process of integrating CSR and law will continue, and we want to try to investigate this process through the collection of articles in this book.

This ambition was born out of our interest in human rights as a part of CSR and in human rights responsibilities for corporations as an emerging discourse of its own. To make the distinction clear between the general CSR discourse and the emerging specific discourse on business responsibilities for human rights, we propose to adopt the acronym BRHR for business responsibilities for human rights. The general CSR discourse embraces social and environmental issues, including climate issues. However, in the current CSR debate, climate tends to dominate. We want to focus on human rights as the key social area within the CSR debate. The CSR debate remains business-centred. We want to explore further the significance of state obligations for human rights problems that also feature in CSR discourse. Even though business has created many social problems, action by companies has also been a driver for the development of human rights as a part of CSR commitment and the work of the UN in this area. We want to explore some implications of the state role to provide the framework for business action.

This chapter sets out some lines of thought that have motivated the book and the collection of articles in the subsequent chapters. In Section 2 we discuss business responsibilities for human rights as a part of CSR and as a line of normative thinking that increasingly takes shape as a discourse of its own. We refer to that discourse as BRHR, to distinguish it from CSR and from human rights responsibilities discussed as part of CSR. The emerging distinction has become particularly clear with the work of the UN Secretary

General's Special Representative on Human Rights and Business (commonly referred to as the 'SRSG'). In fact, the publication of the SRSG's final report from his first mandate term (2005–2008) was decisive for the theme and timing of the conference from which most of the chapters in this book were first prepared. Section 2 discusses some benefits that may result from the distinction between CSR and BRHR. It sketches some aspects of law as a source of norms, legal conflicts including human rights conflicts related to climate degradation, and the insistence among many business leaders and academics that CSR is and should only be 'voluntary'.

Section 3 goes further into the debate on law and CSR, arguing that law and CSR are less distinct than is often claimed in CSR contexts. This section explains that the state-centred character of international human rights law has done much to shield businesses from being held accountable for abuse of human rights. CSR and – perhaps to a lesser extent – BRHR indicate a blurring of boundaries between corporate voluntary action and the law. Opening a debate that we return to at the end of the chapter, we argue that some aspects of law, including process-oriented legal theories, may provide valuable insight into the development of CSR and BRHR norms.

Section 4 addresses global legal and management perspectives of CSR and BRHR. In this section, we introduce the main points of the subsequent chapters of the book.

Section 5 addresses the institutionalization of corporate integration of CSR from a managerial perspective. It discusses the phenomenon of corporate isomorphism and its effects on corporate CSR decisions.

Finally, Section 6 returns to the relationship between law and management in relation to CSR and BRHR. This section argues that the theory of reflexive law may contribute to an understanding of the blurring of boundaries between corporate voluntary action and the law. As a regulatory technique, reflexive law promotes organizational learning and self-regulation. It leaves organizations the choice to determine their own norms but assists them in understanding the concerns and needs of other social actors. The final part of the introduction argues that this particular process-oriented regulatory theory may therefore offer a medium for communication and understanding for law and management to meet in the discussion and solution of CSR and BRHR issues.

2 Business responsibilities for human rights

Business and its impact on human rights is an area within CSR that has been subjected to intense debate, ranging from whether business should consider human rights at all to arguments that business entities should be subjected to international and national regulation and enforceable human rights obligations. Since the 1990s, the issue of business responsibilities for human rights has been put on the agenda of international organizations with a regulatory purpose, especially within the UN. This resulted in the 2003 draft UN Norms on business and human rights[5] and has culminated, so far, in the final report from the 2005–2008 mandate of the SRSG. The 2008 report,[6] which was unanimously 'welcomed' by the UN Human Rights Council, presented the *Protect, Respect, Remedy* framework. This three-pronged framework, which has since come to be known as the 'UN Framework', presents a combination of the state's duty to protect individuals against human rights violations by others (such as companies), a business responsibility to respect human rights through due diligence and other measures, and the need for better access to remedies both within a business sphere and within conventional as well as possibly new public remedial institutions (such as courts or an international ombudsman). The report led to the Human Rights Council extending the SRSG's mandate until 2011, with a request to the SRSG to operationalize the three-pronged framework proposed in 2008 and to continue his coalition building style, which employs a high degree of multi-stakeholder consultations.

The SRSG's work during the first term of his mandate, however, also makes it clear that increasingly, the discourse on BRHR travels on a path distinct from that of CSR.[7] The emerging discourse on BRHR has increasingly come to be a discourse on the state duty to protect. This came out clearly in the *Protect, Respect, Remedy* framework in the SRSG's 2008 report, from which several chapters in this book take their point of departure. In addition to that crucial difference, the corporate responsibility to respect as defined by the SRSG also entails a stronger compliance element than is assumed by the conventional CSR discourse.[8]

---

[5] United Nations Sub-Commission on the Promotion and Protection of Human Rights. *Norms on the Responsibilities of Transnational Corporations and Other Business Enterprises with regard to Human Rights 2003* (UN doc. E/CN.4/Sub.2/2003/12/Rev.2). The document was considered by the Human Rights Commission to contain 'useful elements and ideas' but was not accepted as a document with legal standing.

[6] SRSG (2008) *Protect, Respect and Remedy: A Framework for Business and Human Rights*. Report of the Special Representative of the Secretary-General on the issue of human rights and transnational corporations and other business enterprises, John Ruggie. UN Doc. A/HRC/8/5 (2008).

[7] On the distinction between CSR and Human Rights, see also Zerk (2006) *supra* note 2; Buhmann, Karin (2007) Corporate social responsibility and human rights responsibilities of business. Introductory chapter in *Nordic Journal on Human Rights*, No. 4: 331–352 special issue on Corporate Social Responsibility and Human Rights; and Buhmann, Karin (2009) Regulating corporate social and human rights responsibilities at the UN plane: institutionalising new forms of law and law-making approaches? *Nordic Journal of International Law*, Vol. 78, No. 1: 1–52.

[8] The SRSG's 'Respect, Protect, Remedy' framework is described in SRSG (2008) *Protect, Respect and Remedy*, *supra* note 6. According to the SRSG's framework, the corporate responsibility to respect entails ensuring compliance with national laws as well as

In our view, the emerging distinction between the notions of CSR and BRHR deserves to be noted. They differ in their approach to state and corporate legal obligations and societal expectations. First, the CSR concept also encompasses many other issues besides human rights. Second, the general CSR discourse remains focused on corporate voluntary action. BRHR is narrower than the CSR discourse in that BRHR specifically deals with human rights. Second, the BRHR discourse gives much more attention to state obligations as obligations of (international human rights) law than does the CSR discourse. BRHR discourse, especially as developed by the SRSG, has become highly informed by the legal discourse of obligations, compliance and liability, whereas the CSR discourse continues along a path informed by 'softer' forms of responsibility, self-regulation, 'voluntary action', and sustainability. Further, the development of the BRHR discourse as an independent discourse also has an impact on CSR and on societal expectations of companies. For example, BRHR's increased emphasis on the obligations or responsibilities of states may decrease legal pressure or societal expectations on companies.

This is not to say there are no overlaps. As the 2007 and 2008 reports of the SRSG indicate, social expectations are perceived as an important link to emerging soft law which may in due time lead to harder national or international law. Corporate codes of conduct, corporate voluntarism and corporate economic interest in risk management are important factors in the emergence of the normative expectations on which the SRSG has based his framework. And although the BRHR discourse stresses state obligations based on international human rights law, it retains the idea that corporations bear responsibilities for human rights.

Whereas BRHR may come to be defined – perhaps during the second term of the SRSG – as a relatively precise notion, CSR remains a relatively open term. Scholars continue to debate whether a definitive definition of CSR should be sought, or whether the term should be left open and flexible, within an overall understanding of businesses taking responsibility for their impact on society, including the environment.[9] For many reasons, including the possible social and economic benefits that may result from more room for companies to innovate within an open notion of CSR, CSR may well be

---

managing the risk of human rights harm with a view to avoiding it (see paras. 51–81, esp. paras. 54–56).

[9] See for example Newell, Peter and Jedrzej George Frynas (2007) Beyond CSR? Business, poverty and social justice: an introduction. *Third World Quarterly*, Vol. 28: 669–681, 673; Crane, Andrew, Dirk Matten and Laura J. Spence (2008) *Corporate Social Responsibility*. New York: Routledge: 4–7; Hopkins, Michael (2006) Commentary: what is corporate social responsibility all about? *Journal of Public Affairs*, Vol. 6: 298–306; Wan Saiful, Wan-Jan (2006) Defining corporate social responsibility. *Journal of Public Affairs*, Vol. 6: 176–184.

left as that, an open notion. With a hardening of BRHR, at least the risks posed to human rights protection by leaving CSR relatively undefined may be contained.

In this book, CSR is understood broadly as a concept that requires companies to take responsibility as they engage with society, especially on human rights, labour rights and the environment. In relation to CSR, human rights have typically been addressed as part of the 'people' dimension of the triple bottom line (*People, Planet, Profit*). They are sometimes referred to in terms of international human or labour rights. In other contexts, they are referred to in more general terms. Human rights are not an isolated part of CSR: Whether approached from a legal, organizational or other specific management perspective, human rights relate to working conditions and other workers' rights, community relations, corruption, and interaction with states and state bodies in home and host states, to mention just a few examples. As the SRSG's research indicates, companies may violate a wide range of human rights – not just economic or work-related rights. With particular relevance to the growing concern with greenhouse gas emissions, human rights relate at a very basic level to the living conditions of individual workers, management, suppliers, buyers and communities in which businesses operate. Climate degradation may have severe effects on access to land, water, wood and natural energy resources for individuals as well as companies. It may have severe effects on related social and economic human rights. It may cause more countries to fall into poverty, and those which are already poor to become even poorer. Past experience in understanding and regulating business and human rights in a CSR context may therefore hold important lessons for ongoing and future efforts to handle business impact on climate in a CSR context as well as beyond.

Prevention and resolution of legal conflicts touching on BRHR or CSR are becoming new practice areas for law firms across the globe. At the same time, the notion that CSR is only action not mandated by law is put under pressure by a transnationalization of corporate self-regulation based on codes of conduct that are integrated into contracts with suppliers, which become legally binding as private law arrangements. While we may claim from an academic perspective that CSR and BRHR are distinct, the mere fact that efforts are underway at the level of the United Nations to define human rights responsibilities of business under international law adds to the pressure on the concept of CSR as being only 'voluntary' action. CSR and BRHR may be distinct in terms of attention given to obligations or responsibilities of governments and companies respectively, but the notions and informing discourses also feed into each other.

While human rights form an integrated part of CSR in many contexts, human rights responsibilities of business are taking on a conceptual and legal character of their own with increased focus on a need for public regulation to ensure protection of human rights and accountability. CSR and

BRHR are not only interrelated in several ways as set out above. They are also related in terms of debates on the voluntary or enforceable character of CSR and BRHR, the processes that create CSR and BRHR norms, and through the turn to international law as a source of both.

The legal character of CSR and BRHR is a recurrent theme in many chapters in this book. As elaborated at the end of this chapter, law is not just 'black-letter' enforceable rules. Law may also be understood as theory and practice of the institutionalization of norms of conduct. From this perspective, multi-stakeholder initiatives launched at intergovernmental level to promote and support business self-regulation on CSR through discursive development of norms on CSR and BRHR may be understood as law. Their legal character lies in the process of creating common understanding or agreement on norms of conduct. The consultative SRSG process is one example, the UN Global Compact another. The European Multi-Stakeholder Forum (MSF) on CSR is a third. Although it takes place outside a formal governmental or intergovernmental framework, the ISO 26000 formulation process, which is coming to an end as this chapter is being written, is arguably a fourth example of a legally relevant process leading to an institutionalization of behavioural norms. This is a different way of perceiving law from that which mainly characterizes the alleged 'voluntary-mandatory' dichotomy of CSR and law. It is oriented towards process and co-regulation rather than towards top-down formal regulation issued by governments and the enforcement of such regulation. It may hold benefits for corporate self-regulation but make enforcement and accountability more difficult.

3 The 'Law vs. CSR' debate

CSR is often seen as opposed to mandatory law. This perception probably owes a great deal to the way Western liberal democracies conceive of law. According to the legal theory that underpins the legal systems of liberal democracies in the West, generally known as liberal legal theory, law is a system of social control, which entails the essentially political task of establishing organs authorized with law-applying and law-enforcement powers. Once created, law is then viewed as an autonomous repository of normative standards that creates an objective normative order that is binding on the same individuals who participated in its creation and which rules out the invocation of subjective opinions to escape law's constraining force.[10] In the world of liberal legal theory, talk about business's legal responsibility for human rights becomes intelligible only if one can identify a set of rules, duly adopted according to the rules that apply to lawmaking, which imposes

---

[10] Koskenniemi, M. (1989) *From Apology to Utopia: The Structure of International Legal Argument*. Helsinki: Finnish Lawyers' Publishing Company: 409–410.

specific mandatory obligations on businesses with regards to some specified natural and/or legal person(s). These rules invest the legal subject with rights that can be enforced in the legal system. If the legal order is found not to contain any valid rules about business responsibilities for human rights, these responsibilities are viewed as completely voluntary undertakings, subject only to the whims of management and the market.

Public international law has been and continues to be heavily influenced by Western liberal democratic theories of law. This influence is seen in the positivist approach to international law, which is focused on states as the only proper subjects of international law and as the only proper law-making actors in international law. Thus, human rights in international law were originally conceived as rights held by individuals against the state. This approach to the international law of human rights has done much to shield businesses from being held accountable for activities that, if they had been performed by a state, would amount to violations of human rights. The CSR and BRHR movements challenge these assumptions about the law and the protection of human rights by asking: is the protection of human rights the exclusive domain of states, leaving businesses free to seek their profits solely on the basis of the legal rules of states or do human rights constitute a normative order from which businesses cannot claim exemption on the basis of inadequate state protection of human rights?

However, as several contributions in this book demonstrate, CSR and law are not necessarily as separate or distinct as they may appear when viewed through the lens of liberal legal theory. Nor does CSR always gain from being separated from law. This does not by necessity imply that CSR should be subjected to law, or that CSR is only action which is not required by law. Process-oriented theories of law, such as reflexive law, suggest that law need not only consist of specific rules which require action, but it may also be understood as constituting a theory and a method of institutionalization of norms of conduct. From this perspective, legal theories about regulatory strategies and modalities for institutionalization of norms of conduct could provide valuable insight into the development of CSR and BRHR norms. We return to this perspective at the end of the current chapter.

4 Global legal and management perspectives of CSR and BRHR

Chapters in this book indicate that CSR and BRHR connect to both law and management through a variety of organizational and institutional channels. In his article on international framework agreements, Dominique Bé suggests human rights-oriented codes of conduct may influence the internal regulation and management decisions of multinational enterprises with regard to the terms and coverage of their international framework agreements. From political science and legal perspectives based in practical experience in Africa, Latin America and Austral-Asia, Wambui Kimathi,

Cecilia Anicama and Chris Sidoti demonstrate that CSR and business responsibility for human rights are not just a luxury phenomenon to be invoked by consumers, workers, communities, companies or indeed states in industrialized countries. Both CSR and BRHR are very much pressing realities for individuals as well as states in the less wealthy and developing parts of the world. From varying legal perspectives, Surya Deva, Sara Seck and Ruth Nielsen suggest that regulation of business responsibilities for human rights can come in a range of forms and degrees of binding character, emanating from national as well as supranational and international law-making bodies. Andreas Rasche, on the other hand, taking an organizational and business ethics perspective, suggests that the concern with legislative and enforcement measures should be widened to consider institutional arrangements like the UN Global Compact which provides a learning forum for business, civil society and governments to exchange views and experience. Karin Buhmann argues that some such arrangements which function as reflexive law should be examined in regard to strengthening the representation of weaker actors to achieve a process and normative result perceived as legitimate. Lauren Caplan suggests that greater uniformity in the application of CSR standards and legislative requirements will increase possibilities for investors and others in their efforts to support or promote CSR. Drawing on the example of EU policy efforts and a set of United States guidelines directed at judges when assessing criminal acts committed by corporations, Jacob Dahl Rendtorff argues that business ethics and the capacity of corporations to act as moral citizens may be strengthened by public interventions. Jette Steen Knudsen, on the other hand, takes the perspective of corporate management and in particular the role of boards.

CSR and BRHR are often perceived, at least in the West and North, as related to problems that are particularly acute in developing states. SRSG John Ruggie developed his *Protect, Respect, Remedy* framework with special regard to countries which suffer from what he refers to as 'governance gaps'. The chapters by Nielsen and Sidoti demonstrate that CSR and BRHR are relevant to developed societies too. These chapters show that CSR and BRHR problems may also be encountered in states with well-functioning legal systems, the rule of law, and few governance gaps. This underscores the importance, for companies and legal professionals in all societies, of being attentive to CSR and BRHR challenges in their own organizations, communities, countries and in their transnational relations, and to regard CSR and BRHR as aspects not only of corporate but also of public governance.

The chapters in this book were originally prepared for the International Conference on Business Responsibility and Human Rights which took place in Copenhagen on 5–6 November 2008 organized by the University of Copenhagen and Copenhagen Business School. The conference stimulated debate on the important issues of the blurring of boundaries between company voluntary action on human rights and the law, and on ways in which law and organizational studies may complement each other with regard to better understanding and cooperation on CSR and related topics.

In the CSR and BRHR fields, the terms of obligations, responsibilities and duties often converge and are used somewhat interchangeably, without necessarily intending concretely to indicate the same level of obligation. In this book, we seek to strive towards a uniform use of the terms 'responsibilities', 'duties' and 'obligations', with the following meanings:

- Obligations are legally binding. They may or may not be enforceable, depending on the legal context.
- Responsibilities are not legally binding. From the perspective of law, they may be seen as politically or morally binding.
- We try to avoid the term 'duties' but use it to designate a sense of duty which cannot at this stage be clarified as either legally binding or not legally binding.[11]

Like the conference, several of the chapters take their point of departure from the work of the United Nations Secretary General's Special Representative (SRSG) on Business and Human Rights that culminated in June 2008 with the presentation of the report of the SRSG after his first mandate 2005–2008. The aim of the book is not to assess the SRSG's policy framework, but to take this as a timely point of departure for a multi-disciplinary discussion on the subjects of CSR, business and human rights, and their interaction, differences and complementary character. This book aims to provide theoretical and empirically based perspectives on the understanding and inter-relationship of CSR and business responsibilities for human rights from scholars representing different regions of the world. The book is informed by a desire to establish a globally legitimate understanding of CSR and business responsibilities for human rights, and by the need for legal and management scholars and practitioners to work more closely together to address public sector as well as business needs in relation to the role of business in a globalized society.

This complex subject is addressed through articles organized into three parts. Part I sets the stage for the on-going debate on CSR, business responsibilities for human rights, law and management. Part II provides regional perspectives from Africa, Asia, Australasia, Europe and Latin America. Drawing on additional regional perspectives, Part III offers suggestions for combining law and management in relation to corporate social and human rights responsibilities.

---

[11] On this terminology, see also Solomon, Margot E., Arne Tostesen, and Wouter Vanderhole (2007) Human Rights, development and new duty-bearers, in Solomon, Margot, Arne Tostesen, and Wouter Vandenhole (eds) *Casting the Net Wider: Human Rights, Development and New Duty-Bearers*. Antwerp: Intersentia Publishing: 3–24, at 17.

Taking the work of the SRSG as her point of departure, Sara Seck discusses the home State duty to protect human rights. Seck examines the scope of the permissibility of home State regulation under the public international law of jurisdiction and proposes that the preliminary justification for home State regulation should be rooted in the territoriality principle. Thus, she argues for a different approach from that which considers home State regulation of corporate human rights duties as an exercise of extraterritorial jurisdiction. Seck discusses whether the home State duty to protect should be interpreted to mandate the exercise of home State jurisdiction over transnational corporate conduct in order to both prevent and remedy human rights harms. Seck evaluates her preliminary findings from the perspective of Third World Approaches to International Law (TWAIL). She concludes that the state duty to protect includes a state duty (or obligation) to structure their institutions so as to both facilitate corporate compliance with the responsibility to respect rights, and facilitate access to remedies by victims of human rights abuses. This also includes state regulation of such structures, such as export credit agencies, stock exchanges and financial institutions, and to actively consider the use of corporate laws to bring about compliance with the state duty to protect.

In his chapter, Surya Deva critically discusses the *Respect, Protect and Remedy* framework set out in the SRSG's 2008 report. Noting the background for the appointment of the SRSG and his mandate, Deva recognizes the value of the efforts made by the SRSG and that he deserves credit for bringing attention to a number of important points. These include paying attention to developing countries' lack of capacity or sometimes will to regulate TNC activities, extraterritorial regulation of TNCs activities as a legitimate option, and suggestions that governments should work to change the corporate culture to become responsible. Deva argues that the framework, however, suffers from a serious omission in its failure to address the role that international financial institutions and other international organizations such as the WTO could play in ensuring that business complies with human rights. Deva also argues that the SRSG's suggestion that 'governance gaps' created by globalization are the root cause of business and human rights predicaments is simplistic and fails to consider the background for the development of the international human rights law regime and that of corporate law in relation to the interests to be served. Deva finds that the framework would be stronger if it suggested which human rights are most relevant to be considered for corporate human rights responsibilities. He also argues that the framework's conceptualization of the corporate responsibility to respect human rights could be more specific in promoting corporate human rights responsibility. Deva concludes that a consensus is needed on why corporations have human rights responsibilities, what these are, how they could be implemented and enforced and that such consensus requires not only states and international organizations but also business leaders and civil society to act beyond their own interests and to think beyond what is politically feasible here and now.

Andreas Rasche discusses the UN Global Compact from an organizational and business ethics perspective. His chapter takes issue with what he considers to be common misconceptions of what the Global Compact is. The Global Compact has been criticized for being toothless, a 'blue-washing' instrument for companies, and generally too weak in terms of enforcement. Rasche argues that the Global Compact does not have to be legally binding, but is a supplement, indeed a necessary one, to other ways of regulating company action in a context of global governance. It has the capacity to assist mutual learning and the development of a set of shared values. Rasche argues that the Global Compact must be understood and appreciated in the context of its underlying mandate and supplementary nature with regard to state and non-state regulation. In addition, its dynamic and flexible multi-stakeholder and network-based governance structure can promote necessary reform of the UN system from within.

Karin Buhmann discusses some differences in outcomes between the Global Compact and the EU's efforts to develop a normative framework on CSR through the MSF. Based on differences between the Global Compact and the MSF as regards stakeholder composition, the procedures of adoption, and the impact of international human rights law on the final normative result, Buhmann argues that the Global Compact and the MSF offer instructive lessons on the importance of balancing power disparities between actors in reflexive regulatory processes. Buhmann proposes that Habermasian theory on deliberative law-making, transposed to the intergovernmental level, may provide qualitative normative guidance for dealing with reflexive law theory's failure to address the issue of how to deal with power disparities. While not offering a blueprint solution, Habermasian theory takes the qualitative aspect of the reflexive regulatory process a step further to provide for participation by representative stakeholders. The theory may provide qualitative guidance for the management and design of reflexive regulatory fora to provide participants with an actual say. Based on the perspectives offered by reflexive law and Habermasian theory on deliberative law-making, Buhmann also argues that a stronger integration of legal theory – understood as a theory of institutionalization of behavioural norms – into cross-disciplinary work on CSR may enrich the development and implementation of CSR. The chapter addresses business and human rights only from the CSR perspective. However, similar observations to those made in the chapter may be made with regard to balancing power disparities in multi-stakeholder initiatives on BRHR and work to promote the development and implementation of BRHR.

Addressing the business impact on human rights and the CSR discourse from an African perspective, Wambui Kimathi argues that both debates must aim at making business take greater responsibility for human rights. Kimathi argues from a political science perspective, which is informed by her experience as Commissioner at the Kenyan Human Rights Commission, that poverty in most of Sub-Saharan Africa serves as a trigger for the social engagement of African business. Businesses participate in social and economic services, but unless this is to be just a fig leaf, there needs to be more complementarity between business action, communities' expectations and national development plans. There is a need to change approach in order to make CSR a pathway towards greater realization of human rights. Both the CSR debate and that on business and human rights should be directed towards ensuring an alignment of commercial and societal concerns. These should not be separated but re-embedded in discussion on sustainable development. Kimathi concludes that greater focus by businesses on respecting human rights would enable business to play a greater role in poverty reduction as well as in the general protection of human rights, and would generate increased societal value. National human rights institutions have a role to play in the promotion of CSR and BRHR and they should accept it. Like Chris Sidoti, Kimathi argues that the debates on CSR and BRHR must place stronger emphasis on empowering the individuals for whom human rights and CSR generally are crucial concerns.

Chris Sidoti draws on his background as a human rights activist and former Human Rights Commissioner of Australia to discuss how the process of regulating and enforcing CSR could attain a higher degree of inclusiveness. The profit-seeking aim of business is a legitimate aim. However, business and the rest of society need to recognize that all business activity has or can have human rights dimensions. Based on cases from the Australasian region, Sidoti demonstrates several examples of how people and their human rights are affected by business. These effects may be positive, but many are negative. Sidoti argues that because business affects human rights, it has responsibilities that should be subject to law. Victims of human rights violations by business and others whose human rights are most affected by business are the ones best qualified and most entitled to participate in discussing how to regulate and enforce human rights responsibilities of business. As international law is dynamic, Sidoti argues that it should respond affirmatively to the need to include legal regulation of business and human rights and to the need for inclusion of those whose human rights are the most affected by business.

Ruth Nielsen approaches the SRSG's *Respect, Protect and Remedy* framework from the perspective of the interaction of international labour law and EU law on free movement and public procurement. Including international trade law in her discussion, she argues that CSR and the BRHR paradigm may act as a soft law bridge between international trade law and labour law but that there is need for more hard law in this area. She argues that some of the points raised by the report of the SRSG in relation to human rights and business such as access to remedies are also relevant in a more general EU context.

Cecilia Anicama's chapter reflects a human rights law approach to business and human rights in Latin America. She argues that BRHR is a topic of emerging legal relevance in Latin America. This is evident, inter alia, in the case law of the Inter-American Human Rights Commission and Court. CSR does not necessarily comprise a human rights based approach, and indeed in many countries, businesses engage in CSR without doing so in a framework that could determine the impact activities could have on human rights. Companies' CSR policies therefore do not necessarily indicate that the companies understand or reflect upon their human rights responsibilities in this regard. Anicama proposes that a specific human rights approach should be taken by companies. She argues that a human rights approach to businesses and their impact on society has already been demonstrated by emerging Inter-American human rights case law, which emphasizes the state duty to protect individuals against human rights violations by non-state actors.

Dominique Bé assesses International Framework Agreements (IFAs) as a form of company level governance. Their primary aim is the protection of minimum labour rights. Through an analysis of the extent of reference to international labour standards and human rights in various IFAs, Bé compares IFAs with CSR codes of multinational corporations. Offering a practically as well as research oriented conclusion, Bé finds that a multinational corporation's CSR code tends to reflect the contents of the same multinational corporation's international framework agreements in terms of the issues and stakeholders covered.

Jacob Dahl Rendtorff discusses what he refers to as the moralization of the firm from a perspective in which he integrates elements of business ethics, philanthropy, law and economics. He argues that to understand the ongoing moralization of the firm we need a holistic view of organizations as open systems representing broader values and cultures that cannot be explained sufficiently in terms of individual maximizing and formal contracts. Such relations must be approached with help from a broader view of institutions as expressions of moral relations and culture, different stakeholder claims and conceptions of meanings that are projected on to the organization as an open system responding to different external and internal expectations. What is needed is an interdisciplinary institutional concept of the organization integrating different external and internal value conceptions and views of the goals of the firm. He concludes that the legitimacy of corporations in modern society is founded on the idea of CSR, business ethics or human rights as instruments of social management.

Lauren Caplan addresses management challenges in relation to CSR from the perspective of varying degrees of state regulation of corporations. As a point of departure, the state makes it easier for individuals to try to create profit-making ventures by limiting the risks to which such individuals are exposed; and in exchange, the owners agree to create something of value to society, or at least to minimize the risk that its limited liability transfers to society. Caplan argues that corporate social responsibility advocates ought to take advantage of the capital markets' recognition that issues such as human rights, the environment and governance pose direct risks to corporations' long-term viability and profitability. She suggests application of the International Financial Reporting Standards as a global accounting system that could provide globally comparable and verifiable corporate disclosures not only in relation to capital market disclosure regulations but also in relation to social responsibility. The development of these standards and other related trends in the global capital markets may help society and its individual sectors get the most benefits from the dual relationship between societal and market interests through CSR. Application of such standards could also provide better background for risk analysis and investors' considerations of CSR.

Jette Steen Knudsen discusses how firms organize their Corporate Social Responsibility (CSR) initiatives in order to control their business environment. Drawing on two case studies – information technology giant Hewlett Packard (HP) and organic ice cream producer Ben & Jerry's – the chapter analyses how firms link their CSR initiatives to corporate strategy, organize these initiatives and make key CSR decisions. Discussing the two cases from the perspectives of defensive and offensive CSR, the chapter considers the organizational placement of CSR managers and the role of boards. The chapter concludes with a set of recommendations to managers in relation to links between CSR and business strategy, placement of CSR managers, and the role of boards.

5 Institutionalization of corporate integration of CSR: a managerial perspective

Institutional theory provides some help in understanding why companies engage in CSR even though it is not legally binding and there is no legal system to punish those who do not engage in CSR. Institutional forces explain how the voluntary invitation to (for example) CSR in fact disciplines and controls companies and their managers and employees.[12] Through the regulative force of social norms, organizations have a tendency to subscribe to the same ideas, the same agendas and develop the same solutions as everybody else. As a consequence, organizations are often more similar than their

---

[12] Dimaggio, P. and W.W. Powell (1991) *The New Institutionalism in Organizational Analysis*. Chicago, IL: The University of Chicago Press; Meyer, J.W. and B. Rowan (1977) Institutional organizations: Formal structure as formal myth. *American Journal of Sociology*, Vol. 83: 340–363.

leaders like to believe.[13] Dimaggio and Powell refer to this phenomenon as 'isomorphism' (iso = same; morp = form or shape). Organizations take on similar forms because they want to be recognized as legitimate institutions in society. We find this argument compelling for the case of CSR in particular. Companies compete not only for resources and customers but also for influence and social recognition, and CSR holds promises of legitimacy and social acceptance. In these competitive processes for social recognition, companies often end up imitating each other in spite of differentiation being their competitive ambition.

Meyer and Rowan define the notion of 'ceremonial conformity' to express how companies adapt their structures and norms to signal conformity with societal norms and expectations. First, the state conditions corporate support on particular hierarchical structures (coercive isomorphism). For example, the state encourages – without legislating – companies to take on more social responsibility and imposes more directly legal obligations on companies to, for example, report annually on their CSR activities. Organizational adherence to the same voluntary codes of conduct or ethical norms and cultures can also develop for other reasons. When companies model themselves vis á vis other companies which they regard as being more successful or legitimate, this is what they define as mimetic isomorphism. When Company A observes how Company B improved reputational rankings and social legitimacy as a result of their CSR efforts, Companies A, C and others may want to mimic this endeavour. Finally, as individuals with similar backgrounds share competencies, position, status, orientation and networks across organizations they come to form a certain set of norms and standards to live up to (normative isomorphism). The steadily growing number of CSR networks online as well as offline, private as well as public, is an illustration of this point. According to Dimaggio and Powell, isomorphism makes it easier for organizations to negotiate with other organizations, to attract competent employees, to be recognized as legitimate actors and to fit the administrative categories that are seen as appropriate in order to obtain contracts.

From the perspective of management, corporate social responsibility holds a strong and powerful lever for contributing to a more motivated, integrated, and loyal workforce in the same way as, for example, marketing scholars argue that CSR contributes to improved relations and loyalty among consumers.[14] Interestingly, neither the management literature nor the CSR

---

[13] Christensen, L.T., M. Morsing, and G. Cheney (2008). *Corporate Communications: Convention, Complexity and Critique*. London: Sage Publications.

[14] Brown, T.J. and P.A. Dacin (1997) The company and the product: corporate associations and consumer product responses. *Journal of Marketing*, Vol. 51, January: 68–84; Sen, S. and C.B. Bhattacharaya (2001) Does doing good always lead to doing better? Consumer reactions to corporate social responsibility. *Journal of Marketing Research*, Vol. XXXVIII, May: 225–243.

literature has paid much attention to how managers and employees relate to CSR. The management literature pays attention to the 'inside' of the corporate body while CSR literature has been much preoccupied with analysing its 'outside' relations. In other words: while management emphasizes the analysis and development of psychological competences and interpersonal skills in the organizational context, CSR literature emphasizes how companies manage their relations with external stakeholders.

A few CSR studies have specifically pointed to the importance of managerial and employee support for the corporate CSR policies to be successfully implemented[15] and a few other studies have pointed to the importance of employee welfare as a major concern for organizational CSR policies.[16] Also, in the Academy of Management's special issue on corporations as social change agents (2007), some authors theorize on how internal processes and motives of organizational members determine how organizations shape action and relate to external stakeholders,[17] and one study explores how certified management standards shape socially desired firm behaviour.[18] A few recent empirical studies have demonstrated how organizational structures and cultural norms are aligned with the CSR strategy[19] and how CSR becomes embedded among managers and employees.[20] Yet while this research draws on theories of organizational culture, organizational justice, institutional theory, and social identity, it does not link CSR to the extensive field of management.

If we are to learn more about how corporate management integrates human rights policies into their organization, we think it is very important to understand how legislated law interacts with self-regulating processes in the organization. How are codes of conduct produced and how do they relate to and influence legal issues confronting the company? What challenges occur between the company's claims to take responsibility on human rights and the company's obligation to live up to the law? It is necessary to study such action and dilemmas at the organizational level to get a clearer

---

[15] Jenkins, H. (2006) Small business champions for corporate social responsibility. *Journal of Business Ethics*, Vol. 67, No. 3: 241–256.

[16] Spence, L.J. and J.M. Lozano (2000) Communicating about ethics with small firms: experiences from the UK and Spain. *Journal of Business Ethics*, Vol. 27, No. 1: 43–53.

[17] Terlaak, A. (2007) Order without the law? The role of certified management standards in shaping socially desired firm behaviours. *Academy of Management Review*, Vol. 32, No. 3: 968–985.

[18] Id.

[19] Wit, Monique de, Wade, M. and E. Schouten (2004) Hardwiring and softwiring corporate responsibility: a vital combination. *Corporate Governance*, Vol. 6, No. 4: 491–505.

[20] Morsing, Mette and D. Oswald (2009) Sustainable leadership: management control systems and organizational culture in Novo Nordisk A/S. *Corporate Governance: The International Journal of Business in Society*, Vol. 9, No. 1: 83–99.

picture of how management deals with creating a culture amongst employees to motivate and inspire the production of a 'CSR culture' – and in our case a 'BRHR culture'.

6 Towards an understanding of the blurring of boundaries between corporate voluntary action and the law: reflexive law

As several chapters in this book suggest, corporate isomorphism as a driver for CSR is complemented today by a number of initiatives instigated by public organizations at governmental or intergovernmental level. The public policy interest in CSR and BRHR is increasingly driving authorities at different levels to initiate procedures aimed at inducing corporate self-regulation on CSR. As some of these initiatives are public and refer to international law as a normative source, they challenge both the understanding that CSR is voluntary and the conventional divide between law and CSR.

A theoretical framework is needed to appreciate and analyse the inter-relationship between law and CSR, and the emerging discourse on BRHR which is being developed through the multi-stakeholder consultations of the SRSG (2005–2008 and 2008–2011). Much legal theory is normative and output-oriented. As suggested above, CSR research and debate generally relate to law from that perspective. However, legal scholarship also offers theories which are procedural. In the context of business responsibilities as addressed by this book, we propose to draw on the theory of reflexive law to bring about a framework which has the potential to support an increased integration of the concerns of business, civil society, governments and other actors in regard to CSR and BRHR. Reflexive law offers an attractive theoretical perspective for understanding public-private regulation and collaboration on the development of CSR and BRHR, because it is process- and communication-oriented, and because its emphasis is on the exchange of expectations between different social sub-systems (such as economic, political and legal systems). It offers a regulatory strategy which has the capacity to accommodate the views and concerns of many social actors in a common process which may result in business self-regulation and forms of public-private law-making based on insight into the concerns of others.

The background for the development of reflexive law as a regulatory theory was an observation that regulatory strategies employed by welfare states in the 1970s–1980s were ineffective for addressing societal concerns, such as environmental problems, unemployment and social inequalities, which required the cooperation of non-state actors for their solution.[21] Poverty,

---

[21] Teubner, Gunther (1983) Substantive and reflective elements in modern law. *Law and Society Review*, Vol. 17, No. 2: 239–285; Teubner, Gunther (1986) Introduction, in

inequality, unemployment and environmental degradation and other ecological problems were acute concerns in many welfare states, but states were unable to achieve satisfactory changes through conventional top-down formal and substantive law. This was partly because solutions to the problems required active participation and often a change of conduct among companies and other non-state actors. The concerns which reflexive law addressed for the welfare states of the 1980s in many ways resemble those which global society is facing at the beginning of the twenty-first century. As the BRHR discourse shows, when problems move from the national to the global scale, so does much regulation and other efforts to deal with them.

As a regulatory technique, reflexive law leaves organizations such as companies the freedom and choice to determine their own norms of behaviour discursively. In principle, authorities intervene only by establishing procedures that guide self-reflection, but they may also suggest a substantive normative framework to guide the reflexive process of norm-making. Reflexive law allows public institutions to initiate self-regulation among other societal actors, such as companies, by offering a learning process that enables the latter to reflect on their societal impact and the needs and expectations of other social actors, and to integrate societal needs and demands in their management decisions. In other words, where authorities such as states or intergovernmental organizations such as the UN perceive a need for a change in the behaviour of companies or other social actors, they may set up procedural fora which promote learning and reflection but leave the final regulation to its participants. The process is reflexive in the sense that it promotes reflection at several levels and between different types of actors on mutual and differential concerns and expectations. This leads to an understanding and appreciation of the needs and concerns of other stakeholders and the interests they represent, which in turn leads to an internalization of these interests which results in self-regulation.

By proposing reflexive law as a theoretical framework for understanding CSR and BRHR, we are not claiming to be offering revolutionary ideas. Indeed, reflexive law was related to CSR in early discussions by the author of the theory, Gunther Teubner.[22] Scholars have also applied reflexive law to a range of issues of relevance to CSR, such as to environmental management

---

Teubner, Gunther (ed.) *Dilemmas of Law in the Welfare State*. Berlin and New York: Walter de Gruyter: 3–11; Teubner, Gunther (1993) *Law as an Autopoietic System*. Oxford: Blackwell.

[22] Teubner, Gunther (1984) Corporate fiduciary duties and their beneficiaries: a functional approach to the legal institutionalization of corporate responsibility, in Hopt, Klaus J. and Gunther Teubner (eds) *Corporate Governance and Directors' Liabilities*. European University Institute, Berlin and New York: Walter de Gruyt: 149–177.

and labeling as self-regulation and auditing,[23] non-financial reporting,[24] globalization of law and transnational private regulation,[25] and labour law.[26] However, such discussions of reflexive law have mainly been made by scholars with a background in law or in subjects closely related to law. What we propose is that the paradigm of reflexive law may offer the sort of medium for common understanding and cooperation which is needed to bring law and management scholarship and practice to work closer together on CSR and BRHR. Because of its emphasis on process, communication, exchange of expectations and self-regulation, the paradigm of reflexive law offers a strategic tool and theoretical framework for the economic, political and legal systems to interact and learn about mutual expectations and needs. This offers business the opportunity to learn about expectations of regulators and civil society and to self-regulate, and it offers regulators and the citizenry which they represent the opportunity to shape CSR and BRHR without resort to formal statutory law. The reflexive law approach, however, does not rule out formal law. It complements formal law, and provides a forum for understanding, cooperation and soft guidance.

While it may offer a medium for learning and understanding, reflexive law is no panacea. Some scholars who have otherwise welcomed the contribution of the theory have identified important weaknesses, including

---

[23] Orts, E.W. (1995) Reflexive environmental law. *Northwestern University Law Review*, Vol. 89, No. 4: 1227–1339; Orts, E.W. (1995) A reflexive model of environmental regulation. *Business Ethics Quarterly*, Vol. 5, No. 4: 779–794.

[24] Hess, D. (1999) Social reporting: a reflexive law approach to corporate social responsiveness. *Journal of Corporation Law*, Vol. 25, No 1, Fall: 41–84.

[25] Scheuerman, W.E. (2001) Reflexive law and the challenges of globalisation. *The Journal of Political Philosophy*, Vol. 9, No. 1: 81–102.

[26] For example, Wilthagen, Ton (1994) Reflexive rationality in the regulation of occupational safety and health, in Rogowski, Ralf and Wilthagen, Ton (eds) *Reflexive Labour Law: Studies in Industrial Relations and Employment Regulation*. Deventer and Boston, MA: Kluwer Law and Taxation Publishers: 345–376; Rogowski, Ralf (1994) Industrial relations, labour conflict resolution and reflexive labour law, in Rogowski, Ralf and Wilthagen, Ton (eds) *Reflexive Labour Law: Studies in Industrial Relations and Employment Regulation*. Deventer and Boston, MA: Kluwer Law and Taxation Publishers: 53–93; Rogowski, Ralf (2001) The concept of reflexive labour law: its theoretical background and possible applications, in Priban, J. and David Nelken (eds) *Law's New Boundaries: The Consequences of Legal Autopoiesis*. Aldershot: Ashgate/Dartmouth; Rogowski, Ralf (1998) Autopoietic industrial relations and reflexive labour law, in Wilthagen, Ton (ed.) *Advancing Theory in Labour Law and Industrial Relations in a Global Context*, Amsterdam: North-Holland Press; Deakin, S. and R. Hobbs (2007) False dawn for CSR? Shifts in regulatory policy and the response of the corporate and financial sectors in Britain. *Corporate Governance*, Vol. 15, No. 1: 68–76; Arthurs, Harry (2008) Corporate self-regulation: political economy, state regulation and reflexive labour law, in Bercusson, Brian and Cynthia Estlund (eds) *Regulating Labour in the Wake of Globalisation*. Oxford and Portland, Oregon: Hart: 19–35.

its lack of specificity in explaining how external concerns are to be integrated in internal processes, how to balance them against internal concerns, and how to handle power disparities in general.[27] It is in this light that Buhmann's chapter, as indicated above, proposes that Habermasian theory on deliberative law-making may complement reflexive law in terms of how to balance power disparities by providing qualitative guidance for the management and design of reflexive regulatory fora to provide participants with an actual say.

The reflexive law approach is open to application not only by legal scholars but also by a range of other social scientists, such as management, organizational, communication and political science scholars. The communicative aspects of the interrelationship between management and law which informs CSR and contributes to its on-going development are among the points highlighted by Rasche's chapter on the Global Compact as a necessary supplement to conventional regulation. Assessed from the perspective of reflexive law, the Global Compact need not be seen merely as 'a necessary supplement' to state regulation of company action in a context of global governance. Given its focus on learning, sharing of experience and encouraging business self-regulation based on concerns of other actors (such as the concerns embodied in the international law instruments on human rights, labour, environment and anticorruption which inform the Ten Principles, or the concerns voiced by civil society or participating companies) the Global Compact may be considered an example of reflexive law. This does not mean that the Global Compact is a legal instrument, but it may offer important lessons for future consideration on how governments, business and civil society may interact and communicate with regard to regulation of societal concerns (such as climate change and poverty).

The consultative process of the SRSG during his first mandate is another example of what may be characterized as reflexive law. The process did not result in a regulatory framework (to the extent that the policy framework presented in the 2008 report is not considered soft law, which it may in fact be). The process of consultation did result in business entities and organizations engaging in self-regulation on issues related to human rights and business. In at least one case, it appears to have caused actors who had previously expressed considerable reservations towards the idea that businesses

---

[27] See Scheuerman, W.E. (2001) *supra* note 25 at 86; Neves, M. (2001) From the autopoiesis to the allopoiesis of law. *Journal of Law and Society*, Vol. 28, No. 2: 242–264, at 263–254; compare also Dalberg-Larsen, Jørgen (1991) *Ret, styring og selvforvaltning*. Aarhus: Juridisk Bogformidling: 15–16, 136. Sand goes as far as characterising Teubner's theory of reflexive law as having a preliminary and un-finished character, see Sand, Inger-Johanne (1996) *Styring av kompleksitet: Rettslige former for statlig rammestyring og desentralisert statsforvaltniing*. Bergen: Fagbokforlaget Vigmostad & Bjørke: 94.

should take responsibility for human rights to change stances.[28] Perhaps most importantly, the consultative approach of the SRSG demonstrates a novel way of making international law, and of including participants hitherto excluded from the formal sphere of international lawmaking. The SRSG process until mid-2008 granted a voice to companies, and invited civil society, including representatives of the concerns of individual persons and victims, into the process. The extended mandate (2008–2011) encourages the SRSG to continue this style of consultations, with increased focus on victims. This may not only be an opportunity to include a wider range of groups including the voices of the individuals to whom Sidoti refers in his article. It may also be an indication that intergovernmental organizations are realizing that to be effective with regard to social concerns, regulation needs to involve those concerned and those to be subjected to resulting norms. These are the lessons which many states have realized with regard to national level regulation of environmental and related concerns, and which essentially build on the theory of reflexive law. While the formal structure and law-making process of international society remains state-centred, intergovernmental type multi-stakeholder fora on CSR and BRHR, such as the Global Compact and the SRSG process, may indicate a gradual course towards including non-state actors to a higher degree than before. This may also allow for better integration of the concerns, objectives and insight of law and management as theory and practice. In addition, a regulatory strategy focusing on firms' internationalization of externalities may contribute to the development of corporate cultures respectful of human rights, a need which has repeatedly been highlighted by the SRSG since the presentation of his 2008 report, the *Protect, Respect, Remedy* UN Framework on business and human rights. Such a strategy need not compete with or replace conventional corporate law. Like other instances of reflexive law, it may complement substantive governmental law and provide parts of a pragmatic solution to national, regional and global concerns on CSR and BRHR.

---

[28] For this example of change of stances, see IOE, ICC, BIAC (2006) *Business and human rights: The role of business in weak governance zones: Business proposals for effective ways of addressing dilemma situations in weak governance zones*, Geneva, December 2006.

Part I
Setting the Stage

1
Conceptualizing the Home State Duty to Protect Human Rights

Sara L. Seck

1 Introduction*

The Special Representative to the UN Secretary General on Business and Human Rights (SRSG) has identified the State duty to protect against human rights abuses by non-State actors, including business, as one of the fundamental pillars of the *Protect, Respect, Remedy* Framework [Framework].[1] The Framework 'rests on differentiated but complementary responsibilities', and comprises three 'core principles': the State duty to protect, the corporate responsibility to respect human rights, and the need for more effective access to remedies.[2] However, the jurisdictional scope of the State duty to protect is disputed. According to the SRSG, international law provides that States are required to protect against human rights abuses by businesses 'affecting persons within their territory or jurisdiction'.[3] With regard to home States:

> Experts disagree on whether international law requires home States to help prevent human rights abuses abroad by corporations based within their territory. There is greater consensus that those States are not prohibited from doing so where a recognized basis of jurisdiction exists, and the actions of the home State meet an overall reasonableness test, which includes non-intervention in the internal affairs of other States. Indeed,

---

* The author would like to thank Jennifer Butkus and David Vaughan for their excellent research assistance, and the Social Sciences and Research Council of Canada for funding. I am also grateful to Andreas Rasche and Karin Buhmann for their very helpful suggestions.

[1] U.N. Hum. Rts. Council, *Promotion and Protection of All Human Rights, Civil, Political, Economic, Social and Cultural Rights, Including the Right to Development: Protect, Respect and Remedy: A Framework for Business and Human Rights*, U.N. Doc. A/HRC/8/5 (7 Apr. 2008) (*prepared by* John Ruggie) [hereinafter *Framework*].

[2] *Id.*, ¶9.

[3] *Id.*, ¶18.

there is increasing encouragement at the international level, including from the treaty bodies, for home States to take regulatory action to prevent abuse by their companies overseas.[4]

This chapter will explore the scope of the home State duty to protect, and in the process will underscore the complementary nature of the responsibilities in the Framework. The SRSG has accepted a renewed 3-year mandate to 'operationalize' the Framework by 'providing "practical recommendations" and "concrete guidance" to States, businesses and other social actors on its implementation'.[5] In 2009 keynote presentation at the EU Presidency Conference in Stockholm, the SRSG highlighted the importance of better understanding the jurisdictional aspects of the State duty to protect, and described 'extraterritorial jurisdiction' as the 'elephant in the room that polite people have preferred not to talk about'.[6] Yet, in order to 'achieve practical progress', the SRSG noted that it is necessary to 'pierce the mystique of extraterritorial jurisdiction and sort out what is truly problematic from what is entirely permissible under international law and would be in the best interests of all concerned'.[7] This chapter will seek to contribute to this project. Beyond this, however, the chapter will explore an even larger elephant in the room – whether, beyond permissibility, the home State duty to protect should be interpreted to mandate the exercise of home State jurisdiction over transnational corporate conduct in order to both prevent and remedy human rights harms. The chapter will then briefly examine some practical applications that might flow from this conclusion.

The chapter is structured as follows. First, the scope of the permissibility of home State regulation will be examined under the public international law of jurisdiction. In essence, the permissibility question asks when it is that the exercise of home State jurisdiction over transnational corporate conduct is or is not in violation of the jurisdictional rules of public international law. This analysis will then be evaluated from the perspective of Third World Approaches to International Law (TWAIL), an approach to international legal scholarship adopted by a diverse group of scholars who are

---

[4] *Id.*, ¶19.
[5] U.N. Hum. Rts. Council, *Promotion and Protection of All Human Rights, Civil, Political, Economic, Social and Cultural Rights, Including the Right to Development: Business and Human Rights: Towards Operationalizing the 'Protect, Respect and Remedy' framework*, U.N. Doc. A/HRC/11/13 (22 Apr. 2009) (*prepared by* John Ruggie) [hereinafter *Operationalizing*].
[6] John G. Ruggie, UN SRSG for Business and Human Rights, *Keynote Presentation at EU Presidency Conference on the 'Protect, Respect and Remedy' Framework*, 2, available at: http://www.reports-and-materials.org/Ruggie-presentation-Stockholm-10-Nov-2009.pdf (Stockholm, 10–11 Nov. 2009) [hereinafter, *Stockholm Keynote*].
[7] *Id.*, at 6.

committed to reforming the international legal system by taking seriously the experiences of those States or societies who self-identify as Third World.[8] Second, this chapter will explore whether, beyond permissibility, home States are obligated to comply with the State duty to protect human rights. The international law of state responsibility will be scrutinized here. If, as I conclude, home States should indeed be understood to be obligated to comply with the State duty to protect, then compliance with this duty must include structuring home State institutions so as to both facilitate corporate compliance with the responsibility to respect rights, and facilitate access to remedies by victims of human rights abuses. These home State institutions include export credit agencies, stock exchanges, financial institutions and even corporate laws themselves, which together create the structural conditions of the global economic order without which transnational corporations (TNCs) and other businesses would be unable to operate. Finally, the chapter will explore the practical implications of these conclusions by evaluating a single question: whether mandating that institutional investors adhere to the UN Principles of Responsible Investment would satisfy the State duty to protect human rights.[9]

2 The permissibility of home State regulation

The State duty to protect 'lies at the very core of the international human rights regime'.[10] International human rights treaty bodies recommend that States take all necessary steps to protect against abuse by non-State actors, including prevention, investigation and punishment, and provision of access to redress.[11] The duty has both legal and policy dimensions, and while States have discretion as to how to implement the duty, both regulation and adjudication are considered appropriate measures.[12] However, according to the Framework, home States 'may feel reluctant to regulate against overseas harms' because the 'permissible scope of national regulation with extraterritorial effect remains poorly understood'.[13] Alternatively, this reluctance may be 'out of concern that those firms might lose investment opportunities or relocate their headquarters'.[14] As a consequence, the

---

[8] Obiora Chinedu Okafor, Critical Third World Approaches to International Law (TWAIL): Theory, Methodology, or Both? 10 *Int. Community L. Rev.* 371, 376 (2008) [hereinafter Okafor ICLR].
[9] United Nations Principles for Responsible Investment, available at: http://www.unpri.org/principles/ [hereinafter, UNPRI].
[10] *Framework, supra* note 1, ¶9.
[11] *Id.*, ¶18.
[12] *Id.*
[13] *Id.*, ¶14.
[14] *Id.*

SRSG has recently stated that 'we have the oddity of home states promoting investments abroad – extra-territorially, if you will – often in conflict affected regions where bad things are known to happen, but not requiring adequate due diligence from companies because doing so may be perceived as exercising extra-territorial jurisdiction'.[15]

Many scholars analyse the permissible scope of home State jurisdiction by framing the problem as one relating to 'extraterritorial' jurisdiction.[16] Yet, 'extraterritorial' is not only notoriously difficult to define, but is often associated with notions of illegality.[17] Indeed, continued reference to extraterritoriality may undermine recognition of existing territorial links between home State institutional structures and the global economic activities of TNCs, unintentionally reinforcing home State reluctance to regulate in the first place.[18] Moreover, 'extraterritorial jurisdiction' is not a recognized basis of jurisdiction under public international law.

Despite this, not surprisingly, the SRSG's EU presidency address explicitly incorporates the language of extraterritoriality, in contrast with the Framework itself. The following section will examine the public international law of jurisdiction using the discussion of home State jurisdiction in the Framework as a starting point. The recent comments of the SRSG on extraterritorial jurisdiction will then be explored, followed by an assessment of the problem from a TWAIL perspective.

2.1 The public international law of jurisdiction

The Framework proposes that an analysis of the scope of home State jurisdiction should begin by finding a recognized basis of jurisdiction under

---

[15] *Stockholm Keynote*, *supra* note 6 at 6.
[16] *See, e.g.*, JENNIFER A. ZERK, MULTINATIONALS AND CORPORATE SOCIAL RESPONSIBILITY, 133–142, 145–197 (2006); OLIVIER DE SCHUTTER, EXTRA-TERRITORIAL JURISDICTION AS A TOOL FOR IMPROVING THE HUMAN RIGHTS ACCOUNTABILITY OF TRANSNATIONAL CORPORATIONS, *available at* http://www.reports-and-materials.org/Olivier-de-Schutter-report-for-SRSG-re-extraterritorial-jurisdiction-Dec-2006.pdf (report prepared as a background paper for the legal experts meeting with John Ruggie in Brussels, 3–4 Nov. 2006) [hereinafter DE SCHUTTER REPORT]; Surya Deva, *Acting Extraterritorially to Tame Multinational Corporations for Human Rights Violations: Who Should 'Bell the Cat'?*, 5 MELB. J. INT'L. L. 37 (2004); Christen L. Broecker, *"Better the Devil you Know": Home State Approaches to Transnational Corporate Accountability* 41 N.Y.U. J. INT'L L. & POL. 159 (2008).
[17] ANDREAS R. LOWENFELD, INTERNATIONAL LITIGATION AND THE QUEST FOR REASONABLENESS: ESSAYS IN PRIVATE INTERNATIONAL LAW 15 (1996); Sara L. Seck, *Home State Responsibility and Local Communities: The Case of Global Mining*, 11 YALE HUM. RTS. & DEV. L. J. 177, 186 (2008) [hereinafter Seck in YHRDLJ].
[18] *But see* Austen L. Parrish, *Reclaiming International Law from Extraterritoriality*, 93 MINN. L. REV. 815 (2009) (arguing that extraterritorial regulation is not a solution to global problems).

public international law, and then examining whether the exercise of home State jurisdiction meets an overall test of reasonableness.[19] The nationality principle is often assumed to be the most appropriate basis of jurisdiction upon which to ground a preliminary justification for the regulation of TNCs by home States.[20] However, State practice diverges in the determination of corporate nationality, and the factors that determine corporate nationality may differ even within a single State as the regulatory context changes.[21] Even where corporate nationality is clear, widespread acceptance of corporate entity theory, according to which each foreign affiliate is a separate legal entity from the parent corporation, restricts the ability of the home State of the parent company to directly regulate foreign subsidiary or associate companies.[22]

While the definition of home State in essence depends upon the ability to identify the nationality of a TNC,[23] this is often done in the public international law context by reference to 'the place of incorporation' or 'the place from which control over the corporation's activities is primarily exercised'.[24] The importance of 'place' suggests that an examination of territorial links might serve equally well as a preliminary justification for the exercise of home State jurisdiction. Instinctively, a focus upon territoriality draws attention to the territory of the host State where the impact of the human rights violation is felt, and to any subsidiary or affiliate corporate entity based within host State territory. However, attention is equally due the territory of origin. The home State, as the State of origin of foreign direct investment, will necessarily have a strong territorial connection to conduct that takes place within home State territory. This conduct may take many forms, including decision-making at corporate headquarters, decision-making by a government body or private financial institution in relation to financing

---

[19] *Framework, supra* note 1, ¶19.
[20] *See, e.g.*, ZERK, *supra* note 16, at 106–109; DE SCHUTTER REPORT, *supra* note 16, at 29–34.
[21] Seck in YHRDLJ, *supra* note 17, at 187–188; DE SCHUTTER REPORT, *supra* note 16, at 30; CYNTHIA DAY WALLACE, THE MULTINATIONAL ENTERPRISE AND LEGAL CONTROL: HOST STATE SOVEREIGNTY IN AN ERA OF ECONOMIC GLOBALIZATION 132–137 (2002).
[22] Corporate enterprise theory, a competing theory, is described as an emerging doctrine. LOWENFELD, *supra* note 17, at 85–86; Upendra Baxi, *Mass Torts, Multinational Enterprise Liability and Private International Law*, 276 REC. DES COURS 297, 399–401 (1999). A home State may still regulate a parent company so that it exercises control over a foreign subsidiary without directly regulating that entity. F.A. MANN, *The Doctrine of International Jurisdiction Revisited After Twenty Years*, 186 REC. DES COURS 19, 60–63 (1984); ZERK, *supra* note 16, at 108.
[23] ZERK, *id.* at 146–151.
[24] *Id.* at 147. The 'nationality of owners or those having substantial "control" over the activities or operations of the corporation' may also serve to identify TNC nationality.

or insurance support, or decision-making by a stock exchange in relation to listing to obtain equity financing. While this conduct may not in and of itself directly cause the human rights violation, it does play an essential supporting role without which the human rights violation could not occur. Moreover, all of these home State institutional structures, whether conceived of as 'public' or 'private,' are supported by a network of professionals, including underwriters, auditors, analysts and lawyers, who are primarily based in a city located within the territory of the home State.[25]

Once a recognized basis of jurisdiction is identified providing a preliminary justification for the exercise of home State jurisdiction, the question remains as to whether or not the exercise of jurisdiction is reasonable. In particular, does it constitute an unacceptable intervention into the internal affairs of the host State? Incidents of concurrent or overlapping jurisdiction are quite commonplace; indeed, they are inevitable in a global economic order with both host and home States.[26] On the other hand, incidents of truly conflicting jurisdiction, where it would be impossible for a TNC to comply with the laws of both the home State and the host State, are likely to arise less frequently in the human rights context.[27] In most cases there is no true conflict between the laws of the home and host States, but the home State's exercise of concurrent jurisdiction is understood as intrusive by the host State, touching matters that are considered central to the 'very idea' of state sovereignty.[28]

The reasonableness of an exercise of home State jurisdiction is often said to involve a balancing of State interests, including consideration of factors such as the links to the territory of the regulating state; the character of the activity being regulated; its importance to the regulating state; and the importance of the regulation to the international system.[29] An alternative approach to the resolution of jurisdictional conflicts recognizes

---

[25] On the importance of global cities, *see especially* SASKIA SASSEN, LOSING CONTROL?: SOVEREIGNTY IN AN AGE OF GLOBALISATION (1996); SASKIA SASSEN, TERRITORY, AUTHORITY, RIGHTS: FROM MEDIEVAL TO GLOBAL ASSEMBLAGES (2006).

[26] Seck in YHRDLJ, *supra* note 17, at 192; D.W. Bowett, *Jurisdiction: Changing Patterns of Authority Over Activities and Resources, in* THE STRUCTURE AND PROCESS OF INTERNATIONAL LAW: ESSAYS IN LEGAL PHILOSOPHY DOCTRINE AND THEORY 555, 565 (R. St. J. Macdonald & Douglas Johnston eds., 1983).

[27] Seck in YHRDLJ, *id.* at 192–193. A true conflict would occur only where the host state mandates the TNC to violate human rights, not where the host state omits to regulate the TNC so as to prevent human rights violations.

[28] Craig Scott, *Translating Torture into Transnational Tort: Conceptual Divides in the Debate on Corporate Accountability for Human Rights Harms, in* TORTURE AS TORT: COMPARATIVE PERSPECTIVES ON THE DEVELOPMENT OF TRANSNATIONAL HUMAN RIGHTS LITIGATION 45, 53 (Craig Scott, ed., 2001) [hereinafter TORTURE AS TORT].

[29] Seck in YHRDLJ, *supra* note 17, at 195. *See also* RESTATEMENT (THIRD) OF FOREIGN RELATIONS LAW OF THE UNITED STATES §403 (1987); ZERK, *supra* note 16,

that home States may exercise jurisdiction not only to enforce their own policy goals, but also to enforce international policy goals such as those of international human rights law.[30] According to August Reinisch, where the exercise of home State jurisdiction could validly be described as an attempt to enforce international human rights norms through national legal systems, the substantive international law principles of human rights should override the formal principles from the public international law of jurisdiction.[31] In these situations, 'affected states will have a hard time justifying their disregard of human rights in rejecting the extraterritorial acts of others'.[32]

The most recent statement by the SRSG on the permissibility of extraterritorial jurisdiction takes a slightly different approach. The SRSG explicitly distinguishes between what he describes as 'true extraterritorial jurisdiction exercised directly in relation to overseas actors or activities', and 'domestic measures that have extraterritorial implications'.[33] In the case of direct extraterritorial jurisdiction, the SRSG notes that States 'usually rely on a clear nationality link to the perpetrator'. By contrast, domestic measures with extraterritorial implications 'rely on territory as the jurisdictional basis, even though they may have extraterritorial implications.'[34] Both, according to the SRSG, can be controversial, although domestic measures with extraterritorial implications are most common.[35] In general, 'principles-based approaches' appear 'less problematic than detailed rules-based approaches', due to 'genuine legal, political and cultural differences among states'.[36]

In recognition that extraterritorial jurisdiction 'constitutes a range of measures', the SRSG ultimately proposes a matrix:

> It has two rows: direct extraterritorial jurisdiction over parties or activities abroad, and domestic measures with extraterritorial implications. And it has three columns: public policies, prescriptive regulations, and enforcement action. The combination yields six cells – six broad types of measures with differing extraterritorial reach – not all of which are equally controversial or as likely to trigger objections and resistance.

---

at 136–139; Bowett, *supra* note 26, at 566–572; DE SCHUTTER REPORT, *supra* note 16, at 27.

[30] August Reinisch, *The Changing International Legal Framework for Dealing with Non-State Actors, in* NON-STATE ACTORS AND HUMAN RIGHTS 37, 58 (Philip Alston ed., 2005).

[31] *Id.*

[32] *Id. See also* Seck in YHRDLJ, *supra* note 17, at 195.

[33] *Stockholm Keynote, supra* note 6 at 3.

[34] *Id.* at 3.

[35] *Id.* at 4.

[36] *Id.* at 4.

Yet, the SRSG concludes, 'all cells' are 'under-populated', 'not only the most difficult and controversial'.[37] While the SRSG clearly acknowledges the legitimacy of concerns expressed by home States, host States and corporations about extraterritorial jurisdiction, he is clear: 'the debate [about extraterritorial jurisdiction] must be had because the business and human rights agenda ultimately is about closing governance gaps'.[38]

2.2 Insights from Third World Approaches to International Law

As described above, August Reinisch proposes that where the exercise of home State jurisdiction could validly be described as an attempt to enforce international human rights norms through national legal systems, the substantive international law principles of human rights should override formal principles from the public international law of jurisdiction that might suggest the home State is acting in violation of international law. One of the difficulties with Reinisch's proposal, however, is determining whether a home State is in fact regulating in order to enforce an international norm, or whether its conduct is better described as serving its own national policy goals.[39] A related question is whether home State reluctance to regulate in relation to the State duty to protect is attributable to a lack of understanding of permissible jurisdictional scope, or whether it is more accurately described as arising 'out of concern that those firms might lose investment opportunities or relocate their headquarters'.[40] The SRSG's recent statement on extraterritorial jurisdiction appears premised upon the assumption that there is in fact misunderstanding over the permissible scope of home State jurisdiction. However, if in practice home States only exercise jurisdiction when it would serve to promote internal economic interests, then the reluctance to implement even domestic public policies with extraterritorial implications in the human rights realm as identified by the SRSG becomes easier to understand, although more difficult to justify.

A TWAIL assessment of the jurisdictional rules of public international law may be helpful here. TWAIL, or Third World Approaches to International Law, is an approach to international legal scholarship adopted by a diverse group of scholars who are:

> solidly united by a shared ethical commitment to the intellectual and practical struggle to expose, reform or even retrench those features of the international legal system that help create or maintain the generally unequal, unfair, or unjust global order... a commitment to centre the *rest*

---

[37] *Id.* at 5.
[38] *Id.* at 5.
[39] Reinisch, *supra* note 30. *See also* Zerk, *supra* note 16, at 136–138. Zerk notes that "the motives of the regulating state are rarely (if ever) pure." *Id.* at 137.
[40] *Framework, supra* note 1, ¶14.

rather than merely the *west*, thereby taking the lives and experiences of those who have self-identified as Third World much more seriously than has generally been the case.[41]

While TWAIL is not a unanimous, monolithic school of thought, TWAIL scholarship is united in its broad opposition to the unjust global order.[42] TWAIL historical scholarship has highlighted the colonial origins of international law, revealing how despite international law's universal claims, it was used to justify, manage and legitimize the subjugation and oppression of Third World peoples.[43] Colonialism was central to the formation of international law, and neocolonialism continues to be central to the structure of international law today through contemporary initiatives such as the discourse of development that presents Third World peoples as deficient and in need of international intervention.[44] According to Antony Anghie, the practices of powerful Western states following the establishment of the United Nations and continuing today may be best understood as the 'continuation, consolidation, and elaboration of imperialism'.[45] However, TWAIL scholars do not reject international law, but rather seek to make the people of the Third World the ultimate decision-makers when identifying and interpreting international legal rules. As international law provides Third World peoples with no real voice, TWAIL scholars 'themselves must imagine or somehow approximate the actual impact of specific rules or practices on their daily lives and define or interpret those rules accordingly'.[46] TWAIL scholars have also asked how to define the Third World, with many concluding that a fixed geographic approach is unhelpful; rather, the significance of Third World is tied to a sense of subordination within the global system shared by a group of States or societies that self-identify as Third World.[47]

---

[41] Okafor ICLR, *supra* note 8 at 376.
[42] Obiora Chinedu Okafor, *Newness, Imperialism and International Legal Reform in Our Time: A TWAIL Perspective*, 43 OSGOODE HALL L.J. 176 (2005) [hereinafter, Okafor Newness]. *See also* Makau Mutua, *What Is TWAIL*, 94 AM. SOC'Y INT'L PROC. 31 (2000); Karen Mickelson, *Taking Stock of TWAIL Histories*, 10 INT'L COMMUNITY L. REV. 353 (2008).
[43] Antony Anghie & B.S. Chimni, *Third World Approaches to International Law and Individual Responsibility for Internal Conflict*, 2 CHINESE J. INT'L L. 77 at 187 (2003).
[44] *Id.* at 193.
[45] ANTONY ANGHIE, IMPERIALISM, SOVEREIGNTY AND THE MAKING OF INTERNATIONAL LAW 11–12 (2005). *See also* BALAKRISHNAN RAJAGOPAL, INTERNATIONAL LAW FROM BELOW: DEVELOPMENT, SOCIAL MOVEMENTS AND THIRD WORLD RESISTANCE (2003).
[46] Anne-Marie Slaughter & Steven R. Ratner, *The Method is the Message*, 36 STUD. TRANSNAT'L LEGAL POL'Y 239 at 248–249 (2004).
[47] Okafor *Newness, supra* note 42 at 174–175. *See also* Balakrishnon Rajagopal, *Locating the Third World in Cultural Geography*, THIRD WORLD LEGAL STUDIES (1998–1999).

The unilateral exercise of home State jurisdiction in the human rights realm creates a curious problem from a TWAIL perspective. On the one hand, if home States only exercise jurisdiction to promote internal economic goals, then unilateral home State regulation, even ostensibly addressing human rights concerns, appears innately problematic as an imperialistic infringement of host State sovereignty.[48] Moreover, if home State regulation designed to prevent and remedy human rights harms were to become routine State practice that contributed to the development of customary international law norms, it could unintentionally serve to reinforce the neocolonialist tendencies of international law.[49] On the other hand, to the extent that neocolonial tendencies are already embedded within the structure of international law, the public international law rules of jurisdiction which suggest that extraterritoriality in the business and human rights context is illicit and a violation of international law could themselves be neocolonialist. The language of extraterritoriality thus shields home States from pressure to take action to ensure home State TNCs respect the rights of citizens in Third World host States. It also shields the home State from the fear that another home State might take action to protect the human rights of its own Third World peoples, including perhaps indigenous peoples.

Notably, many TWAIL scholars complain that home State courts have been reluctant to exercise 'justice jurisdiction' over TNC conduct that has violated the human rights of communities within developing countries, while at the same time according protection to developed State investors.[50] Moreover, according to Balakrishnan Rajagopal, despite the problematic reliance of human rights discourse upon the State as the primary duty-holder, human rights should not be dismissed.[51] The problem with human rights theory is that it is linked with the colonial origins of the doctrine of sovereignty, for the State is given a predominant role as the source and implementer of the normative framework.[52] Consequently, the 'radical democratic potential in

---

[48] *See, e.g.*, B.S. Chimni, *An Outline of a Marxist Course on Public International Law*, 17 LEIDEN J. INT'L L. 1, 19–20 (2004).

[49] *See further* Sara L. Seck, *Unilateral Home State Regulation: Imperialism or Tool for Subaltern Resistance?* 46 OSGOODE HALL L. J. 565 (2008) [hereinafter Seck in OHLJ].

[50] Chimni, *supra* note 48, at 20. *See generally* Baxi, *supra* note 22; Muthucumaraswamy Sornarajah, *Linking State Responsibility for Certain Harms Caused by Corporate Nationals Abroad to Civil Recourse in the Legal Systems of Home States, in* TORTURE AS TORT 491, *supra* note 28.

[51] RAJAGOPAL, *supra* note 45, at 186.

[52] *Id.* at 187. Thus, despite its "nominal anti-sovereignty posture", human rights remains a "state-centred" discourse, and protest or resistance movements inside societies are ignored.

human rights' must be sought out, 'by paying attention to the pluriverse of human rights, enacted in many counter-hegemonic frames'.[53]

What might this mean? While TWAIL calls for justice jurisdiction have generally been made in relation to the exercise of adjudicative jurisdiction by courts, the SRSG has correctly noted that courts are reluctant to accept these cases without clear legislative or executive support.[54] This suggests that a TWAIL analysis of home State regulation necessitates a distinction between regulation that enables host State individuals and local communities to seek redress from harm (and to seek to prevent harm in the first place), and regulation that imposes home State values or standards on communities in other States without the participation, consultation or consent of those same communities.[55] It also suggests that asking what the permissible scope of home State extraterritorial jurisdiction is may serve to distract from the real elephant in the room: whether State-created institutional structures of the global economic order must regulate the TNC conduct that they facilitate so as to protect individuals and local communities from human rights violations, and to offer access to remedies in the event of harm.

3 Home state obligations

3.1 Jurisdictional scope and the *ILC articles*

The extent of home State obligations depends upon the scope of jurisdictional clauses in international human rights treaties or as understood under customary international human rights law. According to the Framework, international law provides that States are required to protect against human rights abuses by business 'affecting persons within their territory or jurisdiction'.[56] Thus, while territoriality could serve as a preliminary justification for the exercise of home State jurisdiction under public international law, territoriality does not so easily ground an obligation to regulate where those affected by conduct supported by home State institutions are physically located in the host State. Moreover, although nationality jurisdiction has been invoked in relation to transnational corporate conduct in

---

[53] Balakrishnan Rajagopal, *Counter-hegemonic International Law: rethinking Human Rights and Development as a Third World Strategy*, 27 THIRD WORLD Q. 767 at 768 (2006).
[54] *Stockholm Keynote, supra* note 6, at 3.
[55] Seck in OHLJ, *supra* note 49.
[56] *Framework, supra* note 1, ¶18. Some States claim the scope of the duty is limited to protecting those "both within their territory and jurisdiction". *Id.* at n. 10.

multilateral efforts to regulate transnational bribery,[57] human rights treaties do not make specific mention of the scope of State obligations in relation to TNCs.

The precise scope of obligations under international human rights law hinges upon the meaning of 'jurisdiction'.[58] Despite some controversial jurisprudence from the European Court of Human Rights (ECHR),[59] international human rights treaty bodies generally support a broad concept of jurisdiction that includes where the victim is within the 'power, effective control or authority' of the State.[60] This approach has also found favour with the International Court of Justice.[61] Thus, even if home State conduct is understood as taking place on home State territory, the jurisdictional scope of the obligation must extend to the extraterritorial effect of this conduct. In essence, the problem rests in determining to whom a State owes obligations: merely the public within the State's territorial borders, or all those impacted by home State conduct? Sigrun Skogly and other scholars have persuasively argued that universal respect for international human rights

---

[57] *See, e.g.*, OECD Convention on Combating Bribery of Foreign Public Officials in International Business Transactions art. 2, 17 Dec. 1997, DAFFE/IME/BR(97)20, 37 I.L.M. 1, available at http://www.oecd.org/dataoecd/4/18/38028044.pdf (obliging State parties to exercise jurisdiction in respect of bribery offences committed abroad by their nationals).

[58] *See, e.g.*, U.N. Hum. Rts Comm., *General Comment No. 31*, The Nature of the General Legal Obligation Imposed on States Parties to the Covenant on Civil and Political Rights, ¶3, U.N. Doc. CCPR/C/21/Rev.1/Add. 13 (26 May 2004) (clarifying that while Article 2(1) of the ICCPR refers to both territory and jurisdiction, a state's obligations extend to individuals who are not within the state's territory but who are subject to its jurisdiction). *See* Robert McCorquodale & Penelope Simons, *Responsibility Beyond Borders: State Responsibility for Extraterritorial Violations by Corporations of International Human Rights Law*, 70(4) MODERN LAW REV. 598, 602–605, n. 25 (2007); EXTRATERRITORIAL APPLICATION OF HUMAN RIGHTS TREATIES (F. Coomans & M.T. Kamminga eds., 2004) [hereinafter EXTRATERRITORIAL APPLICATION]. *See also* Smita Narula, *The Right to Food: Holding Global Actors Accountable Under International Law*, 44 COLUMBIA J. TRANSNAT'L L. 691, 728–737 (2006) (discussing the jurisdictional scope of the ICESCR as extending to jurisdiction exercised through "effective control" or international cooperation).

[59] Banković v. Belgium, App. No. 52207/99, 2001-XII Eur. Ct. H.R., 41 I.L.M. 517. *Banković* has been criticised for mistakenly applying principles drawn from the public international law of jurisdiction, rather than following the ECHR's own jurisprudence and that of other international human rights bodies in relation to the extraterritorial scope of obligations. *See* M. Scheinin, *Extraterritorial Effect of the International Covenant on Civil and Political Rights*, in EXTRATERRITORIAL APPLICATION, *id.* 73, 79–80.

[60] McCorquodale & Simons, *supra* note 58, at 605.

[61] *Id.* Citing Legal Consequences on the Construction of a Wall in the Occupied Palestinian Territory (Advisory Op.), 2004 I.C.J. 136, ¶¶107–113 (9 July); Armed Activities on the Territory of the Congo (Democratic Republic of the Congo v. Uganda) (Merits), 2005 I.C.J. 1, ¶¶216–220 (Dec. 19).

must go hand-in-hand with universal human rights obligations.[62] Indeed, according to Skogly and Mark Gibney, 'international human rights treaty law, by definition, is premised on the notion of extraterritorial obligations'.[63] The same conclusion may be reached without resorting to the language of extraterritoriality, however. If the primary rules that specify the content of home State obligations include due diligence obligations of prevention and reparation of harm by non-State actor TNCs, then the home State obligations must extend to the fullest possible exercise of legal authority by the State.[64]

There are no extraterritorial limitations under the secondary rules of the international law of State responsibility as provided by the *Draft Articles on Responsibility of States for Internationally Wrongful Acts* (*ILC Articles*).[65] Moreover, practical considerations commonly associated with an exercise of extraterritorial jurisdiction should also not create insurmountable obstacles, particularly as obligations of prevention under the *ILC Articles* are 'usually construed as best efforts obligations, requiring the State to take all reasonable or necessary measures to prevent a given event from occurring, but without warranting that the event will not occur'.[66] Nor are there any extraterritorial limitations inherent in the companion work of the ILC on the rules relating to the prevention and remediation of transboundary environmental harm

---

[62] SIGRUN I. SKOGLY, BEYOND NATIONAL BORDERS: STATES' HUMAN RIGHTS OBLIGATIONS IN INTERNATIONAL COOPERATION (2006) [hereinafter SKOGLY, BEYOND BORDERS]; Sigrun I. Skogly & Mark Gibney, *Transnational Human Rights Obligations*, 24 HUM. RTS. Q. 781 (2002); Mark Gibney, Katarina Tomaševski & Jens Vedsted-Hansen, *Transnational State Responsibility for Violations of Human Rights*, 12 HARV. HUM. RTS. J. 267 (1999).
[63] Sigrun I. Skogly & Mark Gibney, *Economic Rights and Extraterritorial Obligations*, in ECONOMIC RIGHTS: CONCEPTUAL, MEASUREMENT, AND POLICY ISSUES 267, 273 (Shareen Hertel & Lanse Minkler eds., 2007).
[64] NICOLA M.C.P. JÄGERS, CORPORATE HUMAN RIGHTS OBLIGATIONS: IN SEARCH OF ACCOUNTABILITY 172, generally at 166–167, 169–172 (2002) [hereinafter JÄGERS]. For an environmental perspective, see BRIAN D. SMITH, STATE RESPONSIBILITY AND THE MARINE ENVIRONMENT: THE RULES OF DECISION 36, 41–43 (1988).
[65] Int'l L. Comm'n, *Draft Articles on Responsibility of States for Internationally Wrongful Acts*, in Report of the International Law Commission to the General Assembly, 56 U.N. GAOR, Supp. (No. 10), UN Doc. A/56/10 (2001) [hereinafter *ILC Articles*]. *See also* Rick Lawson, *Life After Bankovic: On the Extraterritorial Application of the European Convention on Human Rights*, in EXTRATERRITORIAL APPLICATION, supra note 58, at 83, 85–86; JÄGERS, id. at 168–169; Robert McCorquodale, *Spreading the Weeds Beyond Their Garden: Extraterritorial Responsibility of States for Violations of Human Rights By Corporate Nationals*, 100 AM. SOC. INT'L L. PROC. 95, 99, n. 30 (2006). On the *ILC Articles* generally, see *Symposium: Assessing the Work of the International Law Commission on State Responsibility* 13 EUR. J. INT'L L. 1053–1255 (2002); D. Bodansky & J.R. Crook eds., *Symposium: The ILC's State Responsibility Articles*, 96 AM. J. INT'L. L. 773–890 (2002).
[66] *ILC Articles*, id. in Commentary to art. 14, ¶14.

(*Prevention Articles* and *Loss Allocation Principles*).[67] The scope of this second project extended in the early days to cover transnational harm associated with the export of hazardous technology by TNCs.[68] While the final drafts of the *Prevention Articles* and the *Loss Allocation Principles* were clearly designed with transboundary environmental harm in the forefront (and as primary rather than secondary rules),[69] their scope may still be read as extending to transnational harm from a State of origin. Both thus provide for the possibility of concurrent home and host State obligations under primary rules addressing the problems of transnational harm.[70]

The fact that internationally wrongful conduct often results from the collaboration of several States is clearly recognized under the *ILC Articles*.[71] The wrongfulness of one State's actions may depend on the independent action of a second State, or a State may be required by its own international obligations to either prevent certain conduct by another State or to at least prevent harm flowing from such conduct.[72] As a general rule, each State is responsible for its own wrongful acts under the principle of independent responsibility.[73] Thus, both the home and host State may be independently responsible for violations of human rights norms committed by TNCs, although the precise nature of the responsibility may differ depending on the nature of their own obligations.[74]

---

[67] Int'l L. Comm'n, *Draft Articles on the Prevention of Transboundary Harm from Hazardous Activities*, in Report of the International Law Commission to the General Assembly, 56 U.N. GAOR, Supp. (No. 10), U.N. Doc. A/56/10 (2001) [hereinafter *Prevention Articles*]; Int'l L. Comm'n, *Draft Principles on the Allocation of Loss in the Case of Transboundary Harm Arising Out of Hazardous Activities* 101–182, 58 U.N. GAOR, Supp. (No. 10), U.N. Doc. A/61/10 (2006) [hereinafter *Loss Allocation Principles*]. But see ZERK, *supra* note 16, at 160.

[68] Shinya Murase, *Perspectives from International Economic Law on Transnational Environmental Issues*, 253 REC. DES COURS 287, 396–398 (1995).

[69] *Loss Allocation Principles*, *supra* note 67, in Commentary to Principle 1, ¶6.

[70] *See* Sara L. Seck, Home State Obligations for the Prevention and Remediation of Transnational Harm: Canada, Global Mining and Local Communities 290–413 (Dec. 2007) (unpublished Ph.D. dissertation, Osgoode Hall Law School, York University) [hereinafter Seck PhD]. On what international human rights law can learn from international environmental law regarding the transnational scope of obligations, *see also* SKOGLY, BEYOND BORDERS, *supra* note 62, 49–54; John H. Knox, *Diagonal Environmental Rights*, *in* UNIVERSAL HUMAN RIGHTS AND EXTRATERRITORIAL OBLIGATIONS (Mark Gibney & Sigrun Skogly eds., 2010).

[71] *ILC Articles*, *supra* note 65, in Commentary to ch. 4.

[72] *Id.*

[73] *Id.*

[74] Where several States contribute to causing the same damage by separate internationally wrongful conduct, the responsibility of each "is determined individually on the basis of its own conduct and by reference to its own international obligations." The responsibility is not reduced nor precluded by reason of the concurrent responsibility of another State. *ILC Articles*, *supra* note 65, in Commentary to art. 47, ¶8.

The *ILC Articles* are concerned exclusively with the responsibility of States to one another,[75] and do not address the question of whether non-State actors hold international rights and obligations.[76] As a result, their relevance to international human rights law is sometimes contested.[77] However, as the human rights treaty bodies themselves have applied the international law of State responsibility to matters before them, and the *ILC Articles* themselves make reference to human rights cases, the relevance of the *ILC Articles* to the business and human rights debate will be presumed.[78] The following section will examine the attribution rules of the *ILC Articles*, which are said to reflect existing international law, rather than being a progressive statement of what the law should be.[79] Accordingly, they may be regarded as a statement of how governments currently perceive the international law of State responsibility.

3.2 Direct responsibility and attribution by agency

Under the *ILC Articles,* an internationally wrongful act that would give rise to State responsibility occurs where there is conduct consisting of an action or omission that is attributable to the State under international law and that constitutes a breach of an international obligation of the State.[80] Scholars who have explored the question of whether home State responsibility flows from the wrongful conduct of TNCs have often focused on asking whether it is possible to attribute the conduct of the TNC to the home State under

---

[75] *Id.* arts. 57, 58.
[76] Emmanuel Roucounas, *Non-State Actors: Areas of International Responsibility in Need of Further Exploration, in* INTERNATIONAL RESPONSIBILITY TODAY: ESSAYS IN MEMORY OF OSCAR SCHACHTER 391, 398–399 (Maurizio Ragazzi ed., 2005) [hereinafter INTERNATIONAL RESPONSIBILITY TODAY]; and R. Pissolo Mazzzeschi, *The Marginal Role of the Individual in the ILC's Articles on State Responsibility* 14 ITALIAN Y.B. INT'L L. 39, 47 (2004).
[77] *Compare, e.g.*, Matthew Craven, *For the 'Common Good': Rights and Interests in the Law of State Responsibility, in* ISSUES OF STATE RESPONSIBILITY BEFORE INTERNATIONAL JUDICIAL INSTITUTIONS 105 (Malgosia Fitzmaurice & Dan Sarooshi eds., 2004) [hereinafter Fitzmaurice & Sarooshi], *with* Malcolm D. Evans, *State Responsibility and the European Convention on Human Rights: Role and Realm, in* Fitzmaurice & Sarooshi, *id.,* 139, *with* Dominic McGoldrick, *State Responsibility and the International Covenant on Civil and Political Rights, in* Fitzmaurice & Sarooshi, *id.,* 161. *See also* ANDREW CLAPHAM, HUMAN RIGHTS OBLIGATIONS OF NON-STATE ACTORS 317–318 (2006); TAL BECKER, TERRORISM AND THE STATE: RETHINKING THE RULES OF STATE RESPONSIBILITY 261–265 (2006).
[78] McCorquodale & Simons, *supra* note 58, at 601–602.
[79] James Crawford & Simon Olleson, *The Continuing Debate on a UN Convention on State Responsibility,* 54 INT'L COMP. L.Q. 959, 968 (2005). *See also* David D. Caron, *The ILC Articles on State Responsibility: The Paradoxical Relationship Between Form and Authority,* 96 AM. J. INT'L L. 857 (2002).
[80] *ILC Articles, supra* note 65, art. 2.

the *Nicaragua* test of effective control,[81] reproduced in essence in Article 8 of the *ILC Articles*.[82] This test provides the nature of the link that must be established for private acts of a TNC to be transformed into the acts of de facto State agents.[83] According to Article 8, the conduct of a person or group who are 'in fact acting on the instruction of, or under the direction or control of' the State in carrying out the conduct, will be considered an act of the State under international law.[84] Notably, the Commentaries to Article 8 explicitly exclude a State's initial establishment of a corporation by special law or otherwise as a sufficient basis for attribution to the state of the entity's subsequent conduct.[85] Aside from the case of private military contractors, it is rarely argued that TNCs are in fact acting on the instructions of the home State.[86] Moreover, it is frequently said that the effective control test from the *Nicaragua* case is extremely difficult if not impossible to meet in the TNC/home State context.[87] While some scholars had speculated that the effective control test had been replaced by a test of 'overall control' in the *Tadić* case,[88] this was not accepted by the ICJ in *Bosnia*.[89]

An alternative approach to establishing an agency relationship between a TNC and a home State is under Article 5 of the *ILC Articles*, according to which the conduct of an entity empowered by state law to exercise elements of governmental authority will be attributed to the state.[90] As the *ILC Articles* suggest that this attribution only occurs where the conduct concerns

---

[81] Military and Paramilitary Activities (Nicar. v. U.S.), Merits, 1986 I.C.J. 14, ¶115 (27 June), cited with approval in Application of the Convention on the Prevention and Punishment of the Crime of Genocide (Bosn. & Herz. v. Serb. & Mont.) 2006 I.C.J. 91, ¶399 (26 Feb.).

[82] *See, e.g.*, JÄGERS, *supra* note 64, at 169–172; Olivier De Schutter, *The Accountability of Multinationals for Human Rights Violations in European Law, in* Alston, *supra* note 30, 227 at 235–237.

[83] BECKER, *supra* note 77, at 67; JÄGERS, *id.* at 169–172.

[84] *ILC Articles*, *supra* note 65, art. 8.

[85] *Id.* in Commentary to art. 8, ¶6.

[86] McCorquodale & Simons, *supra* note 58, at 610. According to Wolfrum, this test does not depend upon whether the non-State actor follows the instructions, but upon whether the authorities giving the instructions "exercise legislative, executive or judicial functions." Rüdiger Wolfrum, *State Responsibility for Private Actors: An Old Problem of Renewed Relevance, in* INTERNATIONAL RESPONSIBILITY TODAY, *supra* note 76, 423 at 427–428.

[87] Narula, *supra* note 58, at 760–762; Gibney, Tomaševski & Vedsted-Hansen, *supra* note 62, at 286; McCorquodale & Simons, *supra* note 58, at 609–610. But see JÄGERS, *supra* note 64, at 171 (arguing that the effective control test may be met due to the "economic, legal and political connection between the corporation and the home State").

[88] Narula, *supra* note 58, at 761–762; Wolfrum, *supra* note 86, at 428–429.

[89] *Bosnia* case, *supra* note 81, ¶403–407.

[90] *ILC Articles*, *supra* note 65, art. 5.

governmental activity, not private or commercial activity with which the entity may be engaged,[91] Article 5 appears of limited use for attributing TNC conduct directly to the home State. This is particularly the case as the entity must be specifically authorized by internal law to exercise public authority.[92] Having said this, Article 7 provides that conduct is attributable to the state where a state organ or entity is empowered to exercise elements of governmental authority and, while acting in its official capacity, acts in excess of authority or contrary to instructions.[93] It is therefore not strictly necessary for the state to have ordered the wrongful conduct itself. Article 11 is similarly of limited use, as it requires the state to have 'acknowledged and adopted the conduct in question as its own'.[94] Home states rarely, if ever, adopt human rights-violating conduct by TNCs as their own.

While the above examples suggest that direct attribution of human rights-violating TNC conduct to the home State is difficult if not impossible under the *ILC Articles*, there is at least one possible exception. Article 9 of the *ILC Articles* could provide a basis for arguing that home States bear direct responsibility for harmful conduct by TNCs exercising elements of host State governmental authority in failed States or conflict zones.[95] Article 9 is designed for exceptional circumstances, such as 'during revolution, armed conflict or foreign occupation, where the regular authorities dissolve, are disintegrating, have been suppressed or are for the time being inoperative'.[96] If an extractive company exercises police powers in order to protect its property in the absence of a functioning host State police force, and violates human rights in the process, then this conduct may be attributable to both the incapacitated host State and the home State under the principle of independent responsibility. The more that the home State is aware that the host State is unable to exercise its regulatory powers, the more onerous the responsibility might be for the home State.

Thus, generally speaking it is difficult to establish an agency relationship between a TNC and a home State. This is in part because an agency

---

[91] *Id.* in Commentary to art. 5, ¶5.
[92] *Id.* in Commentary to art. 5, ¶7. However, it is not obvious what is included in the ILC's definition of governmental authority, nor is governmental authority ever easy to define. *See* Clapham, *supra* note 77, at 242–243, 460–499.
[93] *ILC Articles*, *id.* art. 7.
[94] *Id.* art. 11. Article 11 is derived from the Case Concerning United States Diplomatic and Consular Staff in Tehran (U.S. v. Iran), 1980 I.C.J. 3. (24 May). According to Becker, Article 11 is concerned with explicit ratification and adoption of conduct by the State, not with implied State complicity arising out of a failure to prevent or prosecute the private offender as would be the case if it had cited older cases which supported the condonation theory. BECKER, *supra* note 77, at 72. *See further* below.
[95] *ILC Articles*, *id.* art. 9.
[96] *Id.* in Commentary to art. 9, ¶1.

relationship presumes that the State is in the position of principal while the TNC is a subordinate.[97] Yet, home States are not 'puppeteers' who direct the actions of TNC 'marionettes.' Instead, home State involvement is more about 'acquiescence than direction and control, more about facilitation by quiet encouragement than specific instructions, more about omission than commission'.[98] While the TNC is clearly the driving force behind its own conduct, the home State 'may be a key facilitator' of the activity through 'complex acts and omissions'.[99] Thus, the use of agency as a standard for direct home State responsibility for private actor conduct by TNCs may be 'not just impractical but also self-defeating'.[100] Notably, the agency paradigm 'not only neglects the subtle relationships between the private and public sphere... it encourages them,' as States can pursue indirect support of activities without creating an agency relationship.[101]

The Framework indicates that implementation of the State duty to protect may be accomplished through regulation and adjudication of TNC conduct so as to protect rights.[102] The following section will explore an alternative route to establishing direct home State responsibility for human rights violations by TNCs, by turning our attention to the conduct of State organs.

3.3 The separate delict theory and the conduct of state organs

Under the principle of independent responsibility, a home State would be directly responsible for its own wrongful conduct in failing to regulate or adjudicate a TNC so as to prevent and remedy human rights violations – that is, failing to exercise due diligence. However, this does not mean that the State is directly responsible for the conduct of the TNC. This understanding of responsibility is described by some scholars as indirect responsibility for private actor conduct,[103] and by others as responsibility under the non-attribution and separate delict theory, with the term 'indirect responsibility' reserved for historical cases of complicity or condonation.[104] According to Tal Becker, as the difference between a finding of direct responsibility and

---

[97] *See* BECKER, *supra* note 77, at 258–261, on the problems of the agency paradigm as applied to the power relationship between the State and the non-State actor terrorist. While there are many similarities between Becker's analysis of terrorism and the State and the relationship between home States and TNCs, there are also many differences. *See further* Seck PhD, *supra* note 70, at 258–266.
[98] BECKER, *id.* at 258.
[99] *Id.*
[100] *Id.* at 259.
[101] *Id.*
[102] *Framework*, *supra* note 1, ¶18.
[103] Scott, *Translating Torture* in TORTURE AS TORT, *supra* note 28, at 47.
[104] BECKER, *supra* note 77, at 14–24, and ch. 2 "State Responsibility for Private Acts: the Evolution of a Doctrine". Becker distinguishes between three theories of State responsibility for private actor conduct in historical context: (1) direct responsibility

responsibility under the separate delict theory makes no difference in terms of the remedy available under international human rights law, the different theories of responsibility are often not clearly distinguished.[105] Generally speaking, however, the current 'prevailing perception' of State responsibility is that the State is:

> directly responsible only for the acts of those persons with whom it is in a relationship of agency. For this reason, the State will be responsible for the conduct of its own organs or officials, but not for the conduct of non-State actors that is wholly private in nature. The State can, however, be held responsible for its own violations of a separate duty to regulate the private conduct.[106]

The distinction between direct responsibility and responsibility under the separate delict theory is not specifically endorsed under the *ILC Articles*, which instead provide that a State is responsible for 'all the consequences, not being too remote, of its wrongful conduct.'[107] However, the distinction becomes evident if one focuses upon Article 4 of the *ILC Articles*, according to which:

> The conduct of any State organ shall be considered an act of that State under international law, whether the organ exercises legislative, executive, judicial or any other functions, whatever position it holds in the organization of the State, and whatever its character as an organ of the central Government or of a territorial unit of the State.[108]

The significance of Article 4 becomes clear if 'conduct' is understood to include both actions and omissions, and if the home State is understood to be under a duty to exercise due diligence to prevent human rights violations by non-State actor TNCs, and to provide victims of human rights violations with access to justice through home State courts. The question

---

(the private conduct itself is directly attributable to the State through the historic theory of collective responsibility); (2) indirect responsibility (the private conduct is indirectly attributable to the State on the basis of the historic theories of complicity or condonation); and (3) the separate delict theory (State responsibility is engaged only for the State's own violation of a separate and distinct duty to exercise due diligence in preventing and punishing the private offence). *Id.* at 24. The condonation theory replaced the historic theory of complicity in the 1920s, which itself fell into disrepute in the early twentieth century, to be replaced by the separate delict theory. *Id.* at 19–42.
[105] *Id.* at 57, 62.
[106] *Id.* at 66.
[107] *ILC Articles, supra* note 65, art.31, ¶10, 13.
[108] *Id.* art.4.

then becomes: which State organs are implicated by the State duty to protect human rights – that is, which organs should be expected to engage in the regulation of private actor conduct? States regulate conduct in many ways, and regulation may involve many branches of government:[109]

> Thus, the Legislature may lay down rules by statute, or the Executive may do so by order.... States also regulate conduct by means of decisions of their courts, which may order litigating parties to do or to abstain from doing certain things.... So, too, may the State's administrative bodies, which may apply rules concerning, for example, the issuance of licences to export goods...[110]

The scope of the State duty to protect under Article 4 implicates any branch of government involved in creating and supporting the global economic order and consequently TNC conduct. The conduct of the executive branch of a home State is implicated when it engages in the negotiation of investment protection agreements and bilateral investment treaties with host States without regard to home State obligations to protect human rights[111] or related obligations of international cooperation.[112] Government departments that provide services to support TNCs are also implicated, as are State-owned enterprises carrying out similar public mandates.[113] It follows that trade commissioner services, overseas development agencies, export credit agencies,[114] and even sovereign wealth funds, as executive organs, must exercise due diligence to ensure that the private actor conduct they support does not violate human rights, and that, in the event harm does occur, victims have access to a remedy.

The implementation of non-binding policies requiring environmental, social and human rights impact assessments, along with ombudsperson-type dispute resolution mechanisms might seem sufficient to discharge the

---

[109] Vaughan Lowe, *Jurisdiction*, in INTERNATIONAL LAW 335, 335–336 (Malcolm D. Evans ed., 2006).
[110] *Id.*
[111] *See, e.g.*, McCorquodale, *supra* note 65, at 100–101; Ryan Suda, *The Effect of Bilateral Investment Treaties on Human Rights Enforcement and Realization*, in TRANSNATIONAL CORPORATIONS AND HUMAN RIGHTS 73 at 143 (Olivier De Schutter ed., 2006).
[112] *See* Skogly, *Beyond Borders, supra* note 62.
[113] Depending on the structure of the agencies or enterprises, Article 5 of the *ILC Articles* may be more appropriate to ground attribution for the purposes of the duty to regulate.
[114] On the legal obligations of export credit agencies, *see* ÖZGÜR CAN & SARA L. SECK, THE LEGAL OBLIGATIONS WITH RESPECT TO HUMAN RIGHTS AND EXPORT CREDIT AGENCIES (2006); McCorquodale & Simons, *supra* note 58.

obligation to exercise due diligence by executive organs. However, as the obligation to regulate also attaches to legislative organs, legislation governing these executive organs must arguably also comply with the duty to regulate. To the extent that governing legislation of executive organs could be amended to mandate the protection of human rights, non-binding policies may not be sufficient. For example, such legislation could open the door to judicial review of decisions made by government organs where a decision is not made in accordance with a designated procedure.[115]

As corporate law itself is the product of the conduct of legislative organs, it too should be subject to scrutiny. Facilitating legislation granting separate legal personality to a corporation must surely be in breach of the duty to protect human rights, if the grant of legal personality is made without ensuring that the corporation is given characteristics that would enable it to respect rights. This observation highlights the complementary relationship between the State duty to protect and the corporate responsibility to respect, as within the State duty to protect is an obligation to enable or facilitate implementation of the corporate responsibility to respect.[116] Moreover, if legal personality is granted so as to enable TNCs to operate beyond the effective regulatory spheres of both home and host States as is often claimed, then this too suggests a failure to comply with the State duty to protect.[117]

Private financial institutions and stock exchanges are both creatures of and regulated by statute. Accordingly, legislative schemes that enable them to support the global economic activities of TNCs should also come under scrutiny. While legislation mandating sustainability reporting by companies that list on stock exchanges might be a sound first step in terms of policy, it may not be sufficient to discharge the duty to protect. As with corporate law, legislation that creates a private enterprise such as a stock exchange and enables it to raise global capital in support of TNC conduct may be in breach of an obligation to regulate and adjudicate TNC conduct if the legislation does not integrate mechanisms that could prevent and remedy human rights violations by the TNC that is to receive the equity financing.

Finally, the conduct of judicial organs is also identified in Article 4. National courts are instrumentalities of the State, as much a part of the State

---

[115] *See, e.g.*, Sara L. Seck, *Strengthening Environmental Assessment of Canadian Supported Mining Ventures in Developing Countries*, 11 J. ENVT'L L. & PRAC. 1 (2001).

[116] This is hinted at in the discussion of corporate cultures. *See Framework, supra* note 1, ¶30.

[117] For example, if corporate law does not mandate sufficient territorial links to the State granting legal personality for that State to effectively exercise enforcement jurisdiction over the corporation, then this could be viewed as a violation of the State duty to protect. *See* Seck PhD, *supra* note 70, at 227.

as the executive or legislative branches.[118] If the State duty to regulate and adjudicate includes a duty to provide access to justice for victims of human rights violations, then home State courts are under an obligation to facilitate this access. This could have implications for the interpretation of common law doctrines such as *forum non conveniens*, or for the availability of legal aid to foreign plaintiffs to ensure effective access to justice.[119] This analysis highlights the complementary relationship in the Framework between the State duty to protect and the need for effective access to remedies.

The above are all examples of home State separate delict responsibility, as opposed to direct responsibility. However, separate delict responsibility may give rise to direct responsibility in certain circumstances. One example is under Article 16 of the *ILC Articles*, which McCorquodale and Simons have convincingly argued could, under certain circumstances, make the home State of an export credit agency complicit in the wrongful conduct of the host State in relation to TNC projects, as well as complicit in violations of international criminal law by TNCs themselves.[120] Beyond Article 16, it is possible that direct home State responsibility may arise through separate delict responsibility if principles of 'common sense causation' guide the analysis.[121] According to Becker, drawing upon the work of H.L.A. Hart and Tony Honoré, once separate delict responsibility is engaged, the State may be responsible for unattributable acts that are causally linked to the State's own wrongdoing. While detailed exploration of Becker's analysis is beyond the scope of this chapter, it is worth noting that causes are understood as 'interventions in the existing or expected state of affairs'.[122] Significantly, as

---

[118] *See generally* JAN PAULSSON, DENIAL OF JUSTICE IN INTERNATIONAL LAW (2005); Christopher Greenwood, *State Responsibility for the Decisions of National Courts*, in Fitzmaurice & Sarooshi, *supra* note 77, at 55. State responsibility would only arise once all means of challenging a lower court decision within the national legal system were exhausted. *Id.* at 72–73.

[119] *See, e.g.*, Sara L. Seck, *Environmental Harm in Developing Countries Caused by Subsidiaries of Canadian Mining Corporations: The Interface of Public and Private International Law*, 37 CAN. Y.B. INT'L L. 139 (1999).

[120] McCorquodale & Simons, *supra* note 58, at 611–615; Gibney, Tomaševski & Vedsted-Hansen, *supra* note 62, at 293–294, referring to Article 27 of the 1979 version of the *ILC Articles*. *See* Article 16 and related Commentary, *ILC Articles*, *supra* note 65. Article 16 applies where one State aids or assists another State in wrongful conduct, including by knowingly providing financing for the activity in question.

[121] H.L.A. HART & TONY HONORÉ, CAUSATION IN THE LAW (2nd ed. 1985), cited in BECKER, *supra* note 77, at 289–294.

[122] BECKER, *id.* at 293, citing HART & HONORÉ, *id.* at 29. Causes are distinguished from conditions which are "present as part of the usual state or mode of operation of the thing under inquiry." BECKER, *id.* at 293, citing HART & HONORÉ, *id.* at 35. For the full implications of Becker's analysis of causation for the understanding of home State obligations, see Seck PhD, *supra* note 70, at 274–287.

the inquiry into what is a cause is 'deeply connected to the context in which the inquiry takes place,' and a 'function of human habit, custom, convention or normative expectation', causation is revealed as a relative concept.[123] Thus, what a TNC or home State might view as a normal state of affairs (the provision of home State support to TNC conduct abroad) may appear to be a cause of a human rights violation to the individual victim or impacted local community within the host State. This provides a link to the TWAIL analysis earlier in this chapter. If the international law of State responsibility reflected host State local community perspectives on causation, then home States would be directly responsible for human rights violations associated with TNC conduct.[124] Moreover, as Becker carefully documents, the theories of attribution reflected in the international law of State responsibility have evolved over time to reflect the prevailing understanding of the power relationship between State and non-State actors.[125] The international legal order of the twentieth century emphasized the sovereignty of the State and a strict distinction between the State and the private conduct of non-State actors, a legal order that is reflected in the non-attribution principle and the separate delict theory.[126] A question for the twenty-first century is whether the strict public/private divide reflected in the separate delict theory accurately reflects either the power relationship between home States and TNCs, or the normative principles that should guide the direction of international governance.[127] This is a particularly pertinent issue in light of the recent global economic crisis and the response of States. The line between the public and private sectors of the global economy does not appear to be so clearly drawn today as it did even in the very recent past.

4 The UN Principles of Responsible Investment

If the analysis above is correct, then what in practice is required of home States to comply with the duty to protect? The answer is not obvious. This Part will explore one idea: whether State regulation mandating that institutional investors adhere to the UN Principles of Responsible Investment (UNPRI) might be sufficient for compliance with the State duty to protect.

---

[123] BECKER, *id.* at 293–294.
[124] *See further* Seck in OHLJ, *supra* note 49.
[125] BECKER, *supra* note 77, at 11–42, 361–362. *See also* J.A. Hessbruegge, *The Historical Development of the Doctrines of Attribution and Due Diligence in International Law*, 36 N.Y.U. J. INT'L L. & P. 265 (2003–2004).
[126] Becker, *id.* at 19, 361.
[127] *Id.* at 361–362; Hessbruegge, *supra* note 125, at 306. *See also* Philip Alston, *Myopia of the Handmaidens: International Lawyers and Globalization*, 8 EUR. J. INT'L L. 435, 447–448 (1997).

The UNPRI were developed in 2005 by a group of institutional investors from 12 countries (the Investor Group), and 'supported by a 70 person multi-stakeholder group of experts from the investment industry, intergovernmental and governmental organizations, civil society and academia'.[128] The United Nations Environment Programme Finance Initiative (UNEP FI)[129] and the UN Global Compact[130] coordinated the process, although 'UNEP did not formally supervise the drafting'.[131] The UNPRI are open to signatories from asset owners, including pension funds, investment managers and professional service partners.[132] The UNPRI were launched in April 2006, and as of May 2009 there were 538 signatories and $US 18,087 trillion worth of assets under management.[133]

The UNPRI are specifically designed as voluntary and aspirational principles that provide a 'menu of possible actions for incorporating ESG (environmental, social and governance) issues into mainstream investment decision-making and ownership practices.'[134] Indeed, application of the principles may be qualified by the fiduciary duties that institutional investors owe to act in the best long-term interests of their beneficiaries. The success of the UNPRI rests in part on the belief that 'environmental, social, and corporate governance (ESG) issues can affect the performance of investment portfolios (to varying degrees across companies, sectors, regions, asset classes and through time)'.[135]

The UNPRI consists of six core Principles, supported by 'possible actions'. The Principles are:

1. We will incorporate environmental, social and corporate governance (ESG) issues into investment analysis and decision-making processes.
2. We will be active owners and incorporate ESG issues into our ownership policies and practices.
3. We will seek appropriate disclosure on ESG issues by the entities in which we invest.

---

[128] UNPRI, *About*, *available at:* http://www.unpri.org/about/ [hereinafter, About UNPRI].
[129] United Nations Environment Programme Finance Initiative, *available at:* http://www.unepfi.org/.
[130] United Nations Global Compact, *available at:* http://www.unglobalcompact.org/.
[131] BENJAMIN J. RICHARDSON, SOCIALLY RESPONSIBLE INVESTMENT LAW at 399 (2008).
[132] UNPRI, *Frequently Asked Questions, available at:* http://www.unpri.org/faqs/ [hereinafter, UNPRI FAQ].
[133] ANNUAL REPORT OF THE PRI INITIATIVE (2009) at 6, *available at*: http://www.unpri.org/files/PRI%20Annual%20Report%202009.pdf.
[134] About UNPRI, *supra* note 128.
[135] UNPRI, *supra* note 9.

4. We will promote acceptance and implementation of the Principles within the investment industry.
5. We will work together to enhance our effectiveness in implementing the Principles.
6. We will report on our activities and progress towards implementing the Principles.[136]

State legislation mandating that institutional investors adopt the UNPRI could overcome reluctance among institutional investors to implement the Principles in situations where it might not be clear whether doing so would be in keeping with their fiduciary obligations. This would satisfy a key concern that ESG criteria should still be applied even if to do so were not clearly in the best financial interests of beneficiaries.[137] It would not, however, address the concern that the UNPRI as currently conceived do not in fact require signatories to actually incorporate ESG factors into their ultimate portfolio choices.[138] Nor would it address the question of whether ESG criteria fully incorporate human rights.[139]

Another concern from a human rights perspective relates to the possible actions proposed under Principle 2 on active ownership. Specifically, the proposed active ownership actions include the suggestions that institutional investors: exercise voting rights; develop an engagement capability with companies; file shareholder resolutions; and engage with companies on ESG issues.[140] On the face of it, this sounds like exactly the kind of active shareholder engagement that is essential for the protection of human rights. However, recent experience has shown that shareholder proposals sometimes do not accurately express the concerns of the communities they purport to be advancing.[141] As socially responsible investment firms are themselves businesses that have a responsibility to respect rights, it may be that State regulation implementing the duty to protect should require

---

[136] *Id.*

[137] Mandate of the Special Representative of the Secretary-General (SRSG) on the Issue of Human Rights and Transnational Corporations and other Business Enterprises, *Corporate Law Tools Project: Summary Report: Expert Meeting on Corporate Law and Human Rights: Opportunities and Challenges of Using Corporate Law to Encourage Corporations t Respect Human Rights* (Toronto, 5–6 Nov. 2009), at 11, available at: http://www.reports-and-materials.org/Corporate-law-tools-Toronto-meeting-report-5-6-Nov-2009.pdf [hereinafter, Toronto Report].

[138] RICHARDSON, *supra* note 131 at 400.

[139] Toronto Report, *supra* note 137 at 11.

[140] UNPRI, *supra* note 9.

[141] Toronto Report, *supra* note 137 at 12; Aaron A. Dhir, *Shareholder Engagement in the Embedded Business Corporation: Investment Activism, Human Rights and TWAIL Discourse*, (2009) 5:2 Comparative Research in Law and Political Economy Research Paper 12/2009, online: SSRN http://papers.ssrn.com/sol3/papers.cfm?abstract_id=1416198.

shareholders to exercise their own due diligence and 'recognize the agency of affected communities by consulting with them before devising human rights-focused shareholder proposals.'[142] Related to this point is a concern that the UNPRI in its current form 'suggests a policy of engagement with companies rather than screening or avoiding stocks based on ESG criteria' in part because the Principles 'are generally designed for large investors that are highly diversified and have large stakes in companies, often making divestment or avoidance impractical.'[143] Yet this may create a conflict between the financial interests of investors who hope to profit from the venture and the rights of communities opposed to the project continuing in any form, who might view a shareholder divestment strategy as essential to their struggle.

Thus, while States mandating that institutional investors comply with the UNPRI could lead to improvements in business compliance with the responsibility to respect human rights by exerting soft pressures on businesses to consider ESG issues, it would not alone be sufficient for compliance with the State duty to protect human rights as explored in this chapter. As the SRSG often states, there is 'no single silver bullet'.[144] Detailed study of additional measures is beyond the scope of this chapter; however, some possible suggestions might include statutorily expanding the types of claimants that can bring derivative actions against companies,[145] mandating the creation of company level grievance mechanisms and statutorily ensuring the possibility of private law claims brought by victims of human rights violations against home State TNCs in home State courts.

5 Conclusions

The State duty to protect is best understood as a duty that attaches to State organs, and requires all States, including home States, to exercise due diligence to prevent and remedy human rights abuses by all businesses that benefit from State organ conduct. Preoccupation with the extraterritorial reach of home State laws serves as a distraction from the central issue in the business and human rights debate: how to ensure that the institutional structures of the global economy which facilitate transnational corporate conduct are designed to demand that human rights be respected. Placing the duty to protect squarely on the shoulders of both home and host States acknowledges the difference in the capacity to regulate experienced by home and host States. Indeed, the work of TWAIL scholars suggests that such lack of capacity (or will) on the part of Third World host States is a direct result

---

[142] Toronto Report, *id.* at 12.
[143] UNPRI FAQ, *supra* note 132.
[144] *Stockholm Keynote, supra* note 6 at 6.
[145] Toronto Report, *supra* note 137 at 8.

of the colonial tendencies of the international legal order. This appears to be implicitly acknowledged by the SRSG, for while the State duty to protect is identified as the most fundamental principle of the Framework, the discussion of the duty is never framed as a reprimand of host States. Instead, the State duty to protect includes a clear recognition of the importance of international cooperation and shared responsibility.

The analysis in this chapter has also underscored the complementary nature of the responsibilities in the Framework. If home States are indeed obligated to comply with the State duty to protect, then compliance must include structuring State institutions so as to both facilitate corporate compliance with the responsibility to respect rights, and facilitate access to remedies by victims of human rights abuses. This is not to suggest that without legal reforms the corporate responsibility to respect is meaningless or that non-legal remedies do not have a role to play. Rather, given the complementary nature of the responsibilities in the Framework, compliance by all States with the duty to protect is essential if the root cause of the problem – the 'governance gaps created by globalization'[146] – are ever to be fully filled.

---

[146] *Framework, supra* note 1, ¶3.

2
'A *Necessary* Supplement' – What the United Nations Global Compact Is (and Is Not)*

Andreas Rasche

1 Introduction

Since its operational launch in 2000, the United Nations Global Compact has attracted a good deal of both support and criticism. The Compact represents the world's largest network-based voluntary corporate citizenship initiative.[1] The term 'corporate citizenship' is adopted here from the literature as a descriptor for a voluntary change of business practices to meet the responsibilities imposed on firms by their stakeholders.[2] It is, however, outside the scope of this chapter to undertake a careful delineation of its similarities and differences with 'corporate responsibility'. Although progress has been made in terms of the large number of business and non-business participants (now numbering 7,300) and improvements in business practices have been presented (McKinsey[3] concludes that nine out of ten participants are doing more towards the Compact's principles than they were 5 years ago), this progress also brought about a lot of criticism, largely from non-governmental organizations (NGOs), academics and the wider press. Thérien and Pouliot,[4] for instance, argue that the Compact fosters a 'pro-market spin' that breaks with the UN's traditional position and thus is eroding

---

* The final, definitive version of this paper has been published in *Business and Society*, 48/4, December/2009 by SAGE Publications, Inc., All rights reserved. © SAGE Publications, Inc. The article can be accessed at: http://bas.sagepub.com.
[1] Hemphill, Thomas A. (2005). The United Nations global compact. *International Journal of Business Governance and Ethics*, 1, 303–316.
[2] Norman, Wayne & Néron, Pierre-Yves (2008). Citizenship Inc.: do we really want businesses to be good corporate citizens? *Business Ethics Quarterly*, 18, 1–26.
[3] McKinsey & Company (2007). *Shaping the New Rules of Competition: UN Global Compact Participant Mirror*. London: McKinsey.
[4] Thérien, Jean-Philippe & Pouliot, Vincent (2006). The global compact: shifting the politics of international development. *Global Governance*, 12, 55–75, here: p. 67.

its legitimacy in the long run. Amnesty International[5] complains about the missing accountability of the initiative and asks for a more rigorous assessment of whether participants are really complying with the principles. In a more radical way, Sethi argues that the Compact 'provides a venue for opportunistic companies to make grandiose statements of corporate citizenship without worrying about being called to account for their actions'.[6]

Even though in order to gain a balanced view of the Compact critical concerns need to be voiced (some of which demand institutional changes that run counter to the very idea of the initiative and its reason for existence), these criticisms must be examined and carefully evaluated. For future critical discussions to be meaningful and to provide possible pointers for improvement, the discussion about the Global Compact needs to (a) show more sensitivity to the underlying core idea of the initiative, which is long-term *learning* experience and not regulation, and (b) address the constraints of the institutional framework in which the initiative is embedded. So far, there has been no systematic assessment of the critical voices that are raised, let alone attempts to clarify some of the misconceptions upon which they are based. Given the rise in the number of articles that criticize the Compact,[7] there is a need to clarify what the initiative is and is not.

This chapter has three main research objectives. First, it aims at structuring existing critiques of the Compact and offers an alternative perspective on the demands they place on the initiative. The chapter intends to show that much of the criticism is based on a misunderstanding of the nature and mandate of the Compact. Second, the chapter delineates a perspective that classifies the Compact as a *necessary* supplement to more regulative undertakings within the sphere of corporate citizenship (for example, auditable standards for workplace conditions such as SA 8,000 or regulation by governments). This discussion illustrates what the Compact is and, most of all, what it is *not* and how future critical assessments, although very welcome to further spur its expansion by providing needed expertise, should identify

---

[5] Amnesty International (2003). *Letter to Louise Fréchette Raising Concerns on UN Global Compact*, available at http://web.amnesty.org.

[6] Sethi, Prakash (2003). *Global Compact is Another Exercise in Futility*, available at http://www.financialexpress.com/news/global-compact-is-another-exercise-in-futility/91447.

[7] Deva, Surya (2006). Global compact: a critique of the UN's "public-private" partnership for promoting corporate citizenship. *Syracuse Journal of International Law and Communication*, 34, 107–151; Nolan, Justine (2005). The United Nations global compact with business: hindering or helping the protection of human rights? *The University of Queensland Law Journal*, 24, 445–466; Rizvi, Haider (2004). UN pact with business lacks accountability, available at: http://2qwww.globalpolicy.org; Zammit, Ann (2003). *Development at Risk: Rethinking UN-Business Partnerships*. New York: The South Centre and United Nations Research Institute for Social Development.

the initiative. Third, the chapter outlines future challenges for the Compact and thus highlights the remaining actions that need to be taken in order to secure its continued success.

To achieve these research objectives, the remainder of this paper is divided into five sections. The first section provides a brief introduction to the Global Compact as of 2008. As the Compact is an evolutionary framework that is continuously extended and modified, this descriptive exercise is necessary to paint a fair picture. The second section maps existing critiques of the Compact into three commonly-mentioned categories and assesses their viability when considering the goals of the initiative, as well as the overall institutional context of the United Nations. The third section classifies the Compact as a necessary supplement to regulatory approaches and thus highlights what the initiative is about and on which grounds it should be judged. This discussion helps future criticism to be presented in a way that is more compatible with the nature of the Compact and also allows for a better understanding of the relationship between the Compact and other initiatives (e.g., SA 8000). While the fourth section discusses existing challenges that the initiative has to address in order to achieve future growth and continued relevance, the fifth section provides a brief conclusion, including suggestions for further research.

2 The United Nations Global Compact

2.1 What is the nature and mission of the Global Compact?

On 31 January 1999 United Nations Secretary-General Kofi Annan outlined the need for what he then called a 'global compact' while speaking at the World Economic Forum in Davos. Annan proposed that 'you, the business leaders gathered in Davos, and we, the United Nations, initiate a global compact of shared values and principles, which will give a human face to the global market'.[8] This speech would mark the birth of a global corporate citizenship initiative which was formally launched on 26 July 2000 at UN headquarters in New York with the support of multinational companies, UN agencies, global trade unions and a variety of NGOs.

The Global Compact engages the private sector to collaborate with the United Nations – in partnership with global labour, NGOs and academia to identify and spread good corporate practices in the areas of human rights, labour rights, protection of the environment and anti-corruption.[9] The

---

[8] United Nations (1 February 1999) *Secretary-General Address to the World Economic Forum in Davos* [Press Release SG/SM/6881]. New York: United Nations, here: p. 1.
[9] Ruggie. John G. (2001). Global_governance.net: the global compact as learning network. *Global Governance*, 7, 371–378, here: p. 371; Ruggie, John G. (2002). Trade, sustainability and global governance. *Columbia Journal of Environmental Law*, 27, 297–307, here: 301.

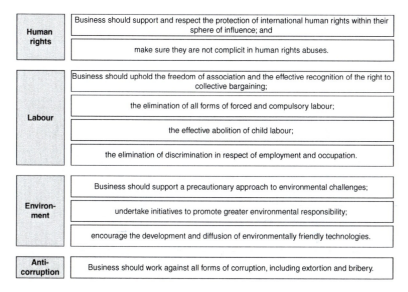

Figure 2.1 The ten universal principles

Compact seeks to weave a web of joint values around the global economy; a web that is based on ten universal principles (see Figure 2.1). The *goals* of the Compact are thus based on the distinction between a macro and micro level: at the macro level the Compact facilitates cooperation, long-term learning and collective problem solving among a full cast of stakeholders, whereas at the micro level it wants participants to internalize its principles into their strategy and daily operations.

The Compact is *not* designed as a certification instrument or tool to regulate and sanction its participants, but instead to foster a dialogue among a diverse set of actors in a non-bureaucratic way. Participating companies are required to be transparent about their engagement by reporting on progress and action with regards to their implementation efforts. The change model that underlies the Compact is based on the idea that corporations, through dialogue and partnership projects, can show responsibility and make a difference once they learn from each other and other actors (such as UN agencies). This is not to imply that binding regulations are not needed, but that regulations must be complemented by a dialogue-based approach that gives recognition to the fact that most companies still have a lot to learn when it comes to managing social, environmental and governance issues. The initiative is based on the idea of 'principled pragmatism' which reflects the need to balance what is ideally expected to exist in the sphere of regulation with what is achievable given the current political environment.

2.2 Why is there a need for a Global Compact?

There are many reasons why a globally valid initiative that fosters the development and dissemination of shared values and their integration into the conduct of corporations makes sense. Some advocates of the Compact argue from a moral perspective. Williams[10], for instance, states that the Compact is needed because corporations have to respect (and cannot simply neglect) that they have a moral purpose as long as they want to be seen as a legitimate part of national societies and the emerging global order. Others, like Ruggie,[11] underline the business case by arguing that some corporations, by learning from other participants, avoid costly mistakes that their peers have committed.

This chapter highlights another dimension of reasoning that is often neglected when it comes to looking at why initiatives such as the Global Compact are needed. When focusing on changes in the global economic order, characterized in part by a globalization of problems facing mankind (e.g., climate change and poverty) and the increased politicized role of multinational corporations,[12] one must recognize that these changes can only be addressed once businesses, civil society, and governments devise for the *global* economy the kind of institutional equilibrium that existed in the postwar *international* economic order.[13] In other words, a stable institutional framework is needed for doing business under the conditions of globalization. The need for such a framework creates two key challenges; at the macro level there is the challenge to embed the global market in a network of shared values, whereas at the micro level these values have to be implemented in the conduct of (multinational) businesses.

At the macro level, the Global Compact is needed to address the omnipresent governance gaps that the rise of the global economy has created (e.g., with regard to environmental policy). The United Nations, as the only truly global intergovernmental organization with a comprehensive mandate,[14] provides the right framework to address these gaps. Although the Compact is by *no means* a substitute for national or international regulations

---

[10] Williams, Oliver F. (2004). The UN global compact: the challenge and the promise. *Business Ethics Quarterly*, 14, 755–774, here: 760.

[11] Ruggie (2001, 2002), *supra* note 10.

[12] Palazzo, Guido & Scherer, Andreas G. (2006). Corporate legitimacy as deliberation: a communicative framework. *Journal of Business Ethics*, 66, 71–88; Windsor, Duane (2007). Toward a global theory of cross-border and multilevel corporate political activity. *Business and Society*, 46(2), 253–278.

[13] Kell, Georg & Ruggie, John G. (1999). Global markets and social legitimacy: the case for the 'global compact'. *Transnational Corporations*, 8, 101–120, here: 103.

[14] Cohen, Jonathan (2001). The world's business: the United Nations and the globalization of corporate citizenship. In J. Andriof & M. Macintosh (Eds.), *Perspectives on Corporate Citizenship*. Sheffield: Greenleaf, pp. 185–197, here: p. 185.

and also not an all-inclusive framework for global governance, it is at least a first pragmatic response to government governance failures and defines an agenda for discussing issues of global governance.[15] Compact participants acknowledge that there is neither the time nor the need to wait until national governments 'get it right' and international law sets binding regulations. The communicative, learning-based framework of the initiative needs to be understood as a *supplement* to existing and emerging regulatory efforts in the global business environment. Understanding the Compact as a supplement reflects the conviction that the governance battle cannot be won until it is based on new forms of social engagement that connect all relevant social actors.[16] Learning about macro-level governance problems is even more important when considering that the Compact has attracted a variety of major firms from emerging markets like China.[17] Since these companies often lack knowledge on the relevance of social and environmental responsibility, they can, as Compact participants, start developing that kind of knowledge.

This discussion raises the question of how the relationship between the problem addressed by the Compact at the macro level (i.e. global governance) and its proposed solution (i.e. learning and shared values) is intended to be understood. Following Rosenau,[18] global governance is the worldwide achievement of order through the issuance of systems of rule to address those governance problems that cannot be solved by sovereign national governments. Mechanisms of global governance include binding international law (e.g., the WTO) and/or soft law approaches (e.g., the Global Compact). Although binding international law is desirable, mutual learning and a set of shared values are indispensable for global governance to function. The complexity of global governance problems requires taking multiple levels (e.g., national and international), as well as a variety of actors from different domains (e.g., the economy, politics and civil society) into account.[19] Learning mechanisms and a set of shared values, as promoted by the Compact, help to establish a ground upon which solutions for complex governance problems can be discussed and advanced. In addition, learning

---

[15] Kell, Georg (2005). The global compact: selected experiences and reflections. *Journal of Business Ethics*, 59, 69–79, here: 78.
[16] Ruggie (2002), *supra* note 10, here: 298.
[17] Nash, Paul (2003). Global Compact challenges firms. *Business Weekly*. Retrieved 29 January 2009, available at: http://www.chinadaily.com.cn/en/doc/2003-04/08/content_162162.htm.
[18] Rosenau, James N. (1992). Governance, order and change in world politics. In James N. Rosenau & Ernst Otto Czempiel (Eds.), *Governance Without Government: Order and Change in World Politics* (pp. 1–29). Cambridge: Cambridge University Press.
[19] Dingwert, Klaus & Pattberg, Phillip (2006). Global governance as a perspective on world politics. *Global Governance*, 12, 185–203.

mechanisms also allow spreading of already available solutions across levels and actors.[20]

At the micro level, the Compact is needed to deal with the challenge of implementing and acting upon the values that are defined at the macro level. Even though the Compact does not sanction or monitor but instead relies upon the enlightened self-interest of corporations to give specific meaning to its underlying principles within their day-to-day conduct, another reason for its existence is to help change corporate behaviour. This goal reflects a specific perspective on corporate responsibility in general and corporate citizenship in particular. Participants are asked to move beyond a philanthropic understanding of citizenship, dominated by charitable donations and other forms of community actions[21] and instead to change their core business practices.[22] Such an expansionist definition of corporate citizenship[23] assumes that businesses promote and participate in multi-stakeholder partnerships in order to identify and learn about their constituencies.[24]

2.3 How does the Global Compact work?

To understand how the Compact 'works', one needs to appreciate its constituent actors and their respective roles. Essentially, there are four core actors that create the Global Compact network.[25] First, there is the *United Nations* system with its various agencies and offices. The Global Compact Office (that belongs to the UN Secretary-General's Executive Office) sets the administrative frame, provides strategic direction and performs quality control tasks. In addition, six UN agencies (i.e. the UN High Commissioner for Human Rights, the International Labour Organization, the UN Environmental Programme, the UN Development Programme, the UN Industrial Development Organization, and the UN Office on Drugs and Crime) offer expertise in special areas in order to set up and steer particular UN-business partnership projects that are created under the umbrella of the initiative.

---

[20] Kell (2005), *supra* note 16.
[21] Carroll, Archie B. (1991). The pyramid of corporate social responsibility: toward the moral management of organizational stakeholders. *Business Horizons*, 34(4), 39–48.
[22] Birch, David (2001). Corporate citizenship: rethinking business beyond corporate social responsibility. In Joerg Andriof & Malcolm McIntosh (Eds.), *Perspectives on Corporate Citizenship* (pp. 53–65). Sheffield: Greenleaf.
[23] Norman & Neron (2008), *supra* note 3.
[24] Poncelet, Eric (2003). Resisting corporate citizenship: business-NGO relations in multistakeholder environmental partnerships. *Journal of Corporate Citizenship*, 9, 97–115.
[25] Kell, Georg & Levin, David (2003). The global compact network: an historic experiment in learning and action. *Business and Society Review*, 108, 151–181.

Second, *businesses are at the heart of the Compact*. With currently over 5,300 corporate participants from developing and developed countries, businesses are encouraged to actively participate in dialogue and integrate the ten principles in their operations. Participating firms are required to not only publicly advocate the Global Compact (e.g., via press releases and speeches) but also to disclose annually how the ten principles are implemented and what progress has been achieved by submitting a so-called Communication on Progress (COP) report. Third, *governments* facilitate the ten principles by setting up regulatory frameworks on a national and supra-national level. The legal environment created acts as an enabling force that underpins and strengthens the ten principles.

Finally, *civil society organizations* and *labour* play a crucial role because they have competence and substantive knowledge with regard to practical problems. On the side of labour, the international trade union movement offers problem-solving competence concerning the implementation of the four labour-related principles. Civil society is mostly represented by non-governmental organizations. Many NGOs are increasingly referred to as partners that provide contextualized knowledge to businesses regarding projects that support the ten principles. NGOs also play a vital role within the dialogue and learning activities since they possess specialized knowledge about particular issues (e.g., HIV/AIDS) that often become even more focused once a national or regional context is taken into account. Furthermore, NGOs act as watchdog institutions that speak up if business participants violate any of the principles.

The Compact links these actors through three engagement mechanisms: *learning events, dialogue events* and *partnership projects*. The three mechanisms serve the two major goals of the Compact (see above) since they (a) enable business and non-business actors to create, discuss, modify and extend a set of shared values within the global marketplace and (b) allow corporations to implement these values into their operations by sharing ideas and best practices. The engagement mechanisms are designed to function both at the global and national/regional level. On the national/regional level engagement is ensured through so-called local networks, which have been established in over 80 countries thus far. Local networks serve as a platform to create a close link between contextualized problems at the local level and the more abstract ideas and commitments that are developed at the global level. Networks are 'translators' of the created global solutions and, at the same time, 'innovators' looking for ways to implement the ten principles given the constraints and opportunities of a local context. In the following section, the three engagement mechanisms are introduced and their role at the global and national/regional level described (see Figure 2.2).

By *partnership projects* the Global Compact means active collaboration between business, civil society and governments under the umbrella of the ten principles. Partnerships seek to discover a common ground of interests

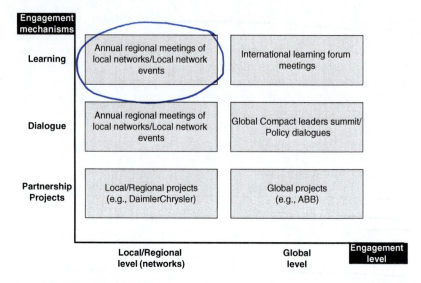

Figure 2.2 The three engagement mechanisms and their role at the global and national/regional level

between the private and the public sector and thus combine and leverage available skills and resources on both sides. Often partnerships occur in direct support of issues discussed at the different loci for dialogue. DaimlerChrysler, for instance, has set up a project together with the German Development Agency (GTZ) to tackle the rise of HIV/AIDS in South Africa. This project is in direct support of the 2003 Global Compact Policy Dialogue on this topic. Whereas some partnership projects are embedded in a local context, others have a more global reach. Deutsche Telekom, for example, has started a Global Communication Initiative that aims to bridge the digital divide across different parts of the world.

Dialogue events are about identifying new and emergent issues that relate to any of the ten principles. However, they also attempt to build relationships and trust with other actors (e.g., by entering into partnership projects). At the global level, the Compact has created a variety of Policy Dialogues that focus on specific issues (e.g., the role of the private sector in conflict zones). These meetings act as an international platform to discuss problems and to gain mutual understanding about possible solutions. Another form of global dialogue is the triennial Global Compact Leaders Summit which brings together executives from business and non-business participants to chart the strategic course of the Compact itself. On the local level, networks are encouraged to facilitate dialogue on issues that are relevant to them and share the ideas developed at regional network conferences. Dialogue at the local level is especially valuable as it allows previously unconnected actors (such as SMEs) to enter into partnerships with other business and non-business participants.

Learning events are closely related to dialogue, but focus more on sharing pre-existing solutions and best practices and thus do not specifically aim to find new ways to promote the ten principles. Learning is crucial as participants can learn from available good practices and thus follow notable examples that were developed under consideration of their region and sector. At the global level, learning occurs through direct interaction, such as at the International Learning Forum Meeting and also the Global Compact website. Corporations are asked to submit case studies and descriptions of best practices to the web portal to enable other participants to replicate and thus propagate available solutions. The Compact Office has also published a case study series that clusters examples.[26] At the local level, network meetings serve as a basis for learning and dissemination of best practices. Networks enable participants to learn from one another taking into account the constraints and opportunities of their region and/or sector. The UK network, for instance, has set up a peer review process of submitted COPs which allows participants to learn how to improve the quality of their COPs.

The three engagement mechanisms work together (e.g., projects also create learning effects) as indicated by the arrows in Figure 2.2. Engagement mechanisms alone do not ensure that a participant fulfills the two goals that the Compact serves. Rather, engagement by participating in learning, dialogue and partnership projects needs to be backed up by implementation of the principles throughout a participant's value chain.

3 The Global Compact and its critics – an assessment

Since its inception, the Global Compact has faced a lot of criticism from a variety of sources. This chapter looks at the three *most often mentioned*: that (1) the Compact supports the capture of the UN by 'big business', (2) its principles are vague and thus hard to implement and (3) it is not accountable due to missing verification mechanisms. The following discussion shows that this criticism is, at least in part, based on a misunderstanding of the initiative and its underlying institutional framework. Other, less frequently-mentioned criticisms include an observed 'non-seriousness' of participants[27]

---

[26] Global Compact (2003a). *HIV/AIDS: Everybody's Business*. New York: Global Compact Office; Global Compact (2003b). *Experiences in Management for Sustainability*. New York: Global Compact Office; Global Compact (2003c). *From Principles to Practice*. New York: Global Compact Office; Global Compact (2004). *Embedding Human Rights in Business practice*. New York: Global Compact Office; Global Compact (2006). *Business Against Corruption: Case Stories and Examples*. New York: Global Compact Office.
[27] Deva (2006), *supra* note 8, here: 113.

and an over-focus on the participation of Western MNCs compared to SMEs from the developing world.[28]

3.1 Allegation 1: the Compact supports the 'capture' of the UN by big business

One common allegation raised by critical parties is that the Compact opens a window of opportunity for business to capture the UN. Zammit,[29] for example, argues that there is a basic inconsistency between the policy interests of developing countries and those promoted by the UN's corporate partners. The fear is that big business will pursue its policy interests within the UN more directly by signing up to initiatives like the Global Compact. Such a view is also adopted by Nolan,[30] who states that '[c]lose relations between the UN and big business provides ample scope for "capture" such that the UN, the supposed rule setter, wittingly or otherwise begins to adopt the agenda of business partners without debate or true democratic procedure.' Thérien and Pouliot[31] thus conclude that the creation of the Global Compact has fuelled concerns about a break in the UN's traditional, non-business position on economic issues. Furthermore, it raises concerns that the institution adopts a 'pro-market spin' that could, in time, lead to its silent privatization.

There are, however, at least two issues that should be taken into consideration here. First, the Global Compact is by no means the first, nor the only attempt to establish partnerships between the UN and business. Almost from its inception, the UN has had partnerships with businesses and business associations. Businesses and NGOs even joined the 51 nations that gathered in San Francisco, CA in 1945 to sign the UN Charter, and were *expected* to be part of the solution to foster peace and development. However, owing to increasing media coverage, most partnerships have only recently entered the wider public consciousness. For instance, at the 2002 Johannesburg World Summit for Sustainable Development (WSSD) over 240 partnerships were announced, most of which were in the field of water and energy use.[32] UN-business partnerships are neither a new nor exclusive feature of the Global Compact, however they have increased in number over the last decade. This increase may be due to the fact that many UN agencies have undergone an ideological change from confrontation to cooperation

---

[28] Transnational Resource and Action Center (TRAC) (2000). *Tangled up in Blue: Corporate Partnerships at the United Nations*. San Francisco: TRAC.
[29] Zammit (2003), *supra* note 8, here: p. xxi.
[30] Nolan (2005), *supra* note 8, here: 465.
[31] Thérein & Pouliot (2006), *supra* note 5, here: 67.
[32] James, Barry (2 September 2002). Partnerships stressed at the summit: Many companies find an opportunity. *International Herald Tribune*. Retrieved 28 January 2009, available at: http://www.iht.com/articles/2002/09/02/joburg_ed3_.php.

with regard to partnerships.³³ There is, of course, the question of why this change has occurred and whether it reflects a 'capture' of the UN by business or whether it is simply in response to the rise of global markets and growing governance gaps at the local and global level. This question brings us to the second point.

It is important to understand that it is not the Global Compact that allows corporations to be closer to the agenda of policy makers at the UN but that corporations *are already* political players, quite independently of the Compact.³⁴ Corporations design and implement social and environmental standards,³⁵ are involved in peacekeeping,³⁶ provide education and healthcare³⁷ and fight corruption.³⁸ All of these issues are also on the UN agenda. This engagement has not been imposed on MNCs but is necessary since (a) national governments, especially in developing countries, increasingly fail to set a regulative framework under which such issues can be resolved and (b) many of today's problems cannot be solved on a national level at all but need to be addressed globally, for example by *multinational* companies.³⁹ Under these conditions, collaboration between the UN and business is not only desirable but also needed as the UN's goals can no longer be achieved without collaboration with business.⁴⁰ In a world of growing interdependencies, neglecting and devaluing UN-business partnerships can only come at the price of sticking to existing ideologies. There is no basic inconsistency between the goals of business and the UN; both are interested in the existence of a stable global market that is sustainable and based on a social consensus of shared values. Neglecting this relationship may be possible in the short run but will go against the UN's mission over a longer time frame.

UN-business partnerships are, of course, not without problems. It is not the direct capture of the UN by businesses but instead the ability of the

---

³³ Cohen (2001), *supra* note 15; Kell (2005), *supra* note 15.

³⁴ Palazzo, Guido & Scherer, Andreas G. (2006). Corporate legitimacy as deliberation: a communicative framework. *Journal of Business Ethics*, 66, 71–88.

³⁵ McIntosh, Malcom, Thomas, Ruth, Leipziger, Deborah, & Coleman, Gill (2003). *Living Corporate Citizenship: Strategic Routes to Socially Responsible Business*. London et al.: FT Prentice Hall.

³⁶ Fort, Timothy L. & Schipani, Cindy A. (2002). The role of the corporation in fostering sustainable peace. *Vanderbilt Journal of Transnational Law*, 35, 389–435.

³⁷ Williams (2004), *supra* note 11.

³⁸ Cavanagh, Gerald F. (2004). Global business ethics – regulation, code, or self-restraint. *Business Ethics Quarterly*, 14, 625–642.

³⁹ Scherer, Andreas G., Palazzo, Guido, & Baumann, Dorothee (2006). Global rules and private actors: toward a new role of the transnational corporation in global governance. *Business Ethics Quarterly*, 16, 505–532.

⁴⁰ Bigge, David M. (2004). Bring on the bluewash – a social constructivist argument against using nike v. Kasky to attack the UN Global Compact. *International Legal Perspectives*, 14, 6–21, here: 10; Kell (2005), *supra* note 16, here: 71.

latter to use the Compact as a means to position a specific idea of what corporate citizenship is about (i.e. learning *not* regulation) that needs to be watched carefully. As discussed below, learning is a supplement, but not a substitute, for regulation. For corporations, the UN is particularly attractive in this context as influencing the public understanding of what 'good' corporate citizenship is about requires discursive legitimacy (among other things), which the UN clearly offers.[41] Since the majority of Compact participants are businesses or business associations, the initiative needs to ensure that the perspectives of multiple stakeholders are taken into consideration when shaping and framing the public understanding and expectation towards corporate citizenship.

3.2 Allegation 2: the Compact's principles are vague and thus hard to implement

The second criticism pertains to the Compact's lack of clarity with regard to its principles. Deva,[42] for instance, notes that the principles hardly provide concrete guidance to corporations about the expected conduct. Requirements such as 'action needs to be taken within a firm's sphere of influence' miss the precision necessary for a viable code of conduct. Deva[43] further argues that 'the language of these principles is so general that insincere corporations can easily circumvent or comply with them without doing anything.' Similarly, Nolan[44] and Bigge[45] claim that the Compact is surrounded by a lack of precision in content that does not even attempt to clarify its principles for its participants. Murphy[46] thus concludes that the Compact is at best a minimalist code of corporate conduct.

First of all, one must recognize that many of these critics want the Compact to be a clearly structured code of conduct against which compliance can be measured. However, as already mentioned, the very idea of the Compact is the creation of a long-term learning network that is used by business and non-business participants to share innovative ideas and best practices as to how the ten principles can be implemented. These principles provide a yardstick for the exchange of ideas, learning and discussion and are not meant to be a benchmark against which to assess compliance. The goal is to establish

---

[41] Levy, David L. (2008). Political contestation in global production networks. *Academy of Management Review*, 33(4), 943–963; Levy, David L. & Prakash, Aseem (2003). Bargains old and new: multinational corporations in global governance. *Business and Politics*, 5(2), 131–150.
[42] Deva (2006), *supra* note 8, here: 129.
[43] *Id.*
[44] Nolan (2005), *supra* note 8, here: 460.
[45] Bigge (2004), *supra* note 41, here: 11.
[46] Murphy, Sean D. (2005). Taking multinational corporate codes of conduct to the next level. *Columbia Journal of Transnational Law*, 43, 388–433, here: 389.

consensus and best practices on what, for instance 'a precautionary approach to environmental challenges' means within a firm's respective region and sector. Over-specified principles could even turn out to be counterproductive as they would limit the scope of possible solutions right from the beginning. The ten principles rather provide corporations with the opportunity and highlight the need to 'fill' their general character with context-specific meaning.

Thinking about context uncovers yet another reason for the general character of the principles. Although regional in its impact, the Global Compact is designed as a global initiative with no restrictions on the size, sector or region of its participants. Currently, 52 per cent of all business participants are small and medium-sized enterprises coming mainly from Europe, Latin America and Asia.[47] The wide variety in corporate size, sector, region and available resources of participating companies does not allow for the introduction of clear-cut principles. For instance, a 'precautionary approach to environmental challenges' has a different meaning for a large MNC operating in the chemical sector, compared to an Indian SME doing business in the IT industry. It is in this spirit that the UNDP-sponsored handbook for implementing the Global Compact recognizes that 'company approaches [toward the ten principles] are very different. It highlights the flexibility of the Compact and the fact that there is considerable scope for adapting the initiative to the specific needs and situation of the individual participant.'[48]

It is the very idea of the Compact acting as a moral compass for participants,[49] a compass that addresses corporate diversity through a learning-based approach, which allows firms to contextualize the general principles within their respective business context. The bottom line is that there are a variety of ways to implement the ten principles: The Compact's values need to be *translated* into action, a task (like any other management task) that can be approached from different angles.

3.3 Allegation 3: the Compact is not accountable due to missing verification

The last allegation, that the Compact is not accountable because it does not independently monitor and verify compliance with its principles, is probably the most well-known critique that has appeared consistently for

---

[47] Global Compact (2007). *UN Global Compact Annual Review*. New York: Global Compact Office.
[48] United Nations Development Program (UNDP) (2005). *Implementing the Global Compact: A Booklet for Inspiration*. Copenhagen: UNDP, here: p. 8.
[49] Kell, Georg (2003). The Global Compact: origins, operations, progress, challenges. *Journal of Corporate Citizenship*, 11, 35–49, here: 47.

the last eight years in the academic and non-academic press.[50] It is in this spirit that Nolan[51] argues that 'accountability, or rather the lack of it, is the crucial issue that faces the Global Compact'. Critics argue that a lack of serious monitoring, sanctions, enforceable rules and independent verification fosters the misuse of the Compact as a marketing tool.[52] In the eyes of these critics the Compact is a public relations smokescreen without substance that allows powerful MNCs to 'bluewash' their damaged image. In other words, they seek to associate their operations with the blue UN flag in order to gain legitimacy. Ultimately, the fear is that such a lack of accountability can lead to adverse selection in that those companies most eager to join are the ones in need of a good public image.[53]

In order to address this allegation in a comprehensive way, two issues need to be discussed and understood. First, one cannot and should not criticize the Compact for something it has never pretended or intended to be; a compliance-based mechanism that verifies and measures corporate behaviour. From its inception, the initiative was never designed as a seal of approval for participating companies as certification would require far more resources than are currently available. The Compact instead expects proactive behaviour from its participants. Its learning approach is advantageous insofar as a code of conduct (that would be needed for monitoring) is always static and thus does not allow participants to react flexibly to varying environmental circumstances.[54] Without a doubt, it should be in the enlightened self-interest of the Compact to prevent free-riders from misusing the initiative. However, the prevention of opportunistic behaviour does not ultimately require close monitoring of corporate actions. The decision faced by rule-setters is not between fully monitoring corporate behaviour *or* not monitoring at all. Rather, there is something in between.

For the Compact this 'in between' is reflected by demanding that its participants report on progress they have made in implementing the principles on an annual basis. The above-mentioned COP policy allows the Global Compact Office to gain an overview of a company's bottom-line activities. Although the Compact does not yet require standardized COP reports, it encourages its participants to follow the recently released G3-guidelines of

---

[50] Recently see, Bigge (2004), *supra* note 41, here: 12; Deva (2006), *supra* note 8, here: 146; Nolan (2005), *supra* note 8; Rizvi (2004), *supra* note 8; Thérien & Pouliot (2006), *supra* note 5, here: p. 67; and Engardio, Pete (2004). Global Compact, little impact. *Business Week*, 12 July 2004, 86–87, here: 86.
[51] Nolan (2005), *supra* note 8, here: 462.
[52] Deva (2006), Rizvi (2004), *supra* note 8.
[53] Williams (2004), *supra* note 11, here: 762.
[54] Ruggie (2002), *supra* note 10, here: 304.

the Global Reporting Initiative.[55] Since COPs are primarily aimed at participants' stakeholders, they foster a social vetting mechanism that is intended to increase report content and quality over time. Social vetting means that other parties (e.g., NGOs) are asked to use submitted COPs as grounds to judge corporate behaviour and file complaints that the Compact can use as a basis for investigations. If a company fails to submit a COP report within a year it is labelled 'non-communicating', while after a second year of non-reporting the firm is labelled 'inactive' and completely delisted after yet another year of non-communication. This policy has already led to over 1,800 firms being permanently delisted (data as of February 2010). The case for ensuring accountability by demanding COPs is a good one as its content needs to be publicized in prominent documents (e.g., the annual report) which are usually approved by a company's board.

A second issue that deserves attention here is the question of whether verification, although not the aim of the Compact, would be achievable at all. Three points are important in this context: (1) the development of indicators; (2) the issuance of a mandate and (3) the accessibility of resources.

(1) First, even if desired by the Compact, monitoring of participants would be nearly impossible as it requires performance indicators relevant to *all* companies in *all* countries and sectors. Without such measures a meaningful comparison of monitoring results, and thus the creation of sanctions, is not only impossible but would also weaken the Compact's accountability as any imposed sanctions would be perceived as arbitrary.

(2) Second, the Global Compact currently has no mandate to monitor or verify compliance with its principles. Since the initiative is embedded within the UN system, the establishment of legally-binding regulations would require the support of the UN General Assembly, which is unlikely given the current international political climate.[56] Even if such a compromise were to be established, it would reflect the 'lowest common denominator' of the currently 193 UN Member States and thus echo a weak mandate. Attempts to transform the Compact into a code of conduct would not only miss political support but also not fit the current climate of cooperation and collaboration between the UN and business.

(3) Third, the logistical and financial resources to effectively and efficiently monitor MNCs and their supply chains, let alone SMEs around the world, are simply not available. Given that there are currently over 5,300 business

---

[55] Global Reporting Initiative (GRI) (2007). *Sustainability Reporting Guidelines on Economic, Environmental, and Social Performance v3*. Boston, MA: GRI.
[56] Ruggie (2002), *supra* note 10, here: 303.

participants, annual (or even biannual) monitoring of corporate behavior would require personal, logistical and financial resources that are way beyond the Compact's current capacity. Nike, for instance, has over 750 direct suppliers in 52 countries. It is precisely for this reason that certification standards such as SA 8000 award certificates for just *one* production facility but never for an entire corporation and/or supply chain.[57] The addressees of the Compact, however, are entire corporations and not single production facilities.

To conclude, a variety of factors prevent the Compact from being a tool for regulation; most of all its underlying idea of creating space for learning and cooperation. Of course, measures such as the annually-required COP reports are essential to strengthen the case for accountability. However, on their own they do not reflect a compliance mechanism in the narrow sense.

This in-depth discussion of the three allegations demonstrates that there is a need to clarify the intent of the Compact. Discussing these allegations should *not* indicate that these critical voices do not deserve to be heard. The tensions they create can lead to productive discussions and even innovations to the initiative. Instead this chapter argues that there is a need to be more careful when judging the initiative for something it never pretended or intended to be. In the following section, the role of the Compact as a supplement to national/international regulation and voluntary regulative standards (e.g., SA 8000) is outlined. This discussion is intended to lead future critical assessments in a more fruitful direction; a direction that enables the initiative to learn from and leverage the suggestions made by its critics.

4 The Global Compact as a *necessary* supplement

Whereas the last section discussed what the Global Compact *is not*, this section focuses on what the initiative *is*, with a focus on the contentious issues that were previously raised (e.g., lack of mandate and resources to monitor). Overall, this chapter argues that the Compact is best understood as something that *necessarily* supplements approaches with a regulative character towards corporate responsibility. Following Baldwin, Scott and Hood,[58] regulation can be defined as something that transcends the law and includes all mechanisms of social control by state and non-state actors to direct corporate behaviour according to predefined standards. In this sense, regulation

---

[57] Gilbert, Dirk U. & Rasche, Andreas (2007). Discourse ethics and social accountability: the ethics of SA 8000. *Business Ethics Quarterly*, 17, 187–216.
[58] Baldwin, Robert, Scott, Colin, & Hood, Christopher (1998). *A Reader on Regulation.* Oxford: Oxford University Press.

is about sustained and focused control.[59] The learning-based approach of the Compact is a supplement to regulation because it should never replace national and international regulatory systems. Instead it is useful where (1) corporations are willing but have trouble putting regulations into practice and thus need to learn about implementation and (2) where regulations fail or are ineffective and need further development. Both of these situations will be explained further.

First, the Compact supplements regulation by national governments, intergovernmental institutions and compliance-based voluntary corporate social responsibility (CSR) standards because it enables a learning process within corporations – a learning process that allows firms to establish compliance with these regulations in the first place. Regulation by itself is often limited in its potential because those who are regulated need to learn how to implement and 'live' the letter of law. The myriad of corporate scandals around the globe shows that regulation by itself is in no way sufficient. Regulated parties need to find out what the letter of law means, how it can be implemented and, most of all, they need to be willing to carry out serious implementation efforts. The Compact helps corporations to address these issues by providing a forum that disseminates best practices and thus translates existing regulations (e.g., international law with regard to human rights issues) into real-life actions. Furthermore, it can also positively stimulate the motivation to comply with regulations by identifying notable best practices and thus exercise peer-pressure on competitors.

Second, the Compact also supplements existing regulations whenever the latter are not working efficiently or are completely absent. For instance, in theory supplier factories in developing countries comply with employee protection codes,[60] whereas in practice there is little enforcement of these rules and voluntary, regulative instruments such as SA 8000 or the FLA workplace code only cover a small share of the overall number of workers. For other problems, for example climate change, there are no binding regulations at all. Of course, the Compact does not define a regulatory framework to tackle climate change; however, it offers a forum where this issue can be discussed to develop measures that can act as a *temporary* solution until binding regulations emerge. The recently launched *Caring for Climate* platform shows that Compact participants (e.g., Deutsche Telekom and Unilever) have come up with a variety of innovative ways to address climate change within their business operations. Setting up the *Caring for Climate* platform does not

---

[59] Selznick, Philip (1985). Focusing organizational research on regulation. In Ed R. Noll (Ed.), *Regulatory Policy and the Social Sciences* (pp. 363–367). Berkeley, CA: University of California Press, here: p. 363.
[60] Webb, Kernaghan (2004). Understanding the voluntary code phenomenon. In Kernaghan Webb (Ed.), *Voluntary Codes: Private Governance, the Public Interest and Innovation* (pp. 3–32). Ottawa, CA: Carleton University Press, here: p. 6.

indicate that there is no need for regulation to fight climate change, but that preliminary results are possible even in the absence of binding rules. Kofi Annan recognized this when referring to the Compact as a pragmatic interim solution with regard to existing governance gaps.[61] Talking about pragmatic solutions, of course, does *not* indicate that learning and the formulation of shared values solely fill the omnipresent governance gaps, nor does it mean that global governance can do without regulation. It merely stresses the fact that (a) interim solutions are necessary as long as binding global regulations are not in sight and (b) regulations should always be supplemented, not replaced, by a learning-based approach towards governance.

In other words, there are two understandings of the Compact's supplementary nature: the Compact as a supplement to learn about and act on existing regulations *and* the Compact as a supplement to missing regulations. These two understandings reflect a *necessity* as every regulatory framework needs to be enacted by its addressees. The Compact provides a forum where such enactment can take place. Regulations, whether they are laws, standards or codes of conduct, need to be understood; otherwise they will be ineffective. The letter of the law remains useless as long as the spirit of the law stays unrecognized. By utilizing a variety of engagement and dialogue mechanisms, participants of the Compact make sense of existing regulations by sharing best practices and innovative solutions. Furthermore, regulations show a strong tendency towards inflexibility and over-formality[62] which can lead to adversarial 'going by the book' attitudes to compliance.[63] The Compact is necessary in this context because it adds flexibility to existing regulations and thus allows for the inclusion of emerging topics (e.g., climate change).

To conclude, in order to appreciate the nature of the Compact there is a need to leave the dichotomy of 'effective regulation by law' *versus* 'ineffective voluntary commitment to non-regulating learning tools'. The choice is not one of an either/or-type but should reflect a both/and way of thinking. That is why this chapter characterizes the Compact as a supplement – something that *adds itself to* regulation but always requires further actions. The International Chamber of Commerce[64] echoes this by claiming that 'the

---

[61] United Nations (24 June 2004). Global compact participants on 'Common Historic Journey' to fairer, more stable world says Secretary-General at UN Summit [Press Release SG/SM/9383, ECO/69]. New York: United Nations.
[62] Bardach, Eugene & Kagan, Robert A. (1982). *Going by the Book: The Problem of Regulatory Unreasonableness*. Philadelphia, PA: Temple University Press.
[63] Coglianese, Cary, & Nash, Jennifer. (2001). *Regulating from the Inside: Can Environmental Management Systems Achieve Policy Goals*. Washington: Resources for the Future.
[64] International Chamber of Commerce (24 June 2004). *The Global Compact: A Business Perspective* [Press release]. Paris: International Chamber of Commerce.

Global Compact's greatest strength lies in its voluntary nature, which acts as a powerful complement to the necessary action by governments themselves to safeguard and advance its principles.'

5 Moving ahead – perspectives and challenges

Although this chapter shows that some of the critical voices are based on a misunderstanding of the nature of the Compact and/or demand changes that are unlikely to occur in the current political climate of the UN, there are a variety of challenges that the Compact needs to address in order to maintain or even increase its relevance. This chapter highlights four issues which represent key success factors for the development of the initiative; (1) the management of *growth*, (2) the management of *diversity*, (3) the continued strengthening of *accountability*, and (4) the inclusion of *financial markets*. Of course, these are by no means the only challenges, as other important issues also exist. For example, the need for collaboration with governments to strengthen the ten principles with binding regulations or the more active consideration of problems that relate to international supply chains. Hence, the following four issues do not represent an exclusive list but are indicative of future challenges, the discussion of which is beyond the scope of this chapter.

5.1 Managing growth

The first major challenge results from the tension that is created between the continued expansion of the initiative – from 50 participants in 2000 to over 7,300 in 2008 – and the constraints of managing such a fast-growing and flexible network of actors within a rather rigid organization such as the UN. It is no secret that the UN system is overly-characterized by a bureaucratic and hierarchical way of management that is not always in a position to provide quick responses to the emerging needs of a proliferating initiative such as the Global Compact. In particular, inter-agency collaboration and also collaboration of UN agencies with non-state actors cannot rely on the rather sticky UN procedures for issuing mandates. Instead it needs to be driven by shared incentives, a decentralized decision-making style and commitment towards the Compact's ten principles.

There is also a danger that the Compact may become politicized in the sense that the UN demands intergovernmental oversight. Although the current mandate, backed by a General Assembly resolution,[65] gives the UN Secretariat clear responsibility for the Compact, this status needs to be

[65] United Nations (3 December 2001). Towards global partnerships [General Assembly Resolution A/56/L.33]. New York: United Nations.

maintained, especially when bearing in mind the expected further growth. The achievements of the Compact and its steady growth are based on its pragmatism and the network-based governance model underlying its operations; politicizing the initiative would put these two success factors at risk.

5.2 Managing diversity

A second challenge deals with achieving greater diversity in terms of corporate size, represented sectors and, most of all, the geographic spread of business participants. Although some areas of the world have not yet attracted a lot of participants (e.g., the Middle East), it is especially remarkable that North American companies only comprise a small portion of the overall share of the Compact's business participants.[66] This is particularly striking because North American (especially US) companies represent a much larger percentage of the world's largest corporations according to the Fortune Global 500 index than their participation rate in the Compact indicates. One major reason is that North America is a more litigious society than Europe or Latin America. Companies are afraid of lawsuits that are filed by adversaries, accusing US participants of not complying with the principles.[67] As Ziegler's[68] empirical study reveals, US participants often cite fear of litigation as an obstacle against membership in the Compact. This participation barely improved even after the Compact, together with the American Bar Association, developed a litigation-proof letter in 2004 which shields US participants from lawsuits based on claims that they failed to comply with the principles. Even though there is no evidence whether this letter holds the force of law, other reasons must also play a role.

The reluctance of US businesses to join the Compact is also reflected by the ongoing fear of public criticism. As mentioned above (Allegation 3), there still is a lot of criticism of the Compact's accountability. Thus, firms fear that once they join they will be accused of 'bluewashing' their operations regardless of how well they implement the principles. In a time of increased transparency and media attention such assertions can be very harmful to a corporation's public image. The Compact can only address this concern by (a) continuing to communicate the purpose of the initiative and strengthen existing integrity measures (e.g., the COP policy) and (b) supporting outreach activities through its established US local network. Since the US hosts

---

[66] Global Compact (2007), *supra* note 48.
[67] Hemphill (2005), *supra* note 2, here: 312; Williams (2004), *supra* note 11, here: 758.
[68] Ziegler, Oliver (2007). Global Compact membership in Europe and the US: a case study of the automobile industry. *Journal of Corporate Citizenship*, 26, 55–68.

> US firms should be encouraged to reject/avoid the GC

many MNCs, increased participation is not only desirable but also necessary to address issues related to global supply chains.

5.3 Ensuring accountability

A third challenge deals with further strengthening the accountability of the initiative in order to protect its integrity and ensure sustainable growth. Accountability is, among other things, directly linked to an organization's ability to provide transparency of its operations and an evaluation of the progress and results against its goals and objectives.[69] To assess the accountability of the Compact, one needs to look at two inter-related issues; on the one hand, information communicated by participants about their progress in implementing the principles and on the other, information regarding the impact communicated by the Compact itself. Concerning corporate reporting, there is a challenge to not only demand annual Communication on Progress, but also to ensure comparable quality of the submitted reports. Although the Compact has no authority to judge the actions of corporations, an industry-specific benchmarking system for the annually-submitted reports would help (a) to provide incentives for participants to submit improved reports as well as a guide to do so and (b) to increase the comparability of report content and thus foster learning and dialogue among participants. Achieving such a benchmarking system means strengthening the already existing relationship with the Global Reporting Initiative to come up with a selection of mandatory core indicators for COP reports. *done 2010*. In addition, the currently existing categories for failed COP reporting (i.e. non-communicating, inactive, delisted) should be merged into one category. This shortens the 'grace period' for non-reporters and thus provides incentives to submit a report on time.[70]

Regarding impact-related information communicated by the Compact itself, there has recently been much improvement. The *UN Global Compact Annual Review* (first introduced at the 2007 Leaders Summit in Geneva) includes specific and comprehensive data on the overall progress of implementing the ten principles throughout the world. The challenge is to make this information more reliable by supplementing the (so far) quantitative survey-based data with more detailed qualitative interview-based data. For first attempts of this approach see Cetindamar and Husoy and McKinsey and

---

[69] Blagescu, Monica & Lloyd, Robert (2006). *2006 Global Accountability Report: Holding Power to Account.* London: One World Trust; Rasche, Andreas & Esser, Daniel E. (2006). From stakeholder management to stakeholder accountability: applying Habermasian discourse ethics to accountability research. *Journal of Business Ethics*, 65, 251–267.
[70] Note: At the time of writing these categories still existed. However, the Global Compact changed its COP policy in July 2009. If business participants do not send a COP report within a year, they are now delisted.

Company.[71] To date, a systematic effort to assess the impact of the Compact in a comprehensive manner has not been attempted, mostly due to the high costs of gathering and evaluating information at different levels of aggregation.[72] The accountability of the initiative could be strengthened if a comprehensive impact assessment can be produced and disseminated on a regular basis. Impact assessments also need to show whether Compact-related projects by business participants are integrated into core-business practices, as indicated by the initiative's understanding of corporate citizenship (see above), or whether such projects reflect philanthropy and are thus isolated from a participant's business. After all, positive results of impact assessments could also prove that the flexibility inherent in the ten principles 'pays off'.

5.4 Including financial markets

Finally, there is the challenge of winning *financial markets* over to base future investment decisions – to a much larger extent than at present – on social and environmental criteria. Although empirical research offers mixed results when it comes to the relationship between corporate social performance (CSP) and long-term financial performance (ranging from no significant relation[73] to a significant positive relation),[74] a meta-analysis finds a generally positive impact of CSP on firms' financial performance across industries and across study contexts.[75] This perspective is also in line with a recent study by Goldman Sachs[76] which finds that business leadership on social, environmental and governance issues can contribute to better market performance. The Compact, by promoting the Principles for Responsible Investment (PRI), can help to set the right institutional framework for responsible investment-decisions. If institutional investors start acknowledging the PRI as a guideline for their decisions, the business case for the Compact will become more obvious. Of course, participation in the Compact should never be *limited* to the business case. However, future growth

---

[71] Centindamar, Dilek & Husoy, Kristoffer (2007). Corporate social responsibility practices and environmentally responsible behavior: the case of the United Nations Global Compact. *Journal of Business Ethics*, 76, 163–176; McKinsey & Company (2004). *Assessing the Global Compact's Impact*. New York: Global Compact Office.
[72] Kell (2005), *supra* note 16, here: 63.
[73] Aupperle, Kenneth E., Carroll, Archie B., & Hatfield, John (1985). An empirical examination of the relationship between corporate social responsibility and profitability. *Academy of Management Journal*, 28(2), 446–463.
[74] Waddock, Sandra & Graves, Samuel B. (1997). The corporate social performance: financial performance link. *Strategic Management Journal*, 18(4), 303–319.
[75] Orlitzky, Marc, Schmidt, Frank L., & Rynes, Sara (2003). Corporate social and financial performance: a meta-analysis. *Organization Studies*, 24(3), 403–441.
[76] Goldman Sachs (2007). *Introducing GS Sustain*. London: The Goldman Sachs Group Inc.

of the initiative will depend on the environment that is set by financial markets. Responsible investment decisions can lead to stable, accountable and thus profitable market conditions which should be in the enlightened self-interest of all market players – especially when considering the recent turbulence of mortgage markets around the world.

6 Conclusions

This chapter seeks to show that (a) the mass of critique of the Global Compact is often, yet by no means always, based on a misunderstanding of the very nature of the initiative as well as its underlying mandate; (b) there is a need to give more credit to its supplementary nature with regard to state and non-state regulation; and (c) to ensure a continued, sustainable growth of the initiative many challenges need to be addressed. Being in its tenth year of operation now, the Compact has achieved much in a rather short period of time; it is not only the largest corporate citizenship initiative in terms of size but also the most inclusive one bringing together a diverse set of business and non-business stakeholders. In addition – and this may be one of the most valuable side effects of the set up of the Compact – its dynamic and flexible network-based governance structure can promote necessary reforms of the UN system *from within*. The Christian Science Monitor,[77] for example, praised the Compact as being 'the most creative reinvention' of the United Nations to date.

Future conceptual and empirical research can and should support the evolution of the Compact. First, researchers can add expertise and insights to develop a more systemic and comprehensive impact assessment. Whereas there are a number of conceptual studies that introduce the content and governance structure of the Compact,[78] there are almost no empirical insights on the implementation of the ten principles in corporations. The academic community can add much-needed information by conducting studies about the impact of the Compact on existing business practices. One key question is, for instance, whether and how participating firms have changed existing routines (e.g., with regard to supplier relations).

Second, academics can also add valuable knowledge on a more conceptual level. For instance, the contribution of the Compact as an institutional arrangement within the emerging system of global governance needs to be explored more closely. Addressing this topic necessitates discussing how the Compact relates to other institutional arrangements that have occurred

---

[77] Christian Science Monitor (2000). *A New Global Compact*. Retrieved 20 July 2007, available at: http://www.csmonitor.com/2000/0908/p10s1.html.
[78] Deva (2006), Nolan (2005), *supra* note 8; Thérien & Pouliot (2006), *supra* note 5; Williams (2004), *supra* note 11.

recently (e.g., stakeholder management standards like AA1000) or are about to occur (e.g., the ISO 26000 guidelines).[79] Scholars can also add valuable insights when it comes to discussing why the Compact, because of its multi-stakeholder nature, is a meaningful and much-needed initiative that addresses declining public trust in traditional state-centered political institutions. The discussion of legitimacy, as recently outlined by Palazzo and Scherer,[80] offers many interesting points of departure here. Third, future research should also advance the initiative itself by critically discussing its existing engagement mechanisms and underlying governance structure. It is our hope that these discussions will take up the issues raised in this chapter to present arguments that consider the nature of the Compact together with its institutional setting to a greater extent.

Without a doubt, the Compact has not yet achieved all of its goals. However, researchers and practitioners should give credit to the fact that neither its goals nor its underlying structure exist in a stable environment and thus reflect steady solutions. A start has been made and the point of departure taken by the initiative is a very promising one. The Compact is by no means a sufficient concept to ensure governance in a global economy; it is only a small part of the overall solution.[81] Whether the Compact succeeds in creating a more inclusive global economy that is embedded in a framework of fundamental, yet indispensable, values remains an open issue. Even the most ambitious journey has to start somewhere and the Global Compact has already helped to propagate the seeds of an emerging solution. History will be the judge of its success.

---

[79] Gilbert, Dirk U. & Rasche, Andreas (2008). Opportunities and problems of standardized ethics initiatives: a stakeholder theory perspective. *Journal of Business Ethics*, 82, 755–773.

[80] Palazzo & Scherer (2006), *supra* note 13.

[81] Rasche, Andreas (2009). Toward a model to compare and analyze accountability standards: the case of the UN Global Compact. *Corporate Social Responsibility and Environmental Management*, 16, 192–205; United Nations (2004), *supra* note 62.

3

Balancing Power Interests in Reflexive Law Public-Private CSR Schemes: The Global Compact and the EU's Multi-Stakeholder Forum on CSR

Karin Buhmann

1 Introduction*

1.1 The topic

The past decade has witnessed the emergence of multi-stakeholder public-private regulatory forums on corporate social responsibility (CSR). The process of the United Nations (UN) Special Representative of the Secretary-General (SRSG) on business and human rights is one such forum. The 2002–2004 EU Multi-Stakeholder (MSF) on CSR is another; the UN Global Compact a third. These are all set within institutional frameworks of intergovernmental organizations. The processes and outputs complement the formal law-making of the UN and the EU. This chapter deals with these types of forums. Set up under intergovernmental auspices, they differ from others, such as development of the ISO 26000 Social Responsibility Standard and the Forest Stewardship Council (FSC) labelling and certification scheme, which function more independently from public bodies. All the above may be considered types of responses to difficulties which formal law-making capacities of international law face with regard to regulation of global sustainability concerns, especially as these are related to human rights abuses or other types of negative impact caused by business action.

Multi-stakeholder forums which function at the level above national law-making as a sort of transnational or global law-making are clearly not conventional law-making institutions but clearly also have normative ambitions. For example, the Global Compact and the EU MSF are instituted with

---

* This chapter builds on research partially made possible through a grant from the Danish Research Council for the Social Sciences for the project "The legal character of CSR: Reflections between public international law and CSR, and implications for corporate regulation". The author is grateful to the Research Council for the support.

an aim to reach agreement on norms of business behaviour to be subscribed to and internalized by business itself. Both forums, however, comprise actors without a formal or limited legislative mandate. [makes rational/democratic action difficult]

This chapter discusses public-private law-making schemes within an intergovernmental setting from a two-pronged perspective: First, these schemes arise and function as responses to difficulties which conventional international law and law-making processes face with regard to encompassing the plurality of actors that have stakes in CSR normativity and regulation to promote CSR. The conventional international law-making system does not include private non-state actors (companies). Although some non-governmental organizations (NGOs, including business NGOs) have observatory roles, their formal law-making roles are also limited. Second, emerging public-private schemes face challenges with regard to their ability to represent the interests of the plurality of actors and views that they claim (or are claimed to) represent, and especially to do so in a balanced way. Under a range of different terms and approaches, a number of scholars working with emerging theories within law and other social sciences have discussed this issue. They generally agree that public-private regulation and multi-stakeholder regulation of global concerns, such as business impact on the environment or human rights, fill a gap in terms of inclusion of non-state actors that do not have access to conventional international law-making, and that these novel procedural forums provide opportunities for regulation across established legal systems in an increasingly globalized society with a powerful private sector. They also generally agree that these initiatives are problematic in the sense of lacking formal publicly granted legitimacy to make rules that pertain to or have effects for others.[1] For

---

[1] For example, Kingsbury, Benedict, Nico Krisch & Richard B. Steward (2005) The emergence of global administrative law. *Law and Contemporary Problems*, Vol. 68, No. 3: 15–61; Krisch, Nico & Benedict Kingsbury (2006) Introduction: global governance and global administrative law in the international legal order. *European Journal of International Law*, Vol. 17, No. 1: 1–13; Herberg, Martin (2008) Global legal pluralism and interlegality: environmental self-regulation in multinational enterprises as global law-making. In Dilling, Olaf, Martin Herberg & Gerd Winter (eds) *Responsible Business: Self-Governance and Law in Transnational Economic Transactions*. Oxford and Portland, OR: Hart: 17–40; Picciotto, Sol (2008) Regulatory networks and multi-level governance. In Dilling, Olaf, Martin Herberg & Gerd Winter (eds) *Responsible Business: Self-Governance and Law in Transnational Economic Transactions*. Oxford and Portland Oregon: Hart: 315–341; McBarnet, Doreen (2007) Corporate social responsibility beyond law, through law, for law: the new corporate accountability. In McBarnet, Doreen, Aurora Voiculescu & Tom Campbell (eds) *The New Corporate Accountability: Corporate Social Responsibility and the Law*. Cambridge: Cambridge University Press: 9–56; Conley, John M. & Cynthia A. Williams (2005) Engage, embed and embellish: theory versus practice in the corporate social responsibility movement. *Journal of Corporation Law*, Vol. 31, No. 1, Fall: 1–38; Trubek, David M. & Louise G. Trubek

example, due to specialization and technicalization of sustainable forestry, ecological food products or human rights impacts on business, public bodies that participate in such law-making are often administrative rather than legislative bodies. They therefore lack a formal law-making mandate, and their mandates generally are to provide topic- or sector-specific expertise rather than to represent the combined interests of their nations' citizens. Another example is provided by sector-wide CSR norms made by companies with or without collaboration with public authorities at administrative level. These norms may have effects for consumers or victims of human rights abuse who were not represented in the regulatory forum.

Against this backdrop, this chapter examines the setting-up of the Global Compact and the 2002–2004 process of the EU MSF as cases. Both cases are approached here as intergovernmentally initiated reflexive law to promote corporate self-regulation on CSR, including on human rights. The Global Compact and the MSF display differences with regard to the representation of interests, balancing of interests, and output in terms of a normative framework to guide companies on human rights as part of CSR. Based on a comparison between the two processes of negotiation that were both intended to lead to normative frameworks on CSR, the chapter discusses newer Habermasian theory (starting from 1992) as a possible explanatory model for the difference in normative outputs from EU MSF compared with the Global Compact. The chapter argues that Habermasian theory on legitimate law-making through deliberation may complement reflexive law theory with regard to balancing of interests among actors through design and management of the reflexive regulatory forum. The objective is to contribute to ongoing development of theory of public-private regulation at the global level, especially with regard to CSR. Due to space constraints and the complexity of both reflexive law and deliberative law-making theory, the chapter does not provide definite answers, but sketches ideas that may feed into further research.

In CSR contexts, law is often perceived narrowly to be about statutes, black-letter rules and enforcement. Law, in this chapter, is perceived as a much wider field: as theory and practice on the institutionalization of behavioural norms (norms of conduct). From that perspective, this chapter argues that law has particular relevance in the context of CSR. Law and

---

(2006) New governance and legal regulation: complementarity, rivalry or transformation. *Columbia Journal of European Law*, Vol. 13: 1–26; Sand, I.-J. (2005) Retten i det polykontekstuelle samfunn: Hvordan skal vi analysere og forstå den? *Retfærd*, Vol. 28, No. 4: 1–28; Lobel, Orly (2005) The renew deal: the fall of regulation and the rise of governance in contemporary legal thought. *Minnesota Law Review*, Vol. 89: 262–390; Haufler, Virginia (2001) *A Public Role for the Private Sector: Industry Self-Regulation in a Global Economy*. Washington DC: Carnegie Endowment for International Peace; Teubner, Gunther (1997) *Global Law Without a State*. Aldershot: Dartmouth: 179–212.

law-making are understood to encompass not only hard law (enforceable and/or legally binding rules) but also soft law, including new and emerging forms of soft law, such as the norms and codes of conduct which result from public-private regulatory forums on CSR. In this perspective, public-private development of CSR norms has legal relevance, especially at the international stage where international law serves as a normative source of considerable importance. This is the case with both the EU MSF and the Global Compact. As indicated in the Introduction to this book, theory on CSR and on law rarely travel on the same path, although many concerns are shared. Addressing CSR from a legal perspective need not challenge the assumption that CSR is voluntary, but may add insight in to our understanding of CSR normativity and the production of CSR norms.

1.2 The cases: The UN Global Compact and EU MSF

The two cases are selected on the following basis: They both relate to human rights as part of the CSR understanding. Both are finalized processes in terms of norm-creation (unlike the drafting of ISO 26000 or the SRSG's operationalization of the *Protect, Respect, Remedy* framework, both still ongoing at the time of writing. The SRSG process, in addition, arguably travels along a somewhat different path on business responsibilities for human rights (BRHR), distinct from CSR inter alia through its emphasis on state obligations through the state duty to protect).

The Global Compact and the EU MSF both include a broad spectrum of non-state actors but still function as extra-parliamentary norm-creating structures. The intergovernmental organizations behind the schemes are basically executive institutions: For the Global Compact, this was originally the UN Secretariat and is now the Global Compact Office which is in charge of ongoing development of the initiative. For the EU MSF, the EU Commission is in charge. These institutions lack the democratic mandate of the UN General Assembly, respectively the formal law-making powers and process in the EU which includes the European Parliament and the Council. The European Parliament is elected by direct suffrage in EU Member States, the Council comprises representatives of the Member States' governments which are based on and ultimately accountable to their national parliaments and electorates.

The Global Compact and the EU MSF are examples of intergovernmentally initiated or framed responses to needs to regulate global sustainability concerns. The Global Compact was established against a backdrop of UN and global civil society concern with sustainability, difficulties in creating a legal framework through past efforts at conventional international law-making, and business willingness to contribute to the UN's aims. The EU MSF was established by the EU Commission in an effort to make business develop a European normative framework on CSR, against a backdrop of political pressure from the EU Parliament and civil society and limited legislative powers of the EU, particularly with regard to regulating European companies' actions in third states.

The Global Compact and MSF represent new forms of developing behavioural norms constituting a cross between international law-making and private norm-setting. The initiatives share procedural features but their outputs differ. This makes for a comparison of aspects of interest to the current analysis. In terms of shared features, both are public-private schemes for regulating CSR through the development of CSR norms. Both are intergovernmental in the sense that they have been launched by bodies within an international organization. Both also contain aspects of global administrative law,[2] because the responsible bodies within both the UN and the EU are executive bodies without formal law-making powers.[3] They are transnational in the sense that they span the international and the private regulatory sphere. In terms of creating CSR norms and producing standards for corporate self-regulation, the outcomes of the Global Compact and the MSF differ considerably. Ten years after its launch, the Global Compact is a relatively successful initiative with continuously rising numbers of participants from the private and also increasingly the public sector. Participants all commit to ten principles and implementing forms of action developed in a public-private process. As an initiative launched under the otherwise state-centrist UN, the Global Compact is almost revolutionary in its approach to public-private norm-creation. The MSF was not very successful in terms of concrete agreement on norms on CSR. A relaunch in 2006 did not have a similar concrete norm-making objective. As described elsewhere,[4] the lack of success of the MSF in relation to norm-creation was likely due to power disparities, particularly power disparities between business organizations and civil society and a lack of balance of interests represented in the process.

1.2.1 The Global Compact

The Global Compact initiative was announced by then UN Secretary General Kofi Annan in January 1999 at the Davos World Economic Forum in a speech

---

[2] Kingsbury, Krisch & Steward (2005) *supra* note 2, Krisch & Kingsbury (2006) *supra* note 2.
[3] The EU Commission lacks such powers with regard to the subject matter in question. Within the EU, the powers to regulate several topics which fall under CSR, such as labour market issues, are as a general rule limited and complementary to those of Member States. For a detailed discussion of the legal basis for EC/EU CSR measures, see Oxford Pro Bono Publico (2009) *Corporate Social Responsibility Soft Law Developments in the European Union*. Oxford: University of Oxford.
[4] Buhmann, Karin (2008) Retliggørelse gennem politisering: EU-tiltag til refleksiv regulering af CSR ved international menneskeret. *Tidsskriftet Politik*, Vol. 11, No. 4: 27–37.

in which he asked companies to become allies with the UN in its efforts to deliver its aims.[5]

The initiative was not originally intended to develop into an actual instrument. However, it was soon realized by staff close to the Secretary General that there was so much interest among companies for substantive guidance on how to follow the Secretary General's appeal that a more detailed move could be made.[6]

As indicated, participants in the Global Compact commit to ten principles on human rights, labour rights, environmental protection and anti-corruption. The Compact Principles are based on instruments of international law. The two human rights principles (Principles 1–2) are based on the Universal Declaration on Human Rights. The labour standards (Principles 3–6) are based on the ILO (International Labour Organization) Declaration of Fundamental Principles and Rights at Work. Among the environmental principles (Principles 7–9), Principle 7 on the precautionary approach is based on the Rio Declaration. Principle 10, which was added in 2004, is based on the UN Convention against Corruption. According to conventional legal theory, these instruments create obligations and responsibilities for states, not for companies or other non-state actors. Nevertheless, the informing international law basis for the Compact Principles was already indicated by the Secretary General in his initial speech on the initiative.

The Compact was developed during 1999 and the first half of 2000 in a multi-stakeholder process comprising the UN Secretary General and representatives for his office, the ILO, the United Nations Environment Programme (UNEP), the Office of the High Commissioner for Human Rights (OHCHR), the International Chamber of Commerce, business organizations and company representatives. The international labour movement decided to become involved only towards the end of the process. NGOs were involved even later, a few months before the official launch in July 2000. After initial opposition by many NGOs who feared that the initiative might compromise the integrity of the UN,[7] selected NGOs were invited to

---

[5] Annan, Kofi (1999/2004) An appeal to world business. 31 January 1999. Reprinted in McIntosh, Malcolm, Sandra Waddock & Georg Kell (eds) *Learning to Talk: Corporate Citizenship and the Development of the UN Global Compact*. Sheffield: Greenleaf Publishing: 28–31.

[6] Kell, Georg (2001) *Remarks*, London School of Economics, Dilemmas in competitiveness, community and citizenship and Human Rights seminar, 22 May 2001, <http://www.unglobalcompact.org/NewsandEvents/speeches_and_statements/london_school_of_economics.html> visited 24 November 2008.

[7] For more detailed overview of the process, see e.g. Nolan, Justine (2005) The United Nation's compact with business: hindering or helping the protection of human rights? *University of Queensland Law Journal*, Vol. 24: 445–466, available at www.austlii.edu.au/au/journals/UQLR/2005/26.html accessed on 23 June 2009.

participate. The selection was based on criteria of global reach and particular competences in a Global Compact issue area.[8] The NGOs were asked, *inter alia*, to contribute to the development of the Global Compact website, which is the key instrument of information on the Compact and for facilitating the adoption, dissemination and implementation of the principles.[9] Despite lack of initial NGO support, the Global Compact did succeed in having major NGOs cooperate in setting up the website and producing comments for it, and in inducing many others to join later as stakeholders.

The Compact promotes corporate self-regulation on the ten principles through three main avenues: a learning forum and learning networks, policy dialogue, and public-private partnership projects. The UN describes the Global Compact as an instrument to promote institutional learning and implementation of best practice based on the ten principles, and the values that these reflect. Despite the explicit links between the principles and the informing instruments of international law, the Global Compact has been promoted as an initiative to realize a vision of a sustainable and inclusive global economy, rather than as an initiative to promote human rights, labour rights and/or environmental protection and anti-corruption. On its website and elsewhere, the initiative is described as a network and forum for dialogue, with an organizational structure and method of operation promoting external consultation process and internal reflection among participating businesses.

The Compact currently (April 2010) has more than 8,000 participants of which more than 5,800 are business participants. The number has been growing steadily since the initiative was launched in 2000.

1.2.2 The EU MSF

The MSF was set up in 2002 by the Commission of the European Communities with the objective of promoting innovation, transparency and convergence of CSR practices and instruments, developing problem understanding, discussing values and relevant action and making recommendations. The Commission specifically suggested that the MSF explore the

---

[8] Kell, Georg & D. Levin (2004) The Global Compact network: an historic experiment in learning and action. In M. McIntosh, S. Waddock, S. & G. Kell (eds) *Learning to Talk: Corporate Citizenship and the Development of the UN Global Compact*. Sheffield: Greenleaf Publishing: 43–65.

[9] Kell, Georg & John G. Ruggie (1999) *Global Markets and Social Legitimacy: The Case of the 'Global Compact'*. Paper presented at an international conference: governing the Public domain beyond the era of the Washington Consensus? York University, Toronto, Canada, 4–6 November 1999, <http://www.unglobalcompact.org/NewsandEvents/articles_and_papers/global_markets_social_legitimacy_york_university.html> visited 29 December 2008.

appropriateness of establishing common guiding principles for CSR practices and instruments. The Commission also suggested that the MSF consider founding such principles on internationally agreed principles, in particular the OECD (Organization for Economic Co-operation and Development) Guidelines and ILO core conventions, as well as environmental standards.[10]

The MSF comprised a range of stakeholders with an interest in CSR. It was chaired by the EU Commission. The role of the Commission was mainly to keep the initiative moving and make suggestions. The Commission does not appear to have taken an active role in the actual negotiations. These were left to the MSF members, who comprised organizations representing trade unions and workers' cooperatives, industrial and employers and commerce organizations, and NGOs engaged in human rights, consumers' interests, fair trade and sustainable development. The industry and workers' organizations that were members of the MSF also regularly participate in EU 'social dialogue' on labour market issues, in some cases with a law-making role. They are large organizations with many members although not representative of all stakeholders within their sectors. Their situation is therefore somewhat advantageous in a negotiation forum like the MSF compared to NGOs that do not participate as often in related forums and do not benefit from the experience of law-making and similar activities involving turning politics into rules.

The working method of the MSF combined plenary ('High Level') meetings and thematic round tables. The end product was a report ('Final Report').[11] Unlike the Global Compact, the MSF did not result in specific principles. The Final Report made only general reference to international human rights law as part of the normative framework for CSR in Europe. In addition, business participants passed responsibility for social or global concerns on human rights and CSR in general back to governments, telling them to act themselves if they wanted public policy goals implemented rather than asking companies to act directly.

The background for the MSF was a 1999 European Parliament Resolution calling for codes of conduct for European TNCs, a 2001 Commission Green Paper and a 2002 Commission Communication on CSR. The Commission asked the MSF to address the relationship between CSR and competitiveness, effectiveness and credibility of codes of conduct based on internationally agreed principles. It proposed that the MSF develop guidelines and criteria for measurement, reporting and verification of CSR reporting. It also suggested that such labelling and other schemes be based on ILO core

---

[10] Commission of the European Communities (2002) *Corporate Social Responsibility: A Business Contribution to Sustainable Development.* EU Doc. COM(2002)347 section 6.
[11] European Multistakeholder Forum on CSR (MSF 2004) Final Results and recommendations. 29 June 2004: 6, <http://forum.europa.eu.int/irc/empl/csr_eu_multi_stakeholder_forum/info/data/en/CSR%20Forum%20final%20report.pdf>.

conventions and the OECD Guidelines for Multinational Enterprises.¹² This indicates the significance which the Commission attached to international law instruments on human rights and other CSR-relevant issues. The Commission clearly intended these instruments to serve as normative sources for the product which the MSF was hoped to deliver.

Among a number of topics addressed by the MSF, however, two were particularly contentious: there was little agreement between business and NGOs on the possible role of international law on human and labour rights as a normative source. There was also considerable disagreement between participants on whether CSR was to be mandatory and subject to (inter-) governmental regulation or continue to be voluntary. NGOs argued in favour of making CSR mandatory and based on international law, amongst others on human rights and labour standards. Influential groups among involved business representatives argued that CSR should remain voluntary. They were hesitant towards awarding international law a normative role and preferred soft and non-specific instruments.

In the end, the MSF did not lead to a concrete framework on CSR. The first and brief part of the Final Report reaffirms international and European agreed principles, standards and conventions of relevance to CSR. As main reference for CSR the report notes the ILO Tripartite Declaration, the OECD Guidelines, and the UN Global Compact.¹³ Indeed, these deal directly with aspects of social and human rights responsibilities of business. However, all these are also non-binding and, at the most, serve as guidance for corporations. Although at least with regard to treaties, this may reflect the fact that those instruments address states, it also indicates the lack of an agreement to base an EU CSR framework on detailed human rights standards contained in those instruments. The Universal Declaration of Human Rights, the European Convention on Human Rights, the 1998 ILO Declaration on Fundamental Principles and Rights at Work which refers to ILO core labour rights and key conventions, and some other instruments are only noted in the introduction to the Final Report. This is done with the somewhat vague comment that they contain values that can inspire companies with regard to CSR.¹⁴

The bulk of the Final Report, which contains its main recommendations and suggestions for future initiatives, focuses on awareness-raising and improving knowledge of CSR, capacity building and competences to help mainstream CSR. It does not mention a common normative framework. Instead, it provides that authorities should ensure that a legal framework and appropriate economic and social conditions are in place to allow companies to benefit market-wise from CSR, both in the EU and globally. Thus, the MSF

---

¹² Commission (2002), *supra* note 11.
¹³ MSF 2004: 6, *supra* note 12.
¹⁴ *Ibid.*

Final Report presents formal law as an instrument for furthering business interests, rather than for setting out a detailed and operative framework for CSR normativity in the EU to assist corporations to self-regulate.

1.3 CSR and law: elaborating the connection

CSR is generally understood to be voluntary, that is, beyond the requirements of binding and enforceable law. Nevertheless, law is not insignificant for CSR. International law on human rights and labour rights informs six of the principles of the UN Global Compact and was suggested by the Commission for the EU MSF as a normative source for EU CSR. International customary and treaty law on human rights also forms a recognized source for several CSR standards drafted outside governmental or intergovernmental auspices, such as the ISO 26000 standards under preparation at the time of writing.

The CSR phenomenon and CSR discourse are not easily accommodated in conventional legal theory (see also the introductory chapter in this book). The claim propounded by the EU Commission[15] and many others that CSR is voluntary action (as opposed to mandatory action required by law that applies directly to the entity in question),[16] CSR's foundation in corporate and therefore private self-regulation and its transnational character all challenge conventional legal theory. That is because this theory is structured on demarcated and defined legal systems which essentially form 'subsystems' of the legal system: lawyers talk about and are familiar with public law and private law as distinct entities, and with national law, supranational law and

---

[15] Commission of the European Communities (2001) 'Promoting a European Framework for Corporate Social Responsibility'. EU Doc. COM(2001)366; Commission (2002) *supra*, Commission of the European Communities (2006) *Implementing the Partnership for Growth and Jobs: Making Europe a Pole of Excellence on Corporate Social Responsibility*. EU Doc. COM(2006)136.final.

[16] The claim that CSR is only voluntary action is problematic in many respects to the extent that it appears to exclude compliance with law. Compliance with law is assumed to be a part of CSR according to the definition of CSR that Archie Carroll presented in his seminal article presenting a three-dimensional conceptual model of corporate performance Carroll, Archie B. (1979) A three-dimensional conceptual model of corporate performance, *The Academy of Management Review*, Vol. 4, No. 4: 497–505, compare Carroll, Archie B. (1991) The pyramid of corporate social responsibility: toward the moral management of organisational stakeholder. *Business Horizons*, July/August: 39–48 and Schwartz, Mark S. & Archie B. Carroll (2003) Corporate social responsibility: a three-domain approach. *Business Ethics Quarterly*, Vol. 13, No. 4: 503–530. Space constraints and the different line of focus of the present article do not allow for more in-depth discussion of the issue. For a more detailed analysis, see Zerk, Jennifer A. (2006) *Multinationals and Corporate Social Responsibility: Limitations and Opportunities in International Law*. Cambridge: Cambridge University Press; McBarnet (2007), *supra* note 2, and Buhmann, Karin (2007) Corporate social responsibility and human rights responsibilities of business. *Nordic Journal on Human Rights*, Vol. 25, No. 4: 331–352.

international law (which is also divided into public and private!) as distinct if somewhat connected systems.

Thus, as an academic field and practice CSR abounds with challenges to law. In particular, the increased public-private character of regulating a phenomenon that claims to be voluntary, and the question of how to handle it in the world of legal notions, established concepts of duty holders, and forms of regulation do not fit neatly into the system created by traditional legal method, theory and concepts. This underscores the need for conceptualizing and theorizing CSR and contested features related to CSR, such as creation of CSR norms and the outputs of public-private CSR norm-creating processes.

As indicated, this chapter takes as its basic premise that although CSR does not easily fit into any of these systemic categories, the CSR phenomenon gains by being addressed from the perspective of law as well as other social science angles. Arguably, law has much to contribute to CSR: CSR is fundamentally about norms of behaviour. Law is basically concerned with normativity and institutionalization of behavioural norms. Law may offer much for ongoing development and implementation of CSR in practice and theory. Better integration and application of law's insight into normativity and regulation, that is, institutionalization of norms, may lead to more legitimate processes of creating CSR norms. This may result in better acceptance among business and other societal actors and better integration in corporate practice.

The development in CSR norm-creation, particularly its increasing transnational and public-private character, parallels that which in recent years has led a range of legal scholars and legal theory-oriented social scientists to seek to conceptualize an adjustment or even a reconstitution of the state-centrist system of international law to allow for the increasing role of non-state actors on the global stage.[17] Some of these developments also lead to a blurring of distinctions between normative forms, with a shift from formal law to quasi-legal or soft law[18] and self-regulation based on morals or societal expectations. As indicated by the SRSG,[19] societal expectations are also a main source of emerging normativity on CSR and BRHR.

---

[17] Ruggie, John G. (2004) Reconstituting the global public domain – issues, actors and practices. *European Journal of International Relations*, Vol. 10, No. 4: 499–531; Teubner, Gunther (2004) Global private regimes: neo-spontaneous law and dual constitution of autonomous sectors in world society? In Ladeur, Karl-Heinz (ed.) *Globalisation and Public Governance*. Ashgate: Aldershot: 71–87; and references above footnote 2.
[18] Picciotto (2008): 328, *supra* note 2.
[19] SRSG (2008) *Protect, Respect and Remedy: A Framework for Business and Human Rights*. Report of the Special Representative of the Secretary-General on the issue of human rights and transnational corporations and other business enterprises, John Ruggie. UN Doc. A/HRC/8/5 (2008).

Partly as a result of globalization and the growth of the private sector, recent decades have witnessed an increased interplay between international, supranational and national public law, between public and private law, and with particular relevance to CSR between state and non-state actors in the creation and implementation of norms. The notion of law increasingly includes norms that cannot be enforced but nevertheless have strong influence on behavioural expectations of societal actors. Like the public-private CSR law-making of the Global Compact, much of this 'new law' is developing from traditional positive top-down enforceable norms made by public bodies with a formal legislative mandate or by private actors through contracts, into a range of new forms, including varieties of non-enforceable or 'soft' norms that nevertheless carry a strong normative weight. Organizations without formal or primarily legislative or adjudicative powers assume or are allowed functions to set and apply rules. Whereas the 'old' law was made by specific actors and applied to specific entities (or in legal language, subjects), many of the new norms and regulatory forms govern networks and are produced by networks, with network actors striving to influence processes and outputs, often without specific democratic mandates to do so.

Some have called for more extensive and formal integration of NGOs in law-making processes of intergovernmental systems like the UN and the EU.[20] Others argue a general need to recognize new forms of law and 'new governance' in order to deal with the democracy deficits which are increasingly apparent with globalization and the growth of the political economy.[21] Still others argue that the creation of new forms of norm-making structures at global level, which include non-state actors in active roles, may provide for a more inclusive and legitimate norm-creating sphere to allow a broad range of stakeholders influence on resulting norms.[22] Such claims hit part of the problem on the head: due to the structure of intergovernmental norm-creating processes, which still builds on the conventional state-centrist international legal order and its law-making system, many of the formal law-making processes taking place at international level exclude a number of actors who may be as close and sometimes even closer to representing relevant concerns of individuals and particular interest groups as are members of parliament or governments.

Later years' growth of public-private schemes for creation of CSR norms underscores the need to understand more about CSR from the legal perspective and to work across disciplines to analyse, discuss, critique and strengthen CSR. Given the past decades' and continuing mushrooming of

---

[20] Decaux, Emmanuelle (1999) Human Rights and civil society. In Alston, Philip (ed.) *The EU and Human Rights*. New York: Oxford University Press.
[21] Lobel (2005), *supra* note 2.
[22] Ruggie (2004), *supra* note 18.

trans-systemic or global regulatory forums, the identification of processes which enjoy procedural and normative legitimacy in terms of representing interests in a balanced way becomes more urgent. The highly consultative process of the SRSG on human rights and business during his first and second mandates indicates that the concern has been taken seriously by the SRSG. The result of the first term of SRSG mandate led to the UN Human Rights Council's unanimously 'welcoming' the *Protect, Respect, Remedy* framework presented in the SRSG's 2008 report to the Council, and support from actors in the business community who had vehemently opposed the draft 'UN Norms' on Human Rights and Business.[23] The consultative process and its results are indicative of the significance of involving actors not normally consulted in international law-making. To appreciate the significance of involving private and non-governmental non-state actors in these processes, this chapter next takes a closer look at public-private CSR norm-creation and the difficulties which conventional international law-making encounters with regard to inclusion of non-state actors.

2 Public-private multi-stakeholder regulation of CSR at intergovernmental level: background and emergence

Conventional international law-making is a well-established way for states to create norms pertaining to themselves and to a limited degree for individuals. It enjoys a high degree of legitimacy to represent and balance interests in that sense. The purpose of this section is to present and discuss some aspects of conventional law-making actors and procedure in order to provide a partial explanation for the emergence of new public-private forms of norm-creation on CSR. This will frame the subsequent discussion of representation of non-state interests in public-private forums.

2.1 Challenges facing conventional international law-making in an increasingly pluralist global society

Under the system of public international law that has developed over centuries, international law is made by states. States are the original and primary subjects in public international law. Conventional international law relates to obligations (or corresponding rights) that states would agree to vis-à-vis each other through bilateral, plurilateral or multilateral agreements or which

---

[23] United Nations Sub-Commission on the Promotion and Protection of Human Rights. *Norms on the Responsibilities of Transnational Corporations and Other Business Enterprises with regard to Human Rights 2003* (UN doc. E/CN.4/Sub.2/2003/12/Rev.2). The document was considered by the Human Rights Commission to contain "useful elements and ideas" but was not accepted as a document with legal standing.

would develop as customary international law over time. Traditionally, obligations under international law would relate to rights for institutions related to other states. Only relatively recently has international law come to regulate states' obligations vis-à-vis individuals within their own territories, and to create rights for these. As indicated by Chris Sidoti in this book, international humanitarian law paved the way, and the development of the international human rights regime since 1945 has led to a comprehensive body of international law that creates obligations for states to respect rights of individuals. Still, as obligations of international law, these obligations are held towards other states, even when they also mean a duty to protect against horizontal human rights violations between individuals (the duty to protect an individual against a violation by a third party, such as a company). Even when individuals are granted the rights to petition against a state under regional human rights systems such as the European Convention (and Court) of Human Rights, the right to petition is based on commitments that states parties to the relevant convention have entered into with each other.

The role of states in international law-making is a logical reflection of the fact that under international law, states not only obtain rights vis-à-vis each other, but also undertake obligations. The law-making process in relation to treaty law and the gradual development of international customary law possessed a measure of democratic legitimacy because those who were subjected to obligations also had a say in devising them.

The situation is more complicated in relation to regulating business responsibilities for human rights. This is a major reason for innovative approaches to development of CSR norms through public-private schemes. Corporations are non-state actors. As legal persons, they may be considered individuals. Certain non-state actors (such as international organizations) are recognized to possess limited international legal personality and therefore enjoy some rights and privileges. The debate on international legal personality has, however, particularly centred on individuals. The traditional view held that individuals do not have an independent position in the international legal system. Under modern international law, this has changed somewhat. Especially with the development of international human rights law, individuals as victims have been granted legal rights at the international level.[24] Corporations, too, have been acknowledged to be holders of human rights and to constitute victims of human rights violations.[25] Obligations have been imposed on individuals under customary international law

---

[24] See also the chapter by Chris Sidoti in this book.
[25] Emberland, Marius (2006) *The Human Rights of Companies: Exploring the Structure of ECHR Protection*. Oxford: Oxford University Press; Addo, M.K. (1999) The corporation as a victim of human rights violations. In Addo, M.K. (ed.) *Human Rights Standards and the Responsibility of Transnational Corporations*. The Hague: Kluwer Law International: 187–196.

(in relation to armed conflict, crimes against humanity, genocide, aggression, terrorism and torture). More recently obligations of individuals have been established through treaties, the establishment of international war tribunals and the International Criminal Court (ICC). The ICC statute, however, did not take the decisive steps to include legal persons (such as corporations) under the ICC jurisdiction.

Technically nothing prevents the creation of obligations under international law for non-state actors, such as corporations. As indicated by Jennifer Zerk, amongst others, obligations for legal persons have been created through treaty law in relation to environmental protection of the sea as well as in some other situations.[26] Wider corporate obligations under international law appear to be held back by a combination of traditional thinking among international lawyers and strong corporate lobbying.[27] The history of the draft UN Norms indicates that the state-centrist system of international law-making is not ready to regulate social or human rights obligations for businesses. The history of the Norms, however, also suggests that part of the failure was due precisely to limited business participation in the process, or at least a perception among parts of the business community and their organizations that they had not been consulted. Whereas international organizations, states and NGOs had been consulted relatively extensively during the drafting process, businesses and their organizations were only consulted late and not to a very considerable extent.[28] The limited degree of consultation seems to have been a significant factor behind the relatively widespread opposition which the business sector held against the Norms and which fed into State reactions to the Norms when they were debated at the UN Commission on Human Rights in 2004.[29]

Although they do not have formal access to the law-making process at the international stage, corporations nevertheless have such political

---

[26] Zerk (2006), *supra* note 17, at 284–295.

[27] Alston, P. (2005) The 'Not-a-Cat' syndrome. In Alston, P. (ed.) *Non-State Actors and Human Rights*. New York: Oxford University Press: 3–36, at 21.

[28] *Report of the Sessional Working Group on the Working Methods and Activities of Transnational Corporations*, 1st session, UN Doc. E/CN.4/Sub.2/1999/9; 2nd session, UN Doc. E/CN.4/Sub.2/2000/12; 3rd session, UN Doc. E/CN.4/Sub.2/2001/9; 4th session, UN Doc. E/CN.4/Sub.2/2002/13; Weissbrodt, David & Muria Kruger (2003) Norms on the responsibilities of transnational corporations and other business enterprises with regard to human rights. *American Journal of International Law*, Vol. 97, No. 4: 901–922; Hearne, Bernadette (2004) Proposed UN norms on human rights: is business opposition justified? *Ethical Corporation*, 22 March 2004; compare Kinley, David, Justine Nolan & Natalie Zerial (2007) The politics of corporate social responsibility: reflections on the United Nations human rights norms for corporations. *Company and Securities Law Journal*, Vol. 25, No. 1: 30–42.

[29] Hearne (2004), *supra* note 29; compare Kinley, Nolan & Zerial (2007), *supra* note 29, at 35–42.

and economic power that they are able to assert considerable influence on decisions of States in relation to CSR topics. Such strong non-state actor lobbying influence was seen inter alia with the UN effort to define Norms for transnational corporations and other business enterprises.[30] The resulting decisions may appear as state decisions but in effect may be heavily imprinted by one particular type of non-state actors through a non-democratic process of access to the informal decision-making process.

Some scholars of international law have argued in favour of allowing non-state actors – both corporations and civil society – a greater role in international law-making to strengthen its legitimacy and provide for more effective regulation of international business and sustainable global development.[31] Such views suggest a growing awareness among certain parts of the community of legal scholars that participation is significant as a condition for effective subjection to the norms, and that the current system is not geared to providing this.

Regardless of the reasons for allowing non-state actors more direct participation in international law-making, there is also reason to be diligent. States' roles as participants in international law-making need not mean a similar role for non-state actors, such as businesses, even if they are the ones subject to regulation. As business opposition to the draft UN Norms suggests, direct participation by businesses in defining duties for businesses with regard to human rights or other social concerns might simply have the effect of obstructing the process. The lesson of the Norms process therefore also demonstrates a need for new forms of norm-creation that are effective in terms of resulting in norms that businesses will adhere to. The history of the Norms suggests that this requires that both business and other parts of society find the process to allow representation of relevant interests in a balanced way.

In sum, the conventional system of international law-making suffers from a two-pronged problem when it comes to the need to regulate social

---

[30] See *inter alia* Kinley, David & Justine Nolan (2008) Trading and aiding human rights in the global economy. *Nordic Journal of Human Rights*, Vol. 7, No. 4: 353–377.
[31] Friedmann, Wolfgang (1964) *The Changing Structure of International Law*. London: Stevens & Sons; Charney, J. (1983) Transnational corporations and developing public international law. *Duke Law Journal*, Volume 1983, 748–788; Muchlinski, Peter (1997) 'Global Bukowina' examined: viewing the multinational enterprise as a transnational law-making community. In Teubner, Gunther (ed.) *Global Law Without a State*. Aldershot: Dartmouth: 79–108; Picciotto, Sol (2003) Rights, responsibilities and regulation of international business. *Columbia Journal of Transnational Law*, Vol. 42, No. 1: 131–152; Hobe, Stephan (2002) Globalisation: a challenge to the nation state and to international law. In Likosky, Michael (ed.) *Transnational Legal Processes: Globalisation and Power Disparities*. Colchester: Butterworths: 378–391; Bianchi, Andrea (1997) Globalisation of human rights: the role of non-state actors. In Teubner, Gunther (ed.) *Global Law Without a State*. Aldershot: Dartmouth: 179–212.

responsibilities or other actions of non-state actors related to CSR: On the one hand, the current system allows for the formal participation of neither those to be subjected to new normative requirements (*in casu*, businesses) nor for representation of the interests of actual or potential victims of business' negative impact on society except for the limited access to influence given to NGOs with observer status. On the other hand, allowing non-state actors more direct access to the process could give some of them disproportionate influence that the current system does not appear to be geared to deal with. When non-state actors are made part of the process, careful thought must be given to the form, role, degree of representativeness and other related issues.

The challenges and dilemmas of the participation of non-state actors in international law-making in conventional international law cannot be directly transposed to the level of European law-making. The legal order of the EU is of a unique type which recognizes the power of the EU institutions to make law that pertains directly to companies. As noted above, in the field of EU law-making on labour law, labour market organizations are included. This allows them to voice concerns and interests of business and workers. However, civil society organizations other than industrial and workers' organizations do not have similar access to participation in law-making.

2.2 The emergence of novel forms of law-making

Against the backdrop of the persisting state-centrist character of international law-making and its corollary, the limited access of non-state actors to the process, non-state actors have invented and engaged in alternative ways of norm-creation. Some of those completely skirt traditional law-making institutions or other state institutions[32] whereas others engage public institutions at national or international level. There is a growing recognition that CSR norms and related norms have legal relevance and may function as soft law.[33]

As indicated, a number of the norm-creating schemes which have appeared at transnational and other levels over the past decade or so comprise mixed groups of government and non-state actors. They often include members of executives at lower levels of the national or intergovernmental organizational levels, representing specialized knowledge of the field in

---

[32] Teubner (1997), *supra* note 32.
[33] Meidinger, Errol (2008) Multi-interest self-governance through global product certification programmes. In Dilling, Olaf, Martin Herberg & Gerd Winter (eds) *Responsible Business: Self-Governance and Law in Transnational Economic Transactions*. Oxford and Portland OR: Hart 259–291; Kingsbury, Krisch & Steward (2005), *supra* note 2; Krisch & Kingsbury (2006), *supra* note 2; Sand (2005), *supra* note 2, Lobel (2005), *supra* note 2; Teubner (2004), *supra* note 18; Trubek & Trubek (2006), *supra* note 2.

question but without formal law-making powers. In addition, they often include non-state actors and give voice to NGOs and other civil society groups who are generally excluded from playing a similar direct role in formal law-making processes.

As described in the introductory chapter of this book, reflexive law is a regulatory theory that counts on procedural forums instituted by authorities, allowing social actors to exchange and learn about social expectations and demands, with a view to (business) internationalization of such expectations through self-regulation. The theory of reflexive law is mainly procedural. It also has a significant but somewhat overlooked normative aspect in that it requires power disparities between participants in reflexive regulatory forums to be balanced. The theory, however, does not describe how such balancing should be achieved. Power asymmetries between various actors – state actors as well as non-state actors, such as business organizations, civil society organizations or the individual NGO, interest group or company – may distort the legitimacy of process and output of transnational norm-creating processes involving actors with diverse interests and varying degrees of economic, political and other forms of power.[34]

What emerges is that processes and outcomes of the type of public-private multi-stakeholder forums which are employed for production of CSR norm-making may be lacking in terms of insight or methods necessary to procedurally provide for balanced and general representation of interests of the actors in these processes, as well as of stakeholders not directly included.

At the same time, however, the new forms of norm-creation in principle enable the participation of actors that have no formal place or direct claim to influence in the formal law-making structures at the international level. As indicated by Picciotto,[35] to properly integrate the public interest and provide for mutual trust there is a need for new approaches to articulate normative interactions that are more conducive to democratic deliberation for such new forms of norm-creation to be legitimate. As elaborated below, providing for deliberation may be the key to dealing with – at least some of – the challenges facing new forms of global norm-creation, including on CSR. First, we will consider the Global Compact and the EU MSF in the light of the way they worked as novel institutional forms of law-making.

2.3 The Global Compact and MSF as reflexive law forums for regulation of CSR

The Global Compact and the MSF both contain features that suggest a reflexive law approach to creation of CSR norms, although not necessarily a 'pure' approach. Both aim at corporate self-regulation but also have co-regulatory

---

[34] See also Ruggie (2004): 522 *supra* note 18.
[35] Picciotto (2008), *supra* note 2; Picciotto (2003), *supra* note 32.

features. As indicated elsewhere, in both cases, the reflexive law character appears to be incidental rather than intended.[36]

The Compact is not a legal instrument in the ordinary sense. However, it is a regulatory instrument drawing heavily on instruments of international (mainly soft) law as sources of normative substance, and on the method of reflexive law to make companies internalize this normative substance through self-regulation. With its principles based on international law, close to 6,000 business participants from around the globe and significant NGO backing 10 years after launch, the Global Compact norms (the now ten principles) and the process of establishing them arguably enjoy a relatively high degree of acceptance in the eyes of stakeholders despite the fact that the principles were developed with business as the main non-state actor together with the UN Secretariat.

The EU Commission's approach to establishing CSR norms for European companies involved a larger range of affected societal actors from the outset than did the Global Compact. The Commission has consistently suggested that corporate CSR self-regulation take certain substantive issues and normative sources into account, especially on human and labour rights, but has also indicated that CSR was not to be expressed as mandatory requirements. Through the MSF the Commission established a reflexive law type procedural modality for stakeholders to meet and learn about concerns of other societal actors and to take part in a shared regulatory process. Non-state actors were given the main stake in defining the substantive output. Commission documents indicate that the process was based on the recognition that public and wider societal interests and expectations require companies to take responsibility for their actions in society and for promoting welfare policy objectives. However, the outcome (Final Report) of the MSF seemed to neither meet the Commission's objective that the MSF would establish a framework for CSR nor, particularly, to meet its objectives with regard to the envisaged role that international law, particularly on human rights, was to play for such a framework.

The differing results of the Global Compact and EU MSF as processes of creating norms suggest a crucial difference in the procedural approach. There are indications that the failure of the EU MSF to create a normative framework and to reference international law widely as sources of CSR norms may be due to power disparities within the MSF, with business having much greater political as well as discursive power than NGOs.[37] Internal power

---

[36] See further Buhmann (2008), *supra* note 5, Buhmann, Karin (2009) Regulating corporate social and human rights responsibilities at the UN plane: institutionalising new forms of law and law-making approaches? *Nordic Journal of International Law*, Vol. 78, No. 1, 2009: 1–52.

[37] Buhmann (2008), *supra* note 5.

struggles in the Commission among proponents of business interests and social affairs may have added to the end result. NGOs were not happy with the general result or with a 2006 decision of the Commission to establish, as a new initiative and in response to the MSF Final Report, a 'CSR Alliance' without NGO representatives. Nor did NGOs support the decision to reconvene the MSF in 2006 as a way of making up for lack of NGO participation in the CSR Alliance.

After these observations we turn to the deliberative approach which assumes that the legitimacy of public-private creation of CSR norms rests on the discursive quality of the process.

3 The added-value of Habermasian deliberative discourse

3.1 Objective

As noted, one of the recognized weaknesses of reflexive law theory is that it assumes that power disparities between actors should be balanced but does not provide directions for how to do so. Scholars who have otherwise welcomed the contribution of the theory have emphasized its lack of specificity in explaining how external concerns are to be integrated in internal processes, how to balance them against internal concerns, and how to handle power disparities in general, as significant weaknesses.[38]

The remainder of this chapter argues that although it does not deliver a blue-print, this aspect of Habermasian theory has the capacity of complementing reflexive law theory with regard to the issue of balancing power through design and management of reflexive regulatory forums.

Teubner's theory on reflexive law predates Habermasian theory on deliberative discourse as a modality for creating legitimate norms. Habermas developed that theory in the seminal work *Between Facts and Norms*,[39] on which the discussion below is based. Teubner therefore did not have the opportunity to consider this part of Habermas' work, while Habermas on the other hand had the benefit of almost 10 years' additional debate on democratic law-making, including the focus on citizens' democratic and human

---

[38] Sand, Inger-Johanne (1996) *Styring av kompleksitet: Rettslige former for statlig rammestyring og desentralisert statsforvaltniing.* Bergen: Fagbokforlaget Vigmostad & Bjørke: 86–94, esp. 94; Scheuerman, W.E. (2001) Reflexive law and the challenges of globalisation. *The Journal of Political Philosophy*, Vol. 9, No. 1: 81–102, at 86; Neves, M. (2001) From the autopoiesis to the allopoiesis of law. *Journal of Law and Society*, Vol. 28, No. 2: 242–264, at 253–254; compare also Dalberg-Larsen, Jørgen (1991) *Ret, styring og selvforvaltning.* Aarhus: Juridisk Bogformidling: 15–16, 136.

[39] Published in German in 1992 as *Faktizität und Geltung*, published in 1996 in English as Habermas, Jürgen (1996) *Between Facts and Norms: Contributions to a Discourse Theory of Law and Democracy.* Translated by William Rehg, Cambridge: Polity Press/Blackwell. References in here are to the English version (Habermas 1996).

rights in public processes of norm-creation which was prevalent in Europe in the late 1980s and early 1990s.

This deliberative democracy theory which Habermas formulated in the 1990s builds on and further develops his previous theory on discourse ethics. Earlier Habermasian discourse theory had focused on the conditions for ideal discourse and on ideal discourse as an avenue for the justification and reasonableness of social claims. With a somewhat different approach, the theory on deliberative democracy formulated in *Between Facts and Norms* is directed at the conditions for production of law as valid norms subject to administration and enforcement in a constitutional-democratic legal order. Such a legal order typically refers to a nation state with its constitutional structure and actors comprising a democratically elected legislature (Parliament, sometimes complemented with government) and a citizenry who, as voters, constitute the democratic basis for the legislative structure. This corresponds neither to the current conditions for production of international law described above, nor to the norm-creation processes that take place within public-private schemes at intergovernmental or transnational level. Habermas' understanding of law mainly relates to binding, enforceable norms. CSR normativity is of a softer kind and being 'voluntary' generally neither legally binding, nor enforceable. Despite these differences between the immediate subject matter of Habermasian deliberative democratic norm-creation and CSR normativity, Habermasian ideas on conditions for the creation of legitimate norms do contain points that may lend inspiration also in the context of creating CSR norms.

Bringing Habermasian theory on deliberative law-making into the context of public-private CSR norm-making at intergovernmental level adds a deeper perspective on requirements of reflexive law procedure to deliver the normative objective of balancing interests. It adds a legitimacy aspect to public-private norm-creation at the intergovernmental level as a new form of international law-making that attempts to incorporate non-state actors into the process. This calls for reflexive or other public-private regulatory forums to consider that the establishment of a procedural forum is not by itself sufficient to ensure legitimate law-making with representation of non-state actors. The procedural forum needs to be complemented by procedural rules or management of power disparities of actors in order for interests to be represented in a balanced way. This not only has the potential to provide for increased legitimacy of CSR-norms through public-private cooperation at intergovernmental level. It may also provide international law-making with guidance and experience on how to adapt to societal conditions at a time when non-state actors make claims to participation in law-making processes at above-state level. Its focus on discourse as a form of communication to provide norms with legitimacy and on procedural conditions for establishing equal opportunities for public participation in law-making makes Habermas' theory relevant in the context of providing participatory input to a process of producing behavioural norms, such as CSR norms. Habermas' theory assumes a qualitative participation, or at least procedural conditions in place for such participation by all actors in the process. This requirement is not similarly developed in reflexive law. We shall now turn to the details of Habermasian theory, looking first at the theory of deliberative law-making as it was developed for national level law-making and next at some related aspects at the international level.

3.2 Habermasian deliberative law-making: the national level

Habermas is one among a number of social science scholars who have contributed to deliberative democracy theory. Also sometimes referred to as discursive democracy, deliberative democracy is political decision-making that relies on popular consultation to make policy. With *Between Facts and Norms*, Habermas seeks to formulate a discourse theory on law and the rule of law (*Rechtsstaat*) and the democratic process. Seeking to integrate legal and political science theory, his discussion considers law based on its normative substance, and in the context of the procedural political reality of society.

In *Between Facts and Norms*, Habermas argues that norms gain validity from the approval of those potentially affected. Approval builds on participation in rational discourses to formulate the substance of norms. The qualitative requirements of the discourse are also normative: It should allow participants to reach a common will by each attempting to convince other participants through arguments. This normative quality of the discourse itself may be ensured through institutionalized procedures and communicative processes which reflect in the legitimacy of resulting norms. Positive law administered or enforced by the state derives its legitimacy through a broad discourse of citizens and their representatives, including the civil society. In deliberative democratic society, public opinions feed into the legislature and regulatory agencies through public participation (for example, consultations and hearings) as well as general elections. Deliberative discourse allows those subjected to legal norms to agree on normative positions for common coexistence and influence the substance of norms during the process of their production. For law-making to be legitimate, participants should have equal rights not just in formal but in actual terms. Balanced discourse is both a condition for legitimate production of law and itself contingent on law, understood as rights which guarantee the procedural equality of participants in the process of producing norms. In this sense, Habermas goes further than Teubner: Teubner's reflexive law is a procedural framework for participation but only assumes balancing of power as a normative principle without specifying how to implement it. Habermas posits that participation must be equal and requires specific procedural steps. In other words, reflexive law simply assumes participation of stakeholders. Habermasian theory on legitimate law-making assumes procedural rights of participation to ensure equal or at least proportional access to shape the normative outcome of the law-making process.

To Habermas, bargaining is an alternative when discourse does not lead to common will. Bargaining aims at identifying compromises. This too is relevant in a context like the EU MSF, when diverging interests such as those held by business need to meet those represented by civil society and those of (inter)governmental organizations. To Habermas, results that are legitimate require bargaining based on procedure to balance conflicting interests. Also relevant in a CSR context, Habermas recognizes that the deliberative will-formation which leads to agreement on norms for collective co-existence may be set off by various factors, including moral or ethical reasons. These relate to interests of our common life, such as protection of the environment, social policies and the distribution of social wealth and resources.

3.3 Deliberative law-making: the international level

In recent work Habermas addresses legitimacy and processes of norm-creation in the context of global governance. Due to basic structural differences between nation-states and the international system in terms of institutional composition and roles of actors, deliberative discourse-based democracy as a foundation for the legitimacy of procedurally created norms cannot be transplanted directly to the international level.[40] However, there is clearly a need for more legitimate procedures at international level, and the basic ideas may be transferred with adaptations to take account of the institutional structure, in particular its state-centrist basis and lack of effective enforcement machinery.[41]

Of relevance for considering aspects related to creation of CSR norms at the international or transnational level, Habermas finds that the current absence of a political system of coordination at transnational market level is a key problem for global will-formation. The practical significance is underscored by the lack of effective powers of the UN to enforce human rights or ensure environmental and social sustainability. There is a need for a common practice for formation of opinions and will at global, international, supranational or transnational level to deal with concerns and needs that

---

[40] Habermas, Jürgen (2004) Folkeretten i overgangen til den postnationale konstellation. *Distinktion*, No. 8: 9–17.
[41] Habermas, Jürgen (2008) The constitutionalization of international law and the legitimation process of a constitution for world society. *Constellations*, Vol. 15, No. 4: 444–455; Habermas, Jürgen (1998) Zur Legitimation durch Menschenrechte, in *Die postnationale Konstellation. Politische Essays*. Frankfurt am Main: 170–194; compare also Willke, Helmut & Gerhard Willke (2007) Corporate moral legitimacy and the legitimacy of morals: a critique of Palazzo/Scherer's communicative framework. *Journal of Business Ethics*, doi:10.1007/s10551-007-9478-1 (no page numbers).

arise as results of globalization and of the deficiencies of current governance systems. Deliberative discursive procedures may provide for legitimacy at these levels too. To provide for wider representation of views of individuals, NGOs and other interest organizations may serve to establish links to deliberative processes at lower levels of decision-making. Indeed, as noted above, a number of NGOs including international business organizations like the International Chamber of Commerce already have consultative status with the UN and therefore have a possibility, if a limited one, to argue the interests that they represent. The formal (state-centrist) organization or procedures of the UN do not provide for adequate procedural structures for deliberative discourse for norm-creation to reflect agreement not just between states but also among other societal actors (such as multinational enterprises) whose interests are not necessarily sufficiently represented by states.

Habermas' ideas suggest that norm-creation at international level may be better able to represent the concerns, will and opinion of the global public if a higher degree of deliberative discourse is established. That means allowing not only states but also other representative entities to take part in a process of collective will-formation leading to the common agreement on norms for co-existence. This may be achieved by involving NGOs and other civil society actors in international negotiations, and through other arrangements and procedures which promote compromises and negotiated results through processes that engages not only states but also non-state actors. Again, this differs from reflexive law theory by stressing the procedural significance for legitimacy of involving non-state actors.

In sum, in a context of transnational or international law making through multi-stakeholder based approaches, reflexive law and deliberative democracy arguably have much in common: Habermasian deliberative law-making theory provides important guidance for legitimacy of the deliberative character of the reflexive regulatory process and its outcome, while the reflexive law paradigm provides the outer procedure to frame the deliberative process. Both Habermas' and Teubner's theories are formulated at a high level of abstraction. Multi-stakeholder public-private schemes on CSR may provide cases to test applicability in practice, assess weaknesses and strengths of the approaches, and operationalize how they may complement each other. With this in mind, we will return to the Global Compact and the MSF.

3.4 Applying Habermasian deliberative law-making theory to reflexive regulation of CSR

The experience of the MSF does indeed indicate that if the procedural design for a reflexive regulatory process does not handle power disparities, such imbalance is likely to affect the process as well as the normative output. The Global Compact, on the other hand, suggests that power disparities can be managed by authorities, even if this means that participation is based on a selection by the authorities. The global adherence to the Global Compact also suggests that such processes may lead to normative results perceived as legitimate in the sense of representing interests in a balanced way. This section aims at discussing whether Habermasian discursive law-making may complement reflexive law by filling out some of the void on how to deal with power disparities between participants.

A distinction must be made between discursive power in terms of cleverly arguing a case, and what we may refer to as politically based power, based on alliances, experience with the politics and negotiation patterns of a particular organization or institutional setting, and sometimes disproportional favourable representation. It is the latter form that is the issue here. Recall in particular that industry and workers' organization in the MSF had experience with EU law-making. Asymmetrical power may result in negotiation outputs that are also disproportionate to the interests sought to be represented. The difference is between the quality of management of the reflexive forum that allows for discursive negotiation, and the discursive quality of the negotiation itself. The former may be addressed through design of the reflexive procedure, criteria for inclusion of actors, and authorities' role in directing the process of negotiation. The latter is basically up to actors themselves, but may also be affected by the composition of the discursive forum. The quality of discourse may be affected by actors' experience with the type of discursive forum or negotiation with similar types of political actors. For this reason too, design and management of discursive reflexive regulatory forums matter. Habermasian theory on deliberative discourse embodies a set of procedural guarantees to ensure public participation in law-making through common will and opinion formation.

As indicated by Scherer and Palazzo,[42] when the CSR debate gets oversimplified, it sometimes neglects to recognize that discourse quality derives from arguments, not from actors *per se*. Transplanted to our purposes, the procedural aspect of discourse for production of norms through reflexive regulatory processes should not only be procedurally structured so as to even out formal or easily observable power disparities and to learn about social expectations. It should also provide for actual participation in a balanced way. Procedural deliberation contains a normative element related to the quality of conditions for an exchange of arguments and a quality of discourse conducive to consensus or at least bargaining, leading to common acceptance of resulting norms. Applying these observations to the EU MSF, analysis suggests that the MSF provided the formal institutional framework for social actors to meet, make speeches, exchange reports and so on. The framework and discussion were soon politicized into non-state participants

---

[42] Scherer, Andreas Georg & Guido Palazzo (2007) Toward a political conception of corporate responsibility: business and society seen from a Habermasian perspective. *Academy of Management Review*, Vol. 32, No 4: 1096–1120 at 1109.

guarding already established positions and the Commission trying to engage business in implementing new political objectives. The procedural framework did not seem appropriate for exchange of arguments at a deeper level to provide for consensus.

The UN Global Compact, on the other hand, appears to have set conditions for an exchange of arguments between individuals from within the UN Secretariat (and now Global Compact Office) and business to engage in a seemingly more successful way of reaching consensus on nine (now ten) principles.

As noted, NGOs only became involved in the Global Compact a few months prior to the official launch, the range of NGOs was initially quite limited, and several NGOs were initially very critical of the Compact. This criticism has been somewhat met by the institution of integrity measures including Communication-on-Progress reporting and de-listing of non-reporting companies. NGOs reacted in a somewhat similar antagonistic fashion to the EU Commission's follow-up to the MSF, 'the CSR Alliance' which comprised business and the Commission and the subsequent re-launch of the MSF. Civil society's reactions to the CSR Alliance confirm the observations above that unless all relevant stakeholders are involved in the process with a qualitative equality of discursive participation, the result will not be perceived as legitimate in the sense of representing interests in a balanced way. This is hardly surprising but worth noting in the context. NGOs had been involved in the MSF from the outset but as described above, business interests prevailed in the outcome.

Reactions by NGOs both to the Global Compact initially and to the EU Commission's follow-up to the MSF underscore an assumption that for the development of CSR norms to be legitimate, procedures should remain open for dissent and promote the expression of marginalized interests and values.[43] This corresponds to Teubner's argument that reflexive regulatory processes should handle power disparities. The Habermasian perspective adds a qualitative aspect, allowing weaker groups real participation, not just formal presence. NGO opposition to the EU MSF outcome and to the Global Compact for lack of accountability underscores this point of the significance of the deliberative approach.

From this perspective it is perhaps surprising that the Global Compact has been relatively more successful than the EU MSF in establishing norms on CSR. This is so even when one allows for the Global Compact being 'global' and the MSF 'only' European. Recall that the Global Compact preparatory process led to agreement on nine and later ten specific principles, all based in international law. The MSF led to a much weaker result in terms of specific normativity on CSR, let alone a normatively principled foundation in

---

[43] *Ibid.* at 1114.

international law. However, several possible reasons related to procedure as well as legitimacy explain the difference despite the fact that NGOs were involved earlier and seemingly with – at least formally – a stronger role in the MSF than in the Global Compact. First, the procedural set-up of the Global Compact appears to have provided the intergovernmental body in charge, that is the UN Secretariat, with a stronger say than that which the EU Commission dealt itself with regard to the MSF. Second, because business was engaged directly with the UN (including UN organizations with mandates related to the ensuring the objectives of the international law instruments that inform the nine original principles) there may have been fewer constraints in terms of getting business-politically sensitive issues on the table and discussing them frankly with the organizations and individuals representing the UN than was the case with the EU MSF. Third and adding to the previous argument, the MSF was developed in a largely public process with speeches, reports etc. made public at the MSF website. The Global Compact was developed in a fashion much less open to the public. On the Global Compact website, information on the development of the Compact remains transmitted mainly through articles and papers written by UN staff and experts involved in the process. This suggests that legitimacy and transparency do not always travel together in development of norms on issues as sensitive to business as human rights, labour, environment and corruption.

Fourth, the Global Compact Principles build directly on international standards agreed within the international law-creating system of the UN and the ILO. It seems that this is what after all provided the Global Compact with legitimacy to make it acceptable even to civil society, which opposed the initiative. Just one or two internet 'clicks' below the ten principles at the Global Compact websites it emerges that each of the principles is informed by instruments of international law, that is, declarations or (in the case of the tenth principle, on anti-corruption) a convention. As indicated, these instruments are conventional international law. They have been agreed to over decades by States according to the conventional system of international law-making. As such, they represent the interests of states that negotiated and agreed on the instruments through a deliberative process of law-making at the international level in which states in principle represent their citizens. The formulation of these instruments of international human rights and labour law marks a particular and somewhat unusual strain in international law-making: The processes towards the pertinent hard law (treaties) or detailed soft law instruments (declarations and recommendations) have been fast, compared with much other multinational international law-making. Since these instruments have been made by members of the UN and the ILO, they have been deliberated, negotiated and agreed to by a large number of the world's states.

This suggests that conventional international law and the new forms of intergovernmentally initiated norm-creation may be combined in ways that provide the new forms with legitimacy through building on conventional instruments whose legitimacy is widely acknowledged among stakeholders. Substantive and procedural legitimacy combine and may even be interdependent: international standards that are perceived to be legitimate serve as sources of normative substance of 'new' soft standards on CSR. These are in turn also perceived to be legitimate, even though they have been developed through a procedure that does not itself fully live up to the legitimacy requirements of deliberative discourse. The MSF in its final report references the Global Compact as one among the few 'internationally agreed instruments' that was to serve as a normative source for CSR for European companies. This suggests that even in the MSF context, the Global Compact was perceived as legitimate, perhaps *the* most widely representative instrument that business in the MSF was prepared to consent to as a normative source of CSR. Indeed, management and policy literature suggests that the Global Compact draws its moral and political legitimacy from the UN.[44]

Finally, the Global Compact's ability to adapt to outside concerns and criticism such as the criticism from NGOs about it being too business-friendly, by engaging civil society more directly and by establishing integrity measures, suggests that a reflexive approach within the multi-stakeholder scheme is significant too. This may be contrasted with the approach taken by the EU Commission when the MSF did not deliver the originally intended results: the Commission instituted a completely new and more exclusive initiative, the CSR Alliance, as a result of or perhaps response to the limited normative outcome of the MSF. Intriguingly, the EU's approach went from being widely inclusive to being more exclusively business-oriented, while the Global Compact went from initially mainly engaging business to being more inclusive, also engaging civil society and more recently public institutions, cities and others as members or stakeholders. This final observation seems to confirm that a Habermasian deliberative law-making approach to public-private CSR-norms development does have the potential to add legitimacy to processes that otherwise function along the lines of the paradigm of reflexive law. In particular, the observation suggests that deliberative discourse may provide an additional normative quality to the procedural aspects of reflexive regulation. With the combination of reflexive law and Habermasian theory, power disparities may be managed not just formally (by granting access) but in such a way as to provide for actual dialogue, negotiation and final agreement on norms on common co-existence. As indicated by Habermas, this ideally requires a set of procedural rights of participation.

---

[44] McIntosh, M., Waddock, S. & Kell, G. (2004) Introduction. In McIntosh, M., Waddock, S. & Kell, G. (eds) *Learning to Talk: Corporate Citizenship and the Development of the UN Global Compact*. Sheffield: Greenleaf Publishing: 13–26; and Waddock (2002) on 'hypernorms'.

4 Conclusion and perspectives

Adapted to the international level, Habermasian deliberative law-making theory provides an explanation for the differences in outcomes of two intergovernmentally initiated forums for the creation of CSR normativity which served as cases for the analysis – the UN Global Compact and the EU MSF. The combination of Habermasian theory and reflexive law suggests that the difference in normative outcomes was due to three interlinked features: First, there was a disproportionate strength of 'social dialogue' actors in the MSF with experience in EU law-making and negotiation compared to NGOs. Industry actors who were opposed to a formalization or juridicalization of CSR in the EU possessed experience in EU-law-making to a higher degree than civil society representatives, especially NGOs. In the Global Compact process, business participants were already in favour of CSR. Second, there was a significant difference between the management style of the UN Secretariat and that of the EU Commission. The UN Secretariat assumed a stronger role with regard to the ongoing management of the reflexive regulatory process than the EU Commission had given itself. Third, the global legitimacy of informing normative sources was clearer in the case of the UN Global Compact. Although the same instruments were brought forward by the EU Commission, this was not done with the same degree of assumption found within the setting up of the Global Compact initiative that instruments passed by UN member states are relevant for CSR. The EU Commission also presented a larger body of possible informing normative instruments as well as topics for CSR in Europe. The problems boil down to design and management of the reflexive regulatory forums, and to the significance of procedural rights to ensure qualitatively balanced participation suggested by Habermas. The analysis suggests that relatively close procedural management of the reflexive regulatory process by the (inter)governmental agency in charge of the process may be required for a balanced process of negotiation and its outcome. The Global Compact case suggests that in the absence of formal rights of participation for non-state actors, a process that is tightly managed by the intergovernmental institution in charge of the regulatory initiative may provide a substitute by ensuring a degree of balancing of interests. Such tight management was absent in the Commission's role in the EU MSF.

Further, the analysis suggests that hand-picking participants for reflexive regulatory forums need not compromise the legitimacy of the normative output, if the output is based on normative sources themselves seen to have a high level of legitimacy.

The combination of Habermasian theory and reflexive law confirms that organizers of reflexive regulatory forums need to pay attention to power disparities between participants, in order for the normative outcomes not to be sidetracked as a result of unbalanced political power. Habermasian theory on deliberative law-making provides qualitative guidance on how to devise a procedure that mitigates power disparities and provides for legitimate norm-creation through involving non-state actors in a process of agreeing on norms of common co-existence and providing them with an actual say. Habermasian deliberative discourse supplements the reflexive law paradigm through which public-private norm-creation intended to promote private self-regulation may be considered. Reflexive law provides a procedural framework within which intergovernmental or other public organizations may engage societal stakeholders to develop and agree on norms for common co-existence while retaining control in order to ensure the primacy of public over private interests. Because it stresses the quality of participation in law-making through common will-formation and not just formal access, Habermasian deliberative discourse provides qualitative guidance for management of reflexive law forums on how to live up to the requirement of reflexive law that power disparities between actors should be balanced.

The analysis of the process and results of the Global Compact and the EU MSF provides guidance on how to enhance legitimacy of new forms of governance and law-making at transnational level through involvement of societal stakeholders from the early stages and providing them with a real stake in the norm-creation process through adequate procedural frameworks. Finally, the analysis suggests that conventional international law and new intergovernmental level forms of public-private development of norms on business ethics may be mutually enriching: international standards on global values, such as human rights, labour standards, environmental protection and anti-corruption, developed through the conventional system of international law-making lend legitimacy to the development of norms for corporate behaviour when the former directly inform the latter. The lessons of both the Global Compact and the MSF suggest that companies are willing to commit to universal principles developed by states and normally intended to apply to states when they are grounded in such universal internationally agreed standards. It also suggests that civil society may regard resulting normative principles on corporate conduct as legitimate, even when civil society has not been engaged directly or strongly in the process of developing the norms for corporate behaviour.

In his 2006–2008 report, the SRSG has highlighted some challenges resulting from globalization. Some of these are human rights abuses that occur when states do not effectively live up to their obligation to protect. They may also occur when multinational enterprises are able to escape jurisdiction for human rights violations due to their transnational character and states' unwillingness to give their laws extraterritorial application. Past experience with international efforts to regulate the conduct of business shows that a significant number of states lack the will to support international law-making to provide for corporate social and human rights responsibility, sometimes due to opposition from business or civil society. In this situation, the case for novel approaches to make businesses self-regulate based on the objectives of relevant normative agreements only grows. The observations in this chapter indicate that it is possible to engage non-state actors in international law-making through innovative procedural forums without threatening the long-standing sovereignty privilege of states. Such concerns have kept many states from acknowledging a role for business and other non-state actors in international law-making. Adding Habermasian insight into reflexive regulatory processes may add to the legitimacy of procedure and spill over on output. In this perspective, the lessons of the Global Compact and the EU MSF hold potential for a more inclusive process of creating international norms to curtail negative business impact on society and promote positive impact through public-private processes of formulation of CSR norms.

4
'Protect, Respect and Remedy': A Critique of the SRSG's Framework for Business and Human Rights

Surya Deva

> My bottom line is that the last thing victims need is more unenforced declarations; they need effective action.... I did not address the implementation provisions [in the UN Norms] because I thought the subject was premature...[1]

1 Introduction

This chapter seeks to critically evaluate the 'conceptual and policy framework to anchor the business and human rights debate' outlined by Professor John Ruggie – the Special Representative of the Secretary General (SRSG) on the issue of Human Rights and Transnational Corporations and Other Business Enterprises – in the April 2008 Report to the Human Rights Council (HRC).[2] I will argue that although the Report lays down a few

---

[1] Professor John Ruggie, Special Representative of the Secretary general for Business and Human Rights, 'Opening Statement to United Nations Human Rights Council' (25 September 2006), http://www.reports-and-materials.org/Ruggie-statement-to-UN-Human-Rights-Council-25-Sep-2006.pdf (2 October 2008).

[2] 'Protect, Respect and Remedy: A Framework for Business and Human Rights', Report of the Special Representative of the Secretary General on the issue of Human Rights and Transnational Corporations and Other Business Enterprises, A/HRC/8/5 (7 April 2008) (hereinafter SRSG, 'The 2008 Report'). After this chapter was written, the SRSG presented two more reports to the Human Rights Council in April 2009 and April 2010. In view of the space limitations, this chapter will not refer to these subsequent reports, which by and large elucidate the operationalization of the three principles of the framework: 'Business and Human Rights: Towards Operationalizing the "Protect, Respect and Remedy" Framework', A/HRC/11/13 (22 April 2009); 'Business and Human Rights: Further Steps toward the Operationalization of the "Protect, Respect and Remedy" Framework', A/HRC/14/27 (9 April 2010).

useful suggestions, it falls short of providing a robust framework that could be employed to promote corporate human rights responsibilities.

The chapter will highlight several drawbacks inherent in the Report. However, before embarking on this ambitious task, an attempt will be made in Section 2 of this chapter to outline the background in which the SRSG was appointed to carry forward the project of mapping the human rights responsibilities of transnational corporations[3] (TNCs) and other business enterprises. This will enable readers to put in context the original as well as extended mandate of the SRSG. Section 3 then will develop a critique of the Report submitted by the SRSG. In particular, I will highlight a few flawed premises and one major omission of the Report. It is explained that the Report is flawed in that it seeks to employ the governance gaps thesis to explain all the current business-human rights challenges and rejects the need for enumerating the human rights responsibilities of corporations. Also critically examined are the problems and limitations inherent in the notion of 'differentiated but complementary responsibilities'. This section further points out one major omission of the Report, that is, the failure of the Report to map the role that international institutions such as the World Bank, International Monetary Fund (IMF) and World Trade Organization (WTO) could play in promoting the business and human rights agenda. Finally, Section 4 will sum up the discussion and also suggest a direction for taking the business and human rights project forward.

Various reports, the accompanying addenda and supporting research material prepared by the SRSG as well as his team have been voluminous.[4] This has been followed by a lot of discussions, papers, submissions, letter exchanges and interviews by a range of stakeholders.[5] For obvious reasons, it will not be possible to analyse all the reports and materials or to cover each and every aspect of the debate. The focus of this chapter will rather be on the 2008 Report, though a reference will be made to other reports or materials at appropriate places.[6]

---

[3] Despite a technical distinction between transnational corporations (TNCs), multinational corporations (MNCs) and multinational enterprises (MNEs), the term TNCs is used here broadly to include all such variations. See Peter Muchlinski, *Multinational Enterprises and the Law*, updated edn (Oxford: Blackwell Publishers, 1999), 12–15 (hereinafter Muchlinski, *MNEs and the Law*); Cynthia D. Wallace, *Legal Control of the Multinational Enterprise* (The Hague: Martinus Nijhoff, 1982), 10–12.
[4] The SRSG has 'produced more than 1,000 pages of documents.' SRSG, 'The 2008 Report', *supra* note 2, para 4.
[5] For a complete list of such materials, see http://www.business-humanrights.org/Gettingstarted/UNSpecialRepresentative (18 September 2008).
[6] See *supra* note 2.

2 SRSG: background, mandate and the progress made

Before looking at the original and revised mandate of the SRSG, it might be useful to understand briefly the context in which the SRSG was invited to break the stalemate in the UN's quest to establish some sort of regulatory framework for TNCs.[7] Putting in place such a framework is fundamental to fulfilling a central mandate of the UN[8] and also keeping it relevant in an era of globalization when non-state actors are playing an important role in the international sphere.

2.1 Background of SRSG's appointment and his mandate

The quest to establish a human rights code for TNCs gained a new momentum in August 1998 when the Sub-Commission on the Promotion and Protection of Human Rights decided to establish a five-member Working Group on the Working Methods and Activities of Transnational Corporations.[9] In mid-2003, the Working Group presented to the Sub-Commission the final draft of the Norms on the Responsibilities of Transnational Corporations and Other Business Enterprises with Regard to Human Rights (UN Norms).[10] The UN Norms attracted, though not unexpectedly, criticism from several leading TNCs and business organizations. The criticisms ranged from lack of adequate consultation during the drafting stage to the Norms laying down a too vague or overly inclusive list of human rights, not properly allocating the extent of responsibilities between states and corporations, having a questionable legal basis for proposed human rights obligations purported, and recommending impractical implementation measures.[11]

---

[7] Even the SRSG considers 'the history that preceded its creation' an important variable. Commission on Human Rights, 'Interim Report of the Special Representative of the Secretary General on the issue of Human Rights and Transnational Corporations and Other Business Enterprises', E/CN.4/2006/97 (22 February 2006), para 3 (hereinafter SRSG, 'Interim Report').

[8] One of the purposes of the UN is to achieve international co-operation 'in promoting and encouraging respect for human rights and for fundamental freedoms for all'. UN Charter, art 1(3).

[9] David Weissbrodt & Muria Kruger, 'Norms of the Responsibilities of Transnational Corporations and Other Business Enterprises with Regard to Human Rights' (2003) 97, *American Journal of International Law*, 901, 903–04.

[10] Sub-Commission on the Promotion and Protection of Human Rights, Norms on the Responsibilities of Transnational Corporations and Other Business Enterprises with Regard to Human Rights, UN Doc E/CN.4/Sub.2/2003/12/Rev.2 (13 August 2003) (hereinafter UN Norms).

[11] See Justine Nolan, 'With Power Comes Responsibility: Human Rights and Corporate Accountability' (2005) 28, *UNSW Law Journal*, 581, 585–605; David Kinley, Justine Nolan & Natalie Zerial, 'The Politics of Corporate Social Responsibility: Reflections on the United Nations Human Rights Norms for Corporations' (2007) 25, *C&SLJ*, 30,

Although the Sub-Commission approved the UN Norms,[12] the Commission on Human Rights in its 2004 session resolved, much to the liking of the business community, that the UN Norms had 'no legal standing'.[13] The Commission also requested the Office of the High Commissioner for Human Rights (OHCHR) to prepare a report setting out, among others, the scope and legal status of existing initiatives and standards relating to the human rights responsibilities of TNCs.

In its 2005 session, the Commission welcomed the report of the OHCHR[14] and requested the UN Secretary General to appoint a Special Representative on the issue of human rights and transnational corporations.[15] In July 2005, Kofi Annan appointed Professor John Ruggie as the SRSG for an initial period of 2 years. Later on, the term of the SRSG was extended for one more year and in June 2008, the HRC extended the mandate further for another 3 years.[16]

The original mandate of the SRSG, as adopted by the erstwhile Commission on Human Rights, was quite wide.[17] The SRSG was requested to 'identify and clarify standards of corporate responsibility and accountability' for TNCs with regard to human rights and also elaborate on the role of states in effectively regulating TNCs. Professor Ruggie was also requested to search and clarify the implications for TNCs of concepts such as 'complicity' and 'sphere of influence'. In addition, the SRSG was requested to 'develop materials and methodologies for undertaking human rights impact assessments' of the activities of TNCs and to compile a compendium of best practices of states and TNCs.

The objective of the mandate, in the words of the SRSG, was 'to strengthen the promotion and protection of human rights in relation to transnational corporations and other business enterprises but that governments bear

---

34–37 (hereinafter Kinley et al., 'The Politics of CSR'); SRSG, 'Interim Report', *supra* note 7, paras 58–69.

[12] Sub-Commission on the Promotion and Protection of Human Rights, Resolution 2003/16 (13 August 2003), E/CN.4/Sub.2/2003/L.11, 52–55.

[13] Commission on Human Rights, 60th Session, Agenda Item 16, E/CN.4/2004/L.73/Rev.1 (16 April 2004), para (c).

[14] Commission on Human Rights, 61st Session, 'Report of the United Nations High Commissioner on Human Rights on the Responsibilities of Transnational Corporations and related Business Enterprises with regard to Human Rights', E/CN.4/2005/91 (15 February 2005).

[15] Commission on Human Rights, 'Promotion and Protection of Human Rights', E/CN.4/2005/L.87 (15 April 2005).

[16] Human Rights Council, 'Mandate of the Special Representative of the Secretary General on the issue of Human Rights and Transnational Corporations and Other Business Enterprises', Resolution 8/7 (18 June 2008), para 4.

[17] *Supra* note 15.

principal responsibility for the vindication of those rights'.[18] The SRSG considered, among others, his mandate to be 'highly politicised' in that it was 'devised as a means to move beyond the stalemated debate' over the UN Norms.[19]

On 18 June 2008, the HRC renewed the SRSG's term for another 3 years with a revised mandate and a request to report annually to the Council as well as the General Assembly.[20] The focus of the revised mandate is on operationalization of the conceptual and policy framework canvassed by the SRSG in the 2008 Report, that is, on providing 'concrete and practical recommendations on ways to strengthen the fulfilment of the duty of the State to protect all human rights from abuses by or involving' TNCs. It is also expected that the SRSG will provide further guidance 'on the scope and content of the corporate responsibility to respect all human rights'.

What is notable in the revised mandate of the SRSG is an acknowledgement that TNCs' activities might affect vulnerable groups such as women and children more. The SRSG is, therefore, invited to pay 'special attention' to persons of such groups. It is hoped that Professor Ruggie will not limit himself to women and children because tribal and indigenous populations in many jurisdictions have suffered the most from TNCs' operations, which are often underpinned by investment-driven development policies of developing states.[21]

Another notable aspect of the revised mandate is that it requests the SRSG to 'explore options and make recommendations, at the national, regional and international level, for enhancing access to effective remedies available to those whose human rights are impacted by corporate activities'.[22] A reference to the access to 'effective remedies' serves at least three important purposes. First, this will caution scholars against asserting anymore that the issue of implementing corporate human rights obligations is premature.[23] It is trite that 'rights' and 'remedies' go hand-in-hand, one

---

[18] SRSG, 'Interim Report', *supra* note 7, para 7.
[19] Ruggie, *supra* note 1. Some commentators, however, argue that the polarization of the debate about the UN Norms into two camps (pro-Norms and anti-Norms) was 'a largely artificial division'. Kinley et al., 'The Politics of CSR', *supra* note 11, 34.
[20] *Supra* note 16.
[21] See Surya Deva, 'The *Sangam* of Foreign Investment, Multinational Corporations and Human Rights: An Indian Perspective for a Developing Asia' [2004] *Singapore Journal of Legal Studies*, 305; 'Human Rights Realisation in an Era of Globalisation: The Indian Experience' (2006) 12, *Buffalo Human Rights Law Review*, 93, and the materials cited therein.
[22] A footnote could be added about the use of the word 'impacted' in the resolution of the HRC. Was it really necessary to use a neutral, politically correct phrase when it is not a moot point that TNCs 'violate' human rights and that effective remedies are required only when rights are violated or infringed?
[23] Professor Ruggie made this remark in 2006. See *supra* note 1.

is redundant without the other. Moreover, the evolution of rights and remedies is a dynamic and evolutionary process and therefore, no attempt should be made to isolate or divide into phases the discussion on rights with remedies.

Second, the focus on remedies reminds us the important direction that the UN Norms provided to the business and human rights project by incorporating specific implementation provisions. The UN Norms had proposed implementation mechanisms, even if preliminary and tentative, not only at the national and international levels but also at the local (corporate) level.[24] Moreover, the Norms did mention the types of civil and criminal remedies that could be employed.[25]

Third, 'access' to remedies which are effective could also fill in one of the gaps which existed in the UN Norms, that is, the failure to respond to the challenges that procedural rules such as the doctrine of *forum non conveniens* pose to the victims of corporate human rights abuses.[26] One could also add here the procedural challenge which the requirement of *locus standi* raises and the financial constraints that poor victims often face in fighting the legal battle against resourceful TNCs. One could hope that the SRSG will consider means to overcome these procedural hurdles which effectively deny any access to legal remedies in order to make TNCs accountable for violations of human rights.[27]

2.2 Progress made by the SRSG

The SRSG has submitted various reports which (along with commentaries on these by various stakeholders) document the progress made during his 2005–2008 mandate term. In early 2006, the SRSG submitted its first Interim Report to the Commission on Human Rights.[28] Among others, the Interim Report found a correlation between alleged corporate human rights abuses and a situation of conflict coupled with bad or weak governance.[29] It also

---

[24] UN Norms, *supra* note 10, paras 15–17. See Surya Deva, 'UN's Human Rights Norms for Transnational Corporations and Other Business Enterprises: An Imperfect Step in the Right Direction?' (2004) 10, *ILSA Journal of International & Comparative Law*, 493, 500, 519–520 (hereinafter Deva, 'UN Norms').

[25] UN Norms, *supra* note 10, para 18.

[26] I had pointed out this lacuna in the UN Norms in 2004. Deva, 'UN Norms', *supra* note 24, 520–22.

[27] In September 2008, the SRSG opened a Consultation Forum on Access to Remedies to be held in November 2008: http://www.business-humanrights.org/Documents/Ruggie-consultation-forum-access-to-remedies-Sep-2008.pdf (2 October 2008).

[28] SRSG, 'Interim Report', *supra* note 7.

[29] *Id.*, para 27. It concluded: '[T]here is clearly a negative symbiosis between the worst corporate-related human rights abuses and host countries that are characterised by a combination of relatively low national income, current of recent conflict exposure, and weak or corrupt governance.' *Id.*, para 30.

offered a brief review of various existing regulatory responses.[30] However, the two strategic directions of the Interim Report – a critique of the UN Norms[31] and the notion of 'principled pragmatism'[32] – proved to be controversial and attracted a lot of criticism from human rights scholars and NGOs.[33] Although this chapter is not the right place to evaluate the SRSG's critique of the UN Norms, it seems that the adverse comments were not always objective.[34] For instance, the SRSG has been quite critical of the UN Norms for imposing higher human rights responsibilities on corporations than on states[35] or for including rights – such as the precautionary principle – which 'states have not recognised or are still debating'.[36] But at the same time, the SRSG apparently seemed comfortable with similar provisions embodying the precautionary principle in the Global Compact[37] or the OECD Guidelines.[38] So, perhaps there might be more reasons for rejecting the UN Norms than the conceptual or doctrinal excesses inherent therein.[39]

The Interim Report was followed by the Main Report, a Companion Report and four addenda in 2007. Whereas the Companion Report dealt with potential methodologies for undertaking human rights impact assessment of business activities,[40] the Main Report mapped international

---

[30] *Id.*, paras 31–54.
[31] *Id.*, paras 56–69.
[32] *Id.*, paras 70–81. Principled pragmatism is defined as follows: 'an unflinching commitment to the principle of strengthening the promotion and protection of human rights as it relates to business, coupled with a pragmatic attachment to what works best in creating change where it matters most – in the daily lives of people.' *Id.*, para 81.
[33] See, for example, David Weissbrodt, 'International Standard-Setting on the Human Rights Responsibilities of Business' (2008) 26, *Berkeley Journal of International Law*, 373 (hereinafter Weissbrodt, 'International Standard-Setting'); Misereor & Global Policy Forum Europe, 'Problematic Pragmatism: The Ruggie Report 2008: Background, Analysis and Perspectives' (June 2008); 'Comments to the Interim Report of the Special Representative of the Secretary General on the issue of Human Rights and Transnational Corporations and Other Business Enterprises, 22 February 2006' (442/2, 15 March 2006), FIDH. But see the reply of the SRSG to the FIDH (letter of 20 March 2006) and to Misereor/GPF (letter dated 2 June 2008).
[34] See, e.g., Weissbrodt, 'International Standard-Setting', *supra* note 33, 383–90.
[35] SRSG, 'Interim Report', *supra* note 7, para 66.
[36] John Ruggie, 'Business and Human Rights: The Evolving International Agenda' (2007) 101, *American Journal of International Law*, 819, 825 (hereinafter Ruggie, 'Business and Human Rights').
[37] UN Global Compact, Principle 7.
[38] OECD Declaration and Decisions on International Investment and Multinational Enterprises, DAFFE/IME(2000)20, reprinted in 40 *ILM* 237 (2001), 243 (para V.4).
[39] The SRSG is likely to reject this suggestion, though: 'I did not reject the Norms on political grounds.' John Ruggie, 'Response to Misereor/GPF' (2 June 2008).
[40] Human Rights Council, 'Report of the SRSG – Human Rights Impact Assessments: Resolving Key Methodological Questions', A/HRC/4/74 (5 February 2007).

standards related to corporate responsibility or accountability for human rights abuses.[41] The 2007 Main Report offered a brief summary and analysis of existing standards and practices by dividing them under the following five clusters:

- states' duty to protect human rights, including against abuses by non-state actors;
- corporate accountability for selected international crimes;
- corporate responsibility for other human rights violations under international law;
- soft-law mechanisms; and
- self-regulation by corporations and/or business organizations.[42]

On reviewing the Main Report, one cannot help but ask if this has made any significant progress or contribution other than providing 'a succinct mapping'[43] of the existing state of affairs.[44] Such a critical review, compilation and classification of existing standards or practices for corporations have been done before on too many occasions to be cited here. In defence of the Report, one could argue that such a background analysis was required to present a conceptual and policy framework which the 2008 Report offered.[45] To avoid duplication, a critical analysis of this report is done in the next section.

On 22 September 2008, the SRSG constituted a Leadership Group to advise him 'on how best to ensure that businesses worldwide respect internationally recognised human rights standards'.[46] A comment at least about the composition of the Group is appropriate. The SRSG deserves credit for inviting to the Leadership Group people like Mary Robinson and Guy Ryder. Similar credit could be given for being gender-sensitive in that 6 out of 15

---

[41] Human Rights Council, 'Report of the SRSG – Business and Human Rights: Mapping International Standards of Responsibility and Accountability for Corporate Acts', A/HRC/4/35 (19 February 2007) (hereinafter SRSG, 'The 2007 Main Report').
[42] *Id.*, paras 10–81.
[43] John Ruggie, 'Presentation of Report to United Nations Human Rights Council' (3 June 2008), 2.
[44] Ruggie justified this as follows: 'my first task under the mandate ... was ... essentially, to "restate" existing standards and indicate emerging trends.' Ruggie, 'Business and Human Rights', *supra* note 36, 827.
[45] SRSG, 'The 2008 Report', *supra* note 2. The Main Report was supplemented by a Companion Report and two Addenda.
[46] 'Global Leadership Group to Advise on Business and Human Rights', http://www.reports-and-materials.org/Leadership-group-22-Sep-2008.pdf (26 September 2008).

members of the Group are women.[47] The commendations end here, though. Of course, it was not possible to include everyone in the Group and one could argue that those who were excluded could still participate in deliberations through other consultation processes. Nevertheless, it is indefensible that the list had no place for even one leading human rights or corporate social responsibility scholar. Also missing from the list are the representatives of NGOs such as Greenpeace, Amnesty International, Human Rights Watch, EarthRights International, Centre for Constitutional Rights, and Corporate Watch.[48] One wonders if these constituents are not there in the Leadership Group merely because they disagree (or might disagree) with the vision of the SRSG.

Apart from the above major omissions, it could not be ignored that out of 15, 6 members come from the corporate world – from Neville Isdell of Coca Cola to Narayana Murthy of Infosys to the former BP Chief Executive John Browne. Although these members are participating in their 'personal capacity' and not as 'representatives of any organisation or constituency',[49] this over-corporatization of the Leadership Group might not augur well for the civil society and victims of corporate human rights abuses.

On a positive side, it should be noted that the SRSG has taken initiatives to reach out to various stakeholders and to organize world-wide consultations.[50]

3 The 2008 report of the SRSG: a critical evaluation

This section offers a critical evaluation of the 2008 Report submitted by the SRSG to the HRC. The Report claims to present 'a conceptual and policy framework to anchor the business and human rights debate, and to help guide all relevant actors'.[51] The critique here focuses on the following two aspects: first it highlights a few flawed premises and one major omission of the report and then explores problems with the concept of 'differentiated but complementary responsibilities'.

The critique below should not be taken to mean that the Report provided no useful suggestions. The SRSG deserves credit for recognizing that

---

[47] It is possible that this gender-sensitiveness was triggered by the revised mandate which requested the SRSG to 'integrate a gender perspective throughout his work', *supra* note 16, para 4(d).
[48] It should be noted that the SRSG, under the revised mandate, is expressly requested to consult 'civil society, including academics', *supra* note 16, para 4(g).
[49] *Supra* note 46.
[50] See http://www.business-humanrights.org/Updates/Archive/UNSpecialRep-Consultationsworkshops (12 May 2009).
[51] SRSG, 'The 2008 Report', *supra* note 2, summary.

developing countries lack capacity or will to regulate TNCs' activities,[52] that extraterritorial regulation of TNCs' activities could be a legitimate option,[53] that governments should work to change the corporate culture of doing irresponsible business,[54] and that the notion of 'sphere of influence' conflates two different meanings of influence (impact and leverage).[55] Professor Ruggie also deserves praise for pointing out that 'defining a limited set of rights linked to imprecise and expansive responsibilities, rather than defining the specific responsibilities of companies with regard to all rights' is probably the better approach.[56] The objective of the critique is to contribute to the ongoing discussion in this complex area.

3.1 Flawed premises and one major omission

Before I highlight two major and some minor flaws underpinning the 2008 Report, let me flag one major omission of the Report. The Report maps a range of judicial and non-judicial mechanisms, operating at different levels, which could be employed to address breaches of human rights obligations by corporations.[57] However, it does not even acknowledge the important role that international institutions such as the World Bank, IMF and WTO could play in ensuring that business complies with its human rights responsibilities.[58] It is possible that the SRSG might consider these institutional options in future because the revised mandate specifically requested him to 'work in close coordination with United Nations and other relevant international bodies, offices, departments and specialised agencies'.[59]

First major flaw of the 2008 Report lies in a suggestion that '[t]he *root cause* of the business and human predicament today lies in the governance gaps created by globalisation'.[60] At best, governance deficits could be one of the

---

[52] *Id.*, para 14.
[53] *Id.*, para 19. See also Human Rights Council, 'Report of the SRSG – Corporate Responsibility under International Law and Issues in Extraterritorial Regulation: Summary and Legal Workshops', A/HRC/4/35/Add.2 (15 February 2007).
[54] *Id.*, paras 29–32.
[55] *Id.*, para 68.
[56] *Id.*, para 51.
[57] *Id.*, paras 88–101.
[58] See Sigrun Skogly, *The Human Rights Obligations of the World Bank and the International Monetary Fund* (London: Cavendish Publishing, 2001); David Kinley & Junko Tadaki, 'From Talk to Walk: The Emergence of Human Rights Responsibilities for Corporations at International Law' (2004) 44, *Virginia Journal of International Law*, 931.
[59] SRSG, 'The 2008 Report', *supra* note 2, para 4(f). The Canadian Network on Corporate Accountability (CNCA) has also requested the SRSG to consider the role of international financial institutions. CNCA, 'Submission to the UN Secretary General's Special Representative on Business and Human Rights' (21 July 2008).
[60] SRSG, 'The 2008 Report', *supra* note 2, para 3 (emphasis added).

reasons, but hardly 'the' root cause of why the UN has been grappling with this issue for almost the last four decades now. Such an analysis underestimates, for example, the significance of the fact that international (human rights) law was traditionally concerned with protecting human rights against state action and not against private corporate actors.[61] It also ignores the fact that corporate law historically did not allow corporations to serve the interests of other than their shareholders,[62] or that a parent company is not generally liable for actions of its subsidiaries, suppliers or contractors. One should not try, as the Report does, to explain all such major conceptual hurdles by a broad brush of governance gaps.

Moreover, the governance gaps thesis is too general to be the root cause of the specific issues that have been and are central to the business and human rights project.[63] For example, one could employ the governance gaps thesis to explain any current or past problem – from child pornography to violence against women, cold war to invasion of Iraq, financial crisis to AIDS, corruption to terrorism, and from poverty to global warming. Will it help much if we say that the root cause of all of these problems is the governance gaps created by globalization? One should not also assume that globalization has merely created gaps in governance; in fact, globalization

---

[61] 'International law – and human rights law in particular – has traditionally concerned itself with state responsibility, rather than the responsibility of non-states actors such as companies.' Sarala Fitzgerald, 'Corporate Accountability for Human Rights Violations in Australian Domestic Law' (2005) 11, *Australian Journal of Human Rights*, 33. 'International law and human rights law have principally focused on protecting individuals from violations by governments.' David Weissbrodt, 'Business and Human Rights' (2005) 74, *University of Cincinnati Law Review*, 55, 59. See also Henry Steiner, Philip Alston & Ryan Goodman, *International Human Rights in Context: Law, Politics and Morals*, 3rd edn (Oxford: Oxford University Press, 2008), p. 1385.

[62] Redmond writes: 'Corporate law does not explicitly address the problem of corporate compliance with human rights standards; indeed, its systemic orientation aggravates the problem of standard setting and compliance... Human rights concerns are, for the most part, extraneous to corporate regulation, culture, and doctrines.' Paul Redmond, 'Transnational Enterprise and Human Rights: Options for Standard Setting and Compliance' (2003) 37, *International Lawyer*, 69, 73, and generally 73–75. The Companies Act 2006 of UK, for example, now imposes a specific duty on company directors to consider 'the impact of the company's operations on the community and the environment' while promoting the success of the company. Companies Act 2006 (UK), s172(1).

[63] I do not want to go into the critique that the good governance thesis has received on another count, that is, a tool of Western hegemony. See Chantal Thomas, 'Does the "Good Governance Policy" of the International Financial Institutions Privilege Markets at the Expense Of Democracy?' (1999) 14, *Connecticut Journal of International Law*, 551; James T. Gathii, 'Retelling Good Governance Narratives on Africa's Economic and Political Predicaments: Continuities and Discontinuities in Legal Outcomes between Markets and States' (2000) 45, *Villanova Law Review*, 971.

has also filled gaps in governance through information sharing and capacity building.

To support the governance gaps thesis, the SRSG makes a reference to the findings of the 2006 Interim Report and writes that corporate human rights abuses 'occurred, predictably, where governance challenges were greatest: disproportionately in low income countries; in countries that often had just emerged from or still were in conflict; and in countries where the rule of law was weak and levels of corruption high'.[64] However, as pointed out above, these governance gaps are not unique to the business and human rights quandary and they could be connected to world's many other problems as well. This linkage also ignores the reality that good governance and sound legal systems do not always ensure robust protection of human rights.[65]

In short, it is too simplistic to identify one variable as the root cause of a complex problem which is caused by several factors. Making such an assumption is problematic because this might result in all remedial efforts focusing on something which is not the sole or even main contributing cause of the problem.[66]

The second major flaw in the 2008 Report is that instead of squarely dealing with the difficult question of precise human rights responsibilities of corporations that operate in diverse business environments, the report debunks any need for cataloguing human rights responsibilities of corporations. The justification runs like this: because 'business can affect virtually all internationally recognized rights... any limited list [as attempted in the UN Norms] will almost certainly miss one or more rights that may turn out to be significant in a particular instance, thereby providing misleading guidance.'[67]

This justification is unsound, in my view, for several reasons. It is, of course, not necessary to create a separate, special list of human 'rights' applicable to corporations. In fact, no one is asking for this – what human rights NGOs are demanding and what the UN Norms tried to do was to outline 'responsibilities' of corporations corresponding to human rights laid down

---

[64] SRSG, 'The 2008 Report', *supra* note 2, para 16. See also SRSG, 'Interim Report', *supra* note 7, para 27.
[65] One could, for example, refer to the human rights struggle faced by the Guantanamo Bay prisoners in the US and the asylum seekers in Australia.
[66] In fact, it seems that Professor Ruggie is already following this trap: 'Insofar as governance gaps are at the root of the business and human rights predicament, effective responses must aim to reduce those gaps.' SRSG, 'The 2008 Report', *supra* note 2, para 17. And again: 'our focus should be on ways to reduce or compensate for the governance gaps created by globalisation.' *Id.*, para 11.
[67] *Id.*, para 6, and also paras 51–52.

in the International Bill of Rights.[68] One might disagree with the nature and extent of corporate responsibilities proposed by the UN Norms, but they were not a limited list of rights by any means.[69]

It is, nevertheless, critical that responsibilities of corporations vis-à-vis rights (defined originally with reference to states) are identified. Professor Raz argues that 'there is no closed list of duties which correspond to the right.... *A change of circumstances may lead to the creation of new duties based on the old right.*'[70] So, a change in circumstances – for example, a shift in powers and functions from states to corporations – justifies that appropriate duties for corporations are identified. This does not mean, however, that the responsibilities of states and corporations should be the same, as explained in the next section. The 2008 Report also sets this out clearly.[71] But the very fact that the responsibilities of corporations should be different from those of states requires that we should catalogue these responsibilities rather than deducing these responsibilities on a case-to-case basis with reference to a general principle.

An identification of corporate responsibilities, which will provide a better guidance to all concerned, is also desirable because corporations are unlikely to abridge all human rights, even though the SRSG takes a different stand.[72] For example, Jägers argues that it 'is difficult to imagine a corporation having a great deal of influence on the right to seek and enjoy asylum or the right to a nationality'.[73] A few other similar examples could be given.[74] One more issue that has not received much attention from the SRSG is: given that

---

[68] Rights (as claims) and responsibilities (duties) are jural correlatives, but still these are two distinct concepts.

[69] From a different perspective, in addition to specific responsibilities, the UN Norms also contained a general provision on human rights obligations. UN Norms, *supra* note 10, para 1.

[70] Joseph Raz, *The Morality of Freedom* (Oxford: Clarendon Press, 1986), 171 (emphasis added).

[71] 'While corporations may be considered "organs of society", they are specialised economic organs, not democratic public interest institutions. As such, their responsibilities cannot and should not simply mirror the duties of states.' SRSG, 'The 2008 Report', *supra* note 2, para 53.

[72] The report notes: 'there are few if any internationally recognised rights business cannot impact... in some manner.' *Id.*, para 52.

[73] Nicola Jägers, *Corporate Human Rights Obligations: In Search of Accountability* (Antwerpen: Intersentia, 2002), 59.

[74] Consider also, for example, Article 11 of the UDHR and Article 14(2) of the ICCPR (right to be presumed innocent when charged for a penal offence) and Article 12 of the ICCPR (liberty to leave and enter his own country). Ratner, however, contemplates the situations in which corporations could be involved in violation of even such rights. Steven R Ratner, 'Corporations and Human Rights: A Theory of Legal Responsibility' (2001) 111, *Yale Law Journal*, 443, 493.

TNCs operate under diverse social, political, economic and cultural environment, which standards of human rights should they follow? To illustrate: what constitutes freedom of speech in the US is different from the meaning that this right has in India. Similarly, corporations would need to identify in each state what constitutes a fair wage. For this reason also, cataloguing responsibilities of corporations is desirable not only at the international level but also at domestic levels.

The 2008 Report also suffers from several minor flaws in that it contains general, unqualified or unsupported assertions. For example, it says that the 'business and human rights debate currently lacks an authoritative point'.[75] Is it possible, or even desirable, to reach such an authoritative point? Does the SRSG expect to achieve this point after completion of the current mandate? Similarly, the report posits that corporations have a responsibility to 'respect [human rights] because it is the basic expectation society has of business'.[76] Is this a theoretical basis, or has it some empirical support? Who represents society: business organizations, civil society, or governments? How do we know what society wants? Could we gather a consensual view from society on this issue? More importantly, will the SRSG and corporations be willing to accept more extensive responsibilities if the expectations of society do change in future?

3.2 Notion of "differentiated but complementary responsibilities": problems and limitations

The 2008 Report proposes an overarching concept of 'differentiated but complementary responsibilities', which has three principles: the state duty to protect human rights; the corporate responsibility to respect human rights; and an access to remedies. The first principle is by and large non-controversial. The only problem is the known limitations of the state's duty to protect human rights from abuses by private corporate actors,[77] which operate at a transnational level and have the capacity to disappear or move from one jurisdiction to another. That is why the quest has been on for some time now to find regulatory alternatives which are not state-focal but are effective at the same time.

The third principle (the access to remedies) is also a welcome step; the only irony being that while the SRSG was critical of the non-voluntary character or implementation provisions of the UN Norms, the 2008 Report itself outlines a range of mechanisms – from judicial to non-judicial, state-based non-judicial, company-led and multi-stakeholder or industry initiatives.

---

[75] SRSG, 'The 2008 Report', *supra* note 2, para 5.
[76] *Id.*, para 9.
[77] Commentators have suggested that the SRSG shares this 'traditional view' of regulating corporations. Kinley et al, 'The Politics of CSR', *supra* note 11, 39.

It is, in fact, critical to employ various mechanisms and strategies to make TNCs accountable in view of limitations inherent in any given mechanism or strategy.

The nature of TNCs' human rights responsibilities need not, and should not, be identical or as extensive as those of states.[78] The SRSG, I think rightly, also points out that the human rights responsibilities of states and corporations should not be identical because 'as economic actors, companies have unique responsibilities'.[79] In order to differentiate the responsibilities of states and TNCs, the 2008 Report proposed that unlike states, TNCs have merely a responsibility to 'respect' human rights: 'To respect rights essentially means not to infringe on the rights of others – put simply, to do no harm.'[80] However, this 'baseline responsibility',[81] which exists independently of states' duties,[82] has an exception, that is, situations where corporations 'perform certain public functions'.[83]

There are, however, a number of problems with the above formulation of the second principle: corporate responsibility to respect human rights. Let me highlight a few here. First of all, the principle has used the term 'responsibility' to respect rather than the 'obligation' to respect human rights. This seems a conscious decision given the distinction that the SRSG has previously maintained between corporate *responsibility* and corporate *accountability*.[84] If states have a duty to respect,[85] why should corporations have merely a responsibility to respect? No explanation has been offered for this difference in terminology. It seems that this conscious distinction is made to dilute further the corporate obligation to respect human rights. An evidence of this dilution is provided by the Report itself: 'Failure to meet this responsibility can *subject companies to the courts of public opinion* – comprising employees, communities, consumers, civil society, as well as investors – *and*

---

[78] Shue writes: '...for every basic right – and many more other rights as well – there are three types of duties, all of which must be performed if the basic right is to be fully honoured *but not all of which must necessarily be performed by the same individuals or institutions.*' Henry Shue, *Basic Rights: Subsistence, Affluence, and US Foreign Policy*, 2nd edn (Princeton, NJ: Princeton University Press, 1996), 52 (emphasis added). Zerk also notes that 'if human rights law obligations are extended to corporate actors they will need to reflect the different roles and capacities of companies vis-à-vis states.' Jennifer A. Zerk, *Multinational and Corporate Social Responsibility: Limitations and Opportunities in International Law* (Cambridge: Cambridge University Press, 2006), 79. See also Kinley & Tadaki, *supra* note 58, 961–66; Thomas Donaldson, *The Ethics of International Business* (New York: Oxford University Press, 1989), 83–4.
[79] SRSG, 'The 2008 Report', *supra* note 2, para 6. See also *supra* note 71.
[80] SRSG, 'The 2008 Report', *supra* note 2, para 24.
[81] *Id.*, para 54.
[82] *Id.*, para 55.
[83] *Id.*, para 24.
[84] SRSG, 'The 2007 Main Report', *supra* note 41.
[85] Ruggie, 'Business and Human Rights', *supra* note 36, 828, footnote 46.

occasionally to charges in actual courts.'[86] Are we then really talking about legally enforceable human rights obligations?

Second, it is clear that the SRSG's conception of corporate responsibilities is trying to turn back the clock in terms of the evolving responsibilities of corporations. For instance, as early as in 1932, Professor Dodd wrote: 'There is a widespread and growing feeling that industry owes to its employees *not merely the negative duties* of refraining from overworking or injuring them, *but affirmative duty of providing them so far as possible with economic security.*'[87] In more recent times, one could easily find provisions in the OECD Guidelines and the ILO Declaration – neither of which has been dismissed by the SRSG – which go far beyond the corporate responsibility to only respect human rights.[88]

Third, it is doubtful if the responsibility of corporations to merely *respect* human rights will prove adequate, for human rights cannot be fully realized unless 'multiple kinds of duties' are imposed on all those actors which could abridge rights.[89] Moreover, the scope of duties should be coterminous with possible ways in which rights could be breached by TNCs. If human rights law could obligate states to ensure that their agents as well as private actors within their respective jurisdictions do not violate human rights,[90] why

---

[86] SRSG, 'The 2008 Report', *supra* note 2, para 54 (emphasis added). See further the following memorandum: 'we have been assured by the Special Representative himself that the distinction between duties/obligations on the one hand, and responsibilities based on expectations on the other, is generally accepted UN terminology; and that his use of the term "responsibility" in the Report refers to the moral obligations and social expectations – *not* binding law.' Weil, Gotshal & Manges LLP, 'Memorandum – Corporate Social responsibility for Human Rights: Comments on the UN Special Representative's Report Entitled "Protect, Respect and remedy: A framework for Business and Human Rights"' (22 May 2008), 2 (emphasis in original).

[87] E. Merrick Dodd, Jr, 'For Whom Are Corporate Managers Trustees?' (1932) 45, *Harvard Law Review*, 1145, 1151 (emphasis added).

[88] The OECD Guidelines, for example, provide that enterprises should '[c]ontribute to economic, social and environmental progress with a view to achieving sustainable development' and '[c]ontribute to the effective abolition of child labour'. OECD Guidelines, *supra* note 38, paras II.1 and IV.1(b).

[89] 'The complete fulfillment of each kind of rights involves the performance of multiple kinds of duties.' Shue, *supra* note 78, 52. Even regarding those rights which are labelled as 'negative', positive duties must be fulfilled: 'It is impossible for any basic right – however "negative" it has come to seem – to be fully guaranteed unless all three types of duties are fulfilled.' *Id.*, 53.

[90] '[T]he positive obligations on States Parties to ensure Covenant rights will only be fully discharged if individuals are protected by the State, not just against violations of Covenant rights by its agents, but also against acts committed by private persons or entities that would impair the enjoyment of Covenant rights in so far as they are amenable to application between private persons or entities.' Human Rights Committee, 'General Comment No. 31 on Article 2: The Nature of General Legal Obligation Imposed on States Parties to the Covenant', 26/05/2004, para 8. See also SRSG, 'The 2008 Report', *supra* note 2, para 18.

cannot we impose an obligation on a parent company to ensure that its de facto agents (subsidiaries, affiliates, contractors and suppliers) respect human rights obligations? In fact, if the responsibility of corporations is limited to respecting human rights, this might encourage them to contract out human rights abuses to their business partners and supply chain participants, over which they often exercise effective control but at the same time keep distance by design.

The fourth problem lies in how the responsibility to respect has been expanded to cover what goes beyond the generally understood meaning of 'respect'. Although the distinction between positive and negative rights may be illusory and misguided, a 'useful distinction', as Shue points out, among the following three duties correlative to rights does exist: (1) duties to *avoid* depriving, (2) duties to *protect* from deprivation, and (3) duties to *aid* the deprived.[91] It seems that the corporate responsibility to respect human rights will correspond to the first category. However, probably being aware of the limitations of the 'respect only approach' highlighted above, the SRSG tries to expand the ambit of responsibilities that respecting human right will entail. This the Report does with the help of concepts such as due diligence, sphere of influence, and complicity.[92] For instance, the 2008 Report mentions that 'where the company's activities or relationships are causing human rights harm... [this is] squarely within the responsibility to respect.'[93] So, if the entry of Wal-Mart in India will affect the right to livelihood of small retailers or farmers, Wal-Mart should probably help these poor people. If that is the case, such responsibilities are more akin to the third category (i.e., duties to aid the deprived) than the first category. The framework is thus not rooted in a clear/coherent duty typology vis-à-vis human rights.

Fifth, the SRSG's 2008 Report suggests that those corporations which perform certain 'public functions' may have additional responsibilities. It is not made clear what these additional responsibilities would be in such exceptional situations. More importantly, what is meant by public functions? A corporation managing a detention centre or a hospital might arguably be performing public functions. But what about a corporation selling milk which was found to contain melamine, or a corporation manufacturing AIDS drugs or carpets?

In short, the corporate responsibility to respect principle is not only inadequate but also presents several problems, which together undermine the usefulness of this principle.

---

[91] Shue, *supra* note 78, 35–46, 52.
[92] See SRSG, 'The 2008 Report', *supra* note 2, paras 56–58, 68–69, and 73–81.
[93] *Id.*, para 68.

4 Conclusion

The aim of this chapter was to examine critically the 2008 Report of the SRSG submitted to the HRC. I have tried to demonstrate that although the Report contains several useful suggestions, it still falls short of what is required to anchor an effective regulatory framework to make corporations accountable for human rights abuses. The three major lacunae of the Report are in particular notable. First, the Report's suggested approach to deal with an important but complex question – the precise human rights responsibilities of corporations – is flawed. It is crucial to identify these responsibilities in advance and with a reasonable certainty (so as to guide the behaviour of all concerned) rather than leaving these to be determined on a case-to-case basis with reference to a given principle. Second, one principle of the concept of 'differentiated but complementary responsibilities' (namely, the corporate responsibility to respect) is not only problematic but also inadequate to meet the societal expectations in the twenty-first century. Third, the conceptual and policy framework outlined in the Report lacks a theoretical foundation; it is critical to identify explicitly an appropriate theory which could underpin any such framework.

In my view, if the business and human rights project has to move forward to a decisive level, a broad consensus (if not agreement) among key stakeholders is necessary on the following issues: *why* corporations should have human rights responsibilities; *what* these responsibilities are, both in abstract and in practical terms; and *how* these responsibilities could be implemented and enforced. However, such a consensus could only be reached if not only states and international institutions but also business leaders and civil society show a strong will to rise above the myopic vision of acting to protect only their respective interests.

During the current mandate, the SRSG should aim to provide not only a concrete theoretical basis on which corporate human rights responsibilities (or perhaps obligations) could be grounded but also the framework to outline precise responsibilities of corporations which operate under vast differences in legal systems, socio-economic conditions, political environments, religions, and cultures. But most critically, the SRSG should aim to propose a clear mechanism to implement and enforce the human rights obligations. The proposed mechanism should encompass multiple regulatory tools and techniques: from voluntary to self-regulatory, non-voluntary, and obligatory. An explicit attempt should also be made to manage societal expectations, for at this point of time we should not expect corporations to deliver everything that we expect from states.

It is also important that principles or underlying objectives are not lost in a desire to achieve consensus. Similarly, it is critical that the above issues should not be settled by the likes or dislikes of corporations (or even

NGOs),[94] but by what would ensure an effective remedy to the victims of corporate human rights abuses. Otherwise, the SRSG would disappoint not only victims but also himself by coming up with another un-enforced or empty declaration. The human rights discourse has not been merely about what was 'politically feasible'[95] at any given point of time but also about what ought to be feasible in the near future.[96]

---

[94] 'Business typically dislikes binding regulations until it sees their necessity or inevitability.' Ruggie, 'Business and Human Rights', *supra* note 36, 822.
[95] Misereor & GPF, 'Problematic Pragmatism', *supra* note 33, 2.
[96] Professor Ruggie asked the question: 'what purpose would be served by making recommendations that are not feasible?' John Ruggie, 'Response to Misereor/GPF' (2 June 2008).

Part II
Regional Perspectives

5
Corporate Social Responsibility in Africa: A Fig Leaf or a New Development Path Worth Pursuing?

Wambui Kimathi

1 Introduction

The discourse of business and human rights is almost absent in Africa while that of corporate social responsibility (CSR) is still largely undocumented, though practised by a few businesses in most of sub Saharan Africa. South Africa may be an exception in relation to the latter. This is perhaps explained by the fact that CSR initiatives are largely seen as an undertaking solely driven by business as and when it chooses to rather than as a framework through which business organizes and takes responsibility for its negative impact on society.

This exclusive drive of CSR by business has left most of its initiatives sitting precariously on a one-legged stool rather than on a solid three-legged one that should include the state and community. This chapter makes the case that moving the conversation of CSR progressively towards assuming a human rights framework will provide the anchorage that it needs to take greater responsibility in society only if the other two 'legs' are built into its infrastructure. The chapter therefore explores the links between greater business responsibility and poverty reduction as a pathway towards greater realization of human rights. It argues that an African-based National Human Rights Institution (NHRI) can only gain legitimacy by taking on rights protection initiatives that make a real difference in the lives of millions of Africans who live in dire poverty. It further argues that the debates on business and human rights and its predecessor, corporate social responsibility, must be used to ensure that commercial and societal concerns are not separated but rather 're-embedded' in any discussions of sustainable economic development.

Using examples from Kenya, this chapter seeks to answer the following questions: What is unique in the African context that calls for a different kind of business conduct? Why is the responsible business seen as a new pathway for enhanced delivery of public policy goals and priorities? And finally, what can be done to enhance committed uptake by business of the responsibility to respect human rights?

The arguments in the chapter are consequently predicated on the understanding that an African National Human Rights Institution must make its contributions as a national protection mechanism by redefining rights from the mostly abstract and aspirational goals of the various human rights conventions to meaningful, relevant actions within a context that is largely shaped by poverty and related deprivations. This redefinition finds a home in the one human rights declaration that captures the uniqueness of developing countries – the UN Declaration on the Right to Development. Article 2 of the Declaration states that the human person must be the 'central subject of development' and that human beings should be the 'active participants and beneficiaries of the right to development' and calls on states to ensure citizens' 'active, free and meaningful participation'. Inevitably then, development initiatives that business claims to undertake through CSR become intrinsically tied to poverty reduction and sustainable development and must therefore be audited for their ability to make the human person the central subject.

It is, however, not the focus of this chapter to go into the detail of the relationship between human rights, poverty and sustainable development.[1] It will suffice here to point out that the legitimacy of human rights work in a poor African country lies in its ability to strengthen people's capabilities to reduce their vulnerabilities and the various 'unfreedoms' that they confront every day. Secondly, in making the case for the re-embedding of commercial and societal concerns through initiatives undertaken by business either through their corporate social responsibility work or, for those that have moved further, in their business and human rights initiatives, the chapter avoids giving any firm definitions of what each of these concepts means but rather expects the chapter's understanding to emerge from the arguments made. However, the arguments made by the Special Representative of the Secretary General (SRSG) on the issue of human rights and transnational corporations and other business enterprises in his recent report to the Human Rights Council, especially his explicit call for NHRIs to pay attention to this

---

[1] For a detailed discussion of this relationship, see 'Human Rights and Poverty Reduction, A Conceptual Framework, United Nations, New York, 2004' at www.ohchr.org/Documents/Publications/PovertyReductionen.pdf accessed on 1 February 2010.

agenda, have informed my proposals on what future work could look like in Kenya.

The fig leaf analogy from which the chapter draws its title seeks to communicate the inadequacy of CSR initiatives that are one-legged – exclusively driven by business – though it also acknowledges the many extremely helpful actions that some businesses have taken through such programmes but which could be improved through making human rights a strong/visible component of such programmes.

It concludes by asserting that by assuming a human rights focus CSR will provide a lot more value to both business and society. This holds great promise for poverty reduction generally and greater protection for human rights specifically, in Kenya and Africa at large.

2 The footprint of CSR in Kenya

Throughout the 1990s most of Africa, Kenya included, went through political transitions that saw the opening up of space for greater freedom of expression and citizens' participation in public affairs. (By the end of that decade, according to Bratton and de Walle, only four countries in sub-Saharan Africa had not held competitive elections.) There were more avenues through which citizens could demand accountability from their governments without excessive fear of retribution. The avenues through which official information and in fact all types of information could be accessed grew in leaps and bounds. Today more people are accessing the internet; cellular phone penetration has grown tremendously as have FM radio stations. Most of Africa has therefore moved from a shortage of information to an overload of it. These happenings are important to note because the lessons derived from this experience by civil society actors from their success in pushing out dictatorships provided the rhythm, the tools and organizing principles that they began using in respect of corporate actors. The history of human rights activism shows that it seeks to challenge existing structures of power wherever they are. It was only a matter of time before such activism was turned on business. In Kenya, the 'splendid isolation' enjoyed by business became a source of attention at the close of the 1990s when the Kenya Human Right Commission's (KHRC) campaign on Del Monte led the 'intrusion' into this isolation.[2] The outcomes of this campaign

---

[2] Between 1999 and 2002, the Kenya Human Rights Commission, an NGO that had been active since the early days of the fight for multipartism in Kenya, led eight other organizations in a campaign that it dubbed 'the struggle for workers' rights at Del Monte Kenya'. For details of this campaign see, KHRC (2002): *Exposing the Soft Belly of the Multinational Beast, the Struggle for Workers' Rights at Del Monte Kenya*.

could be said to have set the tone for several others which included one on workers' rights on flower farms especially in the Rift Valley province, the Export Processing Zones (EPZ), and Tiomin Kenya Limited's titanium mining in Kenya's Coast province.[3]

It is therefore no coincidence that in the same period CSR initiatives by different businesses across all sectors grew, signalling a welcome desire on the part of such companies to acknowledge that they have some responsibility to society. According to a report by the Private Sector Initiative for Corporate Governance, a 1998 workshop by stakeholders in various corporate professional bodies gave rise, unintentionally, to what would develop into what the report describes as 'a major initiative on corporate governance'.[4] Additionally, governance gaps in the corporate sector and especially in state enterprises continued to attract NGOs as the consequences of such gaps began to weigh heavily on individuals and communities.[5] At the close of the 1990s, there were corporate initiatives giving awards aimed at recognizing CSR performance. These include the Kenya Institute of Management (KIM) Company of the Year Award (COYA), which began in 1999 and which has CSR as a key parameter, Financial Reporting Award (FIRE) started in 2002 by the Institute of Certified Public Accountants of Kenya (ICPAK) and joined in 2003 by the Capital Markets Authority (CMA) and Nairobi Stock Exchange (NSE), which also measures a company's CSR work. In 2009 the two attracted a combined total of over 120 businesses including public enterprises and parastatals in Kenya.[6]

---

[3] Tiomin Kenya Limited is a subsidiary of Canada's Tiomin Resources Inc. Its mining interests in Kwale District in Kenya have had many ups and downs since 1999. It has become an example of how failure by a corporation to respect human rights and government to protect human rights can become extremely expensive for all involved. Resistance by Kwale people, human rights groups and environmentalists has ensured that work on the ground has not taken off to date for this $25m project. For recent developments on this project see www.ccr-kenya.com/resources/117.html.

[4] This workshop took place in 1998 and focused on 'The Role of Non-Executive Directors'. It was sponsored by actors such as the Nairobi Stock Exchange (NSE), Capital Markets Authority (CMA), Institute of Certified Public Accountants (ICPAK) and the Kenya Chapter of the Association of Chartered Certified Accountants (ACCA). A subsequent meeting saw the generation of what is probably Kenya's premier document on corporate governance. It was named *Principles for Corporate Governance in Kenya and a Sample Code of Best Practice for Corporate Governance*.

[5] Several state enterprises collapsed alongside other state functions in the 1980s and 1990s (including Kenya Cooperative Creameries, Kenya Meat Commission, Kenya National Assurance occasioning job loss, market infrastructure for milk, livestock and insurance services) enabling ordinary Kenyans to make the connections between bad state governance and misgovernance elsewhere. Demands for good governance therefore cut across state and non-state players.

[6] The KNCHR participates in COYA.

A close look at the CSR programmes covered by several businesses is impressive at a glance. They range from digging boreholes, building hospitals, schools, environment related activities, paying school fees for the needy and supporting vulnerable groups such as persons with disabilities, to charitable deeds such as rebuilding school roofs damaged by winds. The more sophisticated and economically powerful companies have in the recent past set up foundations that accept funding proposals from communities across Kenya.[7] While there has been no uniform Africa-wide approach to corporate social responsibility, the poverty context of the majority of sub-Saharan Africa provides an insight into the triggers of social engagement for most of the companies operating there. Corporations operating in Africa have got involved in building schools and hospitals, launching micro-credit schemes and assisting youth employment programmes. Frynas therefore argues that CSR in the African context has largely been seen from the community issues angle and is consequently more of a reflection of a 'grassroots' African understanding of CSR.[8]

This is hardly surprising. The UN Declaration on the Right to Development, which was largely driven by developing countries following frustrations at the inability of development cooperation to eliminate poverty both through aid and trade, opened a new official front from which developing countries could articulate their development agenda in a human rights language. In its Article II, the Declaration places the human person as 'the central subject of development' and goes on to add that human beings should be 'active participants and beneficiaries of the right to development.' Partially in response to pressure from such initiatives and in pursuit of enlightened self-interest, several corporations have sought to play a role in activities that easily fit the billing of development initiatives. Indeed, such initiatives, if well harnessed, have great potential to make positive contributions to the lives of poor communities deserving of such programmes.

Not unexpectedly though, participation by business in activities that are of service to poor communities has generated increased expectations from the public which, as we shall demonstrate, have assumed a tone of entitlement exposing the inadequacy of the fig leaf of CSR.

However, CSR programmes by business are still the exception rather than the rule. There is no public policy or legislation articulating the place and need for such participation by business. A lot of what is being done falls

---

[7] See, for example, East African Breweries Foundation, Safaricom Foundation, Kenya Commercial Bank Group Foundation etc.
[8] *Ibid*. Quoting research on CSR by the World Business Council on Sustainable Development, Frynas reports that some Ghanaians said they expected business to 'fill in when government falls short'. In the African context this would be most of the time!

largely in the realm of 'should do' initiatives that are informed by traditional benefits of philanthropy. Not much is in the realm of 'ought to do' which would reflect a level of CSR initiatives that are norm-driven. Important documents such as the Companies Act, the Capital Markets Authority Guidelines for Listed Companies and the Central Bank's Prudential Guidelines for institutions licensed under the Banking Act are all silent on what obligations companies might have in relation to CSR. This lacuna is further exacerbated by the fact that over 80 per cent of business in Kenya is made up of small and medium enterprises (SMEs), often in the informal sector and whose context and character of operations lie in a totally different world compared to that of the bigger, often multi-national companies. It is in this world of SMEs that the real building blocks of Social Responsibility and greater responsibility for human rights by business in an African context can be found if the practice is to go beyond a few multinationals. By their very nature, they are located everywhere, usually in their owners' home communities, which gives them greater appreciation and understanding of local contexts and people. Their responsibility to society is expressed in ways that unfortunately have not been studied but which have given such business almost permanent licences to operate. In fact, it is this failure to historicize and contextualize norms and ethical practices underlying the philosophy of CSR that have left its practice looking contrived and largely a preoccupation of the big players who undertake such programmes for reasons that are often unclear to the intended beneficiaries.

2.1 The case of an 'African cultural fingerprint' on CSR

The argument here is that while there are global principles and norms that anchor CSR, each context in which CSR programmes are implemented must take into consideration not only the infrastructure of delivery but, most importantly, the very DNA of the programmes or what Makau Mutua has labelled, in discussing the conception of human rights in Africa, 'the African cultural fingerprint'.[9] When the African Human and People's Charter, unlike the other regional human rights instruments (European Convention for the

---

[9] See Makau Wa Mutua: *The Banjul Charter and the African Cultural Fingerprint: An Evaluation of the Language of Duties* at Makau persuasively argues that the African language of duty by the individual to society '[was] an opportunity for society to contemplate the complex web of individuals and community duties and rights to seek a balance between competing claims of the individual and society'. http://docs.google.com/viewer?a=v&q=cache:G5jNy-PFoigJ:www.kentlaw.edu/faculty/bbrown/classes/HumanRightsSP10/CourseDocs/9BanjulCharterandtheAfricanCulturalFingerprint.pdf+banjul+charter+and+the+african+cultural+fingerprint&hl=en&gl=ke&pid=bl&srcid=ADGEEShAv1z90YEEtC-LJCCKIs3vKRR5HjmPjSEPxk8oz_3ueNzXVGS4n1i NNPfXCzpR2T-7Sf0PmDFFaPrDLak9KjnSW6Xpqae18HCDtCIT8yz5bt1XUKOVE6Jr EtfCLDwBxJNHgqQB&sig=AHIEtbTIvUQ9LLeg0SR59RSBFJfZUUOgPQ.

Protection of Human Rights and Fundamental Freedoms, the American Convention on Human Rights), includes a whole section on individual duties to society, it is an acknowledgment of the underlying philosophy of African societies' conception of the role of the individual in society. To the extent that a significant number of businesses in Africa are small, run by individuals, groups and families, any attempt at ensuring that business organizations take greater responsibility for human rights must take into consideration this unique conception of duties to society.

In the rural areas, for example, small enterprises fill important gaps by offering crucial services as a matter of course rather than as an occasional show of generosity. The local shops, for example, offer credit facilities on the basis of social relationships and in recognition of the reality of the local economy that understands that farmers are paid at the end of the month; some are also 'obligated' to provide free use of their facilities by whole communities; for example, before cellular phone technology permeated most rural areas in Kenya, the rural shop with a landline served as the community's message centre where relatives living away in urban areas would call and leave messages for onward transmission to their village relatives. The letter box was a shared facility as was the ubiquitous Matatu (Taxi), whose owner would be expected to take expectant mothers and the sick to hospital at night. Without glorifying actions that may be rooted more in relative poverty than in social responsibility, there is no doubt that expectation of good neighbourliness is understood clearly between owners of small businesses and their host communities. In this kind of set-up there is little differentiation between business and society. And herein lies the mindset that has defined the business conduct expected and approved of by a majority of people in poor developing countries – meeting unstated expectations that exhibit concern and solidarity with community and which are in consonance with individuals' real needs. Communities expect that business will, without coaxing, conform to such socially expected and approved of conduct. To the extent that most CSR programmes are not seen in this way, they remain a mere fig leaf, satisfying limited needs which are seen as alien and likely to receive expressions of disapproval at the first instance of disagreement between a business and its host community.[10] These examples

---

[10] In one instance where the KNCHR investigated complaints against a salt manufacturing company, the company enumerated the things it had done for the local community, arguing that the community should be grateful rather than seek to bring it to disrepute. The company pointed at the beautiful school they had constructed but which they had named after one of the company's directors. The community rejected this choice of name and with it the gesture. One community leader described this initiative as a 'hoodwink' which aimed at entrenching the company's family in the community on the pretext of serving the community – though they really needed the school.

demonstrate that in the African context, commercial and societal concerns are not separated but rather integrally related. This is what this chapter is calling for in the ongoing debates on business and human rights and corporate social responsibility. Re-embedding CSR initiatives and business responsibilities for human rights in the sustainable development discourse requires that business removes the artificiality of such initiatives by ensuring that there is a clear interlocking relationship between the interests of the business and those of the intended beneficiaries. The more interlocked the interests are, the greater the level of acceptance, support and sustainability for such initiatives.

This is probably not unique. In Ogoniland in Nigeria, Shell was seen as a 'de facto development agency' that should have been delivering on the development expectation of the Ogoni. Likewise, the millennium poll on corporate sustainability conducted in 1999 found that in the West, two in three people want business to go beyond its traditional role of focusing on only its bottom line and obeying laws (Joana, A.Z.). In my view, assuming responsibility for human rights by business would benefit greatly from this understanding of what communities expect by among other things ensuring their participation is real and meaningful, that they have the information they need, the space, the forums and can express dissent notwithstanding the power asymmetry between themselves and the powerful business actors.

On many occasions, the Kenya National Commission on Human Rights (KNCHR) has received complaints from communities that were mostly expressing resentment of business arising out of what is seen as arrogance, failure to recognize that there is a duty of care expected, or simply that a company did not communicate to members in a way that made them feel they 'belonged together'. On the one hand where such resentment exists, it is highly unlikely that a corporation and the community can enter into genuine dialogue unless some key sources of a community's grievances are first dealt with. On the other, simple gestures can forge a productive and lasting relationship. In one example given by Magadi Soda,[11] the fact that they never fenced off the company premises from the larger grazing land was interpreted by the local Maasai community as a good gesture signifying openness. Further, by having a team representing members of the community during corporate planning exercises, Magadi Soda has been able to integrate its CSR initiatives with the community's expectations but more importantly too with the larger development plan of their region

---

[11] Magadi Soda is the biggest soda ash exporter in Africa and is located in Maasailand 60 kilometres south-west of Nairobi.

of operation.[12] This kind of community involvement, especially in the extractive industry, constitutes a big step towards building-in aspects of empowerment, participation and accountability: all critical principles exemplifying a human rights aware approach which also puts the human person at the centre of such activities.

This kind of complementarity between a company's corporate plan, communities' expectations and national/regional plans provides useful synergy for development. Taking on initiatives that exist independently of national/regional plans undermines the effectiveness of such initiatives where business responsibility is understood, as it is in developing countries, to include actions that contribute to sustainable development. Unfortunately, a review of the call for proposal guidelines for funding by some of Kenya's leading businesses, Safaricom, East African Breweries and Kenya Commercial Bank, shows that these guidelines do not require projects seeking funding to demonstrate how their projects fit in with their regions' development programmes.[13] This risks generating stand-alone projects that are likely to have not only limited impact but also limited complementarity with other local programmes.

Where gaps in this understanding exist, business-society relations remain tenuous. It is the view of this chapter that using a human rights framework will stand business in good stead in terms of cultivating better understanding between business and society. Because of its emphasis on both normative and process principles such as participation, non-discrimination, accountability and empowerment of individuals and communities while undertaking development related work, often ignored by other development approaches (see Table 5.1), paying attention to the human rights framework works better at enabling its users to build sustainable relationships with other actors. Clearly then, the insights described in the foregoing paragraph will most likely emerge where business desists from grafting one-size-fits-all CSR 'solutions' and grow such 'solutions' by putting human rights concerns at the centre of business management. Putting human rights concerns at the centre may mean taking on initiatives that are not solely investor-driven as is the case in most CSR initiatives.

3 Making business work for sustainable development

Poverty in Africa remains the biggest affront to the enjoyment of human rights. With 46 per cent of Kenyans living on the so called 'below poverty

---

[12] For more details on Magadi Soda's CSR programme see *Nguzo za Haki* (Pillars of Rights), No. 2, September 2004 by the Kenya National Commission on Human Rights.
[13] See such guidelines: www.safaricomfoundation.org, www.eabl.com/foundation/eabl_funding.htm and www.kcbbankgroup.com.

Table 5.1 Development approaches compared

Principles/Features	Good governance	Sustainable development	Gender analysis	Capabilities	Human rights
Participation	✓	✓	✓	✓	✓
Non discrimination	✓		✓	*	✓
Accountability	✓				✓
Rule of law	✓	*	*		✓
Transparency/access to information	✓				✓ *
Prioritizes poverty	✓	✓	*	✓	*
Empowerment	✓		✓	✓	✓
Availability		*		*	✓
Accessibility		*		✓	✓
Acceptability			✓		✓
Adaptability			✓		✓
Legally binding framework					✓
Effective remedy					✓
Entitlement					✓
Indivisibility					✓
Recognizes future generations' claims		✓	*		*
Capacity building		✓	✓	✓	
Institutional efficiency	✓				
Basic needs and services		✓	✓	*	✓

Source: Table adapted from 'Local Government and Human Rights: Doing Good Service' 2005, p 26.[14]
✓ denotes explicit recognition   * denotes implicit recognition.

line' poverty reduction becomes a core human rights concern. In its blueprint for development over the next 20 years, dubbed Vision 2030, the Kenyan government makes this point by identifying enhanced equity and wealth creation as a crucial foundation for this Vision. It notes that 'no society can gain social cohesion predicted by Vision 2030 if significant sections of the population live in abject poverty'. This nexus between human rights and development and the promise it heralds is a key cornerstone for the human rights based approach which this chapter recommends for making business work for sustainable development. As an ODI Briefing Paper puts it:

---

[14] While this table is useful in helping understand the value adding aspects of the human rights approach (it pays attention to some values and principles that other approaches don't) its authors make no claim to any science in determining which principles and features are recognized by which approach.

A rights-based approach to development sets the achievement of human rights as an objective of development. It uses thinking about human rights as the scaffolding of development policy. It invokes the international apparatus of human rights accountability in support of development action.

(ODI Briefing paper, 1999 (3) September)

Economic growth that puts people at the centre is therefore a necessary condition for enhanced protection of human rights. Since business activities impact on a range of development and therefore human rights issues, business responsibility for human rights must inevitably be expected to concern itself with managing such impacts in ways that reduce possible harm while enhancing the positive impacts.

The dimensions of responsible business practices in a developing country must therefore contribute to outcomes that empower **people, enhance accountability, provide avenues for participation, promote non-discrimination and engage in business conduct that is ethical**. However, given that the business environment in poor countries is characterized by such governance deficits as weak accountability, weak/poor provision of basic public services, weak law enforcement and poor protection of human rights, it is clear that business in Africa faces acute structural constraints. This environment presents unique challenges for business keen on undertaking meaningful CSR work. For CSR to work effectively, it has been argued that a level playing field must exist to enable the market to reward higher standards.[15] To pursue this, one would expect that CSR programmes in developing countries would address and invest in crucial issues of governance. Where this is not the case, unscrupulous organizations are happy to take advantage of governance deficits, hence disincentivizing businesses that would otherwise engage in socially responsible practices. This in effect has continued to undermine the macro-environment in which meaningful CSR initiatives would have been undertaken.

While a number of CSR programmes show credible attempts at acting in socially responsible ways, none of the main actors that this chapter examined had, for example, programmes focusing on improving the general governance framework in the country. Disappointingly too, none had accountability mechanisms that enabled their stakeholders to seek redress in case of harm or even mechanisms through which stakeholders could access information on the various activities by such corporations and their possible effects on them, or even guidelines about how beneficiaries might participate in such programmes. The website of the Kenya Commercial Bank,

---

[15] Fox, T., Ward, H. & Howard, B. 2002. Public Sector Roles in Strengthening Corporate Social Responsibility, Private Sector Advisory Services, The World Bank.

winner of the COYA 2008 Corporate Citizenship Practices Award, has no information regarding the dimensions mentioned above while the tool used to review this area looks at the conventional dimensions of statutory compliance, policy/guidelines on CSR, budgets on CSR, Employees involvement, Evaluation on CSR projects and Business associations.[16]

The foregoing typifies the spread of the fig leaf of CSR in Kenya and points at the direction that human rights groups including the KNCHR have to take to visibilize human rights concerns in business conduct. The willingness exhibited by businesses participating in such awards could be harnessed to reflect human rights concerns in their work. While a commendable 30 businesses have signed up to the UN Global Compact which launched a chapter in Kenya in February 2007, the network's 2007 Annual Report indicates that 'the Global Compact Kenya Network (GNKN) lacks a comprehensive strategic direction and membership strategy'.[17]

4 Conclusion

To give CSR the much needed nudge forward, some meaningful actions are necessary. As Ruggie aptly put it: 'the last thing victims need is more unenforced declarations; they need effective Action';[18] which is why a human rights approach to how businesses manage their responsibilities for human rights holds the greatest promise that CSR can morph into a force for sustainable development particularly in developing countries. This approach, which is a comprehensive conceptual and methodological framework, uses principles, tools and a legal frame which, if deployed appropriately, has great potential in addressing governance gaps and development challenges that most developing countries face. Its organizing principles bring together the key actors for effective action – the state, business and citizens – and specify obligations and responsibilities.

4.1 Taking their place: National Human Rights Institutions as critical actors

National Human Rights Institutions, a creature of international human rights efforts, serve as their country's foremost human rights protection and complaints mechanisms. Most have their country's constitutional mandate to act as interlocutor on all matters of human rights. In Africa, the first

---

[16] See www.kism.or.ke/coya-assessment-areas.php for more information on this Award.
[17] See http://www.unglobalcompact.org/docs/networks_around_world_doc/Annual_Reports_2007/Kenya_Annual_Activity_Report_2007.pdf.
[18] See the full statement of Professor John Ruggie: Opening Statement to the UN Council on Human Rights, 25 September 2006 at http://198.170.85.29/Ruggie-statement-to-UN-Human-Rights-Council-25-Sep-2006.pdf.

such body was established in 1989 in Togo. Since then, they have grown to 30 with a majority of them being accredited with 'A' status by the International Coordination Committee of NHRIs (ICC) of the Office of High Commissioner for Human Rights.[19] In each of the countries where they exist, NHRIs play a pivotal role in anchoring and nurturing emerging human rights issues.

For KNCHR, the constitutive Act, the Kenya National Commission on Human Rights Act 2002, gives it expansive functions under Section 16 including the mandate to investigate all complaints on human rights abuses by any person or group (Sec. 16 1(a)), and to act as the chief agent of the compliance with its (government's) obligations under international treaties and conventions on human rights Sec. 16 1(f). Importantly, under Sec. 19 the Commission is also given the powers of court while in Sec. 22 it has power to hold inquiries into complaints and recommend redress for human rights violations. The infrastructure for providing effective action to victims that lodge complaints with such bodies or for initiating investigations in areas of choice does therefore exist. At KNCHR, work on business and human rights has largely been complaints driven – working on issues ranging from conditions of labour to systemic abuses of rights by business. Finding what constitutes effective action and ensuring that action is taken by whomever it is directed to will be the challenge all NHRIs will face as they seek to operationalize the *Protect, Respect, Remedy* framework.

The SRSG framework with its three key principles of State duty to protect, the corporate responsibility to respect and the need for effective access to remedy is bound to provide a lot of clarity, helping NHRIs to move forward in terms of overcoming the challenges ahead. However, understanding our particular country contexts and that in which different businesses operate will go a long way in determining and shaping the uptake of business responsibility for human rights. Businesses are embedded in political and economic institutions that influence their conduct. To this extent their conduct will probably be as good as their country's other institutions. Where institutions of governance are weak, where respect for the rule of law is wanting and monitoring the conduct of business is still incipient, a lot more work to bring business around will have to be done. This is given credence by a report by the SRSG in 2006 which found that an exceptionally high number of abuses were in low income countries. The report says all but two of those countries fell below the global average of the 'rule of law' index by the World Bank.

Also, the strong presence of what SRSG describes as 'vertical' incoherence – governments taking on human rights commitments without regard to

---

[19] See Chart of the Status of National Institutions as of January, 2010 at www.nhri.net accessed on 30 January 2010.

implementation and 'horizontal' incoherence, where departments work at cross purposes with the State's obligations on human rights, constitute another great challenge to NHRIs in this journey. In developing countries like Kenya this will be compounded by the predominance of informal businesses whose logic of operation is woven around their characteristic ease of entry, unregulated existence, small scale operation among other characteristics all of which make them unsusceptible to formal systems such as are called for in making effective their responsibility to respect human rights. Yet they constitute the majority of businesses and are a key avenue to the achievement of the Millennium Development Goals (MDGs) and Kenya's Vision 2030, which aims at transforming the country into a middle income country. How does the government, for example, ensure that small butchery owners employing hundreds of workers comply with environmental rules relating to disposal of refuse when it has itself not provided basic sanitation infrastructure in their areas of operation?

For developing countries, this will remain a hugely vexed question for the foreseeable future. Given the limited resources of SMEs, their ubiquity and need for survival away from the strict formal demands of law, the bigger corporate players and governments will have to focus their CSR and public policy initiatives on activities aimed at helping incubate SMEs to levels where they reach the threshold of legal compliance. In the absence of this, the discourse of CSR is likely to remain an inadequate cover on the body of social responsibility.

Encouragingly though, the building blocks for moving towards the new pathway for development through supporting businesses to exercise their responsibility for respecting human rights in Kenya are demonstrably present and provide invaluable entry points for beginning this work. Vision 2030 has clear programmes on growing small business and providing supportive infrastructure for the informal sector; the Global Compact Kenya Network is another opening. Because of the requirement of membership to report on progress, it is expected that members will undertake some activities to comply. Partnership with KNCHR in this regard will perhaps find expression.

Ensuring that business takes responsibility to respect human rights is, however, unlikely to be easy; where business has paid attention it has mostly been as a result of public exposure following complaints by individuals or communities. The SRSG has himself observed that business 'typically dislikes binding regulations until it sees their necessity or inevitability'. NHRIs everywhere must make this inevitability real by encouraging and working with businesses that have modelled their operations on avoiding compliance to meet acceptable minimum standards.

In Kenya the draft Companies Bill will be a powerful starting point where clear provisions that can regulate business behaviour in line with human rights standards must be reflected. The second and more important point is to study the informal sector, which is clearly Kenya's economic driver, with a view to understanding how, at that level, human rights standards can be respected in a way that supports rather than undermines this sector's unique competitive edge.

Coupled with this, NHRIs could also use their advisory responsibility to encourage parastatals and state enterprises to embrace social responsibility that is human rights aware as well as ensuring that meaningful incentives are provided to both the big and small business organizations which take up initiatives that complement development priorities spelt out in national development plans.

Finally for Kenya and probably other African countries, deliberate policies spelling out proactive actions supportive of initiatives that will help small and medium-sized businesses respect their human rights responsibilities must be prioritized. Such policies could include encouraging big business to develop supply chain linkages with SMEs in a way that builds the capacity of the latter to progressively take up their human rights responsibilities in a sustainable manner.

6
It's Our Business: Ensuring Inclusiveness in the Process of Regulating and Enforcing Corporate Social Responsibility

Chris Sidoti

1 Introduction

In the best of times business fails to do as much as it could to promote human rights. In the worst of times the harm it will cause human rights can be profound. The global financial crisis is an important time to consider the responsibilities of business for human rights, for human rights responsibilities are in danger of slipping well down the corporate and political agenda.

The global financial crisis is also a most opportune time for this discussion. Whatever analysis economists may develop of this crisis once it is over, some things are clear to most people now. Economic rationalism, the dominant ideology of the past 25 years, has been shown to be irrational. Faith in the free market has been found to be mere superstition. Pure capitalism has failed not only the test of equity but even the test of efficiency. As a result, at last, values can be discussed; values-based ideology, values-based economics and values-based politics. The values that need to be revived and re-inserted into economic and political discourse and decisions are human rights. People can again be the focus of political and economic debate, people-centred business and people-centred law, the human rights of people and the responsibilities of all social and economic entities, including businesses, for human rights. These are the foci of this chapter.

2 The situation of business and human rights

The starting point is not a legal or economic text but the situation of people on the ground. Many factors affect the lives and well-being of ordinary people – weather, families, police, governments, communications system, infrastructure, and so on – but few factors are as influential as business.

Indeed, in a world of interdependence and interconnections, business has an impact directly and through almost all the other factors that affect people.

Business is big. Not all businesses are big businesses, but business as a whole is big. In his interim report in 2006 to the United National Human Rights Council, the Special Representative of the Secretary General on Business and Human Rights, Professor John Ruggie, said that there were '70,000 transnational firms, together with roughly 700,000 subsidiaries and millions of suppliers, spanning every corner of the globe'.[1] Professor Ruggie was speaking of globalization but business is more than globalization. In addition to transnational business, there is national and local business. The total number of business entities must be thousands or even millions of times Professor Ruggie's numbers. In September 2008, in Australia alone, merely the 18th largest economy in the world, there were more than 1.6 million registered corporations.[2] All businesses – large and small, national and transnational – affect human rights for better or worse.

There are many different analytical frameworks to examine the role of business in relation to human rights. This chapter presents examples of my experiences within the framework of aid, investment and trade.[3] By aid, I mean the involvement of private business in the delivery of official and unofficial development assistance. By investment, I mean both financial investment, by way of equity or loan, in another enterprise or business and direct investment in production and trade. By trade, I mean the business of buying and selling goods and services. In each of these three areas, business has the potential to support or undermine the enjoyment of human rights. Let me describe a few of my experiences over the decades.

2.1 Business, aid and human rights

During the early 1980s, the Australian Catholic Commission for Justice and Peace, for which I was working, undertook research into an Australian Government aid project in the Northern Samar province of the Philippines. The project involved the construction of a major road network by an Australian engineering company. Northern Samar was then one of the poorest provinces in the Philippines (and still is). It was an area of intense military activity by the Philippine army and the New People's Army. Grave human

---

[1] J. Ruggie, *Interim Report of the Special Representative of the Secretary-General on the Issue of Human Rights and Transnational Corporations and Other Business Enterprises*, UN Doc. E/CN.4/2006/97 (2006) para. 11.
[2] Australian Securities and Investment Commission at www.asic.gov.au/asic/asic.nsf/byheadline/2008+company+registration+statistics?openDocument.
[3] Professor David Kinley provides an analysis of globalization and human rights in terms of trade, aid and commerce (*Civilising Globalisation: Human Rights and the Global Economy*, Cambridge: Cambridge University Press, 2009). I owe my own triptych to his analysis. Needless to say, he is not responsible for how I interpret and apply it.

rights violations – extra-judicial execution, torture, rape, assault, arbitrary detention – were frequent occurrences. The interior of the province was heavily forested. It was accessible only by water, along one of the major rivers flowing north into the sea. Travelling into the interior by river, as I did on one occasion, was a long, slow journey made dangerous by the activities of the military and the insurgents.

The roads were being constructed, it was said, to open up the interior of the province so that local farmers could send their produce to market. There was some doubt about this rationale. Local farmers in fact produced little surplus and what surplus they did produce was required locally and so was easily sold in local markets. Indeed, had the small local surpluses been exported, the local population would have experienced a significant food shortage. One thing that was clear was that construction of the roads required the compulsory acquisition of fertile land. The landowners were compensated, of course, but the farmers who worked the land were not.

Whether or not the opening of markets for local farmers was the real reason for the project, the fact was that the roads would have two other uses. They were also to be used to enable large-scale logging of the heavily forested interior. This was the period of the Marcos Dictatorship, during which corruption was even worse than it is today in the Philippines. The forestry concession in Northern Samar was owned by a senior government official and he stood to profit handsomely if his logs could be transported out of the province quickly and easily by road rather than being floated down the river. The roads would also be used to assist military deployment in the province. In particular they would enable the military to access the remote areas where the insurgents were strongest (and where, no doubt coincidentally, the official's forest was located).

The Australian company contracted to build the roads had both expatriate and local staff working and living on the ground in Northern Samar. They received military protection and indeed regularly entertained military personnel in their compound. They knew about the logging operations and about the military use of the roads as they were built.

The research on this project was undertaken with and by local people in the province. They knew what was happening, what the military and the insurgents were doing, what impacts the new roads were having on them and their lives. The role of the Australian organization was the analysis of their research and its presentation to the Australian community and government. The role enabled the perspectives of those most affected to be heard in the debate on the worth or otherwise of the project itself.

The study had a significant influence in Australia. It led to changes in Australian aid policy and practice, including a movement away from large infrastructure projects in militarily sensitive areas. It also led to further research and debate on what later became known internationally as the human rights based approach to development, well before there was widespread international interest in the issue.[4]

How are the company's responsibilities in this project to be assessed? There was no doubt that the project was accompanied by human rights violations and led directly to human rights violations, although there was no evidence that the company itself or its employees were directly engaged in violations. The project had been approved by the government of the host country, admittedly at the time a military dictatorship, and funded by the government of the company's home country. But the project had not been discussed with, or approved by, the local people who would be affected by it. Their views had never been sought and then, when expressed, they were ignored.

This experience demonstrates the complicated relationship between business and aid. Aid is delivered under bilateral or multilateral arrangements that require the approval of the recipient state and one or more donor states or intergovernmental organizations. When they are all involved and happy, why should business be concerned about human rights? Because human rights violations can still occur. In fact, neither the recipient state nor the donor state or intergovernmental organization may have any interest in dealing with violations because they are the ones that have approved the project and are responsible for implementing it. States have the legal obligations under international law but they may fail to perform them. Business becomes complicit through its involvement in the project.

2.2 Business, investment and human rights

Between 1989 and 2008 Australian Governments imposed mandatory detention on asylum seekers who came to Australia as boat people. Under these policies, now thankfully changed by the government elected at the end of 2007, boat people coming to Australia to seek asylum were detained in remote centres until they were granted asylum or deported. Men, women and children were detained in their thousands for periods of up to seven years in conditions far worse than in most Australian prisons. Through visits to these centres, the Australian Human Rights Commission was able to allow the voices of the detainees to be heard. They were shut away from public view and media oversight, deprived of any means other than the Human Rights Commission to tell their stories.

---

[4] Human Rights Council of Australia, *The Rights Way to Development: A Human Rights Approach to Development Assistance* (1995) and *The Rights Way to Development: A Manual for a Human Rights Approach to Development Assistance* (1998), republished in one volume in May 2001.

The policies and practices of detention of asylum seekers violated Australia's international human rights obligations. The Australian Human Rights Commission found that they constituted arbitrary detention contrary to the International Covenant on Civil and Political Rights and the Convention on the Rights of the Child.[5] The international Human Rights Committee considered complaints from detainees under the First Optional Protocol to the Covenant and also made findings of arbitrary detention.[6] The Australian Commission also found that conditions in detention centres violated the detainees' rights to humane treatment, to the highest attainable standard of health care and to education and other rights.[7]

The immigration detention centres are under the responsibility of the Australian Government department handling immigration.[8] Until the late 1990s they were run by a government agency, through its own staff. In 1997 the management was put to tender and privatized. Running detention centres became a profit-making enterprise for private corporations. Initially there was a little improvement in the conditions in the centres but that was not sustained. In fact detainees in the centres continued to experience the same human rights violations.

Often the discussion of business and human rights occurs on the basis that problems arise when developed world corporations do business in developing countries whose governments are unwilling or unable to ensure that human rights are fully respected and protected. This Australian experience demonstrates that these kinds of business-related violations can also occur in developed countries. The private operators of the centres were not only complicit in State violations; they were directly responsible for them. They secured the centres, ensuring the arbitrary detention of the asylum seekers contrary to international law.[9] They did so in accordance with Australian law that Australian courts were unable to invalidate, even though it violated human rights under international law.[10] They also conducted

---

[5] Australian Human Rights and Equal Opportunity Commission *Those Who've Come Across the Seas* (1989) and *A Last Resort?* (2004).

[6] *A v. Australia* Communication No 560/1993, UN Doc CCPR/C/59/560/1993 (30 April 1997).

[7] *Supra* note 5. See also the reports by the Human Rights and Equal Opportunity Commission on its inspection visits to detention centres at www.humanrights.gov.au/human_rights/immigration/detention_rights.html#9_3.

[8] The Department has had various names over the years. It was called the Department of Immigration and Multicultural Affairs for much of the past decade and is currently called the Department of Immigration and Citizenship.

[9] International Covenant on Civil and Political Rights Article 9.1; Convention on the Rights of the Child Article 37(b).

[10] *Al Kateb v. Godwin* (2004) HCA 37; *Al Masri v. Minister for Immigration and Multicultural and Indigenous Affairs* (2002) 192 ALR 609.

the centres in a manner that constituted inhumane treatment contrary to international law.[11]

The operating companies were subsidiaries of non-Australian corporations and so there was a transnational dimension but that was not relevant. The legal situation would have been the same if the operators had been fully Australian corporations. Human rights issues arise for business in all circumstances, not only in relation to transnational or globalized activities. Restricting consideration of the issues to transnational business, therefore, would exclude a large part of the field of human rights and business; indeed, I suspect it would exclude by far the largest part.

To provide a measure of balance and a different approach, I want to describe a second experience in relation to investment. From 2000 to 2003 I was part of an initiative to introduce human rights training in Burma, working with several colleagues from Australia, led by Professor David Kinley. The training courses were conducted under two projects, one a bilateral project with the Australian Government and the Government of Myanmar and the other an initiative of a small United Kingdom oil company, Premier Oil, with investments in Burma.[12]

Premier Oil has explicitly committed itself to a human rights policy based on international standards, with an expansive view of the company's human rights role:

> The Premier Oil Human Rights Policy is based on the fundamental rights pronounced in the Universal Declaration of Human Rights and is guided by those rights enshrined in the core labour conventions of the International Labour Organisation. These rights are to be protected and promoted throughout Premier Oil's business operations and in our relations with both business and local community partners. We will also use our legitimate influence to promote the protection of human rights outside of our areas of operation.[13]

Premier Oil operated in Burma from 1990 to 2002 in a context similar to that in the Philippines in the 1980s. There was (and still is) a military dictatorship, though one imposing far greater repression that the Marcos Dictatorship ever imposed. There was (and still is) armed insurgency. There was (and still is) vast corruption.

Premier sought to distance itself from the security forces in its operating zone and to develop direct, positive relationships with local villages. It established a community development fund and provided direct support

---

[11] International Covenant on Civil and Political Rights Article 10.1; Convention on the Rights of the Child Article 37(c).
[12] See www.business-humanrights.org/Categories/Individualcompanies/P/PremierOil.
[13] See www.premier-oil.com/render.aspx?siteID=1&navIDs=19,311,317,402.

to local projects, managed by a well-regarded international non-government organization, through local communities, not through the central government or the military. It also initiated human rights training courses for government officials in agencies with which it was required to engage.[14] It saw its corporate responsibility in the circumstances as extending beyond a negative responsibility to avoid violations to a positive responsibility to promote human rights by contributing to community development and to building human rights knowledge and understanding. In particular it saw an important role for the local communities in commenting on the impact of the company in their lives and also reporting to the company what the military was doing in and around their villages. In all this, its policy and practice were very different from those of other transnational corporations operating in Burma at the time. It did not trumpet its actions for public relations purposes. It did not exaggerate their significance, always recognizing that it was a small contribution. And it had no illusions about the limited impact and the fragility of what it did.

Premier sold its interests in Burma to the Malaysian oil company Petronas in 2002 and the training project came to an end.[15] Indeed, when the very small opening in the military regime at that time was slammed shut in May 2003, the Australian Government initiative also was first suspended and then cancelled.

2.3 Business, trade and human rights

Fair trade groups are small entities that can have little direct impact as actual traders. Rather they seek to effect better trade relationships through consumer education in developed countries, and their own trading activities are primarily educative rather than economic. Nonetheless they do have positive results, directly and indirectly.[16]

Tradewinds, formerly the World Development Tea Cooperative, began working with Sri Lankan tea workers in the late 1970s. At that time most tea production in Sri Lanka was extremely exploitative of the workers, and

---

[14] It sponsored nine courses for around 250 participants during 2001–02. See T. Webb 'Governance and institutions: Big brands' capacity-building success' in *Ethical Corporation*, 16 June 2008 at www.ethicalcorp.com/content.asp?ContentID=5962.

[15] Many human rights groups were sharply critical of Premier Oil's presence in Burma and campaigned against the company. They celebrated Premier's withdrawal as a victory for their campaign. Petronas does not have a human rights policy, does not keep the same distance from the military, does not conduct community development programmes and has not revived human rights training.

[16] The Cooperative Development Center in the United States has produced a comprehensive report on the purposes and history of fair trade cooperatives. See www.coopdevelopmentcenter.coop/New%20Basic%20Documents/fairtrade methodology.pdf.

still is. Most worked on tea plantations where they were poorly paid, poorly housed and poorly treated. Most were descendents of imported workers who continued to live and work on isolated plantations with their families; virtual serfs. They suffered discrimination based on ethnicity and gender. They had poor health, little access to education, especially for girls, and few, if any opportunities to improve their situations and lives. They worked in environments that were sometimes dangerous to health due to the use of pesticides. Large numbers of children were required to work too. Trade unions were weak and ineffective, often because their officials had been bought off. As the descendents of migrant workers the plantation workers were often denied the protection of laws that applied to protect others, even though inadequately.

The restriction of human rights was the result of both local and transnational business practice. Local businesses were the major plantation owners, the direct employers who imposed these conditions on the workers. Transnational businesses were the purchasers of the product who kept prices low, often by colluding in price-fixing through the auction system. A small number of very large transnational corporations dominated and controlled the market for tea and thereby very successfully restricted the profits that were available to be paid to the workers. In 1990 about 90 per cent of Western trade in tea was controlled by only seven transnational corporations. Because there was an excess of supply over demand, they were able to exert pressure on prices through moving from market to market, country to country. Competition among producer countries was intense and damaging to the producers. Long term declines in price accompanied by rising production costs reduced small farmers' incomes and labourers' wages and working conditions.

Tradewinds sought to change this situation even if only for some workers in Sri Lanka. It established direct links with labourer groups, small farmers and small plantations that were not owned by large local or transnational corporations. It encouraged better practices through trade and assistance. It provided greater security to labourers by offering long-term relationships and contracts. By going around the auction system, it guaranteed prices. It provided increased income through purchasing processed and packaged tea rather than bulk tea, enabling the local workers to add value locally. It encouraged environmentally sound production by buying organic tea. It was the first customer of a community development project in which women used traditional weaving skills to produce tea packages. That project now employs 4,500 people. It supports other community development projects in the tea growing areas, bringing together Tamil tea labourers and poor Sinhala villagers, enabling cooperation across traditional ethnic divides. It also supports health, housing and education projects, principally by supporting skills and leadership development among the local people, especially women.

The Tradewinds experience provides a direct contrast between two ways of working, between practices that lead to violations of rights and those that lead to better enjoyment of rights. Tradewinds works through collaboration and partnership across the Global North and Global South. It hears and respects the voices and aspirations of local people and responds positively to their needs and aspirations. The most important aspect of this experience is not that it directs more money from a developed country to a developing country but that it contributes to empowering poor people to take more control of their own lives.

2.4 Drawing some conclusions

These are but a few examples of the relationship between human rights and business. They are not the big examples of the gravest violations of human rights through business activity, such as the role of business in the Nazi genocide or the apartheid regime in South Africa or the poisoning at Bhopal in 1984. They are examples drawn from my own work and the everyday experiences of people. Reviewing my own examples and my own experiences, I come to several key conclusions about the factual situation of business and human rights.

1. All business activity has or can have human rights dimensions. People and their human rights are affected by business.
2. Business activity affects the full range of human rights, civil, cultural, economic, political and social rights and the right to development.
3. The human rights dimensions can be positive or negative. Business can act to promote human rights and, directly and indirectly, to violate human rights. People and their human rights can be benefited and harmed by business activity.
4. Human rights issues arise in transnational business but not only in transnational business. They are equally present in business at local and national levels.
5. Those with most knowledge about the effects of business on human rights, the real experts, are the people affected. They are the ones best placed to comment on situations and their needs, to monitor effects and to propose alternatives.

From these key factual conclusions, I come to two conclusions of principle.

1. Because business affects human rights, it has human rights responsibilities that should be subject to law.
2. Those whose human rights are most affected by business activity are the ones best qualified and most entitled to participate, first, in the discussions of what needs to be done, how adequate existing law is and how

the law needs to be developed, and then in monitoring and enforcing the law.

3 The state of the law

The current legal situation varies from place to place and at the international level it is contested. Nationally, some governments are good at providing a proper and effective framework for human rights protection, at least in their own territory, but many are not. Few provide an adequate legal framework for the activities of their corporate citizens outside their territory. Internationally, the application of human rights law to business entities is not universally accepted and, even when accepted, it is nowhere near adequately enforced.

Business has many more responsibilities than rights. Business activity is directed towards profit-making and that is a legitimate purpose but it is not a human right. The Universal Declaration of Human Rights recognizes a right 'to own property alone as well as in association with others' and a right not to be arbitrarily deprived of property.[17] This is the only right declared in the Universal Declaration that has not found its way into an international treaty obligation.[18] There are other rights in international human rights treaties that are relevant to business, most notably, freedom of association,[19] the right to work[20] and the right to an adequate standard of living.[21] But they are the rights of the individuals who constitute a corporation or are part of a business, not of the corporation or business itself.

In some jurisdictions corporations have been recognized as holders of at least some human rights. The European Court of Human Rights has applied some provisions in the European Convention for the Protection of Human Rights and Fundamental Freedoms and its Protocols for the benefit of legal persons, that is, of corporations, and not only of natural persons, that is, of individuals. Sometimes the wording of the instrument itself makes that clear. The provision on the right to property, for example, refers specifically to every 'natural or legal person'.[22] The European Court has also interpreted the right of non-government organizations to petition the court as applying

---

[17] Article 17.
[18] It is found, however, in regional human rights treaties: African Charter on Human and Peoples' Rights Article 14; American Convention on Human Rights Article 21; Protocol 1 to the European Convention for the Protection of Human Rights and Fundamental Freedoms Article 1.
[19] International Covenant on Civil and Political Rights Article 22.
[20] International Covenant on Economic, Social and Cultural Rights Article 6.
[21] International Covenant on Economic, Social and Cultural Rights Article 11.
[22] Protocol 1 to the European Convention for the Protection of Human Rights and Fundamental Freedoms Article 1.

to corporations.[23] Some national courts, including the Supreme Courts of Canada and the United States, have also interpreted and applied at least some provisions in national bills of rights for the benefit of legal persons, that is, of corporations.[24]

While I have the highest regard for these legal instruments and these courts, I consider that they fundamentally misconceive the nature and purpose of human rights. Human rights derive from and reflect basic human dignity and are inherent in each human being. They are therefore for the benefit of human beings, not human constructs. They can benefit human beings individually or collectively. By 'collectively', I mean human beings as a people or a group of some distinct, identifiable kind, for example, a religious, linguistic or cultural minority. But they must attach to us as human beings. They must attach to our humanity. As a matter of principle, corporations cannot be holders of human rights. However, they can be and are the holders of duties or responsibilities in relation to human rights.

The Universal Declaration of Human Rights itself recognizes that 'everyone has duties to the community':[25]

> [E]very individual and organ of society, keeping this Declaration constantly in mind, shall strive by teaching and education to promote respect for these rights and freedoms and by progressive measures, national and international, to secure their universal and effective recognition and observance.[26]

The Universal Declaration is not specific about the nature of the duties or of this responsibility for 'progressive measures...to secure...universal and effective recognition and observance' of all human rights. Whatever these duties are, however, business shares them.

There are two problems. The first is that there are large gaps in the legal framework to define and enforce these duties. The second is that there is no agreement on what role international law can and should play in filling these gaps.

3.1 Gaps in the legal regime

States bear the primary responsibility for the protection, promotion and fulfilment of human rights. This is well accepted. However, states often fail to discharge this responsibility adequately or sometimes at all. Each of the

---

[23] European Convention for the Protection of Human Rights and Fundamental Freedoms Article 34 (formerly Article 25). See A. Clapham, *Human Rights Obligations of Non-State Actors*, Oxford: Oxford University Press, 2006, p. 80n87 and pp. 81–82.
[24] D. Kinley, *Human Rights in Australian Law*, Federation Press: Sydney, 1998, pp. 10–12.
[25] Article 29.1.
[26] Universal Declaration of Human Rights opening paragraph.

personal experiences related here concerning business and human rights demonstrates state failure of one kind or another, or one degree or another, due to repressive military dictatorship or to governmental corruption or to weak governance structures or simply to bad public policy.

States can and should take all necessary measures, including through national legislation, to protect and promote human rights. Each government must 'use all appropriate means to ensure that actors operating within its territory or otherwise subject to its jurisdiction comply with national legislation designed to give effect to human rights'.[27] However, governments are often unwilling or unable to meet these obligations. Steiner, Alston and Goodman, in their leading human rights compilation, identify four problems in leaving the human rights regulation of business to governments alone, even where a government might be willing enough to act:

1. measures can be seen as costly and beyond the resources of a developing country
2. effective regulation can push up costs and lead to a loss of competitiveness compared with other non-regulating countries
3. with globalization it is harder to identify who is responsible for what activities where
4. especially in relation to labour, there are different levels of minimum acceptable standards from one country to another.[28]

Of course many governments will not be interested in effective human rights regulation at all, due to such factors as authoritarianism or corruption. Then the difficulties are even worse.

3.2 The role of international law

The second general problem is the lack of agreement on a role for international law. The debate is well known, revolving around the question of whether international law can or should impose obligations directly on corporations. If it should, then the second question is the extent to which it should do so. This issue has two points from a practitioners' perspective.

First, international law develops and it has developed to recognize international actors in addition to States and to hold them accountable. It may be true that in the beginning international law was the law governing relations between and among States and that only States were recognized. However, international legal history is a history of legal development. International law is not frozen or fixed. It has shown its developmental nature most clearly

---

[27] H. Steiner, P. Alston and R. Goodman *Human Rights in Context*, 3rd edition, Oxford: Oxford University Press, 2008, p. 1388.
[28] Ibid.

in relation to the protection of the well-being of human beings. Attempting to make a short summary of history is dangerous but let me sketch a couple of examples of this historical development.

In the nineteenth century, international humanitarian law emerged and began to develop, providing protection for certain categories of persons during inter-state wars. It dealt with the obligations of states initially but, as it developed, individuals came to be held accountable for their actions. It was defined in treaties but the substance of those treaties became incorporated into customary law binding all states and not merely binding but binding as unalterable peremptory norms, as *ius cogens*. It dealt at first only with inter-state war but it developed to include other conflict situations, including those involving non-state actors. And these non-state actors became bound by it too and accountable under it for their actions.

In the twentieth century, international criminal law developed, finding its original basis in international humanitarian law but now operating independently of it in customary and treaty law. The Genocide Convention 60 years ago declared genocide an international crime and imposed criminal responsibility on individuals, 'whether they are constitutionally responsible rulers, public officials or private individuals', for their genocidal actions.[29] The Rome Statute more recently recognized individuals as international actors who are accountable for international crimes, giving the International Criminal Court jurisdiction over 'natural persons'.[30] The Court itself is given international legal personality.[31]

International law has developed over the centuries. It is no longer what it was. It can and will continue to develop.

The second point I wish to make about international law is that human need has been one of the driving forces in its development. That is evident in the development of international humanitarian law. What was happening to human beings on and around battlefields drove development not only in the substance of international law but in the very nature of international law. The same is evident in the development of international human rights law. What happened to human beings, especially before and during World War II, drove development in international law that led to legal norms that were superior to the principle of State sovereignty.

When the effects of bad business practices on human rights are examined, human need is again apparent. Businesses exploit workers, dispossess peasants or clear rainforests, produce and release dangerous poisons and other pollutants. Businesses collude with human rights violating governments or,

---

[29] Convention on the Prevention and Punishment of the Crime of Genocide Article IV.
[30] Rome Statute of the International Criminal Court Articles 25. Article 1 refers to jurisdiction over 'persons'.
[31] Rome Statute of the International Criminal Court Article 4.

at least, directly benefit from them. National laws and individual governments have proved to be insufficient and there are clear gaps in international law. Among other necessary responses to this human need, an important one is further development of international law to fill that gap.

There is no credible argument that international law only recognizes States and only imposes obligations on states and only holds states accountable. It has already developed well beyond that. As Professor Andrew Clapham summarizes the situation:

> The point is that international law is already concerned with the duties of individuals both in their public and private capacities. International law has already extended this concern to inter-governmental organisations, and there is no evidence that the international legal order cannot accommodate duties for other kinds of actors.[32]

Professor Clapham summarizes the present need and possible response well:

> ... the strength of the human rights system has always been its ability to adapt to new demands and new needs. There are now demands for protection from the effects of big business and non-state actors. The human rights machinery and norms are pliant enough to be reoriented to cope with these new demands.[33]

What I would add to this comment is that there are not only 'demands for protection from big business and other non-state actors' but a clearly demonstrated need for it. Human rights law has shown itself to be not only pliant but responsive.

4 The politics of business and human rights

The problem is not the law but the politics. This is the third element in the present situation, alongside the facts of the effect of business on human rights and the state of the law. The necessary and possible development of the law is being constrained by political opposition. This opposition is expressed in terms of legal principle, that international law cannot and should not impose direct obligations on non-state actors and that doing so would lessen or even remove the legal obligations of states. Each of these propositions is wrong in fact and bad in theory. They are used not as legal points, however, but as arguments to achieve a political end. Many states, especially in the Global North, simply do not want international

---

[32] *Supra* note 23, p. 31.
[33] *Id.*, p. 32.

legal accountability for their transnational business entities. In many states in the Global South, transnational corporations can do pretty much as they wish. They and their home governments would like to keep it that way. At the same time, many States in the Global South fear that recognition of transnational and other business entities in international law would somehow diminish the status of states.

The political situation is best illustrated by the response to the draft Norms on the Responsibilities of Transnational Corporations and Other Business Enterprises with Regard to Human Rights.[34] The draft Norms are a good attempt to set out what existing international law requires in relation to business and human rights. They were developed and approved by the Sub-Commission on the Promotion and Protection of Human Rights of the UN Commission on Human Rights after four years of consultation and discussion. During the development process, there were arguments about how accurately they reflected existing law, with some commentators asserting that in some places they went further than the existing law. Most arguments, however, were political, with a surprising and disturbing coincidence of interest from international business and labour organizations.

Although many transnational corporations demonstrated a good commitment to human rights principles and were supportive of the process of developing norms, the two major business councils were extremely hostile to the whole process. It suited them to argue that international obligations were properly imposed on states, not non-state entities, because they knew this left business free under international law to do virtually what it wished. They lost sight of the fact that it is not only good for people but also good for business when bad practice is prohibited and prevented. It forces a fair playing field and fair competition on all businesses.

The International Council of Free Trade Unions (ICFTU) (as it was then called) was at least as hostile as business. It did not want anything to occur outside the forum of the International Labour Organisation (ILO) where labour operates in a cosy tripartite arrangement with governments and business. The draft Norms in fact reinforced ILO labour standards but, because they were products of the human rights system rather than the ILO, they were opposed by the ICFTU.

The Sub-Commission's members were individuals, not governments. They persisted with the development of the draft Norms in spite of the opposition. When the Sub-Commission referred the draft Norms to the Commission on Human Rights, however, governments were again in control and the legal process was transformed into a political one. The combined hostility of business and labour led most States in the Global North to take a strong

---

[34] UN Doc. E/CN.4/Sub.2/2003/12/Rev.2, available at http://www.fes-globalization.org/geneva/documents/UN_Norms_Background.pdfOpenElement.

position of opposition. States in the developing world were far less hostile but did not seem especially committed to the draft Norms, certainly not committed enough to become the champions of the document. When the Commission met in 2004, not only were the draft Norms certain to be rejected but the whole project of considering issues of business and human rights was at risk. Without the determination of non-government organizations to keep a process alive, it would have been lost. In the event, a cross-regional group of States, very ably led by the United Kingdom, developed a new approach that led to an independent study commissioned by the Office of the High Commissioner for Human Rights.[35] There was a strong attempt to have the Commission specifically repudiate the draft Norms. Again due to the advocacy and lobbying of non-government organizations, the Commission Decision simply said that the Norms, 'as a draft proposal', had 'no legal standing', a significantly more neutral position. Nonetheless the draft Norms were effectively put to one side.

The Commission Decision of 2004 led to the independent report and to a Commission resolution in 2005 for the appointment of a Special Representative of the Secretary General on Human Rights and Transnational Corporations and Other Business Enterprises.[36] The mandate of the Special Representative has been a successful means of continuing the work of examining the relationship between business and human rights – indeed it salvaged the work after the near disaster of the politics surrounding the draft Norms. However, the draft Norms continue to receive strong support from civil society organizations that regret the way they have been discarded:

> Asian civil society organisations strongly believe that the UN Norms... , unlike many other codes, offer a model for a truly global standard that would help companies assess the compatibility of their activities with relevant human rights standards.[37]

Under the circumstances it was understandable that the Special Representative would want to distance himself from the draft Norms. It is very unfortunate, nonetheless, that the Special Representative has effectively done what the Commission on Human Rights was persuaded not to do in 2004. He has effectively repudiated the draft Norms. That he considered it

---

[35] UN Commission on Human Rights Decision 2004/116.
[36] UN Commission on Human Rights Resolution 2005/69. The mandate of the Special Representative was renewed by the new Human Rights Council in 2008 in Resolution 8/7.
[37] Asian Civil Society Statement to U.N. Special Representative on Transnational Business and Human Rights at the Asia Regional Consultation, Bangkok, Thailand, 27 June 2006, at www.reports-and-materials.org/Asian-civil-society-statement-Ruggie-consultation-27-Jun-2006.pdf.

politically necessary to do so is the most telling indication of the continuing politicization of this important issue and the difficulty in ensuring the necessary development of law.

5 Whose business is human rights and business?

Earlier in this chapter I gave some examples, drawn from my own work, of the experience of business and human rights. I described how the business of aid, investment and trade affected some communities. In each case I referred to the position of the local people and their role in addressing, successfully or unsuccessfully, the effects of business on their lives and their rights. The relationship between business and human rights is the business of many people but, first and foremost and most of all, it is the business of those whose human rights are most affected, positively or negatively, by business.

Many institutions and people have an interest in this issue. Businesses themselves – national and transnational corporations and others – have legitimate interests. So do individual national governments. Intergovernmental institutions, both political (the United Nations generally and the Human Rights Council in particular) and economic (the World Bank and International Monetary Fund), are also interested. National human rights institutions have particular responsibilities for monitoring compliance at national level with international human rights norms and so are also involved. Non-government organizations that are active in or concerned about development and human rights have an interest. Academics and researchers have very important information, analyses and views to contribute. But no stakeholder or category of stakeholder has an interest as great or as personal as those whose human rights are affected by the activities of business. Yet their voices are the ones least heard in debates about what responsibilities business has and should have for human rights and how those responsibilities should be monitored and enforced.

5.1 Inclusion in developing law and standards

The international discussions about business and human rights have been under way through the processes of the UN human rights machinery for many years now. These processes have been commendably open. The Sub-Commission was very consultative in its work. Governments, intergovernmental institutions, national human rights institutions and non-government organizations all participate in the deliberations of the Human Rights Council.

Professor Ruggie, as Special Representative, has made quite extraordinary efforts to consult, including convening three regional consultations, four legal workshops and numerous specialist consultations. He has been particularly concerned to hear the voices of people in the Global South. It is important to state, however, that this has been largely the result of his own effort. As he has pointed out, as Special Representative he has

> a 'research mandate', requiring no field work of any kind. Accordingly, the sole budgetary support I was provided during the first year consisted of three trips to Geneva. Organizing regional consultations, convening legal workshops, and making site visits within different industry sectors all are at my own initiative, and I have had to raise the funding for them.[38]

Professor Ruggie sounds understandably frustrated here. The problem was then and is still a basic unwillingness on the part of those establishing and supporting the mandate to provide the resources and therefore the political endorsement for the work to be done properly. However, due no doubt to the Special Representative's own efforts, his work does seem to be attracting more interest in Geneva and in particular more interest from states in the Global South. Hopefully this will lead to more financial and political support for it as well.

A number of Asian civil society organizations have correctly pointed out that:

> For his recommendations to be useful and relevant, he needs to continue to hear from a range of civil society groups and local communities who are able to make positive and credible contributions, and raise legitimate concerns in the areas of business and human rights.[39]

This is plain commonsense. If the experiences of those affected are not known and their views not taken into account, any law or standards developed may well be ineffective in addressing the problem. They may address the wrong issues or issues that are relevant to one part of the world but not another. That is why it is not sufficient to listen only to non-government organizations from states in the Global North, for example, even though their views are important. They have contributed substantially and effectively to the international discussions but their participation alone is not good enough. The voices of the Global South must be heard as well.

Listening to those voices, we hear a consistent forceful message about the need for better legal regulation. Asian civil society groups have said they are seeking

---

[38] J. Ruggie, *Response to Asian Civil Society Statement*, 2 July 2006 at www.reports-and-materials.org/Ruggie-response-to-Asian-civil-society-statement-2-Jul-2006.doc.
[39] *Supra* note 37.

- a universal normative framework that provides clear, common standards that apply in all sectors in all countries that includes, as a minimum but not sufficient standard, the existing international law standard forbidding aiding and abetting gross human rights abuses;
- effective human rights obligations of States to ensure business does not infringe human rights;
- further recognition of the applicability of international laws to private actors and responsibility of states to ensure business acts accordingly.[40]

Latin American civil society groups have called on the UN system to, among other things

- create and adopt a human rights normative framework which is obligatory for companies, as the best way to respect and guarantee the human rights of persons and communities who have been affected by the actions or omissions of business enterprises;
- promote adequate and effective access to judicial recourses and protections in cases where companies threaten or negatively impact human rights.[41]

There is also a strong message that the focus of these discussions should not be the business activities of large Western transnational corporations alone but those of all business enterprises, transnational and local, large and small. Many Asian civil society organizations have said:

> Not all human rights violators are big companies. Some are small, Asian transnational corporations... Any set of guidelines that is not responsive to the need for accountability for all enterprises and sub-contractors, large and small, across all sectors and regardless of location, will be seriously incomplete.[42]

As the work of standard development proceeds, therefore, it is necessary to ensure that it seeks, takes into account and reflects the experiences and views of those most directly affected. This will require more than has been done to date. Certainly the views of leading international and regional non-government organizations should be heard but those on the ground too

---

[40] Ibid.
[41] Declaration of the Social, Non-Governmental and Union Organizations and Indigenous and Affected Communities Convened at the Regional Consultation of the Special Representative of the Secretary General of the UN on the issue of Human Rights and Transnational and other Businesses Enterprises Bogotá, Colombia, 18–19 January 2007, at www.reports-and-materials.org/Joint-NGO-declaration-on-Ruggie-Lat-Am-consultation-19-Jan-2007.pdf.
[42] *Supra* note 37.

must have opportunities to understand the issues under debate and respond to them, in their own ways.

5.2 Inclusion in monitoring and ensuring compliance

The legal development in relation to business and human rights that is required has three dimensions. The first is the adoption of law and standards. The second is the establishment of systems for monitoring compliance. The third is the creation of mechanisms for enforcement. Monitoring and enforcement are essential to the effectiveness of any new law and standards. Part of the problem with voluntary codes of conduct is that there are no monitoring and enforcement mechanisms.

Inclusiveness, which I have just discussed in relation to standard setting and legal development, is also important in ensuring monitoring and enforcement of norms. Participation in the development of standards enables understanding of the standards and promotes commitment to their implementation. Again the people whose human rights are most affected by business activities are the ones with the best knowledge and the most to gain through their participation. They are best placed to monitor and report on what business is doing. I have learned this through my own work. The local people in Northern Samar province in the Philippines knew what the impact of the Australian aid project was and were able to monitor and report on the human rights violations relating to it. The workers in the tea plantations of Sri Lanka knew best what the effects on them of local and transnational business were. Local villagers in Burma were best able to report on and compare the different effects of different oil companies. Detained asylum seekers in Australia knew exactly how the private security company running the detention centres was violating their human rights.

Monitoring compliance has to be based on community and other networks that can report on what is happening, what the effects of business activity are. National and international non-government organizations can support the work of these networks and bring their findings to national and international attention. National human rights institutions can also play very important roles in providing support and assistance and indeed in undertaking some of the monitoring themselves, in collaboration with local villagers and communities. The international legal system needs to provide processes through which the results and analysis arising from this monitoring can receive international attention.

Finally, there must be some mechanisms for enforcement. Laws and standards will be ineffective and monitoring will be meaningless unless they can lead to enforcement action. The international human rights system is very bad at enforcement. It is very weak and needs to be strengthened. Nonetheless, it is important that existing mechanisms extend their scope, within their jurisdictions, to include issues of business and human rights. The Committee on Economic, Social and Cultural Rights is already doing this and other treaty monitoring bodies should be encouraged and assisted to do the same. There may be a need for new and more effective mechanisms too. The discussions should be open to that possibility and to exploring what would be required to make any enforcement system, new or existing, work effectively.

Enforcement mechanisms will be ineffective unless they are accessible, directly or indirectly, to victims of human rights violations. Here again the role of national and international non-government organizations and national human rights institutions is important. In an increasingly globalized world, globalized responses to human rights violations are increasingly possible and necessary. But the actual victims, with their experiences, needs and views, have to be at the centre of the globalized response, not peripheral or incidental to it. Unfortunately, the individual victims are overlooked far too often by governments, intergovernmental institutions and international mechanisms. Even non-government organizations become so dedicated to their campaigning that they are in danger of losing sight of those for whom the campaign is being conducted.

6 Conclusion

I have said that the relationship between business and human rights is the business of many people but, first and foremost and most of all, it is the business of those whose human rights are most affected, positively or negatively, by business. More broadly, however, it's our business, the business of all of us. Business activity in all its dimensions is too important and its effects are too serious, positively and negatively, to be left to business people or even to governments.

In the last few months of 2008 we saw the economic consequences of bad business practices. We are told that the world is in 'financial crisis' and at risk of 'economic meltdown'. Emergency meetings are held. Heads of government and heads of central banks convene for crisis talks. Literally trillions of dollars are quickly found to address the situation. The human rights consequences of bad business practices are every bit as serious and as severe but attract far less attention. Everyone has come to accept them or at least to feel that nothing can be done about them. One lesson from the current economic crisis is that, where there is political will, anything can be done. Trillions of dollars can be found. The key question then becomes how we can promote the political will to address the human rights consequences of bad business practice.

That political will must be based on the focuses I referred to at the beginning: human rights as the values base for social and economic life and people as the centre of our concerns and responsibilities.

7
Public Procurement, International Labour Law and Free Movement in EU Law: Protect, Respect and Remedy

Ruth Nielsen

1 Introduction

In this paper, I discuss the interaction of international labour law and European Union (EU) law on fundamental rights and free movement in regard to public procurement in the light of the Report[1] of the Special Representative of the Secretary General (SRSG) on Human Rights and Business. In the Report of the SRSG the author states:

> The root cause of the business and human rights predicament today lies in the governance gaps created by globalization – between the scope and impact of economic forces and actors, and the capacity of societies to manage their adverse consequences. These governance gaps provide the permissive environment for wrongful acts by companies of all kinds without adequate sanctioning or reparation. How to narrow and ultimately bridge the gaps in relation to human rights is our fundamental challenge.

The challenge of how to narrow the gaps between economic forces and human rights is, in an EU context, mainly dealt with within the framework of binding legal provisions, in particular the provisions on free movement of services and freedom of establishment that mainly accommodate economic business interests and the equally binding provisions on fundamental rights that also accommodate a number of social rights that may be more or less

---

[1] John Ruggie: Protect, Respect and Remedy: A Framework for Business and Human Rights, 2008. Available at http://www.business-humanrights.org/Documents/RuggieHRC2008.

contrary to the economic interests of business. The social model EU law is based on is often called 'a social market economy'.[2]

The EU has so far not taken a legal approach to corporate social responsibility (CSR) and business responsibilities for human rights (BRHR) as distinct from legally binding human rights/fundamental rights which are generally well integrated into EU law. The Communication[3] 'Implementing the partnership for growth and jobs: making Europe a pole of excellence on corporate social responsibility' states (emphasis added):

> Corporate social responsibility (CSR) is a concept whereby companies integrate social and environmental concerns in their business operations and in their interaction with their stakeholders on a *voluntary* basis. It is *about enterprises deciding to go beyond minimum legal requirements and obligations stemming from collective agreements* in order to address societal needs.

Because there are fairly strong legally binding fundamental rights in the EU, CSR/BRHR – when understood as referring to non-legally binding measures – plays only a rather marginal role as an instrument to narrow the gaps between economic forces and human rights.[4] There is, however, within the framework of the legally binding EU-rules a tension between free movement on the internal market and fundamental rights which may give rise to problems that are parallel to those described in the Report of the SRSG on Human Rights and Business.

---

[2] Since the Treaty of Lisbon came into force Article 3(3) TEU reads (emphasis added): 'The Union shall establish an internal market. It shall work for the sustainable development of Europe based on balanced economic growth and price stability, *a highly competitive social market economy*, aiming at full employment and social progress, and a high level of protection and improvement of the quality of the environment. It shall promote scientific and technological advance. It shall combat social exclusion and discrimination, and shall promote social justice and protection, equality between women and men, solidarity between generations and protection of the rights of the child. It shall promote economic, social and territorial cohesion, and solidarity among Member States. It shall respect its rich cultural and linguistic diversity, and shall ensure that Europe's cultural heritage is safeguarded and enhanced.' See also Christian Joerges and Florian Rödl: ' "Social Market Economy" as Europe's Social Model?', EUI Working Paper LAW No. 2004/8 and Dagmar Schiek: The European Social Model and the Services Directive, in Ulla Neergaard, Ruth Nielsen and Lynn Roseberry (eds): *The Services Directive – Consequences for the Welfare State and the European Social Model*, Copenhagen, 2008.

[3] COM(2006)136.

[4] Some non-European companies established in the EU may underestimate the legal obligations of businesses established in the EU and believe that they are practicing CSR/BRHR while they are in fact only fulfilling legally binding (minimum) requirements.

In this paper, I examine whether EU law on free movement undermines the human rights claims that can be based on international labour law and fundamental rights in the EU in connection with government contracts; for example, the right to take collective action in order for posted workers to obtain equal pay with comparable workers from the host country. This problem has been at issue in European Court of Justice (ECJ) case law during the last ten years or thereabouts. Recent judgments on posted workers such as *Laval*,[5] *Rüffert*[6] and *Commission v Luxembourg*[7] have been much criticized for setting aside collective agreements and workers' rights in favour of free movement. National labour law on collective bargaining and the right to take industrial action in order to obtain a good bargain varies considerably within the EU.[8]

In the pending case *Commission v Germany*,[9] the Commission seeks a judgment declaring that Germany is infringing the procurement rules by awarding contracts concerning occupational pension schemes directly to pension undertakings mentioned in the relevant collective agreement without a European call for tender. In *Albany*,[10] the ECJ did, on the other hand, find that EU competition rules do not prohibit a decision by public authorities to make affiliation to a sectoral pension fund compulsory at the request of organizations representing employers and workers in a given sector.

Finally, I confront my analysis of EU law with the findings in the Report of the SRSG on the duty to protect, respect and remedy. In the case law of the ECJ, the right to take collective action is treated as a fundamental right which must be balanced against free movement. The Report of the SRSG presents a conceptual and policy framework to anchor the business and human rights debate, and to help guide all relevant actors. The framework comprises three core principles: the State duty to protect against human rights abuses by third parties, including business; the corporate responsibility to respect human rights; and the need for more effective access to remedies.

---

[5] Case C-341/05 [2007] ECR I-11767.
[6] Case C-346/06 [2008] ECR I-0000, judgment of 3 April 2008, nyr.
[7] Case C-319/06 *Commission v Luxembourg*, judgment of 19 June 2008, nyr.
[8] See Andrzej M. Swiatkowski (ed.): The Laval and Viking Cases Freedom of Services and Establishment v. Industrial Conflict in the European Union, *Bulletin of Comparative Labour Relations*, No. 69, 2009, Kluwer Law International. The volume includes country reports dealing with how the ECJ rulings in the Laval and the Viking Line cases affect European labour law issues (in both individual and collective matters) as well as how they affect national labour law systems in 12 EU countries and Norway and Russia.
[9] Case C-271/08, pending.
[10] Case C-67/96 [1999] I-5751.

2 CSR/BRHR and public international law

Historically, the first part of the legal system[11] where CSR and BRHR were addressed was public international law. With regard to the labour market,[12] that development started in the 1970s. In June 1976 the OECD governments adopted a 'Declaration on International Investment and Multinational Enterprises'. A set of Guidelines for Multinational Enterprises developed by the IME committee was attached to the declaration as an annex. In 2000, the OECD's Guidelines for Multinational Enterprises were revised.[13] In 1977, the International Labour Organisation (ILO) adopted a 'tripartite declaration of principles concerning multinational enterprises and social policy', which addresses a number of labour law questions and was revised in 2006. There is a Multinational Enterprises Programme (MULTI), which is responsible for follow-up to the 'tripartite declaration of principles concerning multinational enterprises and social policy'. To a limited extent legally binding human rights obligations for businesses have also been addressed by collective labour law.[14]

2.1 The Global Compact

The United Nations Global Compact[15] serves as a framework for businesses that are committed to aligning their operations and strategies with ten universally accepted principles in the areas of human rights, labour, the environment and anti-corruption. The Global Compact is a voluntary initiative with two objectives: (1) to mainstream the ten principles of the Global Compact in business activities around the world and (2) to catalyse actions in support of broader UN goals, such as the Millennium Development Goals (MDGs). Four labour law principles are included in the Global Compact, namely:

> Principle Three: businesses should uphold the freedom of association and the effective recognition of the right to collective bargaining;

---

[11] See for an overview of CSR and business responsibilities for human rights Buhmann, Karin: Corporate Social Responsibility and Business Responsibilities for Human Rights, *Nordic Journal of Human Rights*, 2007, p. 331, who argues that there is a closer relationship between CSR and law than is often recognized. I agree with that view.

[12] See for an analysis of the new methods of transnational labour regulation that are emerging in response to globalization Hepple, Bob: *Labour Laws and Global Trade*, Oxford, 2005.

[13] See further www.oecd.org/.

[14] Collective agreements create legally binding obligations in all EU countries except the UK. Under English law collective agreements are non-legally binding instruments.

[15] See http://www.unglobalcompact.org/.

Principle Four: the elimination of all forms of forced and compulsory labour;

Principle Five: the effective abolition of child labour; and

Principle Six: eliminate discrimination in respect of employment and occupation.

The four labour law principles of the UN Global Compact are taken from the ILO's Declaration on Fundamental Principles and Rights at Work.

2.2 WTO (World Trade Organization): GPA (Government Procurement Agreement)

The General Agreement on Tariffs and Trade (GATT) was negotiated in 1947. GATT 1947 lives on as GATT 1994, which is an integral part of the WTO Agreement currently in force. The Havana Charter for an International Trade Organisation (ITO) was a draft treaty drawn up in 1947 which was intended to set up an International Trade Organisation (a precursor to the WTO) and to facilitate the solution of problems relating to international trade in the fields of employment, economic development, commercial policy, business practices and commodity policy. It was never adopted. The Havana Charter[16] contained a provision on fair labour standards in Article 7 under which the signatories should recognize that measures relating to employment must take fully into account the rights of workers under intergovernmental declarations, conventions and agreements. They should recognize that all countries have a common interest in the achievement and maintenance of fair labour standards related to productivity, and thus in the improvement of wages and working conditions as productivity may permit. The members should recognize that unfair labour conditions, particularly in production for export, create difficulties in international trade. Members which are also members of the ILO should cooperate with that organization in giving effect to this undertaking.

This attempt in the Havana Charter, 60 years ago, to integrate labour law and trade law failed. Labour law has since played only a marginal role in international trade law. Today (2010) CSR may be seen as a soft law bridge between international trade law and labour law.

The GPA[17] is to date the only legally binding agreement in the WTO focusing on government procurement. The GPA dates back to 1979.[18] The first

---

[16] Full text available at http://www.worldtradelaw.net/misc/havana.pdf.
[17] See Evenett, Simon J. and Bernard Hoekman (eds): *The WTO and Government Procurement*, Cheltenham, UK, 2006.
[18] See for details McCrudden, Christopher: *Buying Social Justice. Equality, Government Procurement & Legal Change*, Oxford, 2007.

Agreement on Government Procurement was signed in 1979 and entered into force in 1981. It covered central government entities and procurement of goods only. It was amended in 1987, with this amended version entering into force in 1988. Its present version was negotiated in parallel with the Uruguay Round in 1994, and entered into force on 1 January 1996. It is a plurilateral treaty administered by a Committee on Government Procurement, which includes the WTO members that are parties to the GPA, and thus have rights and obligations under the Agreement. 40 WTO members are covered by the WTO Agreement on Government Procurement[19] and six WTO members have provisions in their respective Protocols of Accession to the WTO with regard to accession to the Agreement.[20]

Article VI of the GPA deals with Technical Specifications in a paragraph which inter alia mentions *the processes and methods of production*. This wording suggests that the technical specification required in public procurement may include reference to the work process – including, for example, prohibition of child labour – by means of which a product has been produced.[21]

2.3 ILO

2.3.1 General

The ILO was set up in 1919. In the Philadelphia Declaration of 1944, the International Labour Conference reaffirmed the fundamental principles on which the ILO is based and, in particular, that

(a) labour is not a commodity.

To a considerable extent the economic rationale of the industrial society was, however, to treat labour as a commodity. Perhaps the economic rationale of the knowledge economy is different; see the free movement of knowledge as the fifth freedom in the EU below in Section 3.2. The ILO formulates international labour standards in the form of conventions and recommendations setting minimum standards of basic labour rights: freedom of association, the right to organize, collective bargaining, abolition of forced labour, equality of opportunity and treatment, and other standards regulating conditions across the entire spectrum of work related issues.

---

[19] These comprise: Canada; the European Communities, including its 27 member States; Hong Kong (China); Iceland; Israel; Japan; Korea; Liechtenstein; the Kingdom of the Netherlands with respect to Aruba; Norway; Singapore; Switzerland and the United States.
[20] These are: Armenia, China, Croatia, the Former Yugoslav Republic of Macedonia (FYROM), Mongolia and Saudi Arabia.
[21] See Kai Krüger, Ruth Nielsen and Niklas Bruun: *European Public Contracts in a Labour Law Perspective*, Copenhagen, 1998, Chapter VII.

The International Labour Conference adopted a Declaration of Fundamental Principles and Rights at Work in 1998. The Declaration called upon all ILO Member States to apply the principles in line with the original intent of the core ILO conventions on which it is based. It identified eight ILO Conventions as being fundamental to the rights of people at work. They are grouped into four categories:

1) Freedom of association[22]
2) Abolition of forced labour[23]
3) Equality[24]
4) Elimination of child labour.[25]

The four labour law principles of the Global Compact are also concerned with these conventions (see above). There is generally only scant reference to ILO conventions in EU law. That has been criticized in the literature.[26] ILO conventions are, for example, not mentioned in the EU Charter on fundamental rights or the explanatory remarks accompanying it.[27] In *Laval* and *Viking*, the ECJ did, however, refer to ILO Convention 87 as a basis for considering the right to take collective action as a fundamental right in EU law.

2.3.2 ILO Convention 94

According to ILO Convention no. 94 from 1949 on labour clauses in public contracts, public works contracts, services contracts and so on must contain clauses ensuring the workers pay, working hours and other working conditions that are no less favourable than the ones applicable by collective agreement, arbitral award, national legislation or administrative acts to similar work within the same trade or industry in the region where the work is

---

[22] Convention no. 87, Freedom of Association and Protection of the Right to Organise Convention, 1948 and convention no. 98, Right to Organise and Collective Bargaining Convention, 1949.
[23] Convention no. 29, Forced Labour Convention, 1930 and convention no. 105, Abolition of Forced Labour Convention, 1957.
[24] Convention no. 100, Equal Remuneration Convention, 1951 and convention no. 111, Discrimination (employment and Occupation) Convention, 1958.
[25] Convention no. 138, Minimum Age Convention, 1973 and convention no. 182, Worst Forms of Child Labour Convention, 1999.
[26] O'Higgins, Paul: Some Problems of Enforcement of Rights under the Community Charter of Fundamental Social Rights of Workers, in Vogel-Polsky, Eliane (ed.): *Quel avenir pour l'Europe sociale: 1992 et après?*, Bruxelles, 1992, p. 73.
[27] See Nielsen, Ruth: The Charter of Fundamental Rights and Migrant Workers' Welfare Rights, in Neergaard, Ulla, Ruth Nielsen and Lynn Roseberry (eds): *Integrating Welfare Functions into EU Law – From Rome to Lisbon*, Copenhagen, 2009.

carried out.[28] ILO Convention 94 is ratified by 59[29] countries including ten EU countries (Austria, Belgium, Bulgaria, Cyprus, Denmark, Finland, France, Italy, the Netherlands and Spain). The United Kingdom ratified the convention in 1950 but denounced it in 1982. One European Economic Area (EEA) country (Norway) has also ratified this convention. ILO Convention 94 applies to contracts which fulfil the conditions that (a) one at least of the parties to the contract is a public authority; (b) the execution of the contract involves the expenditure of funds by a public authority and the employment of workers by the other party to the contract; (c) the contract is a contract for the construction, alteration, repair or demolition of public works; the manufacture, assembly, handling or shipment of materials, supplies or equipment; or the performance or supply of services; and (d) the contract is awarded by a central authority of a member of the ILO. The competent authority shall determine the extent to which and the manner in which the convention shall be applied to contracts awarded by authorities other than central authorities. The convention applies to work carried out by subcontractors or assignees of contracts; appropriate measures shall be taken by the competent authority to ensure such application.

Under Article 2 contracts to which ILO Convention 94 applies shall include clauses ensuring to the workers concerned wages (including allowances), hours of work and other conditions of labour which are not less favourable than those established for work of the same character in the trade or industry concerned in the district where the work is carried on –

(a) by collective agreement or other recognized machinery of negotiation between organisations of employers and workers representative respectively of substantial proportions of the employers and workers in the trade or industry concerned; or
(b) by arbitration award; or
(c) by national laws or regulations.

According to Article 5 of the convention adequate sanctions shall be applied, by the withholding of contracts or otherwise, for failure to observe and apply the provisions of labour clauses in public contracts. Appropriate measures shall be taken, by the withholding of payments under the contract or otherwise, for the purpose of enabling the workers concerned to obtain the wages to which they are entitled.

The ECJ did not consider the relationship between ILO Convention 94 and EU law in *Rüffert*. As Germany has not ratified ILO Convention 94 the

---

[28] See Labour clauses in public contracts. Integrating the social dimension into procurement policies and practices, ILO, 2008.
[29] See http://www.ilo.org/ilolex/cgi-lex/ratifce.pl?C094.

question was not directly relevant in that case. One may, however, ask if it is a consequence of the ruling in *Rüffert* that there is a contradiction between EU law on free movement and ILO Convention 94.

2.4 Codes of conduct and global framework agreements

There have been many unilateral employer statements on CSR, typically in the form of codes of conduct. Since the beginning of the 1990s one can speak of a new generation of codes of conduct.[30] The International Metalworkers' Federation recommends a shift in terminology from Codes of Conduct to Framework Agreements:[31]

> By 2002, the term International Framework Agreement (IFA) had been adopted as a means of clearly distinguishing the negotiated agreements being pursued by IMF (International Metalworkers' Federation) and its affiliates from the type of voluntary codes of conduct that corporations were increasingly adopting unilaterally to ostensibly demonstrate their commitment to corporate social responsibility.

The International Metalworkers' Federation has launched a website on International Framework Agreements (IFA) which includes a list of all IFAs signed so far.[32] The International Metalworkers' Federation recommends that all IFAs must contain the core labour standards of the International Labour Organisation (ILO), clearly referenced by number, cover all company operations throughout the world and include a strong and unequivocal commitment by the transnational corporation that suppliers and subcontractors adopt similar standards for their workers. The core labour standards of the ILO mentioned in the IFA will take precedence over national laws in case the latter are less favourable than the respective ILO Conventions. A representative of the International Metalworkers' Federation, or a duly authorized person of the federation, shall be a signatory party.

3 Fundamental rights and free movement in the EU

3.1 EU Law on Fundamental Rights and the connection to CSR/BRHR

Since 1970, the ECJ has developed a case law on fundamental rights. Starting in the late 1960s, increasing concern was expressed in the courts of Germany

---

[30] André Sobczak: Codes of Conduct in Subcontracting Networks: A Labour Law Perspective, *Journal of Business Ethics*, 2003, Vol. 47, No. 2, p. 225.
[31] International Metalworkers' Federation: Background to International Framework Agreements in the IMF, http://www.imfmetal.org/main/files/06081513541679/Background_document_english-final.pdf.
[32] http://www.imfmetal.org/main/index.cfm?n=47&l=2&c=10266.

and Italy on the question as to whether the fundamental rights guaranteed in their national constitutions were recognized and protected within EU law. In response to the threat that national courts would opt for the supremacy of their own national constitutional provisions on fundamental rights protection, the ECJ held that the protection of fundamental rights was a general principle of EU law. In 1969 in *Stauder*,[33] the ECJ stated for the first time that fundamental rights were enshrined in the general principles of Community law and protected by the Court. In *Internationale Handelsgesellschaft* the reference to fundamental rights was expanded by the Court stating that respect for fundamental rights forms an integral part of the general principles of law protected by the ECJ and that these principles were inspired by the *constitutional traditions* common to the member states.[34] In 1974, the ECJ held in *Nold* that, in addition to Member States' constitutional traditions, *international conventions* could also supply guidelines which could be taken into consideration by the Court on matters concerning claims to fundamental rights.[35] In particular, the European Court of Human Rights (ECHR) has a special significance in this respect.

Fundamental rights were first specifically referred to in a labour law case in 1975 in *Rutili*[36] on trade union rights. In *Defrenne-III*,[37] the ECJ stated that there can be no doubt that the elimination of discrimination based on sex forms part of fundamental rights. In *Maurissen*,[38] the ECJ held that in staff cases an EU institution must respect the principle of good administration. In *Dunnett*,[39] the ECJ stated that the European Investment Bank in a staff case was bound to consult staff representatives under a general principle of employment law before taking a decision to withdraw a benefit. In *Laval*[40] and *Viking*,[41] the ECJ stated that the right to take collective action must be recognized as a fundamental right which forms an integral part of the general principles of EU law. In *BECTU*,[42] the Advocate General argued that the right to paid annual leave is not only guaranteed in the Working Time Directive but also constitutes a fundamental right. In *Mangold*,[43] the ECJ held that the principle of non-discrimination on grounds of age is a general principle of EU law.

---

[33] Case 29/69 *Stauder v Ulm* [1969] ECR 419.
[34] Case 11/70 *Internationale Handelsgesellschaft* [1970] ECR 1125.
[35] Case 4/73 *Nold* [1974] ECR 491.
[36] Case 36/75 *Rutili v Minister of the Interior* [1975] ECR 1219.
[37] Case 149/77 [1978] ECR 1365.
[38] Case 417/85 [1987] ECR 551.
[39] Case T-192/99 [2001] ECR II-813, I-A-65, II-313.
[40] Case C-341/05 [2007] ECR I-11767.
[41] Case C-438/05 [2007] 2007 I-10779.
[42] Case C-173/99 [2001] ECR I-4881.
[43] Case C-144/04 *Werner Mangold v Rüdiger Helm* [2005] ECR I-9981.

In April 1977, the European Parliament, the Council and the Commission issued a joint declaration[44] in which they stressed the prime importance they attached to the protection of fundamental rights, as derived in particular from the constitutions of the Member States and the ECHR. The ECJ has occasionally referred to this Declaration.[45]

In 1989,[46] 11 of the then 12 members of the EC adopted the Community Charter of Fundamental Rights of Workers.[47] There are references to this Charter both in Article 136 EC and in the explanatory remarks to the Charter of Fundamental Rights of the European Union 2000.

In 1999, when the European Council decided to draw up a Charter of Fundamental Rights of the European Union it adopted some broad guidelines on what the Charter should contain. It declared (emphasis added):[48]

> The European Council believes that this Charter should contain the fundamental rights and freedoms as well as basic procedural rights guaranteed by the *European Convention for the Protection of Human Rights* and Fundamental Freedoms and derived from the *constitutional traditions common to the Member States*, as general principles of Community law. The Charter should also include the *fundamental rights that pertain only to the Union's citizens*. In drawing up such a Charter account should furthermore be taken of *economic and social rights as contained in the European Social Charter and the Community Charter of the Fundamental Social Rights*

---

[44] OJ 1977 C 103.
[45] See for example Case 44/79 *Hauer* [1979] ECR 3727 and Case 222/84 *Johnston* [1986] ECR 1651.
[46] Bercusson, Brian: The European Community's Charter of Fundamental Social Rights of Workers, *The Modern Law Review*, Vol. 53, 1990, p. 624.
[47] There is no official publication of this Charter but several private ones. In this article I have used the one found at the internet at http://www.psi.org.uk/publications/archivepdfs/Trade%20unions/TUAPP1.pdf.
[48] Conclusions of the presidency of the European Council of Cologne (3 and 4 June 1999) on the drawing up of a Charter of Fundamental Rights of the European Union, Annex 4, p. 43, available at http://www.consilium.europa.eu/ueDocs/newsWord/en/ec/57886.doc. See on the background to the Charter de Búrca, Gráinne: The drafting of the European Union Charter of fundamental rights, *European Law Review*, Vol. 26, No. 2, 2001, p. 126, Lammy Betten: The EU Charter of Fundamental Rights: A Trojan Horse or a Mouse?, *International Journal of Comparative Labour Law and Industrial Relations*, Vol. 17, No. 2, 2001, p. 151, Deirdre Curtin: The EU Human Rights Charter and the Union Legal Order: The 'Banns' before the Marriage?, in D O' Keeffe and A. Bavasso (eds): *Liber Amicorum in Honour of Lord Slynn of Hadley: Judicial Review in European Union Law*, Kluwer 2000, Engel, Christoph: The European Charter of Fundamental Rights: A Changed Political Opportunity Structure and its Normative Consequences, *European Law Journal*, Vol. 7, No. 2, 2001, p. 151 and Fredman, Sandra, Christopher McCrudden and Mark Freedland: An EU Charter of Fundamental Rights, *Public Law*, 2000, Sum, p. 178–186.

of Workers (Article 136 TEC), insofar as they do not merely establish objectives for action by the Union.

There are seven chapters in the Charter: Title I. Dignity; Title II. Freedoms; Title III. Equality; Title IV. Solidarity; Title V. Citizens' Rights; Title VI. Justice and Title VII. General Provisions. The Charter contains 50 'rights, freedoms and principles' without identifying which of its provisions are rights, which are freedoms and which are principles.

In identical terms, the ECJ held in *Viking*[49] and *Laval*[50] that the right to take collective action is a fundamental right which forms an integral part of the general principles of Community law, the compliance with which must be ensured by the ECJ. It referred to Article 28 of the EU Charter of Fundamental Rights[51] in support thereof.[52]

3.2 Public procurement and the general principles of free movement

Since 1958, the award of contracts concluded in the Member States on behalf of the state, regional or local authorities and other bodies governed by public law entities, is subject to respect for the principles of the EC Treaty and in particular to the principle of freedom of movement of goods (Article 34 TFEU), freedom of establishment (Article 49 TFEU) and freedom to provide services (Article 56 TFEU), and to the principles deriving therefrom, such as the principle of equal treatment, the principle of non-discrimination, the principle of mutual recognition, the principle of proportionality and the principle of transparency.[53]

Article 49 TFEU on the right to establishment and Article 56 TFEU on free movement of services prohibit both direct and indirect discrimination due to nationality as well as nationality-neutral restrictions on free movement. In *Laval*,[54] the ECJ stated that it is clear from its case law that, since the freedom to provide services is one of the fundamental principles of the Community, a

---

[49] Case C-438/05, *International Transport Worker's Federation and Finnish Seamen's Union v Viking Line ABP and OU Viking Line Eesti* [2007] ECR I-10779.
[50] Case C-34 1/05, *Laval un Partneri Ltd v Svenska Byggnadsarbetareförbundet, Svenska Byggnadsarbetareförbundets avdeling 1 Byggettan, and Svenska Elektrikerförbundet* [2007] ECR I-11767.
[51] Article 28 on the right of collective bargaining and action reads: 'Workers and employers, or their respective organisations, have, in accordance with Community law and national laws and practices, the right to negotiate and conclude collective agreements at the appropriate levels and, in cases of conflicts of interest, to take collective action to defend their interests, including strike action'.
[52] See paragraph 43 in Viking and paragraph 90 in Laval.
[53] See Recital 2 in Directive 2004/18/EC on the coordination of procedures for the award of public works contracts, public supply contracts and public service contracts.
[54] See paragraph 101.

restriction on that freedom is warranted only if it pursues a legitimate objective compatible with the Treaty and is justified by overriding reasons of public interest; if that is the case, it must be suitable for securing the attainment of the objective which it pursues and not go beyond what is necessary in order to attain it. A relevant legitimate aim in *Laval* was protection of workers. The ECJ accepted both protection of posted Latvian workers[55] and protection of Swedish home country workers against social dumping.[56] There is abundant case law on the interpretation of these provisions. In *Gebhard*, the Court held[57] that national measures liable to hinder or make less attractive the exercise of fundamental freedoms guaranteed by the Treaty:

1. must be applied in a non-discriminatory manner;
2. must be justified by imperative requirements in the general interest;
3. must be suitable for securing the attainment of the objective which they pursue; and
4. must not go beyond what is necessary in order to attain it.

In the ECJ case law on justification of restrictions on free movement the principles of *proportionality* and *transparency* form an important part.

For the last 25 years, the ECJ has held that the free movement of services under Article 56 TFEU is not only a freedom to provide services but also a freedom to receive services.[58] Under the – Treaty on the Functioning of the European Union (TFEU), the Internal Market is thus both an internal market for producers, seller, service providers and for recipients of works and services. Both groups can rely on the free movement provisions in the FEU Treaty. The classic free movement provisions in the FEU Treaty (Article 34 TFEU, 49 TFEU and 56 TFEU) are complemented by the free movement provision for Union citizens in Article 21 TFEU.

EU policy papers since the publication of the review of the Single Market in 'A single market for 21st century Europe'[59] speak of free movement of knowledge and innovation as the 'Fifth Freedom' in the Single Market. This rhetoric is, for example, used in the renewed Social Agenda where the Commission declared[60] that it will continue to develop a 'Fifth Freedom' by removing barriers to the free movement of knowledge. Stricter rules on free

---

[55] See e.g., paragraph 107.
[56] See paragraph 103.
[57] Case C-55/94, *Reinhard Gebhard v Consiglio Dell'Ordine degli Avvocati e Procuratori di Milano* [1995] ECR I-4165, paragraph 37.
[58] Joined cases 286/82 and 26/83 *Graziana Luisi and Giuseppe Carbone* [1984] ECR p. 377.
[59] COM (2007) 724.
[60] COM(2008) 412, Renewed social agenda: Opportunities, Access and solidarity in 21st century Europe, p. 10.

movement for researchers, students and other knowledge-relevant persons are specifically mentioned. Respect for CSR/BRHR is likely to facilitate free movement of knowledge and innovation and thus is in line with the latest layer of EU policies on free movement.

4 Specific procurement rules

For public contracts above a certain threshold there are additional rules mainly of a procedural nature laid down by directives.[61] The substantive rules in the EC Treaty on free movement have, in matters of public procurement, been complemented by directives coordinating tendering procedures in respect of supplies, works, services and utilities since the early 1970s. The procurement directives contain procedural and remedial provisions aimed at ensuring transparency and equal treatment of different tenderers. There is free choice for the contracting authority or contracting entity between two different tender procedures: open procedures or restricted procedures. There are detailed provisions on selection of candidates to be invited to submit tenders in restricted procedures; on exclusion of potential contractors or service providers and on proof of professional and technical capability and of economic and financial standing. Award of contracts will usually have to be made on the basis of either the lowest price or the economically most advantageous tender. There is no definition in the directives of the concept of 'economically most advantageous tender'. In March 2004, the Community adopted two new directives on public procurement: Directive 2004/18/EC on the coordination of procedures for the award of public works contracts, public supply contracts and public service contracts and Directive 2004/17/EC coordinating the procurement procedures of entities operating in the water, energy, transport and postal services sectors. The new directives came into force on 1 May 2004 and had to be implemented by the Member States by 31 January 2006. There are special directives on remedies in procurement cases.[62]

There are a number of provisions in the procurement directive under which social considerations can arguably be taken into account. This matter is, however, a controversial issue.[63]

In order to meet the Procurement Directive's aim of ensuring development of effective competition in the award of public works contracts, the criteria

---

[61] See in particular Directive 2004/18/EC.

[62] See Directives 89/665/EEC and 92/13/EEC with regard to improving the effectiveness of review procedures concerning the award of public contracts as amended by Directive 2007/66/EC.

[63] See for different views in the literature Martín, José M. Fernández: *The EC Public Procurement Rules: A Critical Analysis*, Oxford, 1996, Krüger, Kai, Ruth Nielsen and Niklas Bruun, *supra* note 21 and McCrudden, *supra* note 18.

and conditions which govern each contract must be given sufficient publicity by the authorities awarding contracts.[64] Contracting authorities can impose contractual clauses relating to the manner in which a contract will be executed. Article 26 of the Procurement Directive provides:

> Conditions for performance of contracts. Contracting authorities may lay down special conditions relating to the performance of a contract, provided that these are compatible with Community law and are indicated in the contract notice or in the specifications. The conditions governing the performance of a contract may, in particular, concern social and environmental considerations.

The clauses or conditions regarding execution of the contract must comply with Community law and, in particular, not discriminate directly or indirectly against non-national tenderers. By way of example, a clause stipulating that a successful tenderer must employ a certain number or percentage of long-term unemployed or apprentices, without requiring the unemployed or apprentices to be from a particular region or registered with a national body, for instance for the execution of a works contract, should not, a priori, amount to discrimination against tenderers from other Member States.[65] In addition, such clauses or conditions must be implemented in compliance with all the procedural rules in the directive, and in particular with the rules on advertising of tenders. Article 24 of the procurement directive on variants empower the contracting authorities to authorize tenderers to submit variants where the criterion for award is that of the most economically advantageous tender. Using variants – for example, contracts with more or less ambitious social content – enables the contracting authority to take the cost of social content into account without using a social criterion as an award criterion, the lawfulness of which is still contested. Under Article 45 of the procurement directive any economic operator may be excluded from participation in a contract where that economic operator:

(c) has been convicted by a judgment which has the force of *res judicata* in accordance with the legal provisions of the country of any *offence* concerning his professional conduct;
(d) has been guilty of *grave professional misconduct* proven by any means which the contracting authorities can demonstrate.

---

[64] See point 21 and 28 in Case 31/87 *Beentjes* [1988] ECR 4635.
[65] See for the same view COM(2001) 566, Interpretative Communication of the Commission on the Community law applicable to public procurement and the possibilities for integrating social considerations into public procurement p. 16, note 61.

Recital 43 in the preamble to the public sector Directive provides that (emphasis added):

> Non-observance of national provisions implementing the Council Directives 2000/78/EC and 76/207/EEC concerning equal treatment of workers, which has been the subject of a final judgment or a decision having equivalent effect may be considered *an offence concerning the professional conduct* of the economic operator concerned or grave misconduct.

Directive 2000/78/EC prohibits discrimination on grounds of religion or faith, age, handicap and sexual orientation in the employment field. Directive 76/207/EEC prohibits discrimination on grounds of sex in the employment field. As can be seen from the above quotation, the Race Directive is not mentioned in the Procurement Directive which must, however, be interpreted so that violations of national provisions implementing the Race Directive may also be considered an offence concerning the professional conduct of the economic operator concerned or a grave misconduct. The Gender Equality (Goods and Services) Directive is also not mentioned in the Procurement Directive from March 2004 but that is because it was only adopted in December 2004. By way of analogy violations of national provisions implementing the Gender Equality (Goods and Services) Directive may also be considered an offence concerning the professional conduct of the economic operator concerned or a grave misconduct.

No workforce-related criteria are explicitly mentioned as award criteria in the Procurement Directive. Article 53 on contract award criteria provides:

1. Without prejudice to national laws, regulations or administrative provisions concerning the remuneration of certain services, the criteria on which the contracting authorities shall base the award of public contracts shall be either:

    (a) when the award is made to the tender most economically advantageous from the point of view of the contracting authority, various criteria linked to the subject-matter of the public contract in question, for example, quality, price, technical merit, aesthetic and functional characteristics, environmental characteristics, running costs, cost effectiveness, after sales service and technical assistance, delivery date and delivery period or period of completion, or
    (b) the lowest price only.

The question discussed here is whether the provisions on award criteria in the Procurement Directives restrict the freedom of Member States to pursue policies by means of procurement further than what follows from the Treaty provisions. Recital 1 in the Preamble to the Directive states that the Directive is based on Court of Justice case law, in particular case law on award criteria, which clarifies the possibilities for the contracting authorities to meet the needs of the public concerned, including in the environmental and/or social area, provided that such criteria are linked to the subject matter of the contract, do not confer an unrestricted freedom of choice on the contracting authority, are expressly mentioned and comply with the fundamental principles mentioned in Recital 2. The above provisions in the Procurement Directive build on the practice of the ECJ, in particular the judgment in the Finnish Bus Case.[66]

In *Commission v France* (Nord Pas Calais)152 the ECJ held on the lawfulness or otherwise of using an additional criterion related to employment as an award criterion:

> 50. None the less, that provision [the provision on award criteria] does not preclude all possibility for the contracting authorities to use as a criterion a condition linked to the campaign against unemployment provided that that condition is consistent with all the fundamental principles of Community law, in particular the principle of non-discrimination flowing from the provisions of the Treaty on the right of establishment and the freedom to provide services. (See, to that effect, *Beentjes*, paragraph 29)

> 51. Furthermore, even if such a criterion is not in itself incompatible with Directive 93/37, it must be applied in conformity with all the procedural rules laid down in that directive, in particular the rules on advertising (see, to that effect, on Directive 71/305, *Beentjes*, paragraph 31). It follows that an award criterion linked to the campaign against unemployment must be expressly mentioned in the contract notice so that contractors may become aware of its existence. (See, to that effect, *Beentjes*, paragraph 36)

> 52. As regards the Commission's argument that *Beentjes* concerned a condition of performance of the contract and not a criterion for the award of the contract, it need merely be observed that, as is clear from paragraph 14 of *Beentjes*, the condition relating to the employment of long-term unemployed persons, which was at issue in that case, had been used as the basis for rejecting a tender and therefore necessarily constituted a criterion for the award of the contract.

---

[66] Case C-513/99 *Concordia Bus Finland Oy Ab v Helsingin kaupunki og HKL-Bussiliikenne* [2002] ECR I-7213.

On a narrow view Article 53 at least allows for the use of equality as an 'additional' award criterion. The concept of an additional criterion was first mentioned in the *Beentjes* case, where the Court held that a criterion relating to the employment of long-term unemployed persons was not relevant either to the checking of a candidate's economic and financial suitability or of the candidate's technical knowledge and ability, or to the award criteria listed in the relevant directive. The Court also held that this criterion was nevertheless compatible with the public Procurement Directives if it complied with all relevant principles of Community law.

5 Confrontation with the Report of the SRSG: duty to protect, respect and remedy when entering into public contracts in the EU

As mentioned in the Introduction, the Report of the SRSG presents a conceptual and policy framework to anchor the business and human rights debate, and to help guide all relevant actors. The framework comprises three core principles: the State duty to protect against human rights abuses by third parties, including business; the corporate responsibility to respect human rights; and the need for more effective access to remedies.

The Report of the SRSG highlights how horizontal and vertical incoherence in the legal framework may make the State duty to protect against human rights abuses less effective. Hepple[67] argues that the opportunities to solve problems concerning labour rights lie in regional regulation such as EU law, CSR, local activities by, for example, trade unions and ILO standards. As appears from the above, there is, however, important incoherence in the legal regulation stemming from these sources of law.

The almost non-existent integration between international trade law (e.g., WTO law) and international labour law (e.g., ILO law) is in itself an example of horizontal incoherence. As mentioned earlier, CSR/BRHR may be seen as a soft law bridge between international trade law and labour law. In my view, there is, however, need for more hard law in this area.

The tension between international trade law (WTO law) and international labour law is mirrored in EU law by the tension between the free movement provisions and fundamental rights, including fundamental labour rights. The ECJ has been confronted with the interface between free movement on the internal market and fundamental rights on a number of occasions and has held that free movement and fundamental rights must be balanced against each other. The one does not automatically take precedence

---

[67] Hepple, *supra* note 12, p. 271.

over the other. In *Omega Spielhallen*,[68] for example, the ECJ held that the freedom to provide services does not preclude an economic activity from being prohibited on grounds of protecting public policy by reason of the fact that that activity is an affront to human dignity. In *Laval*, on the other hand, it held that lawful industrial action under Swedish law was a violation of Article 49 EC even though the right to take industrial action is a fundamental right under Article 28 of the EU Charter of Fundamental Rights. This balancing exercise is governed by the usual justification test for restrictions on free movement which requires that the restriction must pursue a legitimate aim, and the means applied to achieve the legitimate end (the restriction) must be appropriate and necessary, that is, the principle of proportionality must be respected. In *Carpenter*[69] and *Festersen*,[70] the ECJ ruled that in situations where a restriction on the free movement at the same time adversely affects the enjoyment of a fundamental right the restriction is to be considered particularly restrictive.

Since the introduction of Union Citizenship when the Maastricht Treaty entered into force (1 November 1993) there seems to be growing emphasis in the case law of the ECJ on free movement as a fundamental right for all Union citizens. In *Schwartz*,[71] the ECJ thus held that where taxpayers of a Member State send their children to a school established in another Member State, the services of which are not covered by Article 49 EC, Article 18 EC precludes (indirectly) nationality discriminatory legislation.

The corporate/business responsibility to respect human rights requires due diligence. This concept describes the steps a company must take to become aware of, prevent and address adverse human rights impacts. The Report of the SRSG recommends that companies for the substantive content of the due diligence process should look at the minimum provided by the core conventions of the ILO, because the principles they embody comprise the benchmarks against which other social actors judge the human rights impacts of companies. The eight fundamental ILO conventions are all ratified by all 27 EU countries. Consequently they are 'international obligations common to the Member States', see above on the ECJ's case law on fundamental rights and the Preamble to the Charter. Since1 December 2009 when the Fundamental Rights Charter became binding through the coming into force of the Lisbon Treaty, they are directly applicable and take precedence over national law for businesses established in the EU under the general EU rules on direct effect and supremacy of EU law.

---

[68] Case C-36/02 *Omega Spielhallen- und Automatenaufstellungs-GmbH v Oberbürgermeisterin der Bundesstadt Bonn* [2004] ECR I-9609.
[69] Case C-60/00 *Carpenter* [2002] ECR I-6279.
[70] Case C-370/05 *Festersen* [2007] ECR I-1129.
[71] Case 366/04 *Schwarz* [2005] ECR I-10139.

Finally, the Report of the SRSG highlights the need for more effective access to remedies. That is a concern it has in common with EU procurement law where problems relating to remedies have been high on the agenda for at least the last 20 years. The Remedies Directive was amended in 2007 to provide for more effective access to remedies.[72]

6 Conclusion

The EU has mainly taken a hard law approach to narrowing the gap between economic forces and human rights. Notwithstanding this there are considerable similarities between the tensions between free movement on the internal market and fundamental rights and the problems described in the Report of the SRSG on Human Rights and Business. Shifting from a CSR/BRHR agenda to a strictly legal approach will therefore not of itself solve the problems.

The case law dealt with above shows that both the internal market freedoms and the fundamental rights, including the right of collective bargaining and to take collective action in support thereof, must be respected. The opposing rights must be balanced against each other on a case by case basis. It will, however, often be unclear exactly what the concrete outcome of this balancing process will be. There is therefore a rather low level of legal certainty in EU law as it stands at present, making it difficult for a business to predict how much it has a legal obligation to do and from where to start if it wishes to develop a CSR/BRHR policy. The low level of legal certainty results from the lack of coherence between economic and Human Rights EU laws, which leaves a lot of room for interpretation in courts. In my view, there is a need for more precision in the binding legal rules.

---

[72] See Directive 2007/66/EC of the European Parliament and of the Council of 11 December 2007 amending Council Directives 89/665/EEC and 92/13/EEC with regard to improving the effectiveness of review procedures concerning the award of public contracts.

8
Business Responsibilities and Human Rights in Latin America: Lessons and Inspiration for the Future*

Cecilia Anicama

1 Introduction

This chapter addresses the issue of business responsibilities for human rights as an emerging topic of legal relevance in Latin America with the purpose of identifying relevant hints for an analysis of how to proceed after the Report of the Special Representative of the Secretary General (SRSG) on Human Rights and Business in Latin America. In this regard, this chapter is based on the analysis of specific measures adopted in some Latin American countries which have an impact on the sphere of business and human rights and also on the analysis of relevant decisions and jurisprudence of the Inter-American Human Rights organs. The author deems it appropriate to identify the achievements and challenges faced in Latin America in the sphere of business and human rights at the national and regional level as a tool for elaborating a foundation for subsequent debate at the international and national forums in order to support the implementation of the three core principles of the policy framework in the agenda of the SRSG on business and human rights.

In this light, this chapter presents three different sections that address (1) the approach to business responsibilities in the region, (2) the evolution of corporate social responsibility (CSR) in Latin America in relation to the consolidation of democracies in the region and (3) an overview of regional human rights standards relevant to better determine the scope of the state duty to protect in regard to business.

As regards methodology, this chapter is based on the analysis of case studies, decisions adopted by the Inter-American Commission[1] and the

---

* The views expressed in this chapter are those of the author.
[1] For further information on the Inter-American Commission on Human Rights, visit its website at www.cidh.org.

jurisprudence of the Inter-American Court[2] of Human Rights, international and national norms, policies and practices.

The chapter provides some views and recommendations in relation to the effective regulation of CSR and business responsibilities for human rights in Latin America under the policy framework proposed by the SRSG on human rights and business. All of the considerations and recommendations expressed in this chapter are made in the personal capacity of the author.

2 Approaching businesses' responsibilities in Latin America

In this section we intend to differentiate the approach of a merely corporate social responsibility policy in contrast with the incorporation of human rights-based approach by corporations. This distinction is based on the different impacts that both perspectives could have on ensuring sustainable development and respect for human rights.

First, the concept of corporate social responsibility came into common use in the early seventies with the purpose of introducing an ethical approach to business and how they impact on their stakeholders. The author considers that any concept of corporate social responsibility has minimum requirements that refer to stakeholders, win–win relationships, triple results and a management that permits its impact to be monitored and evaluated. Thus, the concept of corporate social responsibility does not necessarily include or require a human rights-based approach. For instance, in Latin America many enterprises have started to work on corporate social responsibility, implementing policies and establishing offices for CSR but without being aware of their role as regards the respect and protection of human rights. It is still possible to find key organizations working on CSR which were created by companies in their countries to promote CSR but which do not work within the framework of the UN Global Compact. Therefore, one cannot state that a company which has implemented a CSR policy is necessarily enacting it because it addresses certain responsibilities in regard to human rights. A clear example of this distinction is that many of the companies extracting natural resources in the region have created CSR offices and policies, but they have failed to respect livelihoods, avoid conflict and countless human rights violations claimed by communities.[3]

For that reason, the author raises this distinction and proposes a change in terminology to shift to business and human rights policies instead of

---

[2] For further information on the Inter-American Court of Human Rights, visit its website at www.corteidh.or.cr.

[3] For detailed information regarding conflicts and human rights violations in relation with companies activities in Latin America, see www.businessandhumanrights.org.

merely CSR policies. In particular, in Latin America the human rights-based approach has a key relevance for the way in which societies relate to other actors, be they states or corporations.

Certainly, the specific link between business and human rights does not go back farther than 16 years. Indeed, it was at the beginning of the 1990s that a combination of factors contributed to the development of this interdependence relationship. These factors include the increasing supervision of the media, constant monitoring by social organizations and public institutions, and more transparency because of the ample access to information. More than a decade ago, any human rights or humanitarian organization talked about business and human rights. But in parallel, practically any corporation at that time used the term human rights. Today, it is more common to use a human rights language and a human rights approach in the relation among corporations and stakeholders in the national and international arena. Nevertheless, if one approaches the Latin American scenario, one will notice that although multinationals operating in the region are working on CSR, and even though an increasing number among them are referring to human rights in their policies, the great majority of medium and small enterprises still do not have or do not know how to implement a human rights approach in their businesses. Indeed between 90 and 98 per cent of all manufacturers in Latin America are small or medium-sized companies.[4] Thus, a major challenge in Latin America refers to a shift from the merely corporate social responsibility discourse to a human rights-based approach on corporate activities.

3 Democracy, human rights and corporations in Latin America

In this section, the author deems it important to analyse the main factors that have influenced the development of CSR and Business and Human Rights during the last 30 years of emerging democracy systems in the region to better understand the way corporations operate in the region and the substantial need for the promotion of a human rights-based approach among corporations. This analysis would be useful in identifying challenges that can be faced in the promotion of a rights-based approach among companies under the umbrella of the SRSG's mandate.

The Latin American scenario differs greatly from those of other regions worldwide. If one focuses on the analysis of the historical trends during the last 30 years, the main trend is the consolidation of democracies after years of authoritarian governments or dictatorships, and in some cases after

---

[4] See Falling behind: the many challenges faced by small companies in Latin America, available at http://www.wharton.universia.net/index.cfm?fa=viewArticle&id=1527&language=english.

years of internal armed conflicts that have badly affected entire countries where the topic of human rights was almost impossible to raise. Nevertheless, since the beginning of the 1990s the scenario has changed favourably due to the establishment of democratic governments that have managed to undertake, in most cases, profound legal reforms that recognize human rights and open an ample sphere of action for civil society organizations, but governments have failed to ensure conditions of life with dignity for a great majority of the population in Latin America. One of the fundamental and structural problems in the region is the persistent breach between law and reality. For instance, United Nations Development Programme (UNDP) indicators show that the inequality between rich and poor people is one of the major problems in the region. Despite the fact that states are the primary duty bearers with respect to human rights, companies have responsibilities to respect and protect human rights within the sphere of influence, and regardless of whether they act directly or in complicity with other actors. Hence, these circumstances place corporations in a privileged situation to adopt a human rights approach to creating welfare and sustainable development for the societies where they operate.

As regards legal reforms undertaken during the years of democracy in the region, one relevant reform was the approval of new Constitutions that are substantially based on the principle of the 'social market economy'. The recognition of this principle in the vast majority of Latin American countries means that although private initiative is free, it cannot be accomplished in contravention of the general or social interest.[5] The manner in which social interest and human rights converge is shown in Article 21 of the American Convention on Human Rights, which enshrines that:

1. Everyone has the right to the use and enjoyment of his property. The law may subordinate such use and enjoyment to the interest of society.
2. No one shall be deprived of his property except upon payment of just compensation, for reasons of public utility or social interest, and in the cases and according to the forms established by law.
3. Usury and any other form of exploitation of man by man shall be prohibited by law.

---

[5] Landa, César The treaty of Free Trade Agreement Peru – United States of America: a constitutional perspective, In Andean Yearly of Property Law, Year II – N° 2, Lima, 2005, p. 19 ('El tratado de Libre Comercio Perú – Estados Unidos: una perspectiva constitucional' En: Anuario Andino de Derechos Intelectuales; Año II – N° 2. Lima, 2005, p. 19, quoting Roldan Xopa, José, Constitución y Mercado D.F. Porrúa, 2004, p. 288 y ss.).

Based on this provision the Inter-American Court of Human Rights has addressed the issue of convergence between social interest and human rights throughout its jurisprudence. For instance, in the Mayagna Awas Tigni case against Nicaragua, the issue of concession was that the Court stated that the human right to communal property of indigenous communities compels the state to 'abstain from carrying out, until that delimitation, demarcation, and titling have been done, actions that might lead the agents of the State itself, or third parties acting with its acquiescence or its tolerance, to affect the existence, value, use or enjoyment of the property located in the geographical area where the members of the Community live and carry out their activities'.[6] Thus, the right to land of indigenous peoples converges with the social interest of the vast majority of society and should be respected by the state in all circumstances. In this regard, the state's obligation to respect and protect is absolutely relevant to ensure that corporations do not contravene human rights.

To this extent, one important example revealing that the majority of Latin American states recognize the importance of their role in regard to companies is the constitutional recognition of the right to commercial freedom or the freedom to conduct business ('libertad de empresa'). As an example, one can refer to Colombia,[7] Ecuador,[8] Peru,[9] El Salvador[10] and Venezuela.[11] Indeed, a constitutional framework is important to determine clearly the scope of the state's obligation to protect all persons within its jurisdiction and specifically to define the scope of the obligation to regulate corporate activities with different stakeholders.[12] For instance, in most countries in Latin America there are norms addressing labour rights, the performance of business activities and the protection of the consumer's right to health, among others. However, the achievements of the legal framework as regards the promotion of business and human rights in the region are still incipient and dispersed in specific norms adopted by different public entities, instead

---

[6] Inter-American Court of Human Rights, Case of Mayagna (Sumo) Awas Tigni Community against Nicaragua, judgment 21 August 2001, merits, reparations and cost, Serie C, paragraph 153.
[7] Constitution of Colombia of 1991, article 333.
[8] Constitution of Ecuador of 1997, article 23.
[9] Constitution of Peru of 1993, article 59.
[10] Constitution of El Salvador, article 110.
[11] Constitution of the Bolivarian Republic of Venezuela of 1999, article 112.
[12] There is no limited list of stakeholders because these change over time depending on geographical grounds or on the type of activities. See: PNUMA, Stakeholder research associate and accountability, Manual for relations with stakeholders. Commitment with stakeholder. From Word to action, Barcelona, Nóos Institute, 2006, p. 25. (Manual para la práctica de las relaciones con los grupos de interés. El compromiso con los stakeholders. De las palabras a la acción. Barcelona: Nóos Instituto, 2006, p. 25.)

of a general legal framework passed by legislative branches. For example, in the Federal Republic of Brazil, the State of Rio Grande do Sul adopted law 11.440[13] in 2000, which stipulates that all social corporate responsibility enterprises operating in that specific state must submit an annual social balance to the authorities. Peru has a Law N° 28611 General Law on the Environment (Ley General del Ambiente), whose Article 78 is titled 'Corporate social responsibility' (De la responsabilidad social de la empresa). In Venezuela there is a Law on Corporate Responsibility on Radio and Television.[14] In Argentina there has been a debate regarding corporate social responsibility legislation aiming to require all enterprises with a minimum of 300 employees to present evidence of a social balance to the authorities.

On the other hand, it is also important to outline the role of national tribunals in the region in promoting business and human rights. For example, the Constitutional Court of Peru has addressed the issue in different cases in order to interpret that the sphere of corporate social responsibility combines mandatory obligations and voluntary actions, stating:

> Being socially responsible does not mean only to respect legal obligations, but it also means going beyond legal compliance to support and improve the local environment and contributing to the development of the communities where they operate, especially local communities.
>
> (Non official translation)[15]

Regarding public policies in the sphere of business and human rights, there are also some interesting initiatives in the region. For instance, in Colombia[16] the government has established a special section on business and human rights that promotes corporate social responsibility with particular focus on the constitutional provisions and the Global Compact. In Chile the Ministry of Labour has created a special award for labour relationships and quality of life of persons working for enterprises.[17]

---

[13] http://www.al.rs.gov.br/legiscomp/arquivo.asp?Rotulo=Lei%20n°%2011440id Norma=219tipo=pdf.
[14] Official Gazzette N° 38.333 of 12 December 2005.
[15] Constitutional Tribunal of Peru Judgment on the file N° 1752-2004-AA/TC paragraph 22.
[16] Vice Presidency of the Republic of Colombia, Business and Human Rights http://www.global-business-initiative.org/News%20Pages/files/GBI%20Roundtable%20 Colombia%2024%20May%202010%20Report.pdf.
[17] Ministry of Labour and Social Provisions, Decree 194, published on 26 November 2004 in http://weblegis1.bcn.cl.

Despite the fact that there are some interesting initiatives and specific measures adopted by different countries in Latin America as regards business and human rights, one can observe that these initiatives are still at a minimum stage in the process of promoting business and human rights through the establishment of systematic and comprehensive legal frameworks and building capacities to implement and promote human rights in this field.

4 Setting regional business and human rights standards: the state obligation to protect

This section focuses on the analysis of how the Inter-American regional system can contribute to 'operationalizing' the policy framework proposed by the SRSG on human rights and business. Definitely, the regional human rights system has an important role for the way ahead to support the work of the SRSG on human rights and business. Specifically, the Inter-American supervisory human rights organs can decisively contribute to one of the three core principles of the SRSG' policy framework, which is the state's obligation to protect. To this extent, the author considers that the Inter-American human rights system could develop in depth considerations regarding due diligence, complicity, sphere of influence and the issue of extraterritoriality as regards business' activities. For instance, the system has not addressed the issue of extraterritorial regulation to prevent overseas abuse by corporations based in a State Party.[18] Thus, this section identifies standards, achievements and shortcomings regarding businesses' responsibilities for human rights in Latin America.

Mapping States Parties' obligations under the American Convention on Human Rights (hereinafter the 'Convention' or 'American Convention') is intended to build on information regarding the scope and content of States Parties' obligations to regulate and adjudicate the actions of business enterprises under the Inter-American legal framework on human rights.

It is pertinent to briefly point out some important details regarding the Inter-American System on Human Rights with the aim to understand better the importance and impact of the decisions and jurisprudence analysed by the author in this chapter.

---

[18] Anicama, Cecilia State Responsibilities to Regulate and Adjudicate Corporate Activities under the Inter-American Human Rights System. Report on the American Convention on Human Rights prepared to inform the mandate of UN Special Representative on Business & Human Rights John Ruggie, April 2008 http://www.reports-and-materials.org/State-Responsibilities-under-Inter-American-System-Apr-2008.pdf.

The Inter-American System of Human Rights is a regional system created within the Organization of American States (OAS).[19] This international organization has 35 Member States,[20] not all of whom have ratified the Convention. States which are OAS members but which have not ratified the Convention are only bound by the American Declaration of the Rights and Duties of Man (ADRDM). The Inter-Amreican Court of Human Rights has confirmed that although this Declaration is not a treaty, it is 'a source of international obligations for the member states of the OAS'.[21] For the States Parties to the Convention, the specific source of their obligations with respect to human rights is, in principle, the Convention itself.[22]

As outlined above, the regional system has two main organs: the Inter-American Commission on Human Rights and the Inter-American Court of Human Rights.[23]

The Commission is an autonomous organ of the Organization of American States.[24] Its mandate is based on Article 106 of the OAS Charter, the Convention and its Statute. The Commission promotes human rights in all of the OAS member states. Its seven members act independently, without representing any particular country.[25] The Commission's headquarters are in Washington DC and the Court sits in San José, Costa Rica.

---

[19] For further information on the Organization of American States, visit its website at www.oas.org.

[20] Antigua and Barbuda, Argentina, Bahamas, Barbados, Belize, Bolivia, Brazil, Canada, Chile, Colombia, Costa Rica, Cuba, Dominica, Dominican Republic, Ecuador, El Salvador, Grenada, Guatemala, Guyana, Haiti, Honduras, Jamaica, Mexico, Nicaragua, Panama, Paraguay, Peru, Saint Kitts and Nevis, Saint Lucia, Saint Vincent and the Grenadines, Suriname, Trinidad and Tobago, United States of America, Uruguay and Venezuela http://www.oas.org/documents/eng/memberstates.asp.

[21] Inter-American Court of Human Rights, Interpretation of the American Declaration of the Rights and Duties of Man within the framework of article 64 of the American Convention on Human Rights, Advisory Opinion. OC 10/89 of 14 July 1989, Series A, Number 10, paragraph 42.

[22] There are other Inter-American treaties on human rights, which can be reviewed at http://www.cidh.org/Basicos/English/Basic.TOC.htm.

[23] Article 33 of the American Convention on Human Rights 'The following organs shall have competence with respect to matters relating to the fulfilment of the commitments made by the States Parties to this Convention: a. the Inter-American Commission on Human Rights, referred to as 'The Commission;' and b. The Inter-American Court of Human Rights, referred to as 'The Court.'

[24] OAS Charter, adopted in 1948, article 106 'There shall be an Inter-American Commission on Human Rights, whose principal function shall be to promote the observance and protection of human rights and to serve as a consultative organ of the Organization in these matters. An inter-American convention on human rights shall determine the structure, competence, and procedure of this Commission, as well as those of other organs responsible for these matters.'

[25] For further details, visit http://www.cidh.org/what.htm.

It is important to observe that while any person, group of persons or non-governmental organization legally recognized in any of the OAS member states can file a petition or a request for precautionary measures to the Commission,[26] only states and the Commission itself can submit a case or a request for provisional measures to the Court.[27]

The Commission's functions are defined in Articles 41–43 of the Convention. Articles 44–51 set forth the procedure for individual petitions and interstate communications.[28] The Commission can provide decisions on individual cases, precautionary measures and country reports, among others. The Commission shall also adopt precautionary measures when there is a situation of gravity and urgency involving irreparable harm to persons.[29] The Commission's decisions are only recommendations to states and are not legally binding.

The Court was created by the Convention and is the only jurisdictional organ within the system. The Court exercises adjudicatory and advisory jurisdiction. It has seven judges who are independent individuals not representing any particular country. The structure, functions and organization of the Court are provided for in Articles 52–69 of the Convention. For example, the Court renders judgments, advisory opinions and provisional measures. In general, judgments determine whether a state is or is not responsible for an alleged human rights violation and provide orders and guidance as to what should happen next. Advisory opinions interpret the Convention and other human rights treaties ratified by the OAS member states. Provisional measures are adopted to avoid irreparable harm to individuals when a situation of extreme gravity and urgency appears.[30] The Court's decisions are legally binding.

For a more comprehensive analysis on the issue of human rights and business within the Inter-American System, please refer to the report prepared by the author to assist the Special Representative of the UN Secretary General (SRSG) on Business and Human Rights, Professor John Ruggie, in implementing sub-paragraph (b) of his mandate to 'elaborate on the role of States in effectively regulating and adjudicating' the activities of business enterprises with regard to human rights.[31]

---

[26] American Convention on Human Rights, article 44 'Any person or group of persons, or any nongovernmental entity legally recognised in one or more member states of the Organization, may lodge petitions with the Commission containing denunciations or complaints of violation of this Convention by a State Party.'
[27] *Id.*, article 61.
[28] See also Rules and Procedure of the Inter-American Commission on Human Rights.
[29] *Id.*, article 25.
[30] American Convention on Human Rights, article 63 '2. Regarding provisional measures.'
[31] *Supra* note 19.

Concerning the state obligation to protect, it must state that under Articles 1.1[32] and 2[33] of the Convention, States Parties must respect and enforce respect of human rights to all individuals under their jurisdiction without discrimination.

Special obligations for states derive from these general obligations, which are ascertainable on the basis of the protection needed by the individual who is the right holder. These special obligations are due diligence and obligation to prevent, the obligation to investigate and the obligation to provide access to redress for violations of human rights. Thus both the Commission and the Court have determined that states shall be responsible for acts of private persons or groups, when these non-state actors act freely and with impunity to the detriment of the rights – in other words, where the state has failed to act with due diligence to prevent such violations. The Court has suggested that this means that states have the obligation to take reasonable steps to prevent human rights violations by non-state actors.

For instance, in the Case of Velazquez Rodriguez:

> Article 1(1) is essential in determining whether a violation of the human rights recognized by the Convention can be imputed to a State Party. In effect, that article charges the States Parties with the fundamental duty to respect and guarantee the rights recognized in the Convention. Any impairment of those rights which can be attributed under the rules of international law to the action or omission of any public authority constitutes an act imputable to the State, which assumes responsibility in the terms provided by the Convention.[34]

In addition, in the *19 Tradesmen v. Colombia*, concerning State responsibility regarding a massacre perpetrated by non-state actors, the Court declared:

---

[32] Article 1. Obligation to Respect Rights '1. The States Parties to this Convention undertake to respect the rights and freedoms recognized herein and to ensure to all persons subject to their jurisdiction the free and full exercise of those rights and freedoms, without any discrimination for reasons of race, colour, sex, language, religion, political or other opinion, national or social origin, economic status, birth, or any other social condition.'

[33] Article 2. Domestic Legal Effects 'Where the exercise of any of the rights or freedoms referred to in Article 1 is not already ensured by legislative or other provisions, the States Parties undertake to adopt, in accordance with their constitutional processes and the provisions of this Convention, such legislative or other measures as may be necessary to give effect to those rights or freedoms.'

[34] *Velazquez Rodriguez v. Honduras*, judgment on the merits, 29 July 1988, Series C Number 4. Also see *Godínez Cruz v. Honduras, judgment* on the merits, 20 January 1989, Series C Number 3 paragraph 164.

141. In order to establish that a violation of the rights embodied in the Convention has occurred, it is not necessary to determine, as it is under domestic criminal law, the guilt of the perpetrators or their intention, nor is it necessary to identify individually the agents to whom the violations are attributed. It is sufficient to demonstrate that public authorities have supported or tolerated the violation of the rights established in the Convention.[35,36]

(Emphasis added)

Furthermore, the Court has recently stated that 'when related to the essential jurisdiction of the supervision and regulation of rendering the services of public interest, such as health, by private or public entities (as is the case of a private hospital), the state responsibility is generated by the omission of the duty to supervise the rendering of the public service to protect the mentioned right'.[37]

Importantly, most of the decisions in the Inter-American System discussing the concept of due diligence and the state duty to protect focus on the activities of paramilitary groups. However, some jurisprudence does discuss due diligence and business activities, suggesting that the concept applies equally to protecting against corporate abuse; even the Court has used the term 'third parties', 'private individuals', 'private persons', and 'private groups' when discussing non-state actors. It has not used the term 'companies' or similar terms, even in a provisional measure concerning the protection of indigenous peoples in Ecuador, where business activities were clearly controversial. However, in this same provisional measure, Judge Antônio Cançado Trindade provides his own opinion, stating that the *erga omnes* nature of the obligations requires protection from all possible abuse, including by corporations.[38] Although these considerations show a very state-centric approach, they are relevant for the discussion of business responsibilities for human rights, considering that States should work

---

[35] *Inter-American Court of Human Rights Case of the 19 Tradesmen v. Colombia, Merits, Reparations and Cost*, judgment of 3 July 2004, Series C, Number 109.
[36] See also Inter-American Court of Human Rights Case of *The Rochela v. Colombia*, paragraph 68, Case of Pueblo Bello Massacre, Merits, Reparations and Cost, Judgment of 31 January 2006, Series C No 40, paragraph 112; Case of the Mapiripán Massacre, Merits, Reparations and Cost, Judgment of 15 September 2005, Series C No 134, paragraph 110; and Case of the 19 Tradesmen, *supra* note 30, paragraph 141.
[37] Inter-American Court of Human Rights, Case of Albán Cornejo v. Ecuador, Merits, reparations and costs, judgment of 22 November 2007, Series C, number 171, paragraph 119.
[38] Inter-American Court of Human Rights, Matter of the Sarayaku people regarding Ecuador, 17 June 2005, Opinion judge Cançado Trindade, paragraph 20. See Part V for a detailed discussion of the concept of *erga omnes*.

in close cooperation with corporations as regards to human rights; otherwise, failure on the part of the State to prevent or to tolerate illicit corporate activities is likely to place the State in a position to be declared as responsible for human rights violation based on a third party activity.

4.1 Inter-American commission on human rights

The author identifies several decisions in which a state violation of rights in the American Convention was related to business operations. The Commission has discussed state responsibility for business abuse in its individual cases, precautionary measures and country reports.

Regarding the analysis of individual cases,[39] the issue has been raised mainly in cases related to violations of indigenous peoples' rights by third parties.

Concerning precautionary measures, the impact of business operations on human rights generating states' responsibility has been addressed when the activities of enterprises have threatened the right to life and the right to personal integrity relating to the physical environment. Where environmental contamination and degradation pose a persistent threat to human life and health, the foregoing rights are implied.

Moreover, there are substantial references to business operations in country reports that detail specific measures a state must adopt to limit the impact of company operations on human rights abuses. For instance, in the Report on the Situation of Human Rights in Ecuador, the Commission analysed the impact of oil exploitation activities by a State-owned oil company on the health and lives of nearby residents. Here, the Commission made important considerations regarding the exploitation of natural resources, concessions and international investment. It stated that international investment has a positive impact in a country, but it is necessary for States Parties to establish appropriate regulations and monitoring when the environment and human rights may be impacted. Moreover, the Commission suggested that the obligation to act with due diligence includes the need to adopt preventive measures regarding the impact of private actors' activities on human rights. Thus the Commission concluded that:

> The State of Ecuador must ensure that measures are in place to prevent and protect against the occurrence of environmental contamination

---

[39] Article 44 of the American Convention on Human Rights provides 'Any person or group of persons, or any nongovernmental entity legally recognized in one or more member states of the Organization, may lodge petitions with the Commission containing denunciations or complaints of violation of this Convention by a State Party'. See also article 23 of the Rules of Procedure of the Inter-American Commission on Human Rights'.

which threatens the lives of the inhabitants of development sectors. Where the right to life of Oriente residents has been infringed upon by environmental contamination, the Government is obliged to respond with appropriate measures of investigation and redress.[40]

This conclusion highlights that the Commission believes states should act with proper due diligence to safeguard rights in the context of development projects and international investment. However, it does not define appropriate due diligence, suggesting that states have discretion in how they choose to fulfil the obligation. The Commission made substantive references to other human rights, including the rights to access to information, to participate in decision-making, and to access judicial remedies that this report analyses in Section 3.

Finally, the Commission's country report suggested that the Commission saw some responsibility for corporations to prevent harm, even if it considered that it was the state that had legal obligations for correcting harm under the Convention.

> As the Commission observed at the conclusion of its observation in loco: 'Decontamination is needed to correct mistakes that ought never to have happened.' Both the State and the companies conducting oil exploitation activities are responsible for such anomalies, and both should be responsible for correcting them. It is the duty of the State to ensure that they are corrected.[41]
>
> (Emphasis added)

This was the first time that an Inter-American supervisory organ had explicitly referred to responsibilities held by both companies and states.

4.2 Inter-American Court of Human Rights

The Inter-American Court of Human Rights is the only judicial organ of the regional system. The Court adopts judgments, advisory opinions and provisional measures. An overview of the judgments on the merits does not show extensive and comprehensive references to states' responsibilities for business operations. The issue has also not been analysed through an advisory opinion. Nevertheless, as highlighted below, the Court has on several

---

[40] Inter-American Commission on Human Rights, Report on the Situation of Human Rights in Ecuador, Chapter IX, OEA/Ser.L/V/II.96, Doc. 10 rev. 1, 24 April 1997, Original: Spanish/English.
[41] Inter-American Commission on Human Rights, Report on the Situation of Human Rights in Ecuador, Chapter IX, OEA/Ser.L/V/II.96, Doc. 10 rev. 1, 24 April 1997, Original: Spanish/English.

occasions granted provisional measures to ensure that states protect human rights threatened by business operations.

4.2.1 Judgments on the merits

Although the issue of business and human rights has not been raised in any of the judgments in depth, this report raises relevant considerations based on seven judgments on the merits. These cases implicitly deal with state responsibility for the actions of corporations, both state and privately owned. The cases are listed below and are only enumerated here, but further information could be found in the report prepared to inform the mandate of the SRSG:[42]

- Case of *Baena v. Panama*[43] (Several public companies)
- Case of the *Mayagna (Sumo) Awas Tingni Community v. Nicaragua* (Logging and indigenous peoples' rights)
- Case of *Ximenes-Lopes v. Brazil* (health services provided by a health care institution)
- Case of *Claude Reyes et al. v. Chile*[44] (Foreign investment project)
- Case of the *Sawhoyamaxa Indigenous Community v. Paraguay*:[45] Although this case does not refer to business operations, it is important to quote a consideration made by the Court regarding the enforcement of trade bilateral agreements, which states that:

   140. [...] the enforcement of bilateral commercial treaties negates vindication of non-compliance with state obligations under the American Convention; on the contrary, their enforcement should always be compatible with the American Convention, which is a multilateral treaty on human rights that stands in a class of its own and that generates rights for individual human beings and does not depend entirely on reciprocity among States.

- Case of the *Saramaka People v. Suriname*[46] (Mining, road construction and logging)
- Case of *Alban Cornejo v. Ecuador* (health services provided by a health care institution)

---

[42] *Supra* note 19.
[43] Inter-American Court of Human Rights Case of *Baena-Ricardo et al. v. Panama, Merits, Reparations and Cost*, judgment of 2 February 2001, Series C, Number 72.
[44] Inter-American Court of Human Rights, *Case of Claude Reyes et al. vs. Chile, merits, reparations and costs*, judgment of 19 September 2006, Series C, Number 151.
[45] Inter-American Court of Human Rights Merits, Reparations and Costs. Judgment of 29 March 2006. Series C No. 146.
[46] Inter-American Court of Human Rights, Preliminary objections, merits, reparations and costs, Judgment of 27 November 2007, Series C, Number 172.

4.2.2 Provisional measures

- Matter of Mayagna (Sumo) Awas Tingni regarding Nicaragua, Provisional measures, Order of 6 September 2002.
- Matter of Indigenous peoples of Sarayaku regarding Ecuador, provisional measures, Order of 17 June 2005.

4.2.3 Advisory opinions

Pursuant to Article 64 of the American Convention on Human Rights, both member states and OAS main organs can request the Court for an advisory opinion regarding interpretation of the Convention, interpretation of other human rights treaties entered into by OAS member states and the compatibility of national laws with the these treaties.

Through its advisory opinions, the Court has examined key human rights issues that, at the time, had not been brought to its attention in an individual case. For instance, advisory opinions have considered issues such as the protection of migrants, the meaning of 'law' and the scope of trade agreements, among others.[47]

While there has not yet been an advisory opinion specifically relevant for business issues with regards to human rights, it is important to note that the Court's second Advisory Opinion titled 'The effect of reservations on the entry into force of the American Convention on Human Rights (Articles 74 and 75)' stated that:

> 29. The Court must emphasize, however, that modern human rights treaties in general, and the American Convention in particular, are not multilateral treaties of the traditional type concluded to accomplish the reciprocal exchange of rights for the mutual benefit of the contracting States. Their object and purpose is the protection of the basic rights of individual human beings irrespective of their nationality, both against the State of their nationality and all other contracting States. In concluding these human rights treaties, the States can be deemed to submit themselves to a legal order within which they, for the common good, assume various obligations, not in relation to other States, but towards all individuals within their jurisdiction. The distinct character of these treaties has been recognized, *inter alia*, by the European Commission on Human Rights, when it declared
>
>> that the obligations undertaken by the High Contracting Parties in the European Convention are essentially of an objective character, being designed rather to protect the fundamental rights of

---

[47] At the time this article was written there were 19 Advisory opinions adopted by the Inter-American Court of Human Rights available in English http://www.corteidh.or.cr/opiniones.cfm.

individual human beings from infringements by any of the High Contracting Parties than to create subjective and reciprocal rights for the High Contracting Parties themselves. [*Austria v. Italy*, Application No. 788/60, *4 European Yearbook of Human Rights* 116, at 140 (1961)][48]

Moreover, in its 17th Advisory Opinion the Court referred to the protection of the rights of the child against non state actors' acts.[49]

Furthermore, in its 18th Advisory Opinion regarding the 'Juridical condition and rights of undocumented migrants', the Court referred to third parties, again confirming that states could be held responsible for failing to prevent abuse by third parties:

> 100. The principle of equality before the law and non-discrimination permeates every act of the powers of the State, in all their manifestations, related to respecting and ensuring human rights. Indeed, this principle may be considered peremptory under general international law, inasmuch as it applies to all States, whether or not they are party to a specific international treaty, and gives rise to effects with regard to third parties, including individuals. This implies that the State, both internationally and in its domestic legal system, and by means of the acts of any of its powers or of third parties who act under its tolerance, acquiescence or negligence, cannot behave in a way that is contrary to the principle of equality and non-discrimination, to the detriment of a determined group of persons.[50]

5 Conclusion

In conclusion, in the region it remains necessary to analyse the issue of business and human rights in relation to the process of strengthening democracies. Democracy and human rights have been key elements for the advancement of development and awareness of social corporate responsibilities in the region. Thus, democracy is key for the promotion of a human rights-based approach among corporations. This factor remains a challenge as regards big, small and medium-sized corporations operating in the region.

---

[48] Inter-American Court of Human Rights OC-2/82 of 24 September 1982, paragraph 29.
[49] Inter-American Court of Human Rights, Juridical condition and human rights of the child, OC-17-02, 28 August 2002, Series A, Number 17, paragraphs 62, 65, and 90.
[50] Inter-American Court of Human Rights, Juridical Condition and Rights of the Undocumented Migrants. Advisory Opinion OC-18 of 17 September 2003. Series A No. 18.

There are some interesting initiatives both at the national and the international level that should serve as inspiration for further developments to set new international standards serving as guidelines for further improvements in the domestic field. Once again, in Latin America the jurisprudence of the international human rights bodies and given by national tribunals is playing a vital role on our way forward for raising awareness for the need to have corporations act on human rights.

Part III
Combining Law and Management

9
Business Commitments in CSR Codes of Conduct and International Framework Agreements: The Case of Human Rights*

Dominique Bé

1 Introduction

Corporate codes of conduct and International Framework Agreements (IFAs) are new forms of governance at company level. Their development has been widely researched. Some research has already compared their respective content, scope, procedures and impact.[1]

This chapter examines the commitments made by multinational enterprises (MNEs), in particular with regard to human rights, in IFAs agreed with Global Union Federations (GUFs) and in codes of conduct covering their social responsibilities. By building upon a comparative analysis of IFAs and corporate social responsibility (CSR) codes of conduct, it argues that the form and content of commitments taken by MNEs and how they are implemented is largely determined by the identity of other parties or stakeholders to the agreement or code.

Sections 2 and 3 analyse the main characteristics of IFAs and CSR codes, their clauses concerning human rights and related international standards, references to the legal framework and implementation mechanisms including requirements concerning business partners, contractors and suppliers. Section 4 examines the differences between CSR codes and IFAs and how they address similar issues. The analysis builds upon three dimensions: IFAs and CSR codes, IFAs of MNEs with or without CSR codes and texts of

---

* This paper reflects solely the author's personal views and may not in any circumstances be regarded as stating an official position of the European Commission.
[1] European Foundation, *Codes of conduct and international framework agreements: New forms of governance at company level*, 2008, http://www.eurofound.europa.eu/pubdocs/2007/92/en/1/ef0792en.pdf.

MNEs having signed both IFAs and CSR codes. Section 5 summarizes the conclusions of the research and concludes that coherence and consistency of the commitments undertaken by MNEs in IFAs and CSR codes are essential for CSR to remain a credible alternative to the legal approach in the area of human rights.

2 International framework agreements

IFAs – which are also referred to as Global Framework Agreements – are agreements signed between MNEs and GUFs. GUFs are international federations of national and regional trade unions organizing workers in industrial sectors or occupational groups. Eight out of the ten GUFs are involved in negotiating and signing IFAs. Only agreements signed by GUFs are called IFAs. Building and Wood Workers' International (BWI), the International Metalworkers' Federation (IMF) and the International Garment and Leather Workers' Federation (ITGLWF) have developed model IFAs.

Since the signature of the first IFA by Danone and the International Union of Food, Agricultural, Hotel, Restaurant, Catering, Tobacco and Allied Workers' Association (IUF) in 1988 a growing number of IFAs have been signed: by mid-2008 60 MNEs had concluded IFAs.

Most IFAs have been signed by MNEs based in continental Europe, in particular in Germany, France, the Netherlands, Sweden, Italy, Spain and Norway. IFAs have also been signed by seven non-European MNEs: National Australia Group [Australia], Quebecor [Canada], Fonterra [New Zealand], Lukoil [Russia], AngloGold Ashanti and Nampak [South Africa] and Chiquita [USA].

MNEs signing IFAs are mostly active in automobile and metalworking, construction, energy and mining, food, commerce and services. Five GUFs have signed most IFAs: 18 IFAs by IMF including a joint one with ICEM, 13 by BWI including a joint one with the ICEM, 13 by ICEM, 11 by UNI and 5 by IUF.

Most IFAs are called an 'agreement' or 'framework agreement' whereas other IFAs are titled '(joint) declaration', 'code of conduct' or 'principles'. Two of the five MNEs having signed IFAs titled 'code of conduct' have also adopted a CSR code. Some 13 IFAs refer in their title to the social responsibility of the signatory MNE and 19 IFAs refer in their text to the CSR code of the signatory MNE.

IFAs cover about 4.5 million workers, which are directly employed by signatory MNEs. The number of employees affected in each MNE varies from less than 1,000 up to half a million, with an average size of 75,000. The number of affected workers is, however, much higher when including those working for business partners, contractors and suppliers when IFAs cover them (see below).

2.1 Objectives of IFAs

GUFs primarily promote IFAs as an attempt to enforce minimum labour rights in MNEs. They aim at dealing with government failure to enforce global minimum labour rights and at getting MNEs to accept some responsibility for the labour rights situation throughout the supply chain. They also promote IFAs to advance trade unions' recognition and social dialogue. One can also argue that GUFs use IFAs as a response to the development of CSR.

Employers see IFAs as a means for developing dialogue with employee representatives but *not* as a collective bargaining exercise.[2] They negotiate IFAs as a means to get the approval or consent of employees' representatives for common policies on employment and social matters and to avoid running parallel local negotiations and their associated costs.

2.2 IFAs and workers' rights

Most IFAs are focused on workers' rights and reaffirm fundamental labour rights defined by the International Labour Organisation (ILO) core labour conventions. The core element of most IFAs is a commitment by the signatory MNE to meet minimum labour standards.

All IFAs refer to ILO core labour standards which are explicitly listed in 33 IFAs. Additional ILO conventions and recommendations are mentioned in a number of IFAs. IFAs primarily state the acceptance of trade unions by the signatory MNE: ILO Convention no. 87 on the freedom of association and protection of the right to organize and no. 98 on the right to organize and collective bargaining are the most commonly cited conventions.

2.3 IFAs and human rights

Besides fundamental labour rights IFAs reaffirm human rights. Both the BWI and the ITGLWF refer to human rights, in particular to the Universal Declaration of Human Rights, in their model IFAs. However, they merely acknowledge the need to observe the fundamental principles of human rights while requiring MNEs to abide by applicable laws insofar as these do not conflict with human rights standards.

Only one IFA refers to human rights in its title (Joint Declaration on Human Rights and Working Conditions in the BMW Group) but most IFAs – 44 out of 60 – refer to human rights and commitments to enforce them. Pledges vary from approval and support for human rights to commitment to respect them. Several IFAs signed by MNEs from different industrial sectors include similar phrasing expressing commitments to respect human rights.

About half of IFAs refer to internationally agreed standards related to human rights, in particular the Universal Declaration of Human Rights, the

---

[2] IOE website, *International Industrial Relations*, http://ioe-emp.org/en/policy-areas/international-industrial-relations/index.html.

ILO Declaration on Fundamental Principles and Rights at Work, the ILO Tripartite Declaration of Principles concerning Multinational Enterprises and Social Policy, the OECD Guidelines for Multinational Enterprises and the UN Global Compact.

IFAs also cite other international standards such as the Declaration on the elimination of all forms of discrimination against women, the Declaration and the Convention on the Rights of the Child, ILO Codes of practice, ILO Guidelines for Occupational Health Management Systems and the Rio Declaration on Sustainable Development.

2.4 Implementation of IFAs

<u>Initially IFAs were very short statements of principle but recent IFAs increasingly include detailed provisions for their implementation, including information, administration, monitoring and problem resolution.</u>

IFAs are, however, not collective agreements. In the absence of a legal framework for international industrial relations or social dialogue, there is no legal obligation for MNEs to enter into the negotiation of IFAs. In the absence of an international court or labour tribunal to which they could resort IFAs are neither legally binding nor enforceable.

Most IFAs thus build only upon the commitment of signatory MNEs to respect them worldwide but a third of them – mostly signed by German-based MNEs – include provisions underlining their binding character. In contrast the IFA signed by Quebecor explicitly states that it 'is not a legally binding document'. The official character of some IFAs has also been reinforced by a signature in the presence of public authorities or an official transmission to them.

The normative framework for workplace issues, in particular working conditions and environmental issues, is usually based on national legislation and local collective agreements. Most IFAs therefore include a commitment of signatory MNEs to respect national regulations and local collective agreements. This ensures that IFAs do not undermine existing workplace standards.

Most IFAs also include a provision for the information of employees of the signatory MNE and in some cases, of the employees of suppliers and contractors. Employees can be informed orally or in writing, by company management or through their trade unions. In some cases the MNE is responsible for informing local management, employee representatives and/or employees themselves, whereas in other cases responsibilities are shared between the MNE, which informs local management and suppliers, and the GUF, which informs its member unions, which in turn inform employees. External communication about the IFA may require the joint agreement of the MNE and the GUF as in Statoil's IFA. Most IFAs, however, are published on the website of the signatory GUF, which also distributes their texts to its member trade unions.

Most IFAs include provisions for their administration and monitoring. A number of IFAs include clauses recognizing the co-responsibility of signatories in administering the agreement. This responsibility lies either with the organizations, their chief officers or ad hoc committees. IFAs may be administered either by a committee of representatives of the signatories of the agreement created for that purpose or by existing works councils. Most IFAs include provisions for regular meetings, including their scope and their financing. Some IFAs include clauses detailing the organization of their monitoring which is often shared between the local level and the group level. Monitoring at the level of the business unit is ensured by management or by joint committees whereas monitoring at group level is usually ensured by joint committees.

Most IFAs provide for the right of signatories, in particular trade unions, to bring complaints concerning their implementation. In some cases all employees have the right to address issues and problems related to the IFA with the guarantee that this will not be to their detriment and neither will it entail any sanctions (e.g., Rheinmetall, GEA, Umicore) whereas other IFAs reserve the right to raise complaints to signatory MNEs.

Most IFAs favour the resolution of differences regarding their interpretation or implementation by the signatories themselves with the possibility of arbitration in some cases. Several IFAs state that disputes concerning their interpretation and application should be handled and settled at the local level (subsidiarity principle), as 'problems that arise between workers and their companies must be resolved at the level closest to the workplace' (Eni's IFA). A procedure for handling and settling disputes unresolved at national level is, however, foreseen by a number of IFAs. Some IFAs foresee a three-step procedure to deal with complaints or infringements which should be raised with local management first, then in a second stage, if needed, referred to national management and trade unions. Only unresolved cases should finally be referred to the GUF, which would then raise the matter with the MNE corporate management.

Although most IFAs state that the resolution of problems arising from their implementation relies on the signatories themselves a few IFAs (e.g., Arcelor and Umicore) are made subject to national law, with disputes being the exclusive competence of national courts. This approach is, however, more an exception than a trend.

Although the responsibility for complying with commitments made in the IFA stays in most cases with the MNE as a whole, some IFAs state that the responsibility to fulfilling their commitments lies with 'the senior managers of each business unit' (Daimler). In the case of the IFA signed by GEA, employee representatives share the responsibility for achieving the objectives of the agreement.

Some IFAs state that 'the parties have a mutual and common responsibility to contribute to the realization of these goals (of the IFA) through an active and constructive cooperation' (e.g., Veidekke, EDF, Nampak). In addition the IFA of Ballast Nedam foresees that trade unions 'will attest vis-à-vis state and international institutions and major private clients [that] Ballast Nedam [plays] a particularly positive role as setting a good example of responsible corporate management'.

2.5 Business partners, contractors and suppliers

Commitments taken in IFAs, in particular with regard to compliance with ILO core labour standards, cover not only operations under the direct control of signatory MNEs but often also concern business partners, contractors, suppliers and their employees, who are not signatories.

In contrast with collective agreements that define precisely which workers are covered, IFAs may therefore cover employees of the signatory MNE and its suppliers, including non-unionized workers. This implies that not everyone who is covered by an IFA, in particular employees of contractors and suppliers, is represented during its negotiation. Furthermore, a number of IFAs – all signed by German MNEs – explicitly state that 'third parties cannot drive or enforce any rights' from them. It means that not everyone who is covered by an IFA may be in a position to claim the observance of the rights agreed in it.

The responsibility of the signatory MNE to extend IFAs to business partners, contractors and suppliers is in most cases limited to informing them of the existence of the agreement and encouraging them to respect its principles. In some IFAs MNEs commit to collaborate only with contractors and suppliers which recognize and implement commitments taken in the IFA and even to reconsider or terminate business relations with those violating labour rights and legislation.

In some cases the implementation of the IFA by suppliers and contractors is monitored by the internal corporate audit (e.g., Leoni and Daimler) or by external compliance organizations (e.g., IKEA and Inditex).

2.6 Main characteristics of IFAs

Although their emphasis varies in relation with their diverse industrial and geographical origins, IFAs share a number of characteristics:

- Within the whole range of human rights IFAs tend to give priority to the respect for labour rights, in particular freedom of association. Next to ILO conventions which are referred to in all IFAs, the Universal Declaration of Human Rights is the most commonly cited international standard.
- IFAs include clauses stating that they will not undermine rights provided by national legislation and collective agreements and often include commitments to go beyond those requirements.

- Most IFAs provide for the information of employees of signatory MNEs and of their contractors and suppliers about their content. GUFs publish most IFAs they sign on their website but MNEs rarely do so.
- GUFs share the objectives of IFAs but seldom the responsibility for their achievement: the responsibility to implement commitments taken in IFAs lies mainly with MNEs or their managers. GUFs are, however, involved in the joint monitoring of most IFAs.
- Whereas IFAs may impact on society as a whole and in particular on contractors and suppliers, third parties are usually excluded from their administration and implementation: only management and employees of signatory MNEs – or their representatives – are involved in them. Most IFAs refer to contractors and suppliers, but in most cases just to inform them of their existence.
- Most IFAs allow trade unions or even individual employees to raise complaints concerning their application. In contrast claims by third parties are sometimes formally excluded.
- Similar wording is found in IFAs signed by MNEs belonging to the same industrial sector and in some instances across industrial sectors. This appears to indicate that GUFs are in a position to influence and to some extent to harmonize the form and content of IFAs.

3 Corporate codes of conduct

In recent years MNEs have increasingly adopted corporate codes of conduct in response to growing public interest in their social and environmental impacts. Codes of conduct are formal statements of principles defining standards for business behaviour. In most cases they are adopted and proclaimed unilaterally by company management. Codes of conduct may relate to a company's own behaviour, to the behaviour of its suppliers or both.[3] Codes of conduct may be all-encompassing, addressing human rights, social and environmental issues, and corporate governance matters or have a specific focus.[4,5] Hereafter the analysis focuses on codes of conduct concerning CSR issues which have been adopted by MNEs having signed IFAs.

Among the 60 MNEs having signed IFAs, 25 have also adopted and published on their website a code of conduct related to their social responsibilities. In addition 17 MNEs having signed IFAs publish on their

---

[3] OECD Secretariat, *Overview of selected initiatives and instruments relevant to corporate social responsibility*, 2008, http://www.oecd.org/dataoecd/18/56/40889288.pdf.

[4] A. Kolk and R.J.M. Tulder, Setting new global rules? TNCs and codes of conduct, *Transnational Corporations*, Vol. 14, No. 3, pp. 1–27, 2005, http://ssrn.com/abstract=894322.

[5] *The promotion of sustainable enterprises*, International Labour Conference, 96th Session, 2007, http://www.ilo.org/public/english/standards/relm/ilc/ilc96/pdf/rep-vi.pdf.

website information related to sustainable development and/or CSR without explicit reference to a code of conduct. Among them seven – six German MNEs and one French – refer to their IFA to define their corporate social responsibility.

Among the 25 CSR codes adopted by MNEs having signed IFAs 20 focus on operations directly controlled by the MNE whereas two codes establish principles and requirements for contractors and suppliers. The last three codes cover both internal business conduct and suppliers' social performance.

Whereas MNEs established in Germany, France and the Netherlands, countries which have strong traditions of social dialogue and legislation, account for almost two-thirds of the IFAs signed so far, they are less likely to adopt CSR codes: less than half of them have adopted CSR codes. In contrast MNEs based in other countries tend to sign both IFAs and CSR codes.

The probability that MNEs having signed IFAs will adopt CSR codes does not vary significantly by industrial sectors: in all of them about half of MNEs have adopted CSR codes.

3.1 CSR codes and human rights

Most CSR codes adopted by MNEs having signed IFAs refer to the promotion of human rights, and a number of them explicitly mention internationally agreed standards related to human rights, in particular the Universal Declaration of Human Rights, the ILO core labour standards, the UN Global Compact and the OECD guidelines for multinational enterprises.

IFAs promoted by MNEs as defining their corporate social responsibility are more likely than CSR codes to refer to human rights, in particular to the ILO core labour standards and the UN Global Compact. They are, however, less likely to refer to the Universal Declaration for Human rights and the OECD guidelines for multinational enterprises.

CSR codes are usually proclaimed unilaterally by MNEs and are not legally binding except regarding misleading advertising rules. Some CSR codes, however, emphasize their binding character for the MNE (e.g., 'These Principles form the basis of compulsory application for all the companies of Groupe Danone') and its staff (e.g., 'These Guidelines shall apply to all the Companies that comprise the Inditex Group, binding all its staff'). Most CSR codes include commitments of signatory MNEs and/or obligations for their employees or suppliers to obey existing regulations. In comparison three of the seven IFAs defining MNE's CSR include clauses stating their binding character and all of them include commitments of signatory MNEs to follow existing regulations.

A number of CSR codes foresee sanctions against employees who would fail to follow their principles (e.g., Danone and Telefónica). Disciplinary action in the event of severe breaches of the rules imposed by CSR codes may lead to dismissal and legal action (e.g., AngloGold Ashanti and Statoil).

3.2 Implementation of CSR codes

Most CSR codes include provisions for their implementation, including information, administration, monitoring and problem resolution.

Employees, and in some cases employees of suppliers and contractors, are to be informed in their own language and/or can participate in training sessions (e.g., Carrefour). Local management is often responsible for informing its employees (e.g., Danone, Lafarge and SKF) and contractors and suppliers for informing theirs (e.g., IKEA). Two-thirds of CSR codes include provisions for their administration and monitoring whilst half of them include a complaint procedure allowing employees to report violations of their principles.

In comparison IFAs defining MNEs' CSR are more likely to include clauses for their implementation. All of them include provisions for the information of employees while most include clauses regarding their administration and monitoring, and half of them describe a mechanism for handling complaints.

3.3 Business partners, contractors and suppliers

CSR codes cover not only operations under the direct control of signatory MNEs but also often apply to business partners, contractors and suppliers. In most cases MNEs merely commit to encouraging business partners and suppliers to respect the principles of their CSR codes. In a limited number of cases MNEs undertake to work only with contractors and suppliers which recognize and implement the principles of their CSR codes. In comparison all IFAs defining MNE's CSR include clauses concerning suppliers. Half of them encourage suppliers to follow their principles whereas the others make contracting conditional on compliance with their requirements.

3.4 Main characteristics of CSR codes

25 MNEs having signed IFAs have adopted CSR codes. MNEs based in countries with a strong social dialogue tradition are, however, less likely to adopt CSR codes. Whereas most CSR codes insist on informing contractors and suppliers of their existence and some condition contracting to compliance with their requirements, very few are suppliers' codes.

Most CSR codes refer to human rights, in particular the Universal Declaration of Human Rights, the OECD Guidelines for MNEs and the Global Compact, whereas labour rights are just one of the issues addressed by them.

Although most CSR codes include commitments to obey existing laws and regulations, relatively few acknowledge their own binding character. MNEs and their management are responsible for the administration and monitoring of most CSR codes. A number of CSR codes foresee sanctions against employees who would not follow their principles.

4 Are CSR codes different from IFAs?

MNEs make commitments related to similar issues in IFAs and CSR codes. One can legitimately ask whether these commitments are consistent and coherent and, if not, how to explain the differences. This analysis focuses on commitments regarding human rights and related international standards. It also compares the degree to which IFAs and CSR codes are binding for MNEs, their employees, contractors and suppliers, how they relate to existing laws and what are their procedures of implementation.

Several samples of IFAs and CSR codes are compared: all IFAs with CSR codes of MNEs having signed IFAs, IFAs of MNEs having adopted CSR codes with IFAs of MNEs without CSR codes, and IFAs and CSR codes of MNEs having adopted both.

A word of caution before proceeding further: the IFA and the CSR code of an MNE may have been adopted years apart and aspirations may have changed for better or worse. Furthermore, this research is based on signed texts and does not assess the extent to which commitments are effectively implemented. One would also expect that when commitments differ in IFAs and CSR codes, MNEs fulfil the commitments which are higher.

4.1 Do IFAs and CSR codes address different issues?

A comparison of all 60 IFAs with the 25 CSR codes adopted by MNEs having signed IFAs shows that IFAs are less likely than CSR codes to refer to human rights, in particular to the Universal Declaration of Human Rights, the OECD guidelines for MNEs and the UN Global Compact. In contrast IFAs are more likely than CSR codes to include references to ILO Conventions and Declarations.

MNEs use a variety of words in IFAs and CSR codes to express their support for human rights: 'respect', 'support', 'endorse', 'commit', 'refer to', 'recognize', 'uphold', 'ensure the application', and so on. The present tense is used in both IFAs and CSR codes to stress the unambiguous commitment taken by MNEs. Some MNEs (e.g., SCA) use the same words, 'respects fundamental human rights', in IFAs and CSR codes. Whereas in CSR codes MNEs commit themselves – and in some instances their employees and suppliers – to respect human rights in their operations, both signatories – MNEs and GUFs – of a number of IFAs (e.g., AngloGold Ashanti, Inditex and Statoil) state their joint commitment to respect human rights.

4.2 Are IFAs more demanding than CSR codes?

IFAs are more likely than CSR codes to include clauses stating their binding character. Most IFAs and CSR codes refer to existing laws and regulations but CSR codes tend to commit MNEs to merely 'comply with the law' whereas several IFAs include pledges to go beyond minimum legal requirements.

IFAs are more likely than CSR codes to include detailed rules for their implementation, including their administration and monitoring, complaint mechanisms and the information of employees and in some cases, of the employees of suppliers and contractors. Some IFAs give an active and sometimes exclusive role to trade unions in their implementation. IFAs are usually made available to employees in local languages. Some IFAs make MNEs solely responsible for informing local management, employees and suppliers (e.g., Italcementi, Telefónica and Umicore) whereas others share the responsibility between both signatories, with MNEs informing local management and signatory trade unions informing employees (e.g., AngloGold Ashanti, Chiquita and Eni). Some IFAs make GUFs responsible for informing their member trade unions which in turn inform employees (e.g., SCA and Statoil) whereas others make contractors responsible for informing their employees (e.g., Inditex). In contrast the responsibility for informing employees of the existence and content of CSR codes lies mostly with (local) management.

MNEs and GUFs often share the responsibility of implementation of IFAs whereas commitments taken in CSR codes are more likely to bind individual employees, in combination with severe sanctions when employees fail to follow the principles of the code. The same phrasing can be found in IFAs negotiated by a given GUF (e.g., both SCA and Statoil IFAs mention 'will meet annually to review practice in the area of the agreed principles and follow up this agreement') or in both the IFA and the CSR code of a given MNE (e.g., SKF 'Group Management' (and the World Works Council presidium) 'will regularly supervise the observance of the Code of Conduct').

Mechanisms for handling complaints related to IFAs rely mainly on signatory trade unions – and individual employees in some IFAs (e.g., SCA) – to raise issues with management. CSR codes give a more exclusive role to employees in identifying and reporting violations of their principles (whistle-blowing) to superiors while offering them protection from retaliation (e.g., AngloGold Ashanti, Chiquita, Eni, ISS, SCA and Telefónica). Some CSR codes give the responsibility to ensure compliance with their principles to a committee composed of management representatives (e.g., EADS, Eni and France Telecom).

IFAs and CSR codes do not differ significantly in the way they address business partners, contractors and suppliers. They are more likely to 'inform, support and encourage' contractors than to 'require' compliance with their principles as a condition for contracting or to include sanctions against those which fail to meet them. Some MNEs use identical clauses in both their IFA and CSR code (e.g., SKF 'encourages its suppliers to adhere to similar codes of conduct' or Umicore 'seeks business partners whose policies regarding ethical, social and environmental issues are consistent with our own Code of Conduct'). Some IFAs refer to subcontracting requirements formulated in the MNE's CSR code (e.g., IKEA and Umicore).

4.3 Does the adoption of CSR codes impact on the content of IFAs?

A comparison of IFAs signed by MNEs having adopted CSR codes with those signed by MNEs which have not ('codeless' MNEs) shows that the adoption of CSR codes reflects an approach embracing a wider range of issues and stakeholders, which in turn influences the content of IFAs signed by those MNEs.

Some 25 MNEs adopted CSR codes besides signing IFAs, whereas 35 MNEs signed IFAs without adopting CSR codes. MNEs adopting CSR codes in addition to IFAs are more likely to belong to the energy, metal and construction sectors.

IFAs signed by MNEs having adopted CSR codes are less likely to mention human rights in general but when they do, they more often make explicit reference to the Universal Declaration of Human Rights. All IFAs name the ILO conventions but IFAs signed by MNEs having adopted a CSR code are more likely to refer to the OECD guidelines for MNEs and the UN Global Compact.

IFAs signed by MNEs having adopted CSR codes are less likely to include clauses acknowledging their binding character and commitments to respect existing laws and regulations than those signed by 'codeless' MNEs. They are also less likely to include detailed provisions for their implementation, in particular their administration and monitoring, the handling of complaints and the information of employees.

IFAs signed by MNEs having adopted CSR codes are likely to include less demanding requirements from contractors and suppliers than IFAs signed by 'codeless' MNEs, as they put more emphasis on informing and encouraging than on obliging contractors and suppliers to respect their principles.

4.4 Do MNEs make consistent commitments in IFAs and CSR codes?

An analysis focused on 25 MNEs having signed and adopted both IFAs and CSR codes shows that their CSR codes are more likely than their IFAs to refer to human rights, in particular to the Universal Declaration of Human Rights, whereas they are less likely to include references to ILO Conventions and Declarations. The OECD guidelines for multinational enterprises and the UN Global Compact are also mentioned more often in CSR codes than in IFAs.

MNEs are more likely to acknowledge the binding character of IFAs than that of CSR codes, whereas they more often commit to respect existing laws and regulations in CSR codes than in IFAs. They tend to agree to more detailed provisions for the implementation of IFAs than of CSR codes, in particular for the administration, monitoring and handling of complaints.

In contrast MNEs tend to impose stricter requirements for contractors and suppliers through CSR codes, which more often condition contracting to the respect of their provisions, whereas their IFAs tend to merely encourage suppliers and contractors to follow their principles.

5 Conclusions

This research – based on a comparative analysis of IFAs and CSR codes of 60 MNEs – examines whether MNEs make consistent commitments concerning human rights in IFAs signed with GUFs and in their CSR codes.

IFAs and CSR codes have been compared in three ways: IFAs versus CSR codes adopted by MNEs having signed IFAs, IFAs of MNEs having CSR codes versus IFAs of MNEs without CSR codes, and IFAs and CSR codes of MNEs having both.

This analysis leads to the following conclusions:

- IFAs and CSR codes appear to reflect the priorities of MNEs' counterparts, trade unions and other stakeholders, which by and large influence the nature and level of commitments taken by MNEs. IFAs agreed with trade unions prioritize labour rights, in particular ILO standards, whereas CSR codes which address the concerns of a wider range of stakeholders deal with a broader scope of human rights and refer more often to broader international standards such as the OECD guidelines for MNEs and the UN Global Compact.
- Stakeholders appear to influence the nature of implementing provisions of IFAS and CSR codes. IFAs, in particular those signed by MNEs without CSR codes, include more detailed provisions for their application within the MNE as trade unions are not only primarily concerned with the impact of business behaviour on employees but also in a position – being co-signatories – to demand stricter commitments from MNEs. In contrast CSR codes, which are often adopted by MNEs in response to pressures from external stakeholders, include more detailed provisions concerning suppliers and contractors. It is also worth noting that IFAs put more emphasis on promoting their principles, in particular concerning workers' rights, and encouraging dialogue with management and also suppliers than on sanctioning employees or suppliers for failing to follow them. Whereas CSR codes impose severe sanctions against employees failing to follow their principles, IFAs usually require remediation measures from corporate management without sanctions against employees.
- The involvement of trade unions, in particular GUFs, in the negotiation and signature of IFAs induces some harmonization of their content and format, which is reinforced by the promotion and use of model IFAs by the IMF, the BWI and the ITGLWF. In contrast MNEs appear less concerned with harmonizing the contents and commitments of their IFAs and CSR codes. Similar wording is therefore more likely to be found across IFAs of different MNEs than in both the IFA and the CSR code of a

given MNE. Similar phrasing is also unlikely to be found across CSR codes as they are drafted and adopted independently by each MNE.
- The uptake of CSR by MNEs is reflected in their approach to international industrial relations, in particular in the characteristics of their IFAs, which integrate elements more usually found in CSR codes. In this respect stakeholders which are not party to IFAs nevertheless exert an indirect influence on commitments taken by MNEs towards trade unions.

Overall MNEs appear to be reactive rather than proactive towards their stakeholders, trade unions and civil society. While commitments taken in IFAs and CSR codes may to a certain extent reflect the values of signatory MNEs, they are still considerably influenced by the priorities and demands of their stakeholders.

As they are co-signed and often co-administered with trade unions IFAs benefit from a greater credibility than unilateral CSR codes. The credibility deficit of CSR codes worsens when commitments and approaches taken by MNEs in them differ from those in IFAs. Trade unions are unlikely to exploit these divergences as their main objective in negotiating and signing IFAs is to establish a positive relationship with MNEs. NGOs in contrast might exploit inconsistencies in commitments taken by MNEs to advocate a legal approach in the area of human rights. For CSR to remain a credible alternative to the legal approach MNEs should ensure coherence and consistency of the commitments they make in IFAs and CSR codes.

Annex I: Acronyms

BWI	Building and Wood Workers' International
CSR	Corporate Social Responsibility
EI	Education International
GUF	Global Union Federation
ICEM	International Federation of Chemical, Energy, Mine and General Workers' Unions
IFA	International Framework Agreement
IFJ	International Federation of Journalists
ILO	International Labour Organisation
IMF	International Metalworkers' Federation
ITF	International Transport Workers' Federation
ITGLWF	International Textile, Garment and Leather Workers' Federation
IUF	International Union of Food, Agricultural, Hotel, Restaurant, Catering, Tobacco and Allied Workers' Association
MNE	Multinational Enterprise
OECD	Organisation for Economic Co-operation and Development
PSI	Public Services International
UN	United Nations
UNI	Union Network International

Annex II: References to human rights and implementing provisions in IFAs and CSR codes

		IFAs	CSR codes	Codeless IFA	Code + IFA
sample		60	25	35	25
references	human rights	44	21	27	17
	Universal Declaration of Human Rights	18	17	8	10
	ILO conventions	60	15	35	25
	ILO Declaration on Fundamental Principles & Rights at Work	14	4	8	6
	ILO Tripartite Declaration of Principles concerning MNEs & Social Policy	5	1	4	1
	OECD Guidelines for MNEs	13	7	7	6
	UN Global Compact	14	10	6	8
implementing clauses	binding character	16	3	10	6
	reference to laws and regulations	50	20	32	18
	information of employees	50	17	31	19
	administration and monitoring	55	16	35	20
	complaint mechanism	41	12	25	16
suppliers' clauses	none	15	7	9	6
	encouraging compliance	29	11	14	15
	conditioning contracting	16	7	12	4

Annex III: List of IFAs and CSR codes

MNE	Country	GUF	IFA year	CSR code	CSR website	IFA = code
Accor	France	IUF	1995		✓	
AngloGold	South Africa	ICEM	2002	✓	✓	
Arcelor	Luxembourg	IMF	2005	✓	✓	
Ballast Nedam	Netherlands	BWI	2002			
BMW	Germany	IMF	2005		✓	✓
Bosch	Germany	IMF	2004		✓	✓
Brunel	Netherlands	IMF	2007			
Carrefour	France	UNI	2001	✓	✓	
Chiquita	USA	IUF	2001	✓	✓	
Club Méditerranée	France	IUF	2004			
Daimler	Germany	IMF	2002		✓	✓
Danone	France	IUF	1988	✓	✓	
EADS	Netherlands	IMF	2005	✓	✓	
EDF	France	ICEM/PSI	2005	✓	✓	
Endesa	Spain	ICEM	2002		✓	
Eni	Italy	ICEM	2002	✓	✓	
Euradius	Netherlands	UNI	2006			
Faber-Castell	Germany	BWI	1999			
Fonterra	New Zealand	IUF	2002			
France Telecom	France	UNI	2006	✓	✓	
Freudenberg	Germany	ICEM	2000	✓	✓	
GEA	Germany	IMF	2003			
H&M	Sweden	UNI	2004	✓	✓	
Hochtief	Germany	BWI	2000		✓	
IKEA	Sweden	BWI	1998	✓	✓	
Impregilo	Italy	BWI	2004			
Indesit Merloni	Italy	IMF	2002		✓	
Inditex	Spain	ITGLWF	2007	✓	✓	
ISS	Denmark	UNI	2003	✓	✓	
ItalCementi	Italy	BWI	2008	✓	✓	
Lafarge	France	ICEM/BWI	2005	✓	✓	
Leoni	Germany	IMF	2003		✓	✓
Lukoil	Russia	ICEM	2004	✓	✓	
Nampak	South Africa	UNI	2006		✓	
National Australia Bank	Australia	UNI	2006	✓		
Norske Skog	Norway	ICEM	2002		✓	
OTE Telecom	Greece	UNI	2001		✓	
Portugal Telecom	Portugal	UNI	2006			
Prym	Germany	IMF	2004		✓	

Company	Country	Federation	Year			
PSA Peugeot Citroën	France	IMF	2006		✓	✓
Quebecor	Canada	UNI	2007			
RAG	Germany	ICEM	2003			
Renault	France	IMF	2004		✓	
Rheinmetall	Germany	IMF	2003			
Rhodia	France	ICEM	2005		✓	
Röchling	Germany	IMF	2005			
Royal BAM Group	Netherlands	BWI	2005		✓	
SCA	Sweden	ICEM	2004	✓	✓	
Schwan-Stabilo	Germany	BWI	2005			
Skanska	Sweden	BWI	2001	✓	✓	
SKF	Sweden	IMF	2003	✓	✓	
Staedtler	Germany	BWI	2006			✓
Statoil	Norway	ICEM	1998	✓	✓	
Telefonica	Spain	UNI	2001	✓	✓	
Umicore	Belgium	IMF/ICEM	2007	✓	✓	
Vallourec	France	IMF	2008	✓	✓	
Veidekke	Norway	BWI	2005		✓	
VolkerWessels	Netherlands	BWI	2007			
Volkswagen	Germany	IMF	2002		✓	✓
Waz	Germany	IFJ	2007			

10
Regulating the Levers of Globalization: Integrating Corporate Social Responsibility into the Capital-Raising Process

Lauren Caplan

1 Introduction

Too many discussions about corporate social responsibility are destined to end in frustration before they even begin because of a disagreement about definitions. The debate about what responsibilities corporations owe and to whom such responsibilities are owed is not a new one and yet there remains broad disagreement about the answer. At its most basic level, a corporation represents a bargain between the state and the owners of the corporation. The state makes it easier for individuals to try to create profit-making ventures by limiting the risks to which such individuals are exposed; and in exchange, the owners agree to create something of value to society, or at least to minimize the risk that its limited liability transfers to society (the 'Bargain').[1]

To be sure, the state's view on what terms constitute an appropriate bargain with corporations has shifted over time: the first joint-stock companies were created by Royal Charter in Britain and company charters were written (and re-written) by state government in the United States. These early charters defined the scope of corporations' activities much more narrowly than the open-ended charters that we are accustomed to seeing today. In the United States, the first state laws allowing for incorporation related to

---

[1] See Micklethwait, John and Wooldridge, Adrian (2005) *The Company: A Short History of a Revolutionary Idea*, The Modern Library, New York, at 50. Interestingly, during the original debate in Britain about the granting of limited liability to corporations, the main proponents of limited liability were the poor and their advocates such as John Stuart Mill. Limited liability was opposed by the wealthy. Mill argued that limited liability would allow the poor to organize their own businesses whereas previously only the wealthy could expose themselves to the risks associated with full liability.

corporations that would build the infrastructure of the new country[2] and the granting of such charters was often conditional on the provision of certain public services.

Over time, the granting of charters in both the United States and Britain became more relaxed and the corporation as an entity began to acquire more distinct private rights.[3] The regulation of corporations has waxed and waned, often in tandem with how well corporations are performing and how much of that wealth is being shared with society through earnings distributions, job creation and improvements in standards of living. Although states have moved away from more narrowly (and some would say more clearly) defining the terms of the Bargain at a corporation's inception, through corporate charters that restrict a corporation's purpose and define a limited life for that corporation, states have regulated corporate conduct through other mechanisms that suggest they are still operating pursuant to some notion of the Bargain. For example, states have passed legislation directly regulating the behaviour of corporations around environmental issues, requiring disclosure to the public about hazardous air emissions, chemical inventories and other projects that could have negative health and environmental impacts on the public.[4] And particularly in the United States, case law has developed the idea of 'piercing the corporate veil' as a way of placing outer limits on the limitation of liability.[5] Since the financial market bubble burst in the 1990s and most recently as a result of the global financial crisis that began in 2008, there have been renewed calls for a closer examination of the responsibilities that corporations owe to society.

Regardless of one's definition of corporate social responsibility or the terms of the Bargain, adequate tools for measuring a corporation's actions against that definition do not currently exist. We have been inundated with voluntary corporate social responsibility codes and legislative efforts aimed at

---

[2] North Carolina enacted a law allowing for incorporation by canal companies in 1795 and Massachusetts did the same for water-supply companies in 1789. See John Micklethwait and Adrian Wooldridge, at 44.

[3] *Id.* at 45–46. In a famous US Supreme Court case in 1810, the Court determined that corporations possessed private rights, invalidating the then-common practice of states rewriting corporations' charters at the government's whim and often for purely political reasons.

Today, the private rights of corporations are still a topic for debate, as is clear in a case that the US Supreme Court recently heard regarding the First Amendment free speech rights of corporations. *Citizens United v. Federal Election Commission.*

[4] Case, David W. (2005) Corporate Environmental Reporting as Informational Regulation: A Law and Economics Perspective, *University of Colorado Law Review*, Vol. 76, at 380.

[5] See Millon, David (September 2006) Piercing the Corporate Veil, Financial Responsibility, and the Limits of Limited Liability, *Washington & Lee Legal Studies Paper No. 2006–08.*

addressing corporate social responsibility issues. Although the existence of such a range of tools is positive evidence that corporate social responsibility issues are beginning to get the attention they require, unfortunately the current system has created a disjointed set of tools that fails to reflect adequately the global nature of business operations today. The implementation of different voluntary codes has led to disclosures that are difficult for society to use meaningfully: variations in reporting content and standards make comparisons across companies difficult. Also problematic is the voluntary nature of many of the codes, which creates an impetus for selective implementation and disclosure. Finally, legislative efforts have, for the most part, been structured on national lines when issues of corporate social responsibility are increasingly global in nature. International treaties and agreements have been piecemeal and are hindered by disagreements about the appropriate scope of corporate social responsibility.

This chapter does not aim to settle the ongoing debate about the definition of corporate social responsibility but instead suggests taking advantage of several trends in the global capital markets that will aid society's (and individual sectors of society's) ability to enforce the Bargain, however one defines it. The simultaneous (i) recognition by corporate risk analysts that many of the issues with which corporate social responsibility advocates are concerned pose direct risks to a corporation's profit maximization; (ii) convergence to a global accounting standard; and (iii) concentration of capital-raising activities in a few major markets, have created a favourable environment for codifying a standard of risk monitoring and disclosure that can satisfy the disclosure society needs in order to enforce the Bargain. Essentially this chapter argues that corporate social responsibility advocates ought to take advantage of the capital markets' recognition that issues such as human rights, the environment and governance pose direct risks to corporations' long-term viability and profitability. One of the most common objections to corporate social responsibility is that the sole purpose of a corporation is profit maximization and that corporate social responsibility distracts the management of corporations from that task. To the extent that corporate social responsibility overlaps with issues that affect profit maximization, most of the objections to consideration of such issues disappear.[6] Corporate social responsibility advocates ought to seize this recognition and take advantage of the development of the International Financial Reporting Standards (IFRS or Standards) as a global accounting system that could provide

---

[6] 'There is one and only one social responsibility of business – to use it[s] resources and engage in activities designed to increase its profits so long as it stays within the rules of the game, which is to say, engages in open and free competition without deception or fraud' Friedman, Milton (13 September 1970). The Social Responsibility of Business is to Increase its Profits, *The New York Times Magazine*, The New York Times Company, quoting Milton Friedman's *Capitalism and Freedom*.

globally comparable and verifiable corporate disclosures, which, although primarily designed to satisfy capital market disclosure regulations, would also provide disclosures that would allow society to more effectively enforce the Bargain.

In Part 2, this chapter will explore the current landscape of voluntary corporate social responsibility codes and legislation to understand the context for the suggestions proposed in Part 5. Part 3 will review the role that accounting standards play in corporations' efforts to raise capital and the convergence around the world to a global accounting system. Part 4 will review the movement in risk analysis circles towards considering corporate social responsibility issues as part of the core risk analysis of companies and will explore examples of how some commercial lenders and institutional investors have already begun to analyse the risks posed by corporate social responsibility issues. Part 5 suggests ways of integrating the mandatory consideration of corporate social responsibility issues into the emerging global accounting system, specifically suggesting amending the current IFRS to clarify the treatment of certain corporate social responsibility issues.

2 The alphabet soup of voluntary codes and legislation

In the past two decades there has been a proliferation of voluntary corporate social responsibility codes and various legislative efforts designed to address corporate social responsibility issues. Although positive as signals of the growing significance given to such issues, these efforts have resulted in a set of tools that (i) are difficult for companies to comply with and (ii) produce confusing and sometimes contradictory disclosures for the public.

2.1 Voluntary codes

A briefing put out by the Global Reporting Initiative and AccountAbility (the 'GRI Report') to assist corporations in making sense of the landscape of voluntary codes explains that there are approximately 300 corporate social responsibility tools in existence.[7] The range of voluntary codes spans from broad principles that apply to all businesses regardless of industry or geography, such as the UN Global Compact,[8] the Global Reporting Initiative Sustainability Reporting Framework (GRI),[9] and the OECD Guidelines for Multinational Enterprises (OECD Guidelines),[10] to codes

---

[7] Ligteringen, Ernst and Zadek, Simon, The Future of Corporate Responsibility Codes, Standards and Frameworks, *An Executive Briefing by the Global Reporting Initiative and AccountAbility*, at http://www.globalreporting.org/NR/rdonlyres/19BBA6F5-9337-42B0-B66D-A3B45F591938/0/LigteringenZadekFutureOfCR.pdf.
[8] See The Global Compact website at http://www.unglobalcompact.org/.
[9] See Global Reporting website at http://www.globalreporting.org/Home.
[10] See The OECD Guidelines at http://www.oecd.org/dataoecd/56/36/1922428.pdf.

that are country-specific, such as the Sudan Divestment Task Force,[11] or industry-specific, such as the Kimberly Process Certification Scheme[12] or the Extractive Industries Transparency Initiative.[13] There are also several assurance and auditing codes, such as the AA1000 Assurance Standard,[14] aimed at verifying sustainability reporting. The GRI Report organizes this array of voluntary codes into a 'global architecture' with a spectrum from normative codes (such as the UN Global Compact and OECD Guidelines), to process and assurance system guidelines (such as GRI, AA1000 Assurance Standard and Social Accountability 8000[15]). This architecture works as follows: a normative framework sets a performance benchmark, a process guideline measures performance of those benchmark goals, and an assurance standard provides a third-party review of the quality of reporting and performance.[16]

Although this architecture is helpful, it does not address the issue that (i) for each of the steps, normative, process, and assurance, there are many different standards to choose from, and (ii) the codes discharge duties through different actors, with some codes aimed at the corporations themselves, others aimed at host and home country governments, and some aimed at lenders. The usefulness of the information disclosed by these different strategies is limited because there is no way to meaningfully compare such information across companies because there is no common benchmark. In addition to voluntary codes, some governments have begun legislating aspects of the corporate social responsibility puzzle.

2.2 Legislation

Similar to the voluntary codes, one finds a variety of approaches being used by governments to legislate corporate social responsibility considerations. Some countries have placed corporate disclosure obligations about corporate social responsibility in environmental legislation, others have put the requirements in securities legislation and still others have housed the obligations in legislation dealing with the management of pensions, state-owned companies or government contracting. Companies operating in several jurisdictions face a maze of overlapping and conflicting reporting requirements.

For example, in Norway and Sweden it is the legislation that regulates corporate financial disclosures that requires companies to report on

---

[11] See The Sudan Divestment Task Force website at http://www.sudandivestment.org.
[12] See The Kimberly Process website at http://www.kimberleyprocess.com/.
[13] See Extractive Industries Transparency Initiative website at http://eitransparency.org/node.
[14] See AccountAbility website at www.accountability21.net.
[15] See http://www.sa-intl.org/index.cfm?fuseaction=Page.viewPage&pageId=487&parentID=472.
[16] Ligteringen and Zadek, *supra* note 7.

environmental impacts. The Swedish government recently passed into law a requirement that state-owned companies produce independently verified sustainability reports in accordance with the GRI.[17] In the United Kingdom, the Pensions Act (2000) requires UK pension funds to disclose how they account for sustainability factors in constructing their investment portfolios and the Companies Act (2006) requires directors of companies to consider the 'impact of the company's operations on the community and the environment'.[18] In the United States, companies interested in securing a government contract must certify that they are not involved in certain businesses, and state and local governments are permitted to divest assets from companies doing business in Sudan, under the Sudan Accountability and Divestment Act of 2007.[19] Various stock exchanges such as the Johannesburg Stock Exchange have corporate responsibility disclosure requirements.[20]

Due to the lack of clarity about what level of climate risk disclosure is required of companies registered in the United States, a group of institutional investors and state officials from New York, California, Maryland, Florida, Rhode Island and five other states have repeatedly petitioned the US Securities and Exchange Commission to clarify what information companies should be disclosing about climate risks. Some have argued that the failure by directors and officers of a company to consider relevant corporate social responsibility issues is a violation of their fiduciary duties.[21] Others have argued that the disclosure and reporting obligations required, for example, under the US securities laws already require disclosure of such information.[22] These two debates make clear that the regulatory system

---

[17] See Sweden Introduces State Sector Sustainability Reporting Regulations, PricewaterhouseCoopers.

[18] See Mathieu, Eugenie (October 2000) Response of UK Pension Funds to SRI Disclosure Regulation, *UK Social Investment Forum*, at http://www.uksif.org/cmsfiles/uksif/ukpfsurv.pdf; and The Companies Act 2006, s. 172(1)(d) (UK).

[19] The Sudan Accountability and Divestment Act, S.2271 (2007) (US), at http://www.thomas.gov/cgi-bin/bdquery/z?d110:s.02271.

[20] See Lydenberg, Steve and Grace, Katie (November 2008) Innovations in Social and Environmental Disclosure Outside the United States, *Domini Social Investments*, at http://www.domini.com/common/pdf/Innovations_in_Disclosure.pdf.

[21] Although the question of the interplay between fiduciary duties and considerations of corporate social responsibility is best left to another chapter, the general idea is that fiduciary duties require directors of companies to perform their duties with that level of care that a reasonably prudent person in a similar circumstance would use. In the context of making business decisions, the analysis often centres on whether an adequate process was used in reaching the decision. If one believes that a reasonable person in similar circumstances would consider certain corporate social responsibility factors, then the failure to consider such factors may be a violation of fiduciary duties.

[22] See Williams, Cynthia (April 1999) The Securities and Exchange Commission and Corporate Social Transparency, *Harvard Law Review*, Vol. 112, No. 6, pp. 1197–1311.

does not adequately address the treatment of corporate social responsibility issues in corporate reporting. Another sign of the growing recognition of the need to provide disclosure about climate risks is the Attorney General of New York's lawsuit against several energy companies seeking to compel those companies to provide additional disclosure on the financial risks that they face due to climate change.[23] In 2007, under a state statute that gives him 'broad powers to access the financial records of businesses', the New York Attorney General subpoenaed utility firms (Xcel, AES, Dominion Resources, Dynegy and Peabody Energy) that were planning to develop coal-fired power plants in New York for information about the climate impact of the potential projects.[24] On 27 August 2008, Xcel Energy agreed to provide detailed annual disclosures in its Form10-K[25] on risks related to current and probable future climate change regulation and legislation; climate change-related litigation; and, the physical impacts of climate change.[26] And on 19 November 2009, AES entered into a similar agreement with the New York Attorney General.[27] As these examples demonstrate, depending on home country legislation and case law leads to a patchwork of requirements that can leave companies confused about what legal obligations they have to whom and when.[28] Such variations in legal requirements may also lead to forum-shopping by companies that choose to base their operations in countries with less restrictive regulatory requirements.

2.3 The result

The proliferation of voluntary codes and legislative requirements has led to an incoherent landscape for corporations and for those who value the practices and disclosures that corporate social responsibility reporting encourages. A review of current corporate social responsibility reports explains that the result is often 'information overload' and lengthy reports

---

[23] See Office of the Attorney General (27 August 2008), Cuomo Reaches Landmark Agreement with Major Energy Company, Xcel Energy, to Require Disclsoure of Financial Risks of Climate Change to Investors, at http://www.oag.state.ny.us/media_center/20008/aug/aug27a_08.html.
[24] See New York General Business Law, Art. 23-A, §352.
[25] The Form 10-K is an annual disclosure that the SEC requires publicly-traded companies to file. It includes an overview of the business, including its financial condition and an audited financial statement.
[26] *In the Matter of Xcel Energy Inc.*, Assurance of Discontinuance Pursuant to Executive Law §63(15), August 2008.
[27] *In the Matter of The AES Corporation*, Assurance of Discontinuance Pursuant to Executive Law §63(15), 19 November 2009.
[28] See Human rights and Transnational corporations: Legislation and Government Regulation (15 June 2006), Note of a meeting held at Chatham House.

that are not very useful.²⁹ Voluntary reporting with a number of reporting regimes to choose from also seems to encourage selective disclosure that does not always paint an accurate picture of a company's interaction with corporate social responsibility factors. In a content analysis of corporate social responsibility disclosures made by 50 publicly traded US firms, the authors found 'a generally self-laudatory tone in the content of the disclosures for the sample firms'.³⁰ For example, approximately 86 per cent of the disclosures were mostly positive or strictly positive with only approximately 14 per cent of the disclosures neutral or mostly negative.³¹ The study also found that 'CSR reporting is not uncommon among US firms, but that the amount and degree of coverage of various elements of CSR is highly variable'.³² This data suggests that in voluntary disclosures companies tend to concentrate on descriptions of their philanthropic and humanitarian endeavours, which tend to be peripheral to the daily operations of the companies, and to report much less on measures taken to address corporate social responsibility issues embedded in the operation of the business itself. The authors also point out that current voluntary disclosures do not require any reconciliation with financial disclosures; this is significant because a conflict between a corporation's voluntary disclosure about corporate social responsibility and its mandatory financial disclosure could signal that selective and potentially misleading disclosure is occurring. Unsurprisingly, the study indicated that disclosures made in an audited document or mandatory filings are less self-laudatory than disclosures made in voluntary formats.³³

The voluntary nature of the majority of corporate social responsibility codes also makes it very difficult to ensure that those who assert compliance with a particular code are in fact adhering to the code in practice. In fact, business concerns about the legal status of a voluntary commitment to adhere to the Global Compact caused the Global Compact Secretariat to issue several statements clarifying that participation in the Global Compact would not lead to any legal liability for signatories who violate the Compact, somewhat undercutting the force of the commitment.³⁴

---

²⁹ KPMG International Survey of Corporate Responsibility Reporting (2005) at 20, at http://www.kpmg.cz/czech/images/but/2005_International_Survey_Corporate_Responsibility.pdf.
³⁰ Holder-Webb, Lori; Cohen, Jeffrey; Nath, Leda and Wood, David (30 November 2007) The Supply of Corporate Social Responsibility Disclosures Among US Firms.
³¹ *Id*. at 37.
³² *Id*. at 14.
³³ *Id*. at 21.
³⁴ See Ward, Halina (September 2005) Corporate Responsibility and the Business of Law, *Swedish Partnership for Global Responsibility*, at 18, and Global Compact Website, FAQ #4 http://www.unglobalcompact.org/AboutTheGC/faq.html.

As this evidence demonstrates, a critical mass of thinking from all sectors has contributed to the development of many sound voluntary codes and guidelines. However, the current environment risks squandering this effort by failing to clarify the mechanisms for considering such issues and failing to ensure the reliability and comparability of such information. The risk is that the multitude of codes, legislation and case law ends up diminishing the value of any one code. Even more worrying is the possibility that such attention will create a false sense that the issues have been adequately addressed, prematurely ending the conversation. The remainder of this chapter suggests that an effective way to codify this progress is to agree on a common, minimum baseline of disclosure about corporate social responsibility issues as a pre-requisite for accessing capital. Financial statements already require the disclosure of various risks facing businesses and there is a growing recognition that corporate social responsibility issues pose direct risks to many businesses' core operations.

3 Accessing capital

Under many countries' securities regulations, in order to raise capital through a country's stock exchanges a company must disclose certain risks to its operations and reflect certain contingencies or uncertainties that may impact its bottom line. As will be discussed in Part 4, there is growing agreement among risk professionals that issues such as human rights, the environment, and governance can pose risks to the long-term viability of a company's operations. Currently securities regulations fail to require the disclosure of such long-term risks in a consistent and comparable manner. As discussed in Part 2 of this chapter, although voluntary codes have developed helpful tools for analysing certain sustainability risks, the current system of codes and uneven national regulation has resulted in a confusing patchwork of disclosures that are difficult (i) for investors and the public to use meaningfully, and (ii) for companies to implement consistently and coherently. This chapter suggests that mandating a minimum level of disclosure about long-term risks through accounting standards would ensure the comparability that has been missing, and would be consistent with the theory of securities regulation based on disclosure that much of the world operates under already. Linking long-term considerations to a company's ability to access capital codifies the central role that long-term factors ought to have in business decisions and forces companies to uphold their side of the Bargain.

Implementing a disclosure requirement through the capital markets takes advantage of the fact that: (i) the architecture of the capital markets is moving towards becoming a global one more quickly than international regulatory structures; and (ii) sources of capital tend to be concentrated. It may be helpful to expand briefly on each of these reasons.

First, while the international community has struggled for years with the issue of extraterritoriality in connection with the regulation of transnational companies, the capital markets have already accepted that in order for a company to raise capital on a country's stock exchanges, it must comply with certain regulatory requirements, regardless of the home or host country of its operations. Financial statements prepared according to a specified accounting standard are a prerequisite to listing on many countries' securities exchanges. For many companies the raising of capital has become unconstrained by national borders and as a result there is currently a movement towards adoption of a global accounting standard. This global accounting standard is necessary to (i) decrease the burden on companies that are required to report in multiple countries, and (ii) allow suppliers of capital to meaningfully compare the financial statements of companies based in different countries, with operations all over the world. Countries across the world are working on convergence projects to make their national accounting standards consistent with the International Financial Reporting Standards and most importantly, the countries through whose exchanges the majority of capital is raised have already committed to such convergence.[35] To be sure, reaching agreement on a common set of accounting standards is rife with its own challenges, not least of which is the debate between using a principles-based or a rules-based system. Ensuring that corporate social responsibility issues are disclosed in financial statements will not replace the need for other types of international regulatory structures to address such issues; but the hope is that ensuring consistent and verifiable disclosure will complement other regulatory efforts, and can be done in parallel with those efforts.

Second, the concentration of sources of capital is important because it means that changes to the accounting standards in a few markets can affect the majority of companies in the world. Although globalization brings shifting trends in the financial markets, a careful look at the per centage of the world stock market capitalization by country shows that affecting the ability to raise capital in a few countries will have a significant impact. For example, 58.3 per cent of all capital raised through stock markets in the world is raised in six countries (US, Japan, UK, France, China and Germany).[36] As countries converge to IFRS, focusing on the convergence efforts of just a few countries will allow corporate social responsibility advocates to improve the disclosure of such issues by a large percentage of companies.

---

[35] See Bespoke Investment Group (11 June 2008) *Percent of World Market Cap by Country* at http://bespokeinvest.typepad.com/bespoke/2008/06/percent-of-worl.html.
[36] *Id.*

3.1 Convergence and the international financial reporting standards

At a conference in June 2008, the Chief Financial Officer of InfoSys Technologies Ltd., an IT and consulting company, explained that the company is based in India, 98 per cent of its revenues are from outside India, and the company is listed on European securities exchanges, all of this requiring it to provide annual reports in accordance with the generally accepted accounting principles of eight different countries.[37] As this example illustrates, clearly the reporting systems have not kept pace with the changes in the operations of corporations. But there is a growing consensus among securities regulators around the world to move towards one global accounting standard, namely the IFRS system. As part of this process the International Accounting Standards Committee Foundation is working to develop 'a single set of high quality, international financial reporting standards for general purpose financial statements'.[38] Many countries already require the use of IFRS or have modelled their national accounting standards on IFRS. In 2005, the European Union began requiring publicly traded companies to prepare their financial statements in accordance with IFRS.[39] In March 2005, Japan initiated the process of converging to IFRS and on 8 August 2007, the Chairman of the Accounting Standards Board of Japan and the Chairman of the International Accounting Standards Board announced that Japan's convergence was being accelerated with a target date of 11 June 2011.[40] In the United States, on 21 December 2007, the SEC began permitting foreign private issuers of securities to submit financial statements prepared in accordance with IFRS without reconciling such statements to US Generally Accepted Accounting Principles (US GAAP). Previously, foreign private issuers were required to reconcile their IFRS financial statements to US GAAP and highlight any variations in reporting that resulted from the different accounting systems.[41] On 27 August 2008, the SEC approved a 'roadmap' to adoption of IFRS for reporting by domestic public companies in the

---

[37] Globalisation of Capital Markets: Impact on Corporate Governance Conference (18–20 June 2008), *Session 4, Corporate Reporting – Trends and Tensions in Convergence, International Corporate Governance Network*.
[38] See International Accounting Standards Committee website at http://www.ifrs.org/The+organisation/IASCF+and+IASB.htm.
[39] Cassese, S.; Carotti, B.; Casini, L.; Macchia, M.; MacDonald, E. and Savino, M. (2008) Global Administrative Law: Cases, Materials, Issues (2nd edition), Institute for International Law and Justice, New York University School of Law at 17.
[40] *ASBJ and IASB meet to review progress in achieving convergence in accounting standards* (11 September 2008) at http://www.accountancy.com.pk/FrameIT.asp?link=http://www.iasb.org/.
[41] US Securities and Exchange Commission Release Numbers 33-8879; 34-57026 at http://www.sec.gov/rules/final/2007/33-8879.pdf.

United States by 2014.⁴² In addition to the European Union (including the United Kingdom), Japan and the United States (which represent the securities exchanges through which more than 50 per cent of the world's capital that is raised on exchanges is raised), Australia, New Zealand and South Africa already use IFRS; Brazil has committed to requiring IFRS in 2010; Canada in 2011; China began a phase-in programme in 2007; and India will fully converge on 1 April 2011.⁴³ Although there is a significant shift towards the use of one global accounting standard, it is important to note that when countries adopt IFRS they do not always adopt the standards in their entirety. As the convergence process progresses, it will be important to ensure that at a minimum, the countries providing the majority of capital have adopted each of the core IFRS that impact most directly on corporate social responsibility considerations.

It is also important to examine the governance structure of those developing IFRS to ensure that such standards are a result of collaboration between a global set of actors. Too often codes or regulations in the sustainability arena are subject to the claim that one country's regulations reach too far into another country, violating that nation's sovereignty. The International Accounting Standards Committee Foundation is the organization tasked with overseeing the development and implementation of IFRS. The International Accounting Standards Committee Foundation is an independent not-for-profit, private sector organization with a board of trustees. The International Accounting Standards Committee Foundation has delegated responsibility for creating IFRS to the International Accounting Standards Board (IASB) and is responsible for appointing the members of the IASB. The International Accounting Standards Committee Foundation's board of trustees is made up of 22 representatives composed of 6 representatives from the Asia/Pacific region, 6 from Europe, 6 from North America and 4 from any region.⁴⁴ This composition is intended to ensure a balanced geographic composition and protect against over-representation of any one region.⁴⁵ The International Accounting Standards Committee Foundation is subject to general guidance that it should consider geographic balance in its appointment of members to the IASB and on 21 July 2008, the International Accounting Standards Committee Foundation published for comment a proposal to specify the IASB's geographic composition as: four representatives

---

[42] SEC Proposes Roadmap Toward Global Accounting Standards to Help Investors Compare Financial Information More Easily, at http://www.sec.gov/news/press/2008/2008-184.htm.

[43] See IAS Plus, Use of IFRSs by Jurisdiction, at http://www.iasplus.com/country/useias.htm.

[44] See International Accounting Standards Board website at http://www.ifrs.org/The+organisation/IASCF+and+IASB.htm.

[45] See Cassese, Carotti, Casini, Macchia, MacDonald, and Savino, *supra* note 39, at 12.

from Asia/Pacific; four from Europe; four from North America; one from Africa; one from South America and two from any region.[46] Supporting such a proposal is important to solidify the global character of the IFRS. The International Accounting Standards Committee Foundation also appoints members to the International Financial Reporting Interpretations Committee, which prepares guidance on the standards developed by the IASB and submits them to the IASB for approval.

The importance of continuing to improve the governance structure of the IASB was recently demonstrated when in October 2008, leaders of the European Commission became concerned that European companies faced a competitive disadvantage against US companies because of changes to a US fair value accounting rule. Because IFRS needs to be ratified by the European Commission to be effective, the European Commission threatened to replace the IFRS fair value standard with its own, essentially forcing the IASB to change its treatment of fair value issues, even though only five of the IASB's members were from Europe.[47] The governance structure and processes of the IASB will need to be improved to prevent political pressure from forcing accounting rule changes in the future. It is also true that once global convergence is further along, there should be less reason for political pressure because such national differences in accounting standards will be minimized.

Before discussing suggestions for how IFRS can more effectively reflect the risks posed by corporate social responsibility issues, it may be helpful to review how some providers of capital are currently analysing such risks. The next section will explore more fully the development among businesses, lenders, and institutional investors of giving a more central role to corporate social responsibility issues in their core risk analysis processes.

4 Risk analysis

Increasingly research is demonstrating that corporate social responsibility issues pose direct risks to a company's ability to maximize shareholder value.[48] Many sources of capital such as commercial lenders and insurance providers have already begun to require additional disclosures about corporate social responsibility issues from potential clients and to reflect such considerations in the products that they offer. This section reviews the growing recognition that corporate social responsibility issues can pose direct

---

[46] See IAS Plus at http://www.iasplus.com/iascf/constreview2008.htm#comment.
[47] Kessler, Glenn (27 December 2008) Accounting Standards Wilt Under Pressure, *The Washington Post*, at A1.
[48] See Emerson, Jed and Little, Tim (2005) The Prudent Trustee: The Evolution of the Long-Term Investor, *Generation Foundation and The Rose Foundation for Communities and the Environment* at 2.

risks to a company's bottom line and provides some concrete examples of how such factors can be analysed.

One area of corporate social responsibility that has gained a lot of attention recently is the issue of sustainability. A report on the changing investment climate explains that there is a 'compelling relationship between a company's financial performance and its performance around sustainability issues'.[49] A workshop organized by the UK Department for International Development and Forum for the Future in response to the release of the Stern Review[50] addressed the need for new models of risk assessment, explaining that climate change 'will require different ways of assessing and managing risk in investments'.[51] The report argues for explicitly linking sustainability factors to concrete business issues, and points to the need for tangible information and measurements to identify the business risks that such factors pose.[52] In addition to the direct impact of corporate social responsibility issues on business operations, businesses are increasingly exposed to secondary impacts of such factors through the global reach of their upstream and downstream operations. A recent example of the production of an 'American' car showed that approximately two-thirds of the value of the car is produced outside of the United States. Specifically, '30 per cent of the car's value goes to Korea for assembly, 17.5 per cent to Japan for components and advanced technology, 7.5 per cent to Germany for design, 4 per cent to Taiwan and Singapore for minor parts, 2.5 per cent to the United Kingdom for advertising and marketing services, and 1.5 per cent to Ireland for data processing.'[53] In connection with this segmentation of operations, many businesses are now exposed to risks from corporate social responsibility issues at several different points within their business operations.

Recognizing the risks posed by corporate social responsibility issues, many commercial lenders have already begun requiring potential borrowers to disclose risk information about such issues and are examining such information before constructing the terms of the loan. Lenders have developed their own tools to evaluate corporate social responsibility factor risks such as the Equator Principles as a framework for examining the environmental and social

---

[49] *Id.*
[50] See Stern, Nicholas (30 October 2006) The Stern Review: the Economics of Climate Change at http://www.hm-treasury.gov.uk/media/4/3/Executive_Summary.pdf.
[51] See Adapting to Climate Change in Developing Countries – what role for private sector finance? (2 February 2007) *Report on a workshop organized by DFID and Forum for the Future* at 10.
[52] *Id.* at 25.
[53] See Blair, Margaret M., Williams, Cynthia A. and Lin, Li-Wen (15 March 2007) Assurance Services as a Substitute for Law in Global Commerce, *Vanderbilt University Law School Law and Economics, Working Paper number 07-06* at 14 (fn 38).

risks of project finance projects.[54] A report examining the risks posed by climate change to the loan portfolios of banks in the US and Canada explains that 'the risk of environmental liabilities to banks, specifically those resulting from the impact of climate change, is determined almost exclusively by the maturity of the bank's financial products'.[55] The report warns lenders that loans with maturities longer than five years should be structured with an ability to be recalled in the event that climate change risks become evident. For example, if the risk of enactment of a cap-and-trade greenhouse gas emissions requirement increases with time, banks may make longer-term loans more expensive by requiring companies that would be impacted by the requirement to maintain a reserve or keep a higher debt service coverage ratio, which effectively decreases the amount that a company can borrow. Lenders may also just choose to lessen their exposure to such risks by shortening loan maturities. Either of these changes would cause disruption to corporate development and operations.

Some institutional investors have also begun evaluating the risks posed by corporate social responsibility issues in their potential investments. The Association of British Insurers (ABI) issued Disclosure Guidelines on Socially Responsible Investment, which ask companies to demonstrate in their annual reports that they have assessed 'ethical, environmental and social risks' and 'are managing them in a manner that will preserve and enhance the company's value'.[56] The Carbon Disclosure Project (CDP) works on behalf of institutional investors to collect information from companies about the 'commercial risks and opportunities from climate change including: regulation, physical risks from extreme weather events, changes in technology and shifts in consumer attitude and demand'.[57]

Investment managers have begun developing methods of reviewing corporate social responsibility issues as well. Generation Investment Management (Generation) builds 'sustainability research into their fundamental equity analysis' by examining 'economic, social and governmental risks and opportunities'.[58] The factors that Generation focuses on are: climate change, poverty and development, ecosystem services and biodiversity, water scarcity, pandemics, demographics and migration and urbanization.[59] It is

---

[54] See The Equator Principles at http://www.equator-principles.com/principles.shtml.
[55] See Global Climate Change: Risk to Bank Loans, prepared by EcoSecurities and the United Nations Environment Programme Finance Initiative, at 61.
[56] See Association of British Insurers: Disclosure Guidelines on Socially-Responsible Investment at http://www.abi.org.uk/Media/Releases/2007/02/ABI_publishes_Responsible_Investment_Disclosure_Guidelines.aspx.
[57] The Carbon Disclosure Project website at http://www.cdproject.net/.
[58] Generation Investment (May 2007) Thematic Research Highlights, at http://www.generationim.com/media/pdf-generation-thematic-research-v13.pdf.
[59] *Id.* at 2.

particularly interesting to examine Generation's framework for analysing the risks due to demographic shifts because demographic shifts can be one of the most amorphous and difficult corporate social responsibility issues to translate into concrete business risks. Generation groups the potential impacts into six financial impact areas: operating costs, revenue, capital expenditures, balance sheet, financing and other. As an example then, if one looks more closely at two of the impact areas, operating costs and capital expenditures, there are several concrete business risks that may be posed as population centres shift. There may be fewer workers available in a region where a company is based and companies may either have to provide incentives to draw workers back to the region, increasing operating costs, or move operations (factories, equipment) to the new population centres, increasing capital expenditures. Changes in the location of workers may also force a company to use different supply chain transportation routes, which may increase operating costs.[60]

Although this is just a brief review of the ways that commercial lenders, institutional investors and investment managers are examining the impact of corporate social responsibility issues on companies' bottom-lines, it is clear that such issues are becoming a part of the core analysis that providers of capital perform. There are also signs that many business executives are beginning to recognize the impact that corporate social responsibility issues can have on their companies' long-term performance. In an article examining the impact of the economic downturn on companies' treatment of corporate social responsibility issues, executives from BT to Microsoft explained the benefit when 'sustainability information became inextricably linked to financial data and therefore started to have strategic import'.[61] For example, BHP Billiton, one of the largest mining companies in the world, states on its website that it has placed its Summary Report on Sustainability as a chapter in its company's annual report to make clear the convergence of risk management and corporate social responsibility considerations in its business operations.[62]

In addition to reporting risks posed by corporate social responsibility issues, many companies have changed their operations to mitigate such risks. Although not currently required to by law, some US companies have begun implementing measures to monitor and control their carbon emissions because they anticipate that future legislation will require such

---

[60] *Id.* at 60.
[61] Bruce, Robert (4 February 2009) Sustainability: Integrated View can facilitate survival, *FT.com* at http://www.ft.com/cms/s/0/900d6f18-f196-11dd-8790-0000779fd2ac.html.
[62] See BHP Billiton Sustainability Report (2007) at 63, *at* http://www.bhpbilliton.com/bbContentRepository/200710338624/sustainabilityreport.pdf.

controls or because it is already required of non-US subsidiaries or affiliates.[63] Some companies have chosen to participate in the Chicago Climate Exchange (CCX).[64] Participation in the CCX is voluntary but once members decide to participate, the commitment to meet greenhouse gas annual emission reduction targets is legally binding. Many large US companies such as Ford, American Electric Power, Dupont, IBM, Dow Corning, International Paper and Honeywell International, Inc. are participating in CCX.[65]

Taken together, the examples outlined in this section suggest a growing consensus by lenders, institutional investors, investment managers and many businesses themselves, that corporate social responsibility issues should be central to any business risk analysis. Unfortunately, the regulatory system has failed to keep pace with this growing consensus and the type of information that these providers of capital are requiring on a one-to-one basis is not available in any consistent manner to those investing through the public markets.

5 A global reporting standard

We are in the middle of a clear shift to a global accounting system that will affect a company's access to capital not only in the United States, Japan, the European Union and the United Kingdom, but also around the world. At the same time there is a growing consensus about the business risks posed by corporate social responsibility issues. The current state of IFRS does not adequately reflect these risks. The next step is to take advantage of the re-examination of IFRS that is currently under way as part of the convergence process, and ensure that corporate social responsibility issues are embedded in its structure. General financial statements are intended to " 'present fairly' the financial position, financial performance and cash flows of an entity", and to the extent that additional information is necessary to 'present fairly' the information in the financial statement, such information is required to be provided.[66]

While it is true that evaluating some corporate social responsibility issues will require assumptions and estimations that are forward-looking in nature, this is true of other items on which companies are already required to report.[67] Financial statements currently contain both backward-looking (reporting on past performance) and forward-looking (valuation of liabilities and the useful life of assets) statements. To ensure that corporate social

---

[63] Pentland, William (July 2008) Here Comes Carbox, *Forbes.com*, at http://www.forbes.com/2008/07/03/sarbanes-oxley-carbon-biz-energy-cx_bp_0703carbox_print.html.
[64] See CCX website at http://www.chicagoclimatex.com/content.jsf?id=821.
[65] *Id.*
[66] See IAS 1, at http://www.iasplus.com/standard/ias01.htm.
[67] *Id.*

responsibility issues are reflected in IFRS, the IASB ought to clarify the existing IFRS's treatment of corporate social responsibility issues, provide guidance to companies on how to apply such standards, and amend any standards that require such amendment to better reflect corporate social responsibility issues. Such efforts should be informed by the many guidelines already developed such as the Principles for Responsible Investment,[68] the GRI, and Assurance 1000.

5.1 Treatment of corporate social responsibility issues by the current IFRS

Certain corporate social responsibility issues may have direct effects on line items of the financial statements, but in many cases it is unclear whether and how to reflect these effects. For example, the need to retrofit a power plant to comply with new emissions regulations may directly affect capital expenditures or the impairment of assets calculations. What if there is a high probability that such regulations will be enacted in the next few years but a company chooses to delay retrofitting its power plants with clean technology? If there is no note in the financial statements about the potential need to make such equipment changes in the future or purchase permits or offsets, the financial statement is misleading and could artificially inflate the value of the company's assets or undervalue its liabilities.[69] The argument that such determinations require too many assumptions is not compelling when one looks at the number of assumptions and estimations that are already reflected in financial statements.

A thorough review of which accounting standards ought to be clarified is beyond the scope of this chapter but two examples of the types of standards that should capture corporate social responsibility factors are IAS 36 Impairment of Assets and IAS 37 Provisions, Contingent Liabilities and Contingent Assets. As currently written it is unclear how a company should comply with these two standards in relation to corporate social responsibility issues.

The objective of IAS 36 is to 'ensure that assets are carried at no more than their recoverable amount' and 'define how the recoverable amount is calculated'.[70] Under IAS 36 an entity is required to perform an impairment test only if certain indicators suggest that the asset may be impaired. Those preparing financial statements must review the balance sheet at each reporting date to determine whether any adjustments are necessary. IAS 36.17 provides a list of specific indicators that would signal a need to reflect an impairment. Indicators are grouped in two categories: (i) external

---

[68] See UNEP Finance Initiative website, at http://www.unepfi.org/ and UN Global Compact website, at http://www.unglobalcompact.org/.
[69] See Generation Investment, *supra* note 58.
[70] See IAS 36, at http://www.iasplus.com/standard/ias36.htm.

sources, such as changes in technology, markets, the economy, or laws; and (ii) internal sources, such as obsolescence or physical damage to an asset.[71] One suggestion is to clarify how these indicators apply to corporate social responsibility issues so that it is clear when corporate social responsibility issues should trigger an impairment of assets. The impairment of an asset may directly impact an asset's useful life, the depreciation method used, or the residual value of the asset. As part of the convergence process the IASB will be re-evaluating IAS 36, making comments on it timely.

The objective of IAS 37 is to ensure that provisions ('a liability of uncertain timing or amount'), contingent liabilities and contingent assets are 'recognized and measured appropriately and that sufficient information is disclosed in the notes to the financial statements to enable users to understand the nature, timing and amount of such uncertainties'.[72] Additional guidance on reflecting contingencies such as regulatory changes, population shifts, and disease vectors in the financial statement should be provided. In particular, guidance on how to define material time horizons and how to determine the materiality of second-order impacts from corporate social responsibility issues would be helpful.

A brief review of financial statements prepared in accordance with IFRS suggests that IAS 36 and 37 are not being applied to corporate social responsibility issues with any consistency. Whereas notes to financial statements do include sensitivity analyses for potential changes in commodity prices or pension liabilities, I have not seen any comparable disclosures in financial statements showing the impact of changes in corporate social responsibility issues. For example, in footnote 26 to BHP Billiton's financial statement for the year ending 30 June 2008, the company shows what the impact of a 10 per cent change in the price of various commodities that they use in their operations would have on the profit of the company.[73] It is not clear why companies do not have similar analyses showing the impact of, for example, proven population shifts in their main consumer or supplier markets, on their cost of operations or revenue. It is also interesting to note the disconnect between the disclosure in financial statements and the disclosure in companies' corporate social responsibility reports. For example, an examination of Exxon's most recent financial statement does not produce much disclosure at all on risks from corporate social responsibility issues but a visit to the sustainability section of their website has much more

---

[71] See IAS Plus, Summaries of International Reporting Standards, at http://www.iasplus.com/standard/ias36.htm.
[72] See IAS 37, at http://www.iasplus.com/standard/ias37.htm.
[73] BHP Billiton Financial Statement for the period ending 30 June 2008, footnote 26, page 211, at http://www.bhpbilliton.com/annualreports2008/_uploads/documents/BHPB-annual-report-2008-notes.pdf.

information.⁷⁴ Without the link to the financial statement and a description of the implications for the business, it is difficult to make good use of such disclosure.

The IASB's current project of providing clarification for the treatment of emissions trading instruments is encouraging. Undertaken in December 2007, the IASB project may result in amendments to IAS 38 Intangible Assets, IAS 39 Financial Instruments: Recognition and Measurement and IAS 20 Accounting for Government Grants and Disclosure of Government Assistance to clarify the treatment of such instruments.⁷⁵ The IASB ought to expand the remit of this project and consider the treatment of additional corporate social responsibility issues such as the impact of climate change on input and output prices, labour issues and the physical environment. A review of requests that have been submitted to the International Financial Reporting Interpretations Committee through September 2008 shows that no such request has been made and denied in the past; the committee may be open to a focused request for review.⁷⁶

One additional note: the IASB is currently engaged in a research project to create a narrative management commentary supplement to the financial statements that would not be part of the financial statements themselves.⁷⁷ Although this is a positive development and would provide additional clarity to the picture painted by the financial statements, it is important that sustainability factors are also reflected in the financial statements themselves to ensure that such disclosures are audited.

5.2 Burden of implementation

The benefit of any new regulatory requirements must be weighed against the increased burden such requirements will inevitably place on businesses. In this case, because the suggestions outlined above are influenced by, and in many ways the culmination of, the widespread implementation of voluntary efforts, the increased burden on businesses may be minimized. Many businesses already have some practice in place for addressing sustainability factors and the requirements suggested herein are narrowly focused on issues that pose direct business risks. For example, in Japan, 80 per cent of companies are issuing separate corporate responsibility reports and 71 per cent of companies in the United Kingdom are already doing so.⁷⁸ In addition, the infrastructure for auditing such reports is rapidly developing. KPMG and

---

[74] Exxon Corporate Citizenship Report, http://www.exxonmobil.com/Corporate/files/Corporate/community_ccr_2007.pdf and Form 10-K for year ending 31 December 2008 at http://ir.exxonmobil.com/phoenix.zhtml?c=115024&p=irol-sec.
[75] See IAS Plus, at http://www.iasplus.com/agenda/emissiontrading.htm.
[76] See IAS Plus, at www.iasplus.com/ifric/notadded.htm.
[77] See IAS Plus, at http://www.iasplus.com/agenda/mda.htm.
[78] See KPMG International, *supra* note 23.

PricewaterhouseCoopers both have developed sustainability practices[79] and the International Register of Certificated Auditors (IRCA) based in London provides assurance services for the auditors of corporate responsibility reports.

Some also argue that such disclosures are already required under national securities regulations. For example, in the US, as discussed earlier, pressure is being put on the Securities and Exchange Commission to clarify reporting requirements and companies are being taken to court on this question because the Securities and Exchange Commission and the legislature have failed to act. In many ways clarification of a company's obligations regarding the monitoring and reporting of corporate social responsibility issues lessens the burden on corporations by providing a more certain regulatory climate. These requirements could be phased in with large companies required to implement the requirements first. This would allow smaller companies more time to build any additional capacity necessary to comply with the new standard.

6 Conclusion

Over the last 10–20 years much hard work has been performed developing methods for companies to evaluate corporate social responsibility issues and there has been a growing recognition by companies that corporate social responsibility issues are not just philanthropic considerations. The practice of performing some type of corporate social responsibility review and reporting on that review through a corporate social responsibility report has become almost mainstream. The proliferation of voluntary codes and the growing recognition in risk analysis circles that corporate social responsibility issues pose real risks to a corporation's long-term viability has caused national legislatures to begin addressing such issues as well. While these are all positive advances, they have developed without a clear framework and the result is a disjointed collection of tools that are difficult to use meaningfully and threaten to overwhelm companies.

Instead, those concerned with developing a more effective means of enforcing the Bargain between corporations and society can take advantage of developments in the global capital markets. This chapter argues that those concerned with corporate social responsibility issues should be paying more attention to the emerging global accounting standards and be working to ensure that they provide some minimum standardized disclosure about corporate social responsibility issues. It is impossible to determine the

---

[79] See PricewaterhouseCoopers website at http://www.pwc.com/extweb/service.nsf/docid/9C4D355FA123525A85257013005B16D2, and Ernst & Young's website, at http://www.ey.com/global/content.nsf/Australia/AABS_-_Sustainable_Development.

terms of the Bargain, let alone enforce it if there is no reliable, consistent and comparable information regarding corporate social responsibility issues. IFRS could provide a clear baseline of comparability across many of the world's largest companies. In order for these mandatory provisions to work effectively, additional support must be given to those engaged in researching methods to quantify the effect of corporate social responsibility issues on corporations,[80] even if some issues can only be quantified across broad ranges. The more analytical tools available to measure such effects, the more effective the mandated disclosures will be within the capital markets disclosure system.

The current situation in the world economy paints a stark picture of the risks of failing to have a robust forward-looking risk management system. Although traditionally viewed in a different arena, it is difficult to divorce the discussion of risks posed by corporate responsibility issues in this chapter from the broader context of current events in world markets. In the past two years or more we have witnessed the failure on several fronts of the capital markets to adequately catch and prevent a taking on of too much risk. Although blame for this lapse can be spread across many different types of entities and can be explained in many different ways, what is clear is that we need to take a more proactive stance towards all risks, in particular the risks that are most difficult to measure, including the risks posed by corporate social responsibility issues. Increasing the transparency about the risks that companies are facing can only improve our chances of preventing another failure and our ability to enforce the Bargain.

---

[80] See Enhanced Analytics Initiative at http://www.enhanced-analytics.com/portal/ep/home.do.

11
Institutionalization of Corporate Ethics and Corporate Social Responsibility Programmes in Firms

Jacob D. Rendtorff

1 Introduction

The last 10–15 years have been characterized by a tremendous development in the ethics and law of values-driven management and corporate responsibility in the United States (US), Europe (EU) and the rest of the world. Many modern corporations have introduced ethics and compliance programmes and values-driven management taking all the firm's stakeholders into account. In many cases reporting procedures and accountability programmes for corporate and social values are introduced into the organization. The corporate boards see them as a means to ensure not only the responsibility and integrity of the organization but also efficient management, competitiveness and legitimacy of the firm in a complex democratic society.

It has been the US government and legal system, US corporations and researchers from the different fields of economics, law, philosophy and political science that have, in particular, contributed to the institutionalization of ethics and compliance programmes in US companies. In the US, the 1991 Federal Sentencing Guidelines for Organizations were very important for developing a policy framework for corporate ethics and corporate social responsibility (CSR). These guidelines are directed towards how judges are supposed to treat cases concerning corporations.

In Europe, the European Community have also introduced important policy initiatives concerning CSR; for example, we can mention the ethics, politics and legal regulation implied in the European Commission's Green Paper Promoting a European Framework for Corporate Social Responsibility published in 2001. In this document, it is argued that CSR should be of a 'voluntary nature' and the concept of 'stakeholder' is seen as very important in the efforts to include different parties in European stakeholder forums concerning CSR-decision-making. This has lead to increased focus on business ethics and many corporations work to integrate CSR in their methods of values-driven management as described by Buhmann in Chapter 3 of this book.

The Caux Round Table discussions involving businesses from most continents were concluded with a proposal for international guidelines for multinational business.[1] These policy developments can be interpreted as efforts to contribute to the institutionalization of corporate ethics and CSR as a central element in the agency and governance of the firm. We may say that the firm is not only conceived as an economic and legal subject but also as an ethically responsible actor.

The ethical and moral responsibilities can be defined as an effort to care not only for economic efficiency and legal compliance, but also to act responsibly in accordance with ethical principles. Ethics is about finding the right balance in the grey in-between zone where things may be economically beneficial but not legally and ethically justified. Ethical duty and legal concerns may override economic concerns in cases of conflict, and ethical responsibility is about formulating values and norms for the corporation that contribute to its performance as a good corporate citizen.

In the following, I will briefly discuss some aspects of the impacts of the institutionalization of business ethics and CSR in the US and in Europe in relation to conceptions of the firm within different theories. In this context, I consider business ethics, CSR and business responsibilities for human rights as closely related aspects of the efforts of the corporation to gain legitimacy in society. So I work with similarities rather than differences between the different elements of the ethics of the firm. My argument is that we can perceive a moralization of the firm within economics, law and business ethics policy, practice and research. I will consider these different conceptions in the light of institutional theory. I will argue that old economic institutionalism and new institutionalism found in sociology most convincingly explain CSR and corporate ethics. Thus, this chapter is theoretical in nature, but therefore also very important for the practitioner. It gives the practitioner the necessary theoretical knowledge in order to understand the foundations and developments of corporate social responsibility and business ethics in corporations. However, in order to clarify the significance for the structure of economic institutions, we will begin with a brief presentation of

---

[1] Georges Enderle (ed.) (1999) *International Business Ethics: Challenges and Approaches*, London: Notre Dame University Press.

the recent policy developments in business ethics and CSR in the US and Europe.[2]

Before I start I would like to propose some important definitions of the central concepts of the chapter: morality; ethics, values-driven management, CSR and corporate citizenship.

While morality and moral convictions are defined as the values, rules, norms and concrete moral points of view that we have in ordinary life, ethics can be defined as the theoretical and practical deliberation and justification of why we have to follow those specific norms and values. In this context, business ethics is the theoretical and practical work that aims at developing well-justified values, rules and norms for the function of business corporations in society.

Values-driven management is closely linked to business ethics, because it represents an effort to formulate correct ethical values that have to govern the strategy of the firm. Values-driven management is defined as management of the firm by values where values relate to foundations of action.

This strategy is important to govern the vision and mission of management and it is a condition for implementation of ethics in the corporation. Corporate social responsibility refers to the activities of responsibility of the firm beyond what is required by the law.

Social responsibility (CSR) must in this context be defined as an integrated part of business ethics and values-driven management, because it relates to

---

[2] Even though we deal with very different situations in the EU, US and United Nations we can perceive a similarity in the developments that focuses on the social and ethical aspects of the corporation in relation to society where the corporation is supposed to assume its ethical and social duties by using either legal instruments, public policy or codes of conduct to in order to make the corporate be aware of these responsibilities. I am aware that I am comparing different elements of law and politics in the US and EU, but this is due to the fact that the ethics agenda and the CSR agenda have developed differently in the two parts of the world. Beginning with a CSR agenda the US went on to focus on ethics and compliance programmes in different legal contexts. In the EU the situation was different because there was not the same institutionalization of legal requirements for business ethics. However, with the policy approach by the European Commission the situation changed and there became more focus on CSR regulation through public policy. It is therefore justified that I compare elements from legal developments in the US with policy developments in the EU. For further clarification of these points see Jacob Dahl Rendtorff (2009) *Responsibility, Ethics and Legitimacy of Corporations*, Copenhagen: Copenhagen Business School Press. See also Paul E. Fiorelli (1992) Fine Reductions through Effective Ethics Programs. *Albany Law Review*, Vol. 56 and Jeffrey M. Kaplan, Joseph E. Murphy, & Winthrop M. Swenson (2002) *Compliance Programs and the Corporate Sentencing Guidelines*, New York: West Publishing Company.

the necessary responsibility that a corporation must have towards its internal and external stakeholders and constituencies.

Corporate citizenship may be defined as the fundamental concept that links together business ethics, values-driven management and corporate social responsibility. Corporate citizenship expresses the necessary involvement of the corporation as a good citizen who realizes that contribution to the common good of society is an essential element of good and ethical business relations.

2 Ethics policy and CSR in the US

A compelling reason for the significant increase in the adoption of ethics programmes in US companies was definitely the US Federal Sentencing Commission's Federal Sentencing Guidelines for Organizations, which became effective in November 1991. They state that an organization's demonstrated record of working to monitor or minimize wrongdoing by its employees can have a significant impact on the sentencing of the organization in case of wrongdoing.[3] This is also the case if the organization accepts its responsibility, cooperates with law-enforcement officials and contributes by self-reporting of the offence. Section 8.A.1.2 of the Guidelines emphasizes that an effective programme to prevent and detect violations of law 'means a programme that has been reasonably designed, implemented, and enforced so that it generally will be effective in preventing and detecting criminal conduct. Failure to prevent or detect the instance of offence, by itself, does not mean that the programme was not effective. The hallmark of an effective programme to prevent and detect violations of law is that the organizations exercised due diligence in seeking to prevent and detect criminal conduct by its employees and other agents'.[4]

Accordingly, organizations that have introduced comprehensive ethics programmes and reporting procedures in compliance with the Federal Sentencing Guidelines for Organizations have a significant chance of having their sentence mitigated. So many organizations according to their size and structure, aim and kind of business, have tried to introduce meaningful and

---

[3] United States Sentencing Commission (1995) *Corporate Crime in America: Strengthening the 'Good Citizen' Corporation*. Proceedings of the Second Symposium on Crime and Punishment in the United States (Sept. 7–8). Washington, DC: United States Federal Sentencing Commission. United States Sentencing Commission (2004), *Federal Sentencing Guidelines*, Chapter Eight, Sentencing Organizations, http:www.ussc.gov/orgguide.htm.

[4] Robert J. Rafalko (1994) Remaking the Corporation: The 1991 U.S. Sentencing Guidelines, *Journal of Business Ethics*, Vol. 13: 625–636, 625.

significant ethics programmes as a kind of insurance against individual as well as collective wrong-doing and criminal behaviour.[5]

The comprehensive ethical perspective on the standards and compliance procedures of the Federal Sentencing Guidelines for Organizations is stressed by many scholars.[6] This becomes evident when considering seven (summarized) steps of the Guidelines (Guidelines, *supra* note 1, §8A1.2.): (1) Establish compliance standards that address potential criminal conduct specially relevant to the organizations business operations; (2) Establish a formal structure for the compliance programme that includes a high level officer assigned responsibility for the programme; (3) Build a system to avoid delegation of substantial discretionary authority to known wrongdoers; (4) Communicate the compliance standards effectively to all employees; (5) Develop effective measures of compliance and of the communication of standards to the organization through monitoring, effective audits, and confidential internal reporting systems (e.g. a hotline); (6) Develop a fair and effective enforcement mechanism to ensure discipline; and (7) Respond appropriately to detect offences and investigations thereof.[7] This formulation of compliance and ethics programmes indeed points beyond the mere submission to legal rules towards a more comprehensive corporate ethics of virtue and excellence.

The 1991 US Federal Sentencing Guidelines for Organizations imply a concept of responsibility where not only individuals are held responsible for their actions, but also where the board of the firm and managing directors as representatives of the firm have responsibility to institutionalize ethics and compliance programmes in the corporation. The use of criminal law to make ethics regulation can be interpreted as an effort to ensure ethical behaviour in the institutions of US business life so that institutional norms can support individuals in complying with the laws and custom of society.[8]

The US regulation is based on a 'stick and carrot approach' to compliance and ethics programmes because it promises firms who have established ethics programmes according to the guidelines a possible mitigation of fines if they are considered as guilty in violation of the law. Thus, establishing an ethics and compliance programme arguably works as a legal insurance for the firm. What is interesting about this element of the US Federal Sentencing Guidelines for Organizations is that they are based on a combination of an economic approach to law regarding economic incentives in institutions as the foundation for obeying the law and a business ethics approach emphasizing the social responsibility of corporations.

---

[5] *Supra* note 3.
[6] Jeffrey M. Kaplan, Joseph E. Murphy, & Winthrop M. Swenson (2002), *Compliance Programs and the Corporate Sentencing Guidelines*, New York: West Publishing Company.
[7] Dave Ozar (1999) *An Idea to Take Away: On the Federal Sentencing Guidelines for Organizations*, Unpublished, Chicago, 1999.
[8] *Supra* note 3.

3 Ethics and CSR policy in the EU

In the EU approach, there is a close link between CSR and sustainable development. CSR management is considered as an application of concepts of sustainability and of triple bottom line reporting,[9] which combines economic (strong financial performance), social (human rights and social security of employees) and environmental (safety, health and ecology) dimensions of CSR. Many stakeholders require increased transparency and focus on CSR in corporate governance, and ask for ethically sustainable leadership practices and values-driven management in modern corporations.

Various European firms work with processes of formulating, implementing, learning and reporting of values-driven management, codes of conduct, reporting and ethical accounting in relation to ethics. EU firms interpret their 'voluntary responsibility' in many different ways according to their size, product, country, culture, management style and so on. We may even talk about changing economic structures in the EU and the emergence of a new 'Stakeholder Economy'.[10] We can detect increased concern for CSR in the interaction between EU institutions, the firm and its different stakeholders; for example, employees, consumers, shareholders and customers.

We can interpret this approach to CSR as based on 'soft law initiatives' as a 'reflexive and pragmatic' approach to legal and political regulation of business life. Viewed in the context of other EU initiatives – for example, use of fine suspension in competition law and initiatives to develop guidelines for corporate governance in general business law – EU CSR regulation can also be said to combine voluntary action in combination with gentle pressure. In general, CSR may be understood as an economic conception of the ethical accountability of the corporation. Moreover we perceive the emergence of a new policy concept of 'corporate citizenship' which is based on new conceptions of the interactions between states and corporate actions.[11]

4 Economic aspects of CSR

An economic interpretation of this institutionalization of moral norms in organizations and economic markets would be to consider ethics and CSR

---

[9] John Elkington (1999) *Cannibals with Forks: The Triple Bottom Line of 21st Century Business*, Oxford: Capstone.
[10] Joseph W. Weiss (2002) *Business Ethics: A Stakeholder and Issues Management Approach*, Canada: Thomson, 3rd ed.
[11] Malcolm McIntosh, Deborah Leipziger, Keith Jones, & Gill Coleman (1998) *Corporate Citizenship, Successful Strategies for Responsible Companies*, London: *Financial Times*, Pitman Publishing.

as a part of the economic responsibilities of the firm of serving stockholders and contribute to economic efficiency in market institutions. But economists also use CSR to be critical of mainstream conceptions of business. We can mention John Maynard Keynes' arguments in the 1920s and 1930s for institutional preconditions for economic efficiency, social justice and individual liberty[12] and John Kenneth Galbraight's criticism of the system of the industrial state in the 1950s and 1960s.[13] These themes re-emerged in the 1970s as a part of the leftist criticism of capitalist economics.[14] However, in opposition to such broad conceptions of CSR most economists accept CSR and ethics as an integrated part of good custom of economic behaviour.

In this context it may even be considered as trivial to the conception of the corporation in modern society that the firm should follow the rule of law, be decent and do some charity.[15] Ethics and CSR can be considered as strategic instruments to ensure long-term shareholder value. Increased pressure on corporations due to economic globalization and new societal expectations requires inclusion of corporate values and improved image as an improved competitive device. CSR and ethics are important values for supporting economic markets in order to create the most effective allocation of resources and goods in society. Economic conceptions of CSR and ethics imply responsibility for production of goods and services according to economic concepts of rationality, utility, efficiency and economic sustainability.

Milton Friedman can be said to define this economic conception of CSR in his infamous article 'The social responsibility of business is to increase its profits' (1970). Friedman restricts ethics and CSR to respect for the rules and norms of free capitalism. The primary responsibility of the firm is to serve the interests of its shareholders, while staying within the rules of the game, that is, respect legal requirements and other rules within the market economy.[16] From this economic point of view we should recognize ethical

---

[12] John Maynard Keynes (1926) *The End of Laissez-faire in Small firms and Economic Growth Volume 1* (ed. J. Zoltan), Cheltemham, UK: Edward Elgar (1996), pp. 292–294; William B. Greer (2000): *Ethics and Uncertainty: The Economics of John M. Keynes and Frank H. Knight*. Cheltenham, UK: Edward Elgar, p. 54.

[13] J. Galbraight ((1967) 1969) The Goals of an Industrial System, Reprinted in H. Igor Ansoff (ed.): *Business Strategy*. London: Penguin Modern Management Readings.

[14] Wim Dubbink (2001) The Fragile Structure of the Free Market Society. *The Radical Implications of Corporate Social Responsibility*, Paper delivered at the Meeting of Society of Business Ethics, Washington.

[15] F. A. Hayek ((1960) 1969) The Corporation in a Democratic Society: In Whose Interest Ought It and Will It Be Run?, Reprinted in H. Igor Ansoff (ed.): *Business Strategy*. London: Penquin Modern Management Readings, p. 225.

[16] Milton Friedman (1962) *Capitalism and Freedom*, Chicago, IL: University of Chicago Press; Milton Friedman (1970) The Social Responsibility of Business is to increase its

and legal responsibilities of the firm as a judicial person. Individuals like managing directors and board members are attributed vicarious responsibility for the actions of the organization and they take responsibility for eventual violation of legal rules and customs of society. Hayek emphasises the responsibilities of professional management.[17] And, indeed, the manager should act for the interests of the owners and the shareholders.[18] The personal values of the CEO need not coincide with his responsibility as an employee in the company.[19] If the manager follows his own social goals, he is misusing his position instead of doing his job making profit for the owners and shareholders of the company.

This economic conception of responsibility emphasizes that the idea of the social engagement of corporations should not transcend the limits of politically neutral economic markets. All other behaviour would be not only illegal, but also not very democratic. The reason is that the CEO and the board have no democratic support in using the money of the firm for social purposes because CSR is not the result of a democratic politics in society. It would also have the damaging effect of increased control of the state by corporations.[20] In this case, the firm is no longer only an economic actor but also functions as a political agent in the same way as the state. In effect, the firm is collecting taxes and reallocating resources between shareholders, consumers and the weakest in society. However, this is the responsibility of the state only.[21]

Nevertheless, 'social responsibility' expresses the firm's interest in economic sustainability. CSR will ensure economic stability and consequently long-term value for shareholders.[22] This may be widely acceptable, but also controversial. CSR may be used as a means to disguise the pursuit of economic interests and profit maximization. It may even be a danger to fair competition, because society is given the false impression that a company has genuine social motives for promoting CSR.[23]

In this sense, economists are generally sceptical towards conceptions of ethics and CSR going beyond the requirements of following 'the rules of the game' of market institutions. New institutional economists, like Williamson, for example, accept that economic efficiency and utility are embedded in

---

profits in *New York Times Magazine*, Reprinted in Rae, Scott, B. & Wong, Kenman, L. (1996) *Beyond Integrity: A Judeo-Christian Approach to Business Ethics*, Grand Rapids, MI: Zondervan Publishing House.

[17] *Supra* note 15, p. 227.
[18] *Id.*, p. 232.
[19] *Supra* note 16.
[20] *Supra* note 15, p. 238.
[21] *Supra* note 16.
[22] *Supra* note 15.
[23] *Supra* note 16.

normative structures and values, but norms and values are considered as given and accordingly as irrelevant for economic decision-making which is seen as guided by utility and efficiency only. Mainstream economists are somewhat critical towards ethics and CSR, when it does not have a direct relation to the economic benefits of the firm. In order to make CSR and ethics acceptable for economics it is necessary to find a strategy of convergence between institutional economics and business ethics as proposed by John Boatright, who builds a theory of business on the tradition of economics of governance of contractual relations from Coase and Williamson.

Boatright (1996) believes that research in business ethics has been too critical of the conception of the firm as a 'nexus of contracts' based on bounded rationality and a system of more or less formal and informal contracts. He argues that it is possible to combine CSR and the contractual theory of the firm. The framework of contract theory should be the framework for corporate ethics.[24] Institutional theory should not propose a pluralistic concept of the values and goals of the firm but rather try to integrate new institutional economics and business ethics. CSR should not be considered as an alternative to contract theory, but instead we should try to integrate business ethics into the already existing legal framework of corporate governance and of the economic market.[25]

Within the framework of this theory of the firm as a nexus of contracts the concerns for economic efficiency and profit maximization are not ignored. However, all goals and values of a firm are ambiguous and concerns for values and stakeholders may be in the interests of owners and shareholders in order to ensure long-term returns. Even though the firm is considered as an instrument for obtaining economic returns, we do not have to exclude ethical concerns and the interests of a broad number of stakeholders in the perspective of the firm as a system of contracts and negotiations.[26] According to institutional theory, a firm's owners and shareholders have an interest in the broad concern for all stakeholders in so far as this helps to increase competitiveness and sustainability of the firm.[27]

As an illustration of such efforts to bridge the tension between business ethics and institutional economics – while staying within the paradigm of economic man and maintaining a strict strategic view on corporate activities – we can mention a conception of CSR which can be seen as an effort to combine the moral and economic agency of the firm. This is

---

[24] John R. Boatright (1996) Business Ethics and the Nature of the Firm, *American Business Law Journal*, Vol. 34, No. 2: 217–238, 238.
[25] *Id.*, 218.
[26] *Id.*, 217–238.
[27] *Id.*, 217–238.

the strategic approach to the competitive advantage of CSR as proposed by Michael Porter and Mark R. Kramer, who suggest a concrete application of corporate philanthropy as a strategic instrument to improve the competitive advantage of the firm.[28] This approach can be said to apply the economic conception of the firm while still being aware of the ethical and legal responsibility of corporations. Such an approach combines economic considerations with a broader engagement of the firm with different stakeholders. This model of CSR addresses social and economic goals simultaneously by improving a company's competitive context. CSR is not considered as something external to the firm, but rather as integrated in its core strategy and business. A proactive and affirmative strategy of CSR would imply that social responsibility is used by the firm to gain a competitive advantage through long-term investments and sustainability strategies.

Nevertheless, this convergence between ethics and economics does not exclude a potential conflict, since strategic management and transaction cost theory first of all focuses on efficiency and economic return.[29] It may be argued that strategic management and the theory of economic organization cannot overcome the economic concept of self-interested utility maximizing subjects that is projected unto the analysis of organizations.[30] We are at the limits of transaction cost economics in so far as this theory does not transcend the neo-classical conception of economic man as self-interested utility and profit maximizer.[31] We may say that contract theory – while being aware of the firm as a contractual form – is limited with regard to the explanation of the firm as a cultural unit and of the institutional role of the firm in society with regard to its impact on social, environmental and ethical values.

Therefore, in order to understand the ongoing moralization of the firm we need a holistic view of organizations as open systems representing broader values and cultures that cannot be explained sufficiently in terms of individual maximizing and formal contracts.[32] Such relations must be approached with help from a broader view of institutions as expressions of moral relations and culture, different stakeholder claims and conceptions of meanings that are projected on to the organization as an open system responding to different external and internal expectations. What is needed

---

[28] Michael E. Porter & Mark R. Kramer (2002) The Competitive Advantage of Corporate Philanthropy, *Harvard Business Review*, Vol. 80, No. 12: 56–68.

[29] *Supra* note 24, at 234.

[30] Francis Fukuyama (2004) *State Building: Governance and World Order in the Twenty-First Century*, London: Profile Books.

[31] Atle Midtun (1999) *Business Ethics and the Logic of Competition: Is There a Scope for the Moral Firm*, Paper, EBEN, p. 3.

[32] Richard W. Scott (1998) *Organizations, Rational, Natural and Open Systems*, Upper Saddle River, NJ: Prentice Hall.

is an interdisciplinary institutional concept of the organization integrating different external and internal value conceptions and views of the goals of the firm.

Therefore, we have to work for careful mediations and dialogue between different concerns when we want to propose an institutional concept of CSR containing all four – economic, legal, ethical and philanthropic dimensions of our definition of CSR. This is necessary to avoid a big gap between economic action and ethically responsible behaviour because companies are contributing to the social good by considering CSR as an integrated part of their core business. If the corporation relates CSR with its core business and organizational culture, there will be a closer connection between business and social concerns and the corporation will appear reliable and trustworthy in society because its core business in itself will express social concerns and contribution to the common good of society.

5 Corporate legal subjectivity: convergence between ethics and law

The ongoing moralization of the firm in legislation and policy making about corporate ethics and CSR in the US and EU also changes our concept of the legal subjectivity of corporations. This legal point of view affirms the idea of new institutional economics of the firm as a nexus of contracts, but it also includes requirements of concern for all stakeholders of the firm.[33] The institutionalization of norms for CSR in organizational procedures and market institutions implies an integration of economic, legal and ethical responsibility, which is reflected in the legal concept of corporate responsibility in so far as the policies, missions, values and institutionally based compliance and ethics programmes of organizations are taken into account when determining legal liability. There is an ongoing extension of corporate legal responsibility and organizations are held responsible for their social behaviour.[34] Ethical concepts of honesty and responsibility are applied directly at the organizational levels.[35] Modern commercial law and the laws of welfare states operate increasingly with collective responsibility where agency and responsibility for errors and damage are attributed to organizations independently of individual human actors.[36] It is because the

---

[33] Edward R. Freeman (1984) *Strategic Management, a Stakeholder Theory of the Modern Corporation*, Pitman Publishing, New York.
[34] Lynn Sharp Paine (2002) *Valueshift: Why Companies Must Merge Social and Financial Imperative to Achieve Superior Performance*, New York: McGraw-Hill, p. 86.
[35] Lynn Sharp Paine (1997) *Cases in Leadership, Ethics and Organizational Integrity. A Strategic Perspective*, Chicago, IL: Irwin.
[36] François Ewald (1984) *L'Etat Providence*, Paris: Le Seuil.

corporation acts as a group that it is responsible for its actions and acquires legal and moral responsibility.[37]

This evolution of the legal status of the corporation enlarges the concept of the firm as a legal fiction (an artificial construct under law that allows certain organizations to be treated as individuals) serving as a nexus of contracts among human individuals.[38] The ongoing moralization of the firm is not satisfied with the view of the corporation as 'contractual relations among individuals with divisional residual claims on cash flows and assets of the corporation'.[39] This legal subjectivity of the firm implies that the firm as a legal subject with rights and duties is not only responsible towards owners and shareholders but also has rights and duties towards stakeholders who are not formal contractors. Legal liability in the present moralization of the corporation implies ethical responsibilities towards customers, suppliers, employees, local communities and the environment.[40]

Such integration of wider social concerns into the objectives of the firm does not have to exclude the *monistic* and contractual conception of the relation between firm, management, shareholders and other stakeholders because CSR and corporate ethics is conceived as a contribution to long-term shareholder value and sustainability of the corporation. This has been the case since the famous *Dodge versus Ford Motor Corporation* case in 1919,[41] where it was decided that management could withhold profit from shareholders for other purposes of the corporation. Moreover, US and EU legislation which protects firms from 'hostile takeovers' illustrates this legal conception of the firm as a legal subject forming part of a broader social system with a plurality of interests.[42] What has happened with recent policy initiatives on CSR and corporate ethics programmes in the US and EU is a reinforcement of this development towards the moral market, creating a much more comprehensive concept of institutional corporate legal and moral responsibility – compared to the one that was proposed by a purely formalist account of the legal responsibilities of the corporation.

In this sense, recent policy initiatives combine the contractual view of the corporation in the tradition of law and economics regarding the firm as a legal fiction to reduce transaction costs with an ethical and social concept of legal subjectivity of the corporation based on notions of 'organizational

---

[37] Peter Cane (2002) *Responsibility in Law and Morals*, Oxford & Portland, OR: Hart Publishing, p. 168.
[38] Michael C. Jensen (2003) *A Theory of the Firm: Governance, Residual Claims, and Organizational Forms*, Cambridge, MA: Harvard University Press, p. 88 and p. 168.
[39] *Id.*, p. 88.
[40] *Supra* note 34.
[41] Jan Schans Christensen (1991) *Contested Takeovers in Danish Law: A Comparative Analysis Based on a Law and Economics Approach*, Copenhagen: GAD, p. 291.
[42] *Id.*

culpability' and 'corporate citizenship'. These concepts may be expressed by the idea of 'due diligence'.[43] This concept can be said to reflect the idea of self-imposed values of corporations through corporate compliance and ethics programmes. In order to be a responsible corporation, it is not sufficient to have beliefs and desires; the corporation must have established compliance and ethical standards to show its good intentions.[44] In addition to actions of specific persons, it is the totality of the policy, strategy, mission statements, and codes of ethics and principles of values-driven management as well as company culture and more or less formal rules and actions that are judged as expressions of the legal subjectivity of the corporation.

Such a legal construction of corporate accountability and liability also operates with the criminal identity and history of the corporation as an indication of the level of culpability.[45] This concept of corporate legal subjectivity may be characterized by intentional structures of agency including the following elements: '(1) Agents whose actions and intentions are related to each other in such a way that they assume the characteristics of a corporate firm (2) Agents whose status in the organization is such that their actions and intentions are those of the organization and (3) Aspects of the organization such as policies, goals and practices, that reflect not merely the sum total of individual agent's intentions, but instead attributes and conditions of the corporation that make it possible for these agents to cooperate and collaborate in legally problematic ways.'[46]

Lynn Sharp-Paine uses the concept of 'organizational integrity' to describe the new approach to corporate ethics and law.[47] Integrity can be defined as coherence and completeness indicating purity of a totality that has not been destroyed. The notion is associated with true identity, honesty, respect and trust. In particular, business ethics has been working with the notion of personal integrity as moral virtue. But this notion of integrity has in modern legal theory been extended to institutional structures and legal entities.[48] We should not only focus on responsibility of the Moral Manager but also look at the organization in interaction with the environment, which can

---

[43] William S. Laufer & Alan Strudler (2000) Corporate Intentionality, Desert, and Variants of Vicarious Liability, *American Criminal Law Review*, Vol. 38, No. 4, Fall, 1285–1312, 1295.
[44] William S. Laufer (1996) Integrity, Diligence, and the Limits of Good Corporate Citizenship, *American Business Law Journal*, Vol. 34, No. 2, 157–181, 160.
[45] *Supra* note 43, 1305.
[46] *Id.*, p. 1309.
[47] Lynn Sharp Paine (1994) Managing for Organizational Integrity, *Harvard Business Review*, March–April, 106–117.
[48] Ronald Dworkin (1986) *Law's Empire*, Cambridge, MA: Harvard University Press.

be described as the Moral Market.[49] The Federal Sentencing Guidelines for Organizations and the work of the European Commission on CSR represent an indication of the fact that legal ethics is not merely a personal issue but is influenced by organizational culture and market behaviour.

Accordingly, realization of CSR and ethics programmes can help the corporation to improve corporate liability as the basis for social legitimacy in economic life. Managers need to institute systems that encourage ethical conduct and corporate social responsibility. Such procedures 'will not prevent all illegalities or improprieties but they can help to influence the character of an organization and its employees'.[50] The institutional account of business ethics moves the perspective from individual morality towards the analysis of 'the ethical logic' of basic concepts of modern economies; organizations, markets, property, information and so on.

6 Towards ethical firms: CSR as moral responsibility

We now analyse these economic and legal aspects of corporate social responsibility in the light of business ethics discourse. This research tradition focuses on ethical aspects of economics and law. CSR and ethics programmes imply a development towards increased emphasis on the moral responsibility of the firm. Scholars of business ethics emphasize that the corporation should be considered as a morally responsible agent.[51] The recent development of the ethics and law of CSR and ethics programmes in US and Europe manifests a concern of corporations to go beyond compliance towards organizational ethics when they are working with the implementation of values-driven management.[52] Therefore, the instrumental explanation is not sufficient. Firms are no longer only interested in economic efficiency, strategic legitimacy or just following the law, but they also want 'to do the right thing' and to 'do no harm' according to their ideal of virtuous behaviour. 'Integrative business ethics' proposes mediation between economics, political rationality and ethical reasoning within the field of institutional analysis.

Consequently, business ethics argues for critical reflection on economics that is not restricted to the paradigms of efficiency, egoism and rational utility maximization, but discusses the foundations of economics as a truly

---

[49] John R. Boatright (1998) Does Business Ethics Rest on a Mistake? Presidential Address to the Society for Business Ethics, 1998, Printed in *Business Ethics Quarterly*, 1999.
[50] Dawn-Marie Driscoll Michael W. Hoffmann (2000) *Ethics Matters: How to Implement Values-Driven Management*, Boston, MA: Center for Business Ethics, Bentley College.
[51] RichardDe George (1999) *Business Ethics*, Prentice Hall, Upper Sadle River, NJ, 5th ed.
[52] *Supra* note 47.

'value-creating' (moral) science.[53] Therefore, we should not separate economics from ethics but rather see them both as serving the purpose of the good life and justice in social institutions. We can say that the aim of business ethics in institutional analysis is to contribute to the evaluation of requirements for just institutions in economic life. The problem of moral agency and responsibility of institutions as a collection of individuals is very important. Institutional actors may be said to reflect a dialectics of what Max Weber calls an 'ethics of conviction' (of personal beliefs) on the one hand and an 'ethics of responsibility' (consequences of actions) on the other.[54]

An ideal concept of CSR would therefore combine economic and legal conceptions with ethical and philanthropic conceptions of the firm. Companies are required to merge social and financial imperative to achieve superior performance based on a value-shift in the economy where the firm is conceived no longer as exclusively as an amoral instrument for profit maximization, but as a morally responsible actor with values and ethical principles.[55] This is the essence of the moral concept of the corporation as a good citizen that in addition to earning money is concerned about caring for its social and ecological environment.

The work of the philosopher Peter French can be used to develop an institutional argument for CSR in the perspective of ethical theory.[56] The argument rests on the presupposition that it is possible to ascribe intentions and purposeful actions to corporations. The concept of intentionality (Donald Davidson) is promoted as the foundation for such an argument for understanding the moralization of the firm. According to this position, intentionality is not a notion of human consciousness, but is rather redefined as 'planned intentionality'. In order to understand action in organizations we can operate with a notion of agency that is not restricted to human persons. This concept of agency makes it possible to develop a notion of the firm as an institutional agent that is attributed liability and responsibility for its actions.[57] The basis of this argument is that corporations as organizational unities of individuals can be morally dangerous agents that are able to do much more harm than solitary individual agents.

---

[53] Peter Ulrich & Thomas Maak (1997) Integrative Business Ethics – A Critical Approach, *CEMS Business Review*, Vol. 2: 27–36, 28.

[54] Marc Maesschalck (1999) L'Éthique professionelle et son champ de compétence in R. Cobbaut & M. Maesschalck (eds.): *Éthique des affaires et finalité de l'entreprise*, DUC: Université catholique de Louvain, p. 7.

[55] *Supra* note 34.

[56] Peter French (1984) *Collective and Corporate Responsibility*, New York: Columbia University Press, p. 133.

[57] *Supra* note 37.

Planned intentionality as the basis for CSR can be defined by the concept of corporate 'internal decision making structure' (CID Structure).[58] This structure may be understood as the unity of value codes, formulated policy statements and strategies as well as formal and informal understandings of corporate traditions and cultures. Corporations make many decisions, which are based on routines and habits, but though they sometimes seem arbitrary this does not mean that they do not originate in the CID structure. The CID structure is the totality of meanings and intentions which make up the corporate ethos, and culture constructs the collective identity of a company. The CID structure defines the goal of the organization and its level of liability and integrity. It is constituted by the identity and history of the organization.

Against this position, institutional individualism, defends the idea that it is only individuals and not groups and organizations that can be socially responsible. It is only in cases where it is possible to find a direct relation to agents – conceived as human beings in flesh and blood with freedom and conscience – that we can talk about 'moral responsibility'. Only the individual can be morally responsible for his or her direct bodily actions. Responsibility originates directly in the intentions of an agent, which are executed in a bodily movement of the individual. There does not have to be a specific intentionality of the corporation, which is qualitatively different from the aggregates of individual intentions. When we attribute intentions to groups, we do it in a metaphorical or analogous sense, signifying that corporate intentionality may be determined as an 'as if intentionality', a kind of prescriptive intentionality, where intentions are ascribed to groups, for example, their policies and procedures, that is their CID structures, which are dependent on actions and intentions of individual actors.

In this sense, moral responsibility of the firm is considered as a kind of group responsibility based on the fact that people work together in corporations with common purpose. Together they can do much more harm and/or good than solitary individuals. This is the basis for ascribing responsibility to groups in law and morals.[59] Concrete practices of purposeful action are the basis for corporate responsibility because we can observe particular actions that corporations are responsible for as groups. However, it is not possible to reduce collective intentionality to individual intentionality.

To ascribe responsibility to the corporation means that it, in addition to economic and legal duties, has the capacity to take a moral point of view making rational and respectful decisions with honesty, integrity,

---

[58] *Supra* note 56.
[59] *Supra* note 37, p. 146.

trustworthiness, reliability and accountability.[60] From the constructivist and institutional sociological and philosophical point of view it makes perfect sense to evaluate the responsibility of corporations in terms of ethical behaviour. Some corporations have been establishing systematic features of ethics and compliance programmes and internal monitoring systems, which help them build their reputation as reliable institutions which distinguish them from other corporations who are behaving in a much less trustworthy manner.[61]

In summary, the analysis of the moralization of the firm in the light of business ethics emphasizes that economic activity and legal status of the firm should be considered as responsible activities of the corporation as a moral agent in society. Business ethics theory can make visible that the firm is evaluated according to its ethical and philanthropic performance. In this sense, moralization of the firm means that internal and external stakeholders are considering firms as morally responsible. Thus, companies are evaluated both for their economic performance and for their position in society as responsible agents.[62] We may say that CSR expresses the capacity of the corporation to act as a moral agent in tension with the economic constraints of the market.

7 CSR, ethics and the social legitimacy of corporations

The view of the firm in business ethics as a responsible subject mainly operates at the level of organizational theory. In order to conceive the interactions between economic, legal and ethical views of corporations in the context of social institutions we may shift to other institutional approaches if we want to understand the rationality of policies on CSR and ethics programmes in modern society. It is possible to integrate the developments of economics, law and ethics in the framework of old institutional economics and new institutional sociology. Within such a framework CSR policies and their normative requirements are conceived as expressions and manifestations of the social embeddedness of economic behaviour. This explains the increased social legitimacy of corporations which is generated from CSR and ethics programmes initiatives.

Old institutional economics not only makes us aware of the importance of governance structures, institutions and institutional environments for economic action, but also considers these institutional factors from the perspective of society as a whole. Whereas new institutional economics is

---

[60] Kenneth E. Goodpaster & John B. Matthews, Jr. (1982) Can a Corporation have a Conscience in Harvard Business Review, pp. 132–141. Reprinted in *Harvard Business Review on Corporate Responsibility*, Cambridge, MA: Harvard Business School Press, 2003, p. 138.
[61] *Id.*, p. 140.
[62] *Supra* note 51.

reluctant to abandon the view of the economic actor as fundamentally rational, self-interested, goal maximizing and opportunistic (self-interested with guile),[63] the approach of old institutional economics is more suitable for understanding CSR and corporate ethics programmes in the general framework of economics, law and ethics because it conceives the economy from the perspective of social custom and culture of society.

In contrast to new institutional economics, old institutional economics is a 'holistic and organicist alternative' to atomism and reductionism.[64] Human beings are not reduced to rational utility maximizing agents, but seen as driven by culture and moral values. Moreover, the focus is not on individuals but on institutions as 'self-reinforcing' or 'even alternative analytical units'.[65] The economy is not exclusively considered as a 'mechanical equilibrium', but as an 'evolving open system' which is in constant interaction with its social and political environment. Individuals are situated and their preferences are 'not given and fixed but in a process of continuous adoption and change'.[66] Normative behaviour, human and institutional welfare are not evaluated exclusively in terms of efficiency or utility and pleasure, but focus is on the 'identification of real human need' in the design and evaluation of institutions.[67]

New institutionalism in sociology emphasizes the importance of social institutions and phenomenological scepticism towards the view of social institutions as a result of individual rational choice.[68] Individuals operate under conditions of limited knowledge and bounded rationality. The focus moves from individuals to institutional arrangements, cultures, values, rules and collective assumptions. New institutionalism in sociology represents a reaction against functionalism and rational choice theory in organizational analysis when the establishment of social relationships in the perspective of phenomenology of daily life (Schütz) and phenomenological social constructivism (Berger and Luckmann) are viewed as being based on creations of common rationality conceived as cognitions, values and customs shaping individual narratives and understandings.[69]

From this point of view, we can interpret the concept of the corporation as the unification of the totality of regulative, normative and cognitive

---

[63] Oliver E. Williamson (1984) The Economics of Governance: Framework and Implications, *Journal of Institutional and Theoretical Economics*, Vol. 140, 195–223.
[64] Geoffrey M. Hodgson (1994) The Return of Institutional Economics, in Niel J. Smelser & Richard Swedberg (eds): *The Handbook of Economic Sociology*, Princeton, NJ: Princeton University Press, pp. 68–69.
[65] *Id.*, p. 69.
[66] *Id.*, p. 69.
[67] *Id.*, p. 69.
[68] *Supra* note 32, p. 13.
[69] Powell & Paul J. DiMaggio (1991) *The New Institutionalism in Organizational Analysis*, Chicago, IL and London: The University of Chicago Press, p. 21.

pillars of organizational behaviour in a common governance structure.[70] As such, organizations are intentional forms based on contracts and interactions among individuals. This institutional unity is nothing other than the systematization of regulative, normative and cognitive elements in common purposeful action where individuals determined by their organizational roles unites with a particular organizational and behavioural project.[71] We can define the organization as a 'loosely coupled system'. It is a subsystem constituted by different institutional structures and forms. Processes of institutionalization of CSR and business ethics programmes in the EU and US imply changes in the regulative, normative and cognitive elements of organizations.[72] These provide 'stability and meaning to social behaviour'. They are 'transported by various carriers – cultures, structures and routines' – and 'they work at multiple levels of jurisdiction'.[73] Institutional structures submit individuals to particular roles and patterns of behaviour. Such collections of regulative, normative and cognitive pillars form the institutional framework of an organization as an agent of collective action.

In this context, CSR and business ethics represent new challenges and societal expectations to business corporations.[74] Many employees, business managers, NGOs, consumer movements and the democratic public consider human rights and standards of labour conditions, codes of good business conduct, ethics and values as indispensable for long-term sustainability and good corporate governance.[75] Many governments make efforts to facilitate the creation of social partnership between corporations and public authorities.[76]

Due to such public expectations of corporations, efforts of extensive stakeholder management and good corporate citizenship are becoming the licence to operate the firm. The theory of 'embeddedness' helps us to interpret this development when it argues that economic actions cannot be separated from their specific social context.[77] This means that the values of the firm reflect a number of organizational goals,[78] which are dependent

---

[70] *Supra* note 32.
[71] *Id.*
[72] *Supra* note 70, p. 33.
[73] *Id.*, p. 33.
[74] *Supra* note 11.
[75] *Supra* note 9.
[76] Cris Gribbon, Kate Pinnington & Andrew Wilson (2000) *Governments as Partners – The Role of Central Government in Developing New Social Partnerships. The Findings from Seven European Countries*, Copenhagen: Asridge & The Copenhagen Center.
[77] Marc Granovetter, (1985) Economic Action and Social Structure. 'The Problem of Embeddedness', *American Journal of Sociology*, Vol. 91(3), 481–510.
[78] H. A. Simon ((1964) 1969) The Concept of Organizational Goal, Reprinted in H. Igor Ansoff (ed.): *Business Strategy*. London: Penguin Modern Management Readings.

on its specific economic context and embedded in the social expectations of society. Many observers argue that there are important mutations in preferences, rationales and reasons for decision-making functioning as normative foundations for economic actions.[79] Uses of strategic values-driven management in firms indicate the efforts of companies to define value-based justifications for their economic activities. Thus, economic activities are forms of social action governed by values, rules and norms.

According to new institutionalism in sociology, the corporation is considered as an integrated part of society and the values of the organization are shaped by the perceptions of internal and external actors and stakeholders.[80] CSR is necessary for strategic management because it ensures the social legitimacy of the corporation as a good corporate citizen. This is because the institutional environment of the organization, which reflects social and cultural expectations of specific appearance and behaviour of the corporation, determines legitimacy. In order to cope with social expectations, the organization is required to construct its image and social appearance in accordance with values and norms of the institutional environment. This institutional legitimacy is not always directly visible but may also be a tacit and presupposed structure of norms and habits as the basis for legitimate rational action.[81]

We can therefore identify a number of different and maybe even contradictory expectations of different stakeholders to corporations that embody economic, social and environmental expectations.[82] Indeed, the institutional view of the firm as a 'loosely coupled system' is necessary to account for these different expectations and stakeholders in organization theory. Although these expectations are ideal they are often reflected in the factual demands of corporations. Shareholders want returns on their money, good risk management, economic transparency and ethics of social and environmental management. Governments want corporations to contribute to the wealth of society, respect the laws and the environment and be good citizens.

---

[79] *Supra* note 9.

[80] Michel Capron & Quairel-Lanoizeelée, Françoise (2004) *Mythes et réalités de l'entreprise responsable. Acteurs, Enjeux, Stratégies*, Paris: La Decouverte, p. 105; M. C. Suchman (1995) Managing Legitimacy: Strategic and Institutional Approaches, *Academy of Management Review*, Vol. 20, No. 3, 571–610, 572.

[81] C. Oliver (1991) Strategic Response to Institutional Processes, *Academy of Management Review*, Vol. 16, No. 1, 145–179. J. W. Meyer and B. Rowan (1977) Institutionalized Organizations: Formal Structure as Myth and Ceremony, *American Journal of Sociology*, Vol. 83, No. 2, 340–363; P. J. Di Maggio & W.W. Powell (1983) The Iron Cage Revisited: Functional Isomorphism and Collective Rationality in Organizational Fields, *American Sociological Review*, Vol. 48, No. 2 (Apr., 1983), 147–160.

[82] Michel Capron & Quairel-Lanoizeelée, Françoise (2004) *Mythes et réalités de l'entreprise responsable. Acteurs, Enjeux, Stratégies*, Paris: La Decouverte, pp. 155–156.

Banks and creditors want risk management and economic security but also respect for social and environmental issues. Employees and trade unions want corporations to ensure equality and good social conditions and they want the firm to have ethical values and ensure motivation, learning and development at work. Customers and clients want fair prices, good product quality, respect for the environment and respect for ethics and law. Suppliers want stable relations, acceptable payments and respect for ethics of contract and control of production so that they themselves will not have to violate law and ethics. Competitors expect corporations to be fair and respect the rules of the game, for example, by abstaining from environmental and social dumping. Local communities want engagement and the contributions of companies to communities and they expect companies to help with community development. International organizations and NGOs want transparency, respect for human rights and sustainability, and they want corporations to abstain from bribery and follow legal rules of countries where they operate.

According to the view of the firm as an open social system, we may say that CSR and business ethics make it possible for the corporation to respond to social expectations.[83] The corporations can use CSR and corporate ethics programmes to increase its capacity to react to social expectations and go into dialogue with stakeholders. CSR manifests the capacity of corporations to be socially reliable and trusted in the community.[84] CSR lays emphasis on the company's concrete contributions to social betterment[85] and in this sense it reinforces its legitimate position in the community.

According to institutional theory, the firm can more or less consciously choose different strategies to cope with such social expectations concerning corporate performance. An organization can ignore or try to avoid such claims of legitimacy. This reactive strategy can be combined with the symbolic manipulation of expectations or dramaturgy in order to be a free rider in regard to legitimacy claims. Another strategy would be a proactive conformation to social expectations. We can argue that strategic management of values and ethics corresponds to such a proactive search for legitimacy. CSR contributes to the maintenance of legitimacy.[86] The strategies of CSR and business ethics can be considered as conscious and rational initiatives to correspond to society's expectation of best practice and virtuous behaviour.

---

[83] William C. Frederick (1994) From CSR1 to CSR2: The Maturing of Business and Society Thought, *Business and Society*, Vol. 33, August, 155.
[84] Rogene A. Buchholz & Sandra B. Rosenthal (2002) Social Responsibility and Business Ethics, in Robert E. Frederick (ed.): *A Companion to Business Ethics*, Oxford: Blackwell publishing, p. 306.
[85] *Supra* note 33, p. 160.
[86] *Supra* note 82, p. 107.

In this sense, CSR can be considered as a symbolic reaction to social expectations in order to protect and develop the brand, image and reputation of the firm.

8 Conclusion

In conclusion, recent policy initiatives on corporate ethics programmes and CSR in the US and Europe imply a moralization of the firm, which is reflected in the conceptions of CSR and business ethics in economics, law and ethical discourse. In order to understand interactions between these different approaches, we have applied the organicist and holistic view of economic action as embedded in the culture and history of old institutional economics and the view of new institutional sociology of the organization as a 'loosely coupled system' in search of adjustment to social expectations as a basis for its sustainability and legitimacy in society. We have seen how this movement of legitimation and institutionalization is working on the economic, legal, ethical and legal level of the interaction of the firm with society. Accordingly, the nutshell of the argument is that legitimacy of corporations in modern society is founded on the idea of CSR, business ethics or human rights as instruments of social management. It is this connection between business ethics, corporate social responsibility and values-driven management that defines the basis for social and political legitimacy of corporations in democratic societies.

12
The Organization of CSR as a Means of Corporate Control: From Do-Gooding Sideshow to Mainstream?

Jette S. Knudsen

1 Introduction

Taking as its starting point Neil Fligstein's well-known claim that firms strive to control their internal and external environment to secure firm survival,[1] this chapter asks the following question: how do firms organize their Corporate Social Responsibility (CSR)[2] initiatives in order to control their business environment? This question has become increasingly important because during the last few decades normative expectations about the role of the firm in society have shifted from a traditional shareholder focus to include a diverse range of stakeholder interests. Investors, NGOs, employees, customers and the media have become adept at holding firms accountable for social and environmental activities.[3] Many firms have therefore adopted a

---

[1] Fligstein, N. (1990) *The Transformation of Corporate Control*, Cambridge, MA: Harvard University Press.
[2] CSR is defined by the European Commission as 'a concept whereby companies integrate social and environmental concerns in their business operations and in their interaction with their stakeholders on a voluntary basis' at http://ec.europa.eu/enterprise/csr/index_en.htm, accessed April 25, 2009. In short, CSR is defined as a 'beyond compliance' strategy.
[3] For example Aguilera, R.V., Rupp, D.E., Williams, C.A. & Ganapathi, J. (2007) Putting the S Back in Corporate Social Responsibility: A Multilevel Theory of Social Change in Organization, *Academy of Management Review*, Vol. 32, No. 3: 836–863; Berger, I.E., Cunningham, P.H. & Drumwright, M.E. (2007) Mainstreaming Corporate Social Responsibility: Developing Markets for Virtue, *California Management Review*, Vol. 49, No. 4: 132–157; Brown, D., Vetterlein, A. & Roemer-Mahler, A. (forthcoming, 2010) Theorizing Transnational Corporations as Social Actors: An Analysis of Corporate Motivations, *Business and Politics*, Vol. 12, No. 1; Porter, M. & Kramer, M. (2006) Strategy and Society: The Link Between Competitive Advantage

range of CSR initiatives in order to ensure that their actions are seen as legitimate, such as labor rights or human rights requirements in the supply chain, anti-corruption schemes or gender equality programmes.[4] The focus of this chapter extends beyond human rights to include a wider range of voluntary corporate social and environmental initiatives.

The CSR agenda is to a large extent driven by globalization, which is a phenomenon that includes new technology, the rapid and extensive fragmentation of production systems to developing countries, a reduction of transportation costs and deregulation of markets. The spread of the internet has also made corporate actions more transparent, including in the increasingly global supply chain. Furthermore, as firms produce in and source from developing countries their sphere of influence has widened yet national institutions are often weak and unable to cope with the large powerful firms operating in these countries. In addition, deregulation has led to growing trade and financial transactions across borders. Firms are therefore often left to find solutions on their own when it comes to handling complex social and environmental demands. One response has therefore been to adopt CSR initiatives in order to meet these emerging demands. Firms are hiring CSR managers, establishing CSR units, preparing CSR reports, etc. However, while many firms spend more and more money on CSR initiatives, little evidence exists regarding how firms define and implement their CSR initiatives.

The purpose of this chapter is to examine how CSR front-runner firms such as information technology giant Hewlett Packard (HP) and organic ice cream producer Ben & Jerry's define and implement their CSR initiatives. We have chosen front-runner firms in order to show that CSR initiatives, like other corporate initiatives, are continually evolving and that even front-runner firms do not have a magic wand when it comes to defining and implementing CSR initiatives. Their strategies for CSR (like any other strategy) have several strengths but also possess some weaknesses. Our focus is on 'expressed CSR' – initiatives that companies themselves label as CSR. A weakness is that this may lead us to miss actions that companies themselves do not explicitly label as CSR even though they are voluntary social and environmental initiatives. IBM's Global Innovation Outlook effort is an example of an initiative that IBM has not labelled as CSR but that could have

---

and Corporate Social Responsibility, *Harvard Business Review*, Vol. 96, No. 16: 78–92; Porter, M. & Kramer, M. (2002) The Competitive Advantage of Corporate Philanthropy, *Harvard Business Review*, Vol. 80, No. 12: 56–68. For a critique see Devinney, T. (2009) Is the Socially Responsible Corporation a Myth? The Good, the Bad and the Ugly of Corporate Social Responsibility, *Academy of Management Perspectives*, Vol. 23, No. 2: 44–56.

[4] Aguilera et al. 2007, *supra* note 3; Margolis, J.D. & Walsh, J.P. (2001) *People and Profits? The Search for a Link Between a Company's Social and Financial Performance*, Mahwah, NJ: Lawrence Erlbaum Associates, Publishers.

been labelled as such. This is a project where IBM collaborates with outside thought leaders to try and develop solutions to global challenges such as the world's finite water supply. A few months after its Global Innovation Outlook effort, IBM launched a new line of smart technologies to help utilities and firms more effectively monitor their water suppliers.[5] However, since our main aim is to clarify how firms define and organize initiatives, a focus on expressed CSR captures key developments.

The chapter is structured in the following manner: Section 2 presents Fligstein's claim that different conceptions of corporate control have emerged during the period 1880–1980 in the US and that each conception of control has resulted in different organizational strategies. Section 3 builds on Fligstein's argument and suggests that CSR initiatives can be perceived as reflections of two different conceptions of corporate control: (1) an offensive business driven approach (business-driven CSR) and (2) a more defensive image-making approach (image-making CSR). Each conception of control implies different ways of organizing CSR. Section 4 presents evidence from HP and Ben & Jerry's regarding the definition and implementation of CSR initiatives. Section 5 concludes and discusses future research ideas and proposes practical recommendations for firms regarding how best to organize CSR initiatives.

2 Fligstein's conception of corporate control in the US from 1880–1980

Focusing on large US firms during the period 1880–1980, Fligstein claims that the viability of the large industrial enterprise in the US is related to long-term shifts in the conception of how the largest firms should operate to preserve their growth and profitability. These shifts have occurred in response to a complex set of interactions between the largest firms, those who have risen to control those firms and the government. They originated with managers who sought more control over their internal and external environments. When one solution was blocked, new solutions were created and diffused. The result was a shift to a new conception of the large corporation and hence a new set of strategies and structures. Managers constructed new courses of action based on their analyses of the problems of controls that they faced. The way managers tried to achieve and exercise control was dependent upon their perspective of what constituted appropriate behaviour.

Fligstein makes a distinction between (1) *a conception of appropriate organizational action in order to achieve control* and (2) *an organizational strategy*.

---

[5] Hollender, J. & Breen, D. (2010) Opinion: Time for an End to Corporate Responsibility, *Ethical Corporation*, February 24: 2–5.

For example, diversification is an example of an organizational strategy but the conceptions of appropriate action that support diversification provide different reasons for pursuing diversification as a course of action. A sales and marketing executive may diversify product lines in order to have a full line of goods to sell to customers. On the other hand, a finance executive may view diversification as a way to spread risk. The strategy is the same but the meaning each attaches to the action is different. In short, managerial actions are justified as ways to extend their control over the situation at hand and managers are assumed to construct rationales for their behaviour based on how they view the world.

How have the conceptions of control been transformed in the past 100 years? Fligstein describes four distinct conceptions. First, from 1900–1924 the conception of control focused on ensuring *direct control of competitors*. Strategies included intensified regulation of the trade practices of large firms. These tactics failed because ultimately they could not prevent the entry or existence of firms in similar product lines.

Second, from WWI until the Depression the concept of control focused on *controlling manufacturing*. Strategies changed from confronting one's competitors and instead the manufacturing conception relied on the size, integration and relative effectiveness of the large firm as a potential threat to competitors. By controlling the input of raw materials and the sales output, managers and entrepreneurs could lower their vulnerability to the threats of their competitors or the vagaries of their markets. The manufacturing conception of control failed because the dominant firms often lost their market share over time as they clung to set prizes. This opened the door to competitors to enter the field and lessen the clout of the market leaders.

Third, from the Depression until the mid 1950s control focused on *sales and marketing*. Strategies changed from a focus on price stability to selling goods. Firm survival no longer depended on threatening one's competitors directly. Instead firms sought outlets for their goods where no other firms were selling. The marketing conception of control viewed the corporation as a growth machine powered by new products and marketing tactics. Differentiation and diversification of products were two tactics to expand the firm and increase its profitability. The marketing mentality of finding products to meet these needs as well as helping to create those needs permeated the entire organization.

Finally, even as the marketing conception of control triumphed, in the 1950s a new conception from of control emerged: *finance control*. How was the finance conception of control different from the sales and marketing conception? The key difference revolved around how each point of view conceived of the firm and its purpose. The sales and marketing conception pursued growth by increasing sales while the finance conception pursued growth by evaluating the contribution of each product line to the overall profit and goals of the firm. The finance conception of control viewed the central office as a bank and treated divisions as potential capital borrowers. The central office would invest in divisions that showed great potential and divest those in slow-growing markets. Profitable divisions supported mergers of new divisions. From this perspective mergers were attractive because product lines could be purchased at a lower price. Strategies included the use of financial tools to evaluate product lines and divisions. The multidivisional firm became the accepted organizational structure and control was achieved by decentralizing decision-making while paying close attention to financial performance.

Fligstein's account ends in 1980. Certainly the financial conception of control still holds sway although recent scandals such as Enron and the Lehman Brothers have resulted in an ongoing reappraisal of how best to ensure financial control. However, during the past 30 years the internationalization of production has taken off particularly rapidly. Today US firms increasingly source from or produce in developing countries and therefore firms face a new range of demands concerning social and environmental issues. Thus, in 2005 a special report by *The Economist* declared that 'the CSR movement has won the battle of ideas'.[6] As a result many firms have been forced into a role as a private regulator of social and environmental issues. We therefore claim that CSR today can be perceived as another important conception of appropriate organizational action in order to achieve control. How do firms seek to organize control of their increasingly international business environment by adopting CSR initiatives?

3 Internationalization of production: CSR as a means of corporate control

Many firms have a long tradition of social responsibility initiatives but in the past, these initiatives have largely been philanthropic. Firms have supported the local sports club, funded affordable housing projects, provided light employment for people who for various reasons were unable to hold a regular job, and so on. Furthermore, firms with daughter companies in developing countries have supported school projects, healthcare clinics, etc., because companies have seen philanthropy as 'the right thing to do'. Philanthropy has been particularly prevalent in the US because of its weaker welfare state compared to in Europe.[7] However, in the past 10–15 years a new perception of CSR has gained a solid hold on firms that now find that writing checks to charities is no longer enough.

---

[6] *The Economist* (2005) Survey: The Good Company, January 22: 8.
[7] Matten, D. & Moon, J. (2008) 'Implicit' and 'Explicit' CSR: A Conceptual Framework for a Comparative Understanding of Corporate Social Responsibility, *Academy of Management Review*, Vol. 33, No. 2: 404–424.

Simplifying somewhat, two competing conceptions of appropriate organizational action in order to achieve control dominate corporate thinking on CSR. Each conception implies different strategies for how CSR initiatives are organized within corporations. One conception views CSR initiatives as a way to improve overall business operations. This conception can be labelled *offensive CSR* or business-driven CSR. The second conception views CSR initiatives as a way of striving for control in a defensive manner by using CSR primarily as a means to enhance corporate image. This conception can be labelled *defensive CSR* or image-driven CSR.

3.1 Offensive CSR

The offensive or business-driven understanding of CSR has been strongly influenced by US thinking, in particular Michael Porter and Mark Kramer's two articles in the *Harvard Business Review* on the competitive advantage of corporate philanthropy (2002) and on the link between CSR and competitiveness (2006).[8] Porter and Kramer argue that CSR can become part of a company's competitive advantage if it is approached in a strategic way. CSR should be embedded into the core business operations so that it influences decisions across the company. Porter and Kramer argue that corporations use CSR initiatives as a way to link core business initiatives with their CSR initiatives in order to strengthen business operations, promote innovation and so on.[9] Examples include Toyota's hybrid electric/gasoline Prius, which has provided Toyota with a competitive advantage as well as environmental benefits. Furthermore, French Crédit Agricole has developed a new financial product, which finances energy efficient home improvements. Paraphrasing Milton Friedman's famous 1970 claim that 'the business of business is business'[10], according to Porter and Kramer, today the business of business is a different kind of business – a kind of business that incorporates social and environmental concerns into a company's DNA.

3.2 Defensive CSR

A defensive understanding views CSR initiatives as marketing or greenwashing.[11] The focus here is on improving the image of business not business creation. One example of this view can be found in a recent study published by the magazine *Ethical Corporation*, which showed that customer satisfaction surveys indicate that 'many firms that hog the limelight in corporate responsibility rankings and conferences are often at the wrong

---

[8] Porter, M. & Kramer, M. (2006) and (2002) *supra* note 3.
[9] *Id.*; Werbach, A. (2009) *Strategy for Sustainability: A Business Manifesto. How to Sustain a Business in Turbulent Times*, Cambridge, MA: Harvard Business Publishing.
[10] Friedman, M. (1970) The Social Responsibility of Business is to Increase its Profits. *New York Times Magazine*, September 13.
[11] Devinney (2009) *supra* note 3.

end of customer satisfaction indices'.[12] According to Chhabara, in most firms corporate responsibility is cosmetic and superficial and is primarily a function run by public relations departments. Critics argue that a CSR industry has created a myth that corporate responsibility is at the core of company behaviour. Almost every company that produces an annual corporate responsibility report includes a section that explains how it cares for customers, but 'Sustainability reports have become cosmetic exercises taken over by corporate communications departments. Many of the things they say in the report they have no way to verify. And they have no way to integrate it into their daily business... [C]orporate responsibility teams have no power. Saying that corporate responsibility teams have any power is a fundamental intellectual dishonesty that permeates the CSR industry.'[13]

Many NGOs are also suspicious of the CSR movement and view this phenomenon as corporate PR or regulation-dodging. The British NGO Christian Aid stated in a report, which examined the CSR record of several major firms, that 'the image of multinational firms working hard to make the world a better place is often just that – an image'.[14] Critics also include Robert Reich, a former labor secretary in the Clinton administration. Robert Reich in his book *Supercapitalism* argues that CSR is not working.[15] Hyper-competition among global corporations has led to a sole focus on extracting profits. CSR is a public relations fantasy created by big management houses and marketing agencies. More importantly, CSR tends to divert attention from establishing democratically based laws and regulations.[16]

3.3 Different stages of CSR development

Defensive and offensive CSR should not be seen as mutually exclusive but as representing different ends of a continuum. Some researchers distinguish between even more stages. For example, David Grayson has characterized five different stages of CSR development: (1) deniers (it's not our fault); (2) compliers (we'll only do what we have to do); (3) case-makers (it's business needs); (4) innovators (it gives us a competitive advantage) and

---

[12] Chhabara, R. (2009) Corporate Responsibility and Corporate Service Disconnect, *Ethical Corporation*, September/October: 22–25.
[13] *Id.* at 25.
[14] Christian Aid (2004). *Behind the Mask – the Real Face of CSR*, London, the UK.
[15] Reich, R.B. (2007) *Supercapitalism: The Transformation of Business, Democracy and Everyday Life*, New York, NY: Alfred A. Knopf.
[16] Doane, D. (2005) The Myth of CSR: The Problem with Assuming that Companies can do Well while also Doing Good is that Markets Don't Really Work that Way, *Stanford Social Innovation Review* at http://www.google.dk/search?source=ig&hl=da&rlz=1R2ADRA_daDK353&q=doane+the+myth+of+CSR&aq=f&aqi=&aql=&oq=&gs_rfai= accessed May 31, 2010; Kapstein, E.B. (2001) The Corporate Ethics Crusade, *Foreign Affairs*, September/October: 105–119.

(5) trail-blazers (we need to make sure that everybody does it). Each stage will result in different outcomes in terms of how CSR is organized within a firm. As Grayson points out: 'A business that is at a higher stage may have integrated its Corporate Responsibility and Sustainability function to the degree that it facilitates operational managers to run the business ethically and to incorporate sustainability directly into their work'.[17]

3.4 Organization of CSR: methodology

This chapter identifies three key elements of an organizational conception of CSR control. A justification for the selection of the three elements is presented below:

1. Link to business strategy
2. The organizational placement of CSR managers
3. The role of boards.

3.4.1 Link to business strategy

Porter and Kramer argue that CSR should be embedded into the core business operations so that it influences decisions across the company.

3.4.1.1 Offensive: clear link to business strategy. According to Porter and Kramer, 'the more closely tied a social issue is to a company's business, the greater the opportunity to leverage the firm's resources and benefit society'.[18] In short, the CSR strategy constitutes a component of the firm's overall strategy, CSR initiatives are clearly aligned with corporate strategy, and CSR decisions are integrated into basic business systems and decision processes. CSR initiatives reflect a clear prioritization of issues related to broader strategic concerns, and the corporate website, annual reports and so on display a link between CSR initiatives and corporate strategy.

3.4.1.2 Defensive: lack of clear link to business strategy. A company that focuses on CSR as image-making has a primary focus on communicating and marketing its CSR efforts to internal and especially external stakeholders. However, CSR initiatives remain focused on communications or marketing and no particular efforts are made to integrate CSR initiatives into core business areas.

In conclusion, if CSR is primarily about image-making we expect that the corporate website, annual reports and so on do not display a clear link

---

[17] Grayson, D. in collaboration with Odgers Berndtson (2009) *Who Should Head up your Corporate Responsibility Approach?* at http://www.odgers berndtson.co.uk/gb/knowledge-insight/article/who-should-head-up-your-corporate-responsibility-approach-1074 accessed on May 31, 2010: 4.
[18] Porter & Kramer (2006) *supra* note 3, at 88.

between CSR initiatives and corporate strategy. If CSR is business-driven we expect the corporate website and so on to present a clear link to corporate strategy as well as concrete examples.

3.4.2 The organizational placement of CSR managers

CSR managers are important private regulators yet we don't know much about these people, their training and background and how they perceive CSR. It is possible that the required skills of CSR managers are changing as CSR matures, with communication skills essential in the early stages of awareness-raising, to operations skills in the later stages of business implementation. It has also been suggested that once CSR is embedded, then somebody who can continue to lead the CSR agenda at a higher level and develop the proposition further will probably be more suitable.[19] In HP, for example, originally the head of CSR had a marketing background, the successor had an NGO background, and recently a new person was appointed with a background in supply chain management. A similar change has taken place at Nike. Criticism has also started to emerge that some CSR managers lack commercial awareness. For example, Adam Werbach, former CSR director at Wal-Mart and now director of Saatchi and Saatchi S, the global advertising firm's sustainability practice, has criticized CSR managers for not being able to explain how their work drives company sales.[20]

MIT Professor Peter Senge has warned that we should not count on a new 'sustainability department or corporate social responsibility department, a renamed EHS function, or any other add-on department to meet the company's strategic goals. At best such a group or function can be a temporary catalyst to develop initial projects and momentum for change, but it cannot be expected to carry the accountability for how business will be conducted as it fully embraces sustainability. That becomes everybody's job in different integrated ways, but especially should be the concern of the line managers...'.[21] Some have even argued that firms which have truly made CSR an integral part of the business will no longer need a separate specialist function.[22]

In order to determine if a position within an organization can be labelled a supporting activity or a primary activity, we use Michael Porter's value chain diagram as a rough approximation.[23] According to Porter, *supporting activities* include: (1) firm infrastructure (investor relations and financing);

---

[19] *Supra* note 17, at 13.
[20] Werbach, A. (2009) *supra* note 9.
[21] Senge cited in Grayson (2009), *supra* note 17, at 4.
[22] *Id.*
[23] Porter, M. (1990) *The Competitive Advantage of Nations*, Cambridge, MA: Harvard University Press.

(2) human resources management; (3) technology development (product design, market research), and (4) procurement (components, advertising and services). *Primary activities* include: (1) inbound logistics; (2) operations; (3) outbound logistics; (4) sales and marketing; and (5) after sales services.

Some CSR managers disagree with the claim that an organization can be characterized as having a 'defensive CSR strategy' if CSR responsibility formally rests with communication, marketing or human resources. They argue that this view undervalues the important informal role that many CSR managers play in terms of linking CSR issues and business strategy. They claim that often CSR managers serve as 'process facilitators' and therefore a focus on their formal placement within the corporate hierarchy does not offer adequate information about the role they play, their importance and how their employers view CSR. Nonetheless, while this criticism has some merit, formal structures do provide an indication of how firms perceive the role of CSR initiatives.

A discussion of how best to incorporate certain issues or concerns into corporate functions is by no means a discussion that is unique to CSR. The management literature is rich in examples including human resources management, health and safety, diversity and equality. Representatives from each field have traditionally sought to have their agenda become a critical element of corporate strategy. For example, in the 1980s in the US, human resource management featured prominently in national debates over competitiveness, and human resource professionals were expected to ascend to positions of greater influence in corporate strategy making and implementation.[24] Yet, while important innovations in practice were implemented in many US firms and these changes were accompanied by numerous calls for a paradigm shift towards a more 'strategic' focus for human resource management research, developments in both practice and research fell far short of expectations.[25] According to Kochan and Dyer, this transformational process fell short because the strategic human resources management model of the 1980s depended too narrowly on the necessary support from human resources line managers and top executives but ignored the need to incorporate more active roles of other stakeholders in the employment relationship including government, employees and union representatives (as well as line managers and top executives).[26]

3.4.2.1 Offensive: CSR managers in core business functions. A company with a business-oriented approach to CSR is expected to link CSR initiatives to business operations. For example, production sites may take care to integrate

---

[24] Kochan, T. & Dyer, L. (1992) *Managing Transformational Change: The Role of Human Resource Professionals*, Cambridge, MA, MIT Sloan School working paper: 3420-92-BPS.
[25] *Id.*
[26] *Id.*

social and environmental issues into day-to-day operations, and responsibility for managing and reporting on such issues rests with production managers. CSR managers may also have experience from core business functions and possibly from the same company or a similar firm or related sector.

3.4.2.2 Defensive: CSR managers in support functions.
A company that focuses on CSR as image-making is expected to have a primary focus on support activities such as communicating and marketing its CSR efforts to internal and especially external stakeholders. However, no particular efforts are made to integrate CSR initiatives systematically into core business areas. According to David Grayson, '[I]f CSR sits in corporate communications or marketing it will not be taken seriously but will be seen as mainly a PR stunt'.[27]

In conclusion, if CSR is primarily about image-making the organizational placement of the CSR manager is either unclear or the manager is located in support functions such as marketing, communications or human resources. If CSR is business-driven we expect the CSR manager to collaborate closely with relevant corporate business units and to respond to someone responsible for core business tasks.

3.4.3 The role of boards

What is the board's role in terms of providing oversight, strategy and disclosure of a firm's environmental, social and governance performance? Few firms have included sustainability explicitly in their governance mandates. A 2007 study from Canada found that fewer than ten Canadian firms reported having CSR or sustainability explicitly in their governance mandates.[28] However, some firms have begun to lay out a CSR mandate for boards that suggests that boards should take stakeholder views into account in their decision-making and strategy setting. Firms in the US and Europe are increasingly establishing CSR committees. The committees are often mandated to review, recommend and monitor compliance with policies such as CSR codes of conduct, management systems and regulations. To take an example: Nike's CSR committee is made up of five board members. The board chair or the CEO (or both) attend every meeting of the CSR committee, which meets several times a year and regularly reports to the board.[29] According to Nike, CSR is discussed frequently at every board meeting and is seen as a factor in product innovation, supply chain management and

---

[27] *Supra* note 17.
[28] Strandberg, C. (2008). *The Role of the Board of Directors in Corporate Social Responsibility (report)* at http://www.corostrandberg.com/publications_Corporate_Sustainability_Governance.html accessed June 4, 2010.
[29] *Id.*

several business priorities. The stated intention is to fully integrate social responsibility into the business model. However, a study by the Canadian Conference Board showed that there is no strong orientation among boards towards incorporating CSR into firm strategy nor are boards reviewing and approving CSR reports.[30] Direct board engagement is also limited although there is a literature stream that recommends this.[31]

3.4.3.1 Offensive: The board plays a key role in shaping the CSR agenda. The role of boards is becoming more important for the CSR agenda. For example public firms face growing pressure, including from institutional investors, to split the role of chairman and CEO. In 2009 US Senator Charles Schumer of New York, a prominent Democrat on the Senate Banking Committee, proposed a bill known as the Shareholder Bill of Rights, which recommends a split. According to Timothy Smith of Walden Asset Management, 'if you have the CEO of the company chairing the board meeting, it sends the message that he is in charge, and you oppose him at your own peril. But if you have an independent chair, it sends the message that the CEO is the chief employee of the company and works for the board'.[32]

If the board views CSR as a means to create value, one indication could be that the terms of reference of the CSR committee should include a focus on CSR strategy as an element of risk management. Furthermore, according to Leonard and Rangan, boards must examine the coherence of the CSR strategy as a component of the firm's overall strategy by asking questions such as:

- How do these actions fit with another and with our general strategy?
- Is the CSR strategy internally coherent?
- Does our approach to CSR take advantage of our key skills and distinctive competences or does it require us to develop new capabilities that we do not otherwise need?
- Are decisions about CSR integrated into our basic business systems and decision processes?[33]

3.4.3.2 Defensive: The board does not play a key role in shaping the CSR agenda. If CSR primarily serves an image-making purpose the board is not likely to play a key role in terms of ensuring that CSR actions fit with the general

---

[30] *Id.*

[31] Paine, L.S. (2002) Bad People Do Not Have a Monopoly on Bad Deeds: Taking an Organizational Approach to Ethics, *Regional Review*, Vol. 12, No. 4: 6–8.

[32] *Sustainability Investment News*, September 9, 2009 at http://www.socialfunds.com/news/article.cgi/article/article2776.html accessed June 4, 2010.

[33] Leonard, H.B. and Rangan, V.K. (2006) Corporate Social Responsibility Strategy and Boards of Directors, *Boardroom Briefing*, winter: 12–14, accessible at: http://www.exed.hbs.edu/assets/board-responsibility.pdf, accessed May 31, 2010.

Table 12.1 CSR impact on corporate functions: business-driven and image-making CSR

Indicators	Business-driven (offensive)	Image-making (defensive)
Link to business strategy[34]	Corporate website, annual reports, etc. display a link between CSR initiatives and firm strategy (official company documents provide illustrative examples)	Corporate website, annual reports, etc. display no clear link between CSR initiatives and firm strategy
Organizational placement of CSR manager in corporate hierarchy[35]	CSR manager responds to someone with core business responsibilities such as operations or sales	Organizational placement of CSR manager in non-core business areas such as marketing, communications or human resources
Role of boards[36]	Clear role of boards in terms of making sure that CSR actions: fit with general strategy; are internally coherent; are integrated into business systems and processes	No clear role of board in terms of making sure that CSR actions: fit with general strategy; are internally coherent; are integrated into business systems and processes
	Role of CEO and chairman often split	Role of CEO and chairman often not split

firm strategy, are internally coherent, and are integrated into basic business systems and processes. Also, the positions of CEO and chairman are often not split.

In conclusion, if CSR is business driven we expect boards to evaluate and determine how CSR actions fit with general business initiatives, to show how they are internally coherent, and how they are integrated into general business systems. If CSR is image-driven, boards will not play much of a role in terms of linking CSR to business strategies (Table 12.1).

4 Leading CSR firms: HP and Ben & Jerry's

Next, we focus on two of the undisputed CSR leaders in the United States: HP and Ben & Jerry's. What take-home lessons can front-runner firms provide

---

[34] Grayson 2009 *supra* note 17; Porter and Kramer, *supra* note 3.
[35] *Ibid*.
[36] Leonard and Rangan, 2006, *supra* note 33.

in terms of how to define and organize CSR initiatives and which challenges remain? The main focus is on HP, which is a Fortune 100 company, while Ben & Jerry's is included as an example of a company that has successfully developed a business model around a social mission.

4.1 HP

HP is renowned for its values-based approach to business (named 'the HP Way') that includes a long tradition for philanthropy and more recently the embedding of social and environmental initiatives into its business strategy. For example, HP was the first firm in Silicon Valley to provide all employees with a health insurance plan; HP also fostered flexi-work allowing employees to choose their own teammates and team leaders and in times of recession HP sought to avoid layoffs by ordering pay-cuts and requesting employees to stretch their working weeks.[37] Finally, HP has been named as 'best place to work in Silicon Valley'.[38]

We therefore expect HP to have undertaken significant initiatives in order to integrate CSR initiatives and firm strategy (offensive CSR). Critics might argue perhaps that 'the bar is set too high': the concept of CSR is so broad and fuzzy that it is always possible to find examples of limited integration of CSR initiatives. Furthermore, critics might also note that integrating CSR initiatives is a process that is never fully complete. There is some merit to these criticisms. However, the intention here is not to set up a 'straw man' so that in order for a company to be seen as organizing CSR initiatives in an offensive manner, initiatives must be so wide-ranging and so deeply integrated into corporate strategy that no company could possibly meet such a standard. The purpose is only to reasonably evaluate how HP has sought to integrate CSR initiatives within its business operations and to point to possible challenges even in this CSR front-runner company.

4.1.1 The definition of CSR and link to business strategy

HP is the world's largest information technology company. Its portfolio spans printing, personal computing, software, services and IT infrastructure. HP's headquarter is in Palo Alto California and with 321,000 employees HP does business in more than 170 countries around the world. The HP 2008 Global Citizenship Report seeks to demonstrate the relevance of many of HP's CSR programmes and in particular its environmental efforts for HP's overall business. Already in the first paragraph of HP's extensive 89-page HP

---

[37] Jacobson, D. (2007) *Founding Fathers* at http://www.stanfordalumni.org/news/magazine/1998/julaug/articles/founding_fathers/founding_fathers.html, accessed May 31, 2010.
[38] ICFAI Business case '*Hewlett Packard – Culture Change Through Acquisitions*', reference number 408-123-1.

Global Citizenship Report 2008, Mark Hurd,[39] HP's CEO, notes that '[customers] also value ways we can help them be more successful. That could mean an energy-efficient data center that cut costs while reducing their carbon footprint, or a centrally managed printing environment that increases productivity and saves resources.' Additional examples include how HP has cut its greenhouse gas emissions and how it has led the industry in reporting GHG emissions of first-tier suppliers, representing more than HP's total product manufacturing spend.[40] Other examples include an innovative device produced in collaboration with UPS to print labels directly on packages thereby saving million in operational costs as well as saving over 1,200 tons of paper each year.

HP has one of the largest supply chains in the industry and therefore points out that it sees an opportunity to lead when it comes to protecting human rights, improving working conditions and protecting the environment. HP works with NGOs to find joint solutions to a range of social and environmental challenges throughout its first, second and third-tier suppliers. Furthermore, Mark Hurd states that 'Global Citizenship is strategic to the worth of our business. Developing solutions for the low-carbon economy offers tremendous potential to reinvent or create entirely new markets. Tightening standards in our supply chain can improve consistency and wring out inefficiencies, while protecting us from risks from unethical suppliers. Investing in transforming education and training entrepreneurs is helping to cultivate the next generation of skilled workers, innovators and customers.'[41] In sum, HP has developed a set of impressive social and environmentally friendly initiatives that are seen as strengthening the overall business strategy. However, it is not clear how HP decides which initiatives to focus on or which decision-making criteria to apply.

4.1.2 The organizational placement of CSR managers

In terms of organizing CSR within HP, several initiatives stand out. For example, HP has a Global Citizenship Council which was created in 2008. Members of the Council include senior executives from each of HP's five focal CSR areas: ethics and compliance, human rights and labor practices, environmental sustainability, social investment and privacy. The Global Citizenship Council meets bi-monthly. It is chaired by the Vice President (VP) of global citizenship. According to the annual report the Council seeks input

---

[39] On August 6, 2010 Chairman, CEO and President Mark Hurd resigned his positions with HP effective immediately. See http://www.hp.com/hpinfo/newsroom/press/2010/100806a.html, accessed August 11, 2010.
[40] HP, 2008. *HP Global Citizenship Report 2008* at http://www.hp.com/hpinfo/globalcitizenship/ accessed May 31, 2010: 1.
[41] *Id.* at 2.

from investor relations and research and development and advises HP's Executive Council, which retains overall responsibility for global citizenship.

However, it is not clear how the Global Citizenship Council and the Executive Council collaborate. No examples are provided of how strategic business decisions are made and in particular how decisions are made that may pose conflicts between global citizenship and business objectives. Nor do we learn about the role of the HP Board of Directors. In short, the link between the Global Citizenship Council, the HP Executive Council and the HP Board of Directors is not very clear. In 2008 HP created two new senior positions – VP for compliance and VP for ethics. They report to HP's chief ethics and compliance officer who oversees HP's ethics and compliance programme and chairs the Ethics and Compliance Committee. The chief ethics and compliance officer reports to the general counsel, the independent director responsible for HP's compliance with legal and ethical requirements related to the conduct of investigations, and to the Board's Audit Committee on HP's investigative practices and ethics and compliance programme. In addition, HP has a VP for corporate citizenship. Based on publicly available evidence, it is not a simple task to determine the organization of HP's CSR work.

4.1.3 *The role of boards*

The Board of Directors has several primary responsibilities relating to ethics and compliance: provide oversight of ethics and compliance at HP, set and enforce the 'tone at the top' and encourage a company culture of ethical conduct and compliance.[42] The board has ten members with the CEO serving as chairman and president. Thus, HP does not follow the recommendation from a growing number of institutional investors that public firms split the role of chairman and CEO. The other nine members are independent directors as defined by the listing standards of NYSE and HP's Corporate Governance Guidelines. The board's Audit Committee guides HP's ethics and compliance programme and is a direct resource for the chief ethics and compliance officer. The role of the board is not clear in terms of setting CSR goals.

4.2 Ben & Jerry's

Ben & Jerry's Homemade Ice cream, Inc. was founded in 1978 in Vermont by two hippies named Ben Cohen and Jerry Greenfield. Today the company boasts an almost 40 per cent share of the premium ice cream market in the US. Early on the company developed its business identity around a social vision. For example, in 1985 the company established a non-profit charitable foundation through a donation of stock from Ben & Jerry's. Traditionally the company has also donated seven percent of pre-tax profits to philanthropy.

---

[42] *Id.* at 23.

4.2.1 The definition of CSR and link to business strategy

Three interrelated objectives comprise the company's mission. First, Ben & Jerry's aims to produce the finest quality all natural ice cream in a wide variety of innovative flavors. A second objective is to operate the company on a sound financial basis, increasing value for shareholders and creating career opportunities for employees. Finally, the company adheres to a social objective to initiate innovative ways to improve the quality of life of the local community where it operates. CSR initiatives include the development of an ecological footprint including measurement and management of water, energy use, waste and emissions reductions and recycling. Social issues have included a cap on management remuneration, a focus on diversity in hiring, work-life balance, generous health insurance and pension plans, dental plan, disability plan and maternity leave. Supply chain issues are also high on the list including sustainable cocoa farming in Africa, which faces substantial problems due to widespread use of forced child labor. In short, CSR initiatives are clearly linked to the production of natural high quality ice cream including input of raw materials, provision of employee benefits and support for the local community.

However, it is not clear how Ben & Jerry's prioritize initiatives or which decision-making criteria are applied. It is also not clear how the company deals with potential conflicts between CSR goals and profitability. For example, a cornerstone of Ben & Jerry's social responsibility identity has been the salary cap on the compensation of its highest paid employees. Historically, the highest paid employee was to be paid no more than five times the salary of the lowest paid employee. This salary cap was removed in 1994 but it is not clear why this was decided or if and how the removal may have affected Ben & Jerry's broader CSR goals. Furthermore, following the acquisition of Ben & Jerry's by Unilever, criticism has mounted that Ben & Jerry's misleads franchisees on their likely earnings. After Unilever's takeover, Ben & Jerry's embarked on an expansion strategy to triple its franchises network by opening shops that critics have claimed are not financially viable.[43] Also, another challenge is that Ben & Jerry's manufactures a costly product that may have serious health ramifications due to its high fat content.

4.2.2 The organizational placement of CSR managers

While Unilever is well-known for its CSR policies, Unilever is clearly not a social mission company. However, Unilever's stated goal when acquiring Ben & Jerry's was that it should retain its unique social profile. Ben & Jerry's is the only Unilever brand with its own board and CEO. Ben &

---

[43] Entine, J. (2008) From Evil Empire to Jolly Green Giant, *Ethical Corporation*, July/August: 36–38.

Jerry's publishes an annual Social and Environmental Assessment Report.[44] The Report describes social initiatives, CSR elements of production and economic targets. The description of business decisions is integrated with a description of CSR initiatives. Ben & Jerry's does not have a CSR manager and in this respect can be said to have progressed to 'full integration of CSR'. However, as Unilever owns Ben & Jerry's it is to be expected that certain Unilever CSR guidelines and standards will also pertain to Ben & Jerry's but this relationship is not addressed in publicly available data sources.

4.2.3 The role of boards

The CEO of Ben & Jerry's 'receives feedback and counsel on the Company's direction from an independent Board of Directors, established at the time of the Unilever acquisition. The Board is responsible for advising and supporting Ben & Jerry's senior management in maintaining and strengthening the company's three-part Mission Statement and protecting Ben & Jerry's brand. This Board, which meets quarterly, includes several former directors of the company with longstanding ties to the brand.'[45] Unilever has a well-developed sustainability programme reflecting the company's diverse operations. Sustainability issues are well-integrated into a committee system supervised by top management. However, as in HP no examples are provided of how strategic business decisions are made and in particular how decisions are made that may pose conflicts between sustainability and business objectives. Furthermore, the possible impact of Unilever's board decisions on Ben & Jerry's is not addressed.

Summing up, we can conclude that both HP and Ben & Jerry's have made tremendous progress in terms of adopting and implementing CSR initiatives. However, the overall link to strategy is not as well developed in HP as it is in Ben & Jerry's. Furthermore, in both cases decision-making processes could be further clarified and in particular how the companies deal with potential conflicts between CSR initiatives and profitability; finally, the role of boards in making CSR decisions could also be further explained. Tables 12.2 and 12.3 provide an overview of CSR impact on corporate functions in HP and Ben & Jerry's.

5 Conclusion

Several implications follow from this exploratory analysis of how CSR initiatives are defined and organized within firms both in terms of research and in terms of practical advice to managers. From a research perspective

---

[44] Ben & Jerry's (2009) *Ben & Jerry's Social and Environmental Assessment Report* at http://www.benjerry.com/company/sear/ accessed on May 31, 2010.
[45] *Id.*

Table 12.2 CSR impact on corporate functions in HP: business-driven and image-making CSR

Indicators	Business-driven (offensive)	Image-making (defensive)
Link to business strategy	Corporate website, annual reports, etc., display link between CSR initiatives and firm strategy including: energy efficiency and productivity increases due to energy efficient data-centers; a centrally managed printing environment; HP as leader in reporting GHG emissions partnerships with NGOs to find solutions to social and environmental challenges in the supply chain	Prioritization of CSR initiatives is unclear Lack of clarity concerning decision-making criteria
Organizational placement of CSR responsible in corporate hierarchy	Global Citizenship Council reports to Executive Council (top management)	Unclear how Global Citizenship Council and executive Council collaborate Unclear how potential conflicts between CSR goals and business goals are dealt with
Role of boards		Unclear role of board in terms of evaluating if CSR initiatives fit with company strategy; are internally coherent; are integrated into business systems and processes CEO is also chairman of the board (roles are not split)

knowledge is clearly lacking about how firms define which among multiple social issues are most relevant to their interests and how they set and evaluate priorities? *Business studies* inform us about how firms are undertaking social initiatives, what they engage in and why, but studies rarely extend beyond a short-term time horizon and focus somewhat narrowly on the opinions of a few managers and stakeholders.[46] *The international relations*

---

[46] Porter & Kramer (2006) *supra* note 3.

Table 12.3 CSR impact on corporate functions in Ben & Jerry's: business-driven and image-making CSR

Indicators	Business-driven (offensive)	Image-making (defensive)
Link to business strategy	Corporate website, annual reports, etc. display link between CSR initiatives and firm strategy. Extensive list of initiatives including: ecological footprint; diversity management; very good employee perks; focus on local community	Prioritization of CSR initiatives is unclear Lack of clarity concerning decision-making criteria). For example, why did Ben & Jerry's end the salary cap? Unclear how potential conflicts between CSR and profitability are solved (e.g., is franchise profitability 'oversold'?) No information provided regarding how Ben & Jerry's deals with negative side effects of its product (weight gain; health problems, etc.)
Organizational placement of CSR responsible in corporate hierarchy	CSR initiatives fully integrated into Ben & Jerry's business model as a social mission company	Unclear how decisions are made regarding CSR initiatives Unclear how link to Unilever may affect Ben & Jerry's CSR profile in the future
Role of boards	Ben & Jerry's CEO receives feedback from an independent Board of Directors. Board advises senior management on CSR to determine if it fits with general strategy; is internally coherent; is integrated into business systems and processes	Unclear how Unilever's board may affect Ben & Jerry's CSR policy

literature provides an extensive list of reasons why actors who hold 'private authority' may behave in certain ways, especially in stressing the complex political environment of national and international rules and regulations (including international organizations and NGOs) in which firms exist.[47] But this literature also often treats firms as black boxes and relies too heavily on

---

[47] Barnett, M. & Finnemore, M. (2004) *Rules for the World: International Organizations in Global Politics*, Ithaca, NY: Cornell University Press.

monitoring and enforcement in a realm where there is often little.[48] *The comparative political economy literature* such as, for example, the 'Varieties of Capitalism' literature highlights how complex domestic institutional structures shape policy outcomes but also does not look inside the black box of the firm. In short, how firms prioritize and evaluate their CSR agenda constitutes a promising new research agenda.[49]

In terms of practical implications we can provide three take-home lessons for managers. First, there is no doubt that the CSR agenda has arrived. Demands are likely to grow for more voluntary corporate social and environmental initiatives from institutional investors, customers, employees, the media and even regulators as globalization poses new challenges to firms. Companies therefore need to identify the larger social consequences of their core business processes. The list of possible CSR issues is constantly expanding and firms will have to clarify how they prioritize social and environmental initiatives. No firm can or should do 'everything'. Firms should

Table 12.4 Recommendations to managers

Core issues	Recommendations
Link to business strategy	Identify social consequences of core business processes
	State openly that company resources are limited
	Prioritize CSR issues and clarify decision-making criteria
Organizational placement of CSR manager	Place CSR manager in core business unit or make CSR manager respond to core business unit
	Ensure that CSR manager is business savvy and understands and can drive corporate strategy
Role of boards	Provide sufficient information to the board to enable the board to shape, monitor and evaluate the CSR strategy as a key element of risk assessment

---

[48] For example Hall, R. and Biersteker, T.J. (eds.) (2002). *The Emergence of Private Authority in Global Governance*, Cambridge Studies in International Relations, Cambridge, the UK: Cambridge University Press; Ruggie, J.G. (2004) Reconstituting the Global Public Domain – Issues, Actors, and Practices, *European Journal of International Relations*, Vol. 10, No. 4: 499–531.

[49] Gourevitch, P. & Shinn, J. (2007) *Political Power and Corporate Control: The New Global Politics of Corporate Governance*, Princeton, NJ: Princeton University Press; Hall, P.A. & Soskice, D. (eds.) (2001) *Varieties of Capitalism: The Institutional Foundations of Comparative Advantage*, Oxford, the UK: Oxford University Press.

not be afraid to openly state that they cannot do everything because of limited resources, limited relevance and/or limited expertise. Second, CSR managers need to be business savvy and much could be gained if they are placed in core business functions in the corporation. We need more CSR managers with a business strategy background or a production background. Third, a focus on CSR initiatives will become increasingly important to boards. According to *The Economist* in the UK in 2007, 20 per cent of top 100 companies had board committees consider CSR issues, another 10–15 per cent had regular board agenda items related to CSR, and 30–40 per cent had ad hoc conversations on a regular basis.[50] This is an important element of corporate risk assessment. It is therefore crucial that boards have sufficient information to shape, monitor and evaluate CSR strategies. An overview of recommendations to managers is provided in Table 12.4.

---

[50] *The Economist* (2008) A Special Report on Corporate Social Responsibility, January 19.

Index

accountability, 65–8, 111, 139, 155–6
advisory opinions, 199–200
African Human and People's Charter, 134–5
aid, 145–7
Alban Cornejo v. Ecuador, 198
Albany case, 167
American Commission on Human Rights, 192–3
American Convention on Human Rights, 188, 191
American Declaration of the Rights and Duties of Man (ADRDM), 192
American Electric Power, 238
AngloGold Ashanti, 206
arbitrary detention, 147–9
assurance system guidelines, 226
attribution rules, 39–47

Baena v. Panama, 198
BECTU case, 174
Beentjes case, 182
Ben & Jerry's Homemade Ice cream, Inc., 15, 281–3
Between Facts and Norms (Habermas), 96–7, 98
BHP Billiton, 237, 240
boards, 9, 276–8
business ethics, 252–3, 257–8
business responsibilities for human rights (BRHR)
 character of, legal, 7
 discourse of, 4
 on European Union law, 166
 on human rights, discourse, 5–6
 legal conflicts on, 6
 by SRSG, development of, 5
 see also CSR
business strategy, 273–4

capital, 230–4
 globalization and, 230–4
 international financial reporting standards for, 232–4
 principles-based *vs.* rules-based systems of, 231
Caring for Climate platform, 69–70
Carpenter case, 183
Caux Round Table discussions, 245
Charter of Fundamental Rights of the European Union, 175
Chiquita, 206
Claude Reyes et al. v. Chile, 198
Coca Cola, 116
Codes of Conduct to Framework Agreements, 173
Commission v. France, 181
Commission v. Germany, 167
Commission v. Luxembourg, 167
Communication on Progress (COP) report, 59, 66–7
Companies Act (2006), 134, 227
compliance programmes, 244
complicity, 111
conduct, 214–7
corporate accountability, 122–3, 256
corporate citizenship, 52, 247, 255–6
corporate codes, 214–17
corporate codes of conduct, 211–13
 IFA's *vs.*, 214–17
 International Framework Agreements (IFA) *vs.*, 214–17
corporate ethics, 244–65
 corporate citizenship and, 247
 corporate legal subjectivity and, 254–7
 CSR and, economic aspects of, 249–54
 morality and, 246
 US on, ethics policies in, 247–8
 values-driven management and, 246
corporate integration, 15–18
 institutional theory and, 15–16
 isomorphism and, 16
 management and, 16–18
corporate isomorphism, 16, 18
corporate philanthropy, 271
Corporate social responsibility (CSR), *see* CSR

Index 289

CSR
    EU CIliance, 96, 102, 104
    BRHR and, distinctions between notions of, 5–6
    concept of, 5, 6, 7
    EU's concept of, 1, 166
    on human rights, discourse, 6–7
    institutional concept of, 254
    law vs., 7–8
    MSF on, 7, 84
    voluntary-mandatory dichotomy of, 7
    see also European Union law
CSR, economic aspects of, 249–54
    ethics on, 251–3, 260–5
    moralization and, 253–4
CSR, legal/management perspectives of, 8–15
    boards, role of, 9
    challenges of, 9
    Corporate Social Responsibility (CSR) initiatives on, 15
    corporations and, state regulation of, 14–15
    duties and, 10
    "governance gaps" and, 9
    home state regulation and, 11
    human rights and, 8–9, 11–14
    Inter-American Human Rights Commission and Court and, 14
    International Framework Agreements (IFAs) on, 14, 206–11
    National Human Rights Institutions role in, 13
    reflexive law and, 9
    Special Representative (SRSG) on Business and Human Rights and, 10–13, see also SRSG
    UN Global Compact and, 12
CSR Codes of Conduct, 205–21
    corporate codes of conduct and, 211–13
    Global Union Federations (GUFs) on, 205, 206
    IFAs and, 206–11

DaimlerChrysler, 60
Danone, 206
Declaration of Fundamental Principles and Rights at Work, 82, 169, 171, 208

Declaration on International Investment and Multinational Enterprises, 168
Defrenne-III case, 174
deliberative law-making theory, 97, 100
Deutsche Telekom, 60
dialogue events, 59, 60–1
differentiated but complementary responsibilities, 121–4
direct extraterritorial jurisdiction, 31
Directive 2000/78/EC, 180
Disclosure Guidelines on Socially Responsible Investment, 236
Dodge vs. Ford Motor Corporation, 255
due diligence, 255–6
Dunnett case, 174
Dupont, 238
duty to protect
    home state obligations and, 35–47
    home state regulation and, 27–35
    international law and, 27, 32–5
    SRSG's identification of, 25
    state institutions for, 27
    TWAIL perspective of, 26–7, 32–3
    UN Principles of Responsible Investment (UNPRI) on, 27, 47–50

EarthRights International, 116
East African Breweries, 137
effective remedies, 112
engagement mechanisms, 59–61
Enron, 270
equal treatment, 178
Equator Principles, 235–6
equity analysis, 236–7
ethics
    business of, 252–3
    conception of, 251–2
    corporations and, social legitimacy of, 260–5
European Communities policy initiatives, 244–5
European Convention
    on Human Rights, 85, 90
    for the Protection of Human Rights and Fundamental Freedoms and its Protocols, 153
European Council, 175
European Court of Human Rights (ECHR), 36, 153, 174

European Court of Justice (ECJ), 167, 173–4
European Economic Area (EEA), 172
European Multi-Stakeholder Forum (MSF), 7, 77, 83–6
European Parliament, 80, 175
European Union, 77, 83–6
  law, *see* European Union law
  Multi-Stakeholder Forum on CSR (MSF), 77, 83–6
EU Charter on Fundamental Rights, 183
EU Commission, 80, 86, 95, 104
EU Green Paper Promoting a European Framework for Corporate Social Responsibility, 244–5
EU Multi-Stakeholder Forum (MSF) on CSR, 77–107
  Final Report, 85–6, 95
  public-private multi-stakeholder regulation, 89–96
  see also Habermasian deliberative discourse; Reflexive law
European Union law, 165–84
  BRHR and, legal approach to business responsibilities for human rights, 166
  Codes of Conduct to Framework Agreements on, 173
  collective bargaining and, national labour law on, 167
  collective labour law and, 167–168
  and, gaps between, 165–6
  on free movement, 165, 167, 176–8
  on fundamental rights, 165, 173–6
  procurement rules and, specific, 178–82
Extractive Industries Transparency Initiative, 226
extraterritorial home state jurisdiction, 35
extraterritorial jurisdiction, 28, 31–2, 37
extraterritorial limitations, 37–8
extraterritorial regulation, 117
Exxon, 240–1

Federal Sentencing Guidelines for Organizations, 244, 247–8
Festersen case, 183
financial statements, 231, 238–9
Finnish Bus Case, 181

FLA workplace code, 69
Fonterra, 206
Ford, 238
Forest Stewardship Council (FSC), 77
forum non conveniens, 46, 113
free movement, 13, 176–8
French Crédit Agricole, 271
fundamental rights, 165, 173–7

Gebhard case, 177
Gender Equality Directive, 180
General Agreement on Tariffs and Trade (GATT), 169
Generation Investment Management (Generation), 236–7
Global Compact, 12, 52–76, 81–3, 100–4, 140, 168–9, 171, 212
  see also United Nations (UN) Global Compact
Global Compact Kenya Network (GNKN), 140
Global Compact Leaders Summit, 60
Global Compact Office, 58, 66, 80
Global Reporting Initiative (GRI), 73, 225
global reporting standard, 238–42
  IFRS treatment of CSR issues, 239–41
Global Union Federations (GUFs), 205
  CSR Codes of Conduct by, 205, 206
  International Framework Agreements (IFA) *vs.*, 215
GPA (Government Procurement Agreement), 169–70

Habermasian deliberative discourse, 12, 96–104
  deliberative law-making theory and, 97, 100
  international level of, 99–100
  objective of, 96–8
  reflexive law and, 12, 98–9, 100–4
Hewlett Packard (HP), 15, 279–81
home state duty to protect, 25–51
  home state obligations and, 35–47
  home state regulation and, 27–35
  international law and, 27, 32–5
  SRSG's identification of, 25
  state institutions for, 27
  TWAIL perspective of, 26–7, 32–3
  UN Principles of Responsible Investment (UNPRI) on, 27, 47–50

Index 291

home state jurisdiction, 28–9, 30–1, 32, 34, 35
home state obligations, 35–47
  see also home state duty to protect; ILC articles (*Draft Articles on Responsibility of States for Internationally Wrongful Acts*); jurisdiction
Honeywell International, Inc., 238
human rights theory, 34–5
human rights violations, 145–6, 147
Human Rights Watch, 116
Hurd, M., 280

IAS standards, 239–41
IBM, 238, 267–8
ILC articles (*Draft Articles on Responsibility of States for Internationally Wrongful Acts*), 43–4, 45–6
  jurisdictional scope and, 35–9
  Loss Allocation Principles and, 37–8
  Prevention Articles and, 37–8
ILO Declaration on Multinational Enterprises and Social Policy, 208
InfoSys Technologies Ltd., 116, 232
institutional investors compliance, 50
institutional theory, 15–16, 264, 252–3
Inter-American commission, 196–7
Inter-American Court of Human Rights, 189, 192–3, 197–200
Inter-American Human Rights Commission and Court, 14
Inter-American System on Human Rights, 191–2, 195
International Accounting Standards Board, 232
International Accounting Standards Committee Foundation, 232, 233–4
Internationale Handelsgesellschaft, 174
International Financial Reporting Standards (IFRS), 231, 232–4, 239–41
  accounting standards for, 239–40
  financial statements prepared for, 239, 240–1
International Framework Agreements (IFA), 206–11
  Codes of Conduct to Framework Agreements and, 173

core ILO labour standards of, 173, 207, 210, 212
corporate codes of conduct *vs.*, 214–17
CSR Codes of Conduct and, 206–11
International Labour Organization (ILO), 82, 158, 170–3, 207
  Codes of Conduct to Framework Agreements and, 173
  core labour standards of, 173, 207, 210, 212
  fundamental principles of, 170–1
  Tripartite Declaration of Principles, 85, 208
  United Nations Global Compact, 171
international law-making, 81, 89–93
International Register of Certified Auditors (IRCA), 242
international trade law, 13, 182–3
ISO 26000 Social Responsibility Standard, 7, 77, 86

jurisdiction, 35–9
  extraterritorial, 28, 31–2, 37
  extraterritorial limitations, 37–8
  home State, 30–1, 32
  internationally wrongful conduct, 38
  resolution of conflicts concerning, alternative approach to, 30–1
  states, responsibilities of, 39
  transnational harm, 38
  see also extraterritorial jurisdiction
jurisdictional rules, 32–3

Kenyan CSR approach, 133
Kimberly Process Certification Scheme, 226

labour standards, 168–9, 212
  see also International Labour Organization (ILO)
Latin America approach to CSR, 185, 186–7
Laval case, 167, 174, 176–7
law-making, 93–6
  Habermasian deliberative discourse, 98–9
  EU Multi-Stakeholder Forum (MSF), 93–6
  non-governmental organizations, 93–4
  reflexive law, 94–6

law-making, emergence of novel forms of, 93–6
learning, 57
  -based approach, 69
  events, 59, 61
  mechanisms, 57–8
Lehman Brothers, 270
liability, 256
  limitations of, 223
liberal legal theory, 7–8
Loss Allocation Principles, 37–8
Lukoil, 206

Magadi Soda, 136–7
Mangold case, 174
Maurissen case, 174
Mayagna (Sumo) Awas Tingni Community v. Nicaragua, 189, 198
"mechanical equilibria," 261
merits, judgments on, 198
moralization, 253–4, 260
MSF, *see EU Multi-stakeholder (MSF) Forum on CSR*
multinational enterprises (MNEs) and International Framework Agreements (IFA), 205, 206, 210, 212, 216–17

Nampak, 206
National Australia Group, 206
National Human Rights Institution (NHRI), 13, 129, 140–3, 141, 160
nationality jurisdiction, 35–6
nationality principle, 29
Nicaragua test of effective control, 40
Nike, 276–7

Omega Spielhallen case, 183
OECD
  OECD Declaration on International Investment and Multinational Enterprises, 168
  Guidelines for Multinational Enterprises, 84, 85, 168, 208, 212, 216
OECD Guidelines, 85, 114, 123, 208, 212, 213, 214, 216, 217, 219, 225, 226
OECD Guidelines for Multinational Enterprises, 85, 168, 208, 216
  see also OECD Guidelines

Petronas, 150
Premier Oil, 149–50
Principles of Responsible Investment (PRI), 27, 47–50
Procurement Directives (EU), 178–82
Public procurement, 178–82
  clauses/conditions regarding, 179–80
  equal treatment, 178
  Procurement Directives on, 178–82
public-private law-making schemes, 78–9
public-private multi-stakeholder regulation, 89–96
public procurement, 13, 178–82

Quebecor, 206, 208

reflexive law, 3, 8, 9, 12, 18–22, 77–107
  development of, 18–19
  and Habermasian deliberative discourse, 12, 100
  EU Multi-Stakeholder Forum (MSF) as, 79
  regulatory technique as, 19
  SRSG, consultative process of, 21–2
  theory on, 18, 96, 98–9
  UN Global Compact, 21, 81–3
  weaknesses of, 20–1, 96–8
Regional human rights standards, 191–200
  American Commission on Human Rights for, 192–3
  Inter-American commission on, 196–7
  Inter-American Court of Human Rights and, 192–3, 197–200
  Inter-American System on Human Rights and, 191–2, 195
  Latin America's, 191–200
  SRSG's framework on, 191, 193
  state obligations to, 194–6
remedies, 112–13
Respect, Protect and Remedy framework, 11–12, 22, 25–7, 28, 31, 32, 33, 35, 37, 39, 49, 50, 51, 77, 80–3, 85–6, 87, 88, 89, 91–2, 95, 99, 100, 102–5, 106, 108–126, 165, 166, 167, 168, 169, 182–4, 185, 186, 187, 188, 191, 193, 198

responsibilities for human rights
  of business, 3–7, 139–40
  for CSR, 10
  differentiated but complementary, 121–4
  TNCs, 39–42, 122, 123
  UN Norms, 121–2
right to property, 153–4
risk analysis, 234–8
Rüffert case, 167, 172–3
Ruggie, John, *see* Special Representative of Secretary-General (SRSG) on Business and Human Rights
Rutili case, 174

Saatchi and Saatchi S, 274
SA 8000, 69
Safaricom, 137
Saramaka People v. Suriname, 198
Sawhoyamaxa Indigenous Community v. Paraguay, 198
Schwartz case, 183
self-regulation, 94–5
separate delict theory, 43
Shell, 136
Special Representative of Secretary-General (SRSG) on Business and Human Rights, 9–13, 21–2, 89, 108, 111–16, 119–21, 145, 182–4, 160
  BRHR, development of, 5
SRSG, *see* Special Representative of Secretary-General (SRSG) on Business and Human Rights
SRSG and 'principled pragmatism', 55, 114
SRSG's Interim Report, 113–14
Statoil, 208
Stauder case, 174
Sudan Accountability and Divestment Act of 2007, 226
Sudan Divestment Task Force, 226

Tadic test of overall control, 40
Third World Approaches to International Law (TWAIL), 26–7, 32–3
Tiomin Kenya Limited, 132
trade and human rights, 150–2
Tradesmen v. Columbia, 194–5
Tradewinds, 150–2

Unilever, 282–3
Union Citizenship, 183
United Nations (UN), 2, 4, 6, 7, 9, 10, 12, 19, 22, 25–7, 33, 37, 39, 47–50, 52–76, 77, 80–3, 85–6, 88, 89, 91–2, 95, 99, 100, 102–5, 108, 110, 111–14, 115, 117, 118, 119, 120, 121, 123, 130, 133, 140, 145, 148, 158, 159, 160, 162, 168, 169, 186, 188, 191, 193, 208, 212, 214, 216, 217, 219, 225, 226, 236, 246
United Nations (UN) Global Compact, 12, 52–76, 81–3, 100–4, 140, 168–9, 171, 212
United States Federal Sentencing Guidelines, 247–8

Velazquez Rodriguez case, 194
Viking case, 174, 176
voluntary codes, 224, 225–7
voluntary-mandatory dichotomy, 7

Walden Asset Management, 277
Wal-Mart, 124
World Bank, 109, 117
World Trade Organization (WTO), 109, 117, 169–70

Xcel Energy, 228
Ximenes-Lopes v. Brazil, 198